The Long Hard Road

An autobiography

by

Ron Hill

Part Two: To the Peak and Beyond

RON HILL SPORTS LTD.

1982

Ron Hill Sports Ltd.,

P.O. Box 11, Hyde, Cheshire.

First published 1982

© Ron Hill

ISBN: 0 9507882 2 8 (Hardback)
       0 9507882 3 6 (Paperback)

Printed by Waddington & Sons (Printers) Ltd.,
Fielden Square, Rochdale Road, Todmorden, Lancs.

ACKNOWLEDGEMENTS

I would like to thank those people who read through the whole of my original manuscript, especially Cliff Temple and Mel Watman, and who corrected my mistakes and made helpful suggestions. I am also grateful to those newspapers which made available their picture files and gave permission for use of many of the photographs in this book.

ᐧ I owe a great debt to my wife, May, who has stood by patiently, literally for years, whilst this autobiography has been written, corrected and collated, to the great neglect of our social life, business and work on our house.

Finally I give thanks to all those friends May and I have met around the world, and in Britain, runners and non-runners, who helped to make our life that much richer.

This book is dedicated
to
my wife, May

INTRODUCTION

PART ONE of my autobiography entitled "Nearly to the Top" dealt with my life up to and including the Mexico Olympics, October 1968, where, shortly after my 30th birthday, I finished 7th in the 10,000m.

My birthplace was Accrington, Lancashire, and my studies were at Accrington Grammar School followed by Manchester University where, over six years, I gained first a B.Sc.(Tech.), then a Ph.D., from the Textile Chemistry Department of the Faculty of Technology. In September 1960 I married May, who had been a weaver in Accrington, and we now had two sons, Steven born in 1963 and Graham born in 1965.

My job was as a research and development chemist in the dyeing research department of Courtaulds Ltd., in Droylsden, near Manchester, where I had worked since leaving University in January 1964.

The running side of my life had become intense to say the least and I loved to compete in cross-country, track, and road-racing. After training twice a day from late 1957 onwards, unguided and with a multitude of experimentation, I slowly improved from moderate schoolboy ability, through university to county and eventually, in 1962, to international standard.

Up to and including 1968, my first love in running was cross-country and I had won the East Lancashire Championships seven times in succession, the Lancashire Championships six times in succession, the Northern Counties four times in 1964 and '65 and 1967 and '68, the National twice, 1966 and 1968, and was second in the International twice, Dublin, 1964 and Tunis, 1968. 1968 proved to be my best ever year "over the country" with victories in the East Lancs., Lancs., Inter-Counties, Northern and National and my defeat at the hands of Mohamed Gammoudi (Tunis) in the International Championships was by a mere 1.4 seconds.

On the roads my international representative honours for the marathon were the European Games in Belgrade—1962 (did not finish), and Budapest—1966 (12th), and the Tokyo Olympics—1964 (19th). My best time for the marathon was 2:14:12 set behind Basil Heatley's then world best of 2:13:55 in the classic Polytechnic Marathon (Windsor to Chiswick), 1964. In 1968 I had clocked a World Best for 20 miles on the road of 1:36:28 in the Pembroke '20', Liverpool. I had been hoping to be selected for the Mexico Olympic Marathon but in the trial race, when I was just starting to train towards an Olympic peak, all I could manage was 4th, clocking my second fastest time 2:17:11, and I was not selected.

On the track I represented Britain on numerous occasions at 6 miles and 10,000 m (once at 5,000 m!) and ran the 10,000 m in the Tokyo Olympics (18th), and 6 miles at the Commonwealth Games, Jamaica, 1966 (5th). I was the proud possessor of three track World Records: 10 miles, 47:02.2 (1968); 15 miles, 1:12:48.2, and 25 km, 1:15:22.6 (1965), these latter two being the last of the great Emil Zatopek's world marks.

At October, 1968, my personal best track times stood at:

400 m.	55.1 (1968)	2 miles	8:41.0 (1965)
880 yds.	1:58.9 (1963)	3 miles	13:27.2 (1967)
1 mile	4:10.1 (1965)	6 miles	27:26.0 (1966)
		Marathon	2:14:12 (1964)

As for marathons, I had attempted 13, but until 1968 was never serious about them as a means of fulfilling long term ambitions in running. I dearly wanted to be a great track runner. The marathons I had run were:

1961 Liverpool (August 12) 2:24:22 (1st)
1962 Polytechnic (June 16) 2:21:59 (1st)
  European, Belgrade (September 16) d.n.f.
1963 Polytechnic (June 15) 2:18:06 (2nd)
1964 Beverley (March 30) 2:19:37 (1st)
  Polytechnic (June 30) 2:14:12 (2nd)
  Olympics, Tokyo (October 21) 2:25:34 (19th)
1965 Beverley (April 19) 2:26:33 (1st)
1966 Polytechnic (June 11) 2:20:55 (3rd)
  European, Budapest (September 4) 2:26:04 (12th).
1967 Beverley (March 27) 2:27:21 (3rd)
  Enschede (August 26) 2:23:43 (2nd)
1968 Cwmbran (July 27) 2:17:11 (4th)

The ultimate symbol of the success in running I was striving so hard to achieve was a gold medal in the Olympics, or failing that a gold medal in either of the two other major games, the European or the Commonwealth.

For years it looked as though I would always get close but always fall down at the last hurdle. However, the Mexico Olympics provided a slim hope that at last I was on the right lines with my finely developed training techniques and my yearly planning of racing and training. 1967 had seen me at 100 miles per week in full training, whereas in 1968 I had stepped up to 120 miles per week. Within this, I needed at least two one month periods of active "rest".

The way my mileage developed over the years (my training log commences in 1956) is shown in the accompanying diagram.

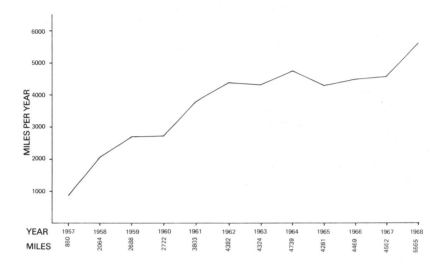

YEAR	1957	1958	1959	1960	1961	1962	1963	1964	1965	1966	1967	1968
MILES	850	2064	2638	2722	3803	4392	4324	4739	4281	4469	4552	5565

My specific weekly mileage for 1968 is shown in the second diagram overleaf. The majority of this was achieved by running to work and back from our home in Romiley, near Stockport, Cheshire. Since December of 1964, a training sequence of twice a day, weekdays and Saturdays, with just one run on Sundays, had been unbroken.

Our home in Romiley.

7

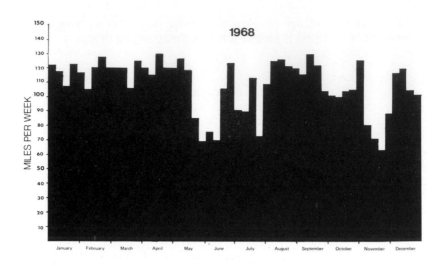

CHAPTER ONE

I forsook the holiday in Acapulco, which most of the British Team were to enjoy, in order to return to my family and job more quickly. My journey was long and tiring, halting in Jamaica and Bermuda before flying through the night to London. There I changed planes and landed in Manchester weary and tired. May and the boys were there to meet me.

I was anxious to get home, but two reporters collared me and started asking questions. This led to trouble for me.

I should never have got involved with them, being tired and having changed time zones, but one of them from the Daily Mail started on about having done well and I must have received a lot of congratulatory telegrams. I said that a s a matter of fact I hadn't, but it didn't bother me. This was later printed as: "Arrived home with a grievance. His employers failed to cable their encouragement or congratulations, he complained," followed by the completely ficti- tious "described how he had watched other athletes opening greetings cables from their firms". Utter rubbish. All I was saying was "Yes" and "No" to questions.

Admittedly I was a little peeved and puzzled before I left; the news of my selection for Mexico was carried on a three line paragraph at the bottom of a page of our company newspaper, and although my manager was away the day I left my office, it would have been reassuring to have a "cheerio" the day before. As it was, the silent treatment made me wonder whether my absence was being frowned upon or not.

But at the end of the interview I could see the way things were heading and said, "For God's sake don't blow this up into some- thing big"; then, "When I win a Gold Medal they can all get stuffed", meaning that then I wouldn't care what anyone thought about my running. I later found out that the bloody reporter had rung up my manager, mis-quoted me several times including, "When I win a Gold Medal the company can get stuffed", and asked, "What have you got to say to that?"

I was furious when I saw the next day's papers. The Daily Express carried a sensible story, but the Daily Mail headlined, "The bitter- ness of the Long Distance Runner" — "Not even a cable, says Ron". Not surprisingly there was a beautiful memo waiting for me when I got into the office, with copies to everyone — "seems you are dissatisfied with response . . . selection . . . performance in 10,000 metres . . . firm in general . . . . immediate colleagues . . . to suggest your colleagues in the firm were at fault . . . just plain impudence." God, it took me a full day to sort everything out, and I decided next time that I would keep my trap shut. As usual all my work-mates were great, congratulating me, and welcoming me back.

A couple of years later, that same reporter on some other story appeared late at night, wavering on my doorstep, drunk; he had been waiting in the Spread Eagle for me to return from some appointment and had the cheek to say, "I'm the one who interviewed you at Manchester Airport when you came back from Mexico." He wasn't granted an audience I can assure you.

So it was back to reality, work, family life, catching up with correspondence and jobs around the house. The faithful A35 van was giving me trouble in the shape of a leaking petrol tank and I wasted hours trying to mend it — draining it, drying it, putting pitch on the outside, metallic paint, soap, all to no avail and I decided that I needed a new car. With about £45 part exchange on the van, we bought a white, second-hand Mini for £300, a faster and more comfortable drive than the van.

I carried on my training as I had a big race on November 9th, a special One Hour race on the all-weather track at Leicester, which Jim Alder had fixed up, hoping to make use of his altitude training, in the Mexico Olympics, to take my One Hour British Record which he had narrowly missed the year before. This race clashed with the Waterloo Road Race, but if my record were going to be broken, I wanted to be there to defend it.

My training at home was marred by stomach troubles. Ironically I had had no bother at all in Mexico, but here I was back in England and having to dive into the bushes on each of my training runs. Pink pills, Streptotriads, solved that problem; but the weather in England was atrocious, miserably cold and raining. It's no wonder I felt tired and depressed on the runs home from work. For one week I kept up to full training — 125½ miles, then, in the week before the Leicester One Hour race, I eased down the intensity and the distance to 80½ miles.

Bonfire night, November 5th, fell just before the race; it wasn't the neighbourhood "bonfire plot" I remembered from my school days. We had a fire in our back garden, but the whole evening was spoiled when Steven was hit by a fire fizzing "aeroplane", which burnt all his hair away on the right side of his head and left a large brown mark near his right eye. I guess he was lucky it didn't hit his eye. I took him to our doctor's surgery and he told us to take him to Stockport Infirmary; a neighbour ran us down, Graham came too, and after much form filling and waiting the burn was dressed and an anti-tetanus injection was stuck rather ineptly into his backside. We got the bus home, the neighbour had lent me 10 shillings for this, and we had some sweets and a bottle of Tizer. On our return, in happy relief, we sat round what remained of the bonfire with three "spuds" roasting in the embers.

Conjure up the vision of an athlete breaking a world record. A long lie-in in bed on the morning of the race, the attention of coaches and a masseur, chauffeuring to the race to give the most restful preparation, huge crowds to cheer on all the contestants, and if the record attempt were successful a champagne celebration, perhaps a T.V. appearance. In reality it wasn't like that at all.

November 9th, 1968, I got up at 7.30 a.m., had a shave with my electric razor, got on my shorts, vest, track suit, training shoes and gloves and ran 3 miles along the canal bank, which took me to the aqueduct and back. It was slightly foggy, no wind, and extremely cold. We didn't have a shower, I only bathed twice a week, so I just swilled my face with cold water, and got dressed. For breakfast I had a bowl of raw Scots' porridge oats with milk and sugar, two eggs and bacon with two slices of brown bread, a honey butty and a pint pot of tea. We set off in the Mini for Stockport at 9.15, did the shopping for groceries and fruit and vegetables, came back via Seventeen Windows and got a dozen eggs at a farm near there. Once home I packed my bag with special light weight running shoes, vest and shorts and towel, had a cup of tea and three "Golden Shred" butties, and left for Leicester, with May and the lads, at 11.20 a.m., driving via Chesterfield and the M1. On the M1 I had the car up to 75 m.p.h. and we were there by 1.40 p.m. There was a little fog in the Midlands and it was still bitterly cold when we stepped out of the car.

I talked to some of the runners before the 3 o'clock start. Jim Alder reported that he was physically very fit but mentally at a very low ebb. Ron Grove had had to get time off work to run and was dashing back as soon as the race was over — what a guy!

I did two laps of the dark red rubberized surfaced track including a couple of strides. It was very cold. I decided to start the race with my gloves on.

The field of 10 competitiors toed the line, with about two dozen spectators looking on. Five schoolboys, a vicar, one or two reporters, race officials and wives, children, girl friends and one or two other athletes. Nothing unusual.

As soon as the gun went, a breeze seemed to spring up on the back straight and first bend, but we had agreed to share the pacemaking so that no one person was doing all the work. Don Shelley, now a City of Stoke A.C. athlete, led off with a fast lap, I heard 68 as

11

I passed, and followed it with a 70 second lap; it was time for us to take over, which we did with 69 - 70's, regular as clockwork, firstly me for three laps, then Ron Grove for three laps, then Jim Alder for three laps. At the end of Jim's stint we had slowed to a 71 second lap, and I took over the lead, passing three miles in 13:53.0. On the next lap Jim's voice floated over from behind, "I'm adrift". I spoke back to Ron Grove, "Two laps apiece?" "O.K.", came the reply.

We alternated through 6 miles in 27:53, very encouraging, well inside world record schedule, even though I was suffering a little stitch. The lap before 7 miles I threw off my gloves, took on my two laps, and at 7¼ miles, when it was Ron's turn to take over, I realised that he had dropped. There was nothing to do but to press on, even though I was starting to feel very tired. I was now only thinking of the 10 mile world record; just once I allowed the thought of how many laps there were to creep into my mind, and I panicked. I didn't think that I could keep it up; but after such a good start I knew it would be daft to jack it in, so I just kept my head down.

With 6 laps to go for 10 miles, I started a count down; 6 more times into the wind, 5, 4, . . . with 3 laps to go a memory flashed to my mind of the Mexico 10,000 metres, how hard those last three laps had been and how I managed it. I could do it again. I ran on. One lap to go, I knew I had the world record, I tried to speed up, but couldn't manage much and ran across the line. Peace. I could jog. I didn't have to force myself with legs and stomach hurting, head throbbing, I could get down the air I needed for recovery.

The race officials must have wondered what was happening. They couldn't have read my thoughts as I'd run at that 10 miles record. They couldn't have understood that on that day, after such a long season, I hadn't enough in me for a one hour record. The 10 mile record was enough! I just jogged. Allan Rushmer and Dick Taylor were there at the track side, "Go on, Hilly! Go on! Go for the 1 hour record." "Too knackered," was all I could whisper.

I had resigned myself to walking for the rest of the hour if necessary. I knew I couldn't drop out, otherwise the record would not be valid and I would suffer the same fate as Mike Freary, who lost his British Records for 20 Km and One Hour, set during my World Record 15 miles and 25 Km run at Bolton in 1965, because he had dropped out. I jogged. I guessed Grove and Alder would catch me soon, but I didn't care. On the back straight, Don Shelley, who I had lapped twice, passed me, so I tucked in behind him, to shelter from the wind, and ran behind him until 11 miles. During this time I recovered sufficiently to calculate that only another six times into the wind and I could have the British records for 20 Km and One Hour and off I went lapping in 71 and 72's to do just that.

Quite a tally. World Record for 10 miles — 46:44.0, British Records for 20 Km — 58:39.0 and One Hour — 12 miles 1,268 yards.

There were no prizes in this race, no need to hang around. I jogged one lap of the track, got my track suit from the infield, rinsed my face in the changing rooms, got in the car and was home by 6.30 p.m., after calling in at the off-licence for 5 pint bottles of Family Ale, a quart bottle of Forest Brown, and some salted peanuts.

May lit the open fire and we put the electric fire on too; it was cold in the house. We got the kids to bed at 7.45, but they kept on coming down. After two bottles of Family Ale I drove up to the chip shop, got fish, chips and peas twice, put the car in the rented garage at the back of the house and settled down to watch T.V., the end of a film, then Match of the Day, in which Sunderland drew with Manchester United, 1-1 at Sunderland. I slept very well when we went to bed at 11.00 p.m.

It was a nice end to a long season.

CHAPTER TWO

The week up to the World Record, 80½ miles, I counted as the first week of my month's active "rest". There followed weeks of 71, 63 and 88½ miles before I started training for the 1969 cross-country season. The "rest" was welcome as I was very busy at work and socially.

Work-wise I was fully occupied with the development of "deep-dye viscose" in all sorts of end uses, and this involved me in a lot of laboratory development work, and dyeing trials in various factories elsewhere. It was interesting working with other people, making friends both outside and within my own company, people like Joe Whitehead, of our Viscose Sales Development Department, who himself was involved in the coaching of ladies' athletics and was a firm friend.

But, underlying all this, I had an uneasy feeling that, to the company, I was something of an anomaly, possibly a nuisance, with requests for time off. I knew I had support at the highest director level, and similarly at ground level, with fellow colleagues and workers, but in between there was no encouragement and possibly the reverse. I had patched up the trouble of the "return from Mexico" news articles, but I couldn't see things getting any easier in the future, and I was grieved at the difference of my treatment and that of Olympic athletes in other countries. So much so, I actually applied for a couple of other jobs at that time, but these applications came to nothing.

Socially, if you could call it that, I was asked to do a lot of things; give slide shows to groups of people, housewives' registers, I started two local guys off on the London to Sydney car rally, I went to Buckingham Palace with the rest of the Olympic team to meet the Queen and have a buffet lunch, and May and I attended a great dinner at the London Hilton, given by Birds Eye, to all the Mexico finalists.

I was busy at home, making Steven do his reading and keeping control of him and Graham, as they got up to the usual lads' tricks, Steven squirting after-shave lotion all over Graham and the walls of the bathroom, and both of them filling the bath with toilet paper whilst they were both in the water.

In December I started to train hard again, after what was really very little of a "rest". I decided I was going to go semi-teetotal, that is drinking just shandies to see if I could get "super-fit". I must admit, this went by the board at Christmas.

The mini car turned out to be a duff job. It continually pulled towards the left and I found some peculiar weldings near the roof; more inquiries revealed that the bloody car had been a write-off and re-built. A further £35 and another exchange got me a pale blue Austin 1100, and skint us.

I always had a keen sense of loyalty and supported my club whenever I could. Ten miles running on the track was not my idea of an ideal Saturday afternoon the first week of December, but I turned up at Leverhulme Park, Bolton, for the club 10 miles championships, which I had won consecutively the previous 6 years, despite having had two weeks of a chest infection and head cold.

The track was in good condition, it was a cold day and I ran in gloves and a scarf wrapped round my neck, first warming up two miles to get some extra training in. Freary wasn't running; the lads guessed rightly that I wasn't looking for a fast race and from the start set a really cracking race, sharing the lead and trying to take me by surprise, which they did to a certain extent. Eric Haslam and Mike Chapman went through the first mile in 4 mins 40 seconds, whilst I jogged round in 5:08. I was going to have to be careful. I put in a 66 second lap and seemed to cut their lead by about half; after jogging two laps behind Roger Swann I put in another 66 lap and was with the leading pair shortly after 2 miles. Chapman soon dropped and to punish Eric I sat on him until 5 miles, making him do all the work into the wind. Midway through the race I relented and said, "Half a mile apiece", and we shared the lead, me having arranged it so that he was leading the last two laps in order that with 300 metres to go I could take him by surprise and zip away to a 62 second last lap, and a 48:31 championship record. Eric ran 48:35.

To keep my interest alive I had a trip to a race in Belgium, through a private invitation, to Erembodegem, and there I made a long standing friendship with my host Josef Lampbrecht and his family.

Josef picked me up in his VW beetle and took me to the Hotel Des Arcades in Aalst. I didn't have a good race. The start was held up until the T.V. was ready to transmit, and it was a typical Belgian creeping, pushing, scrambling start. Gaston Roelants was the winner, Willy Polleunis was 2nd and I had a battle with Mohamed Gammoudi on the last lap, which he won, to give me 4th place.

After the race I had a steak in the hotel and went with Josef, first to the local club headquarters at the cafe "In de Jager", where in a back room we celebrated the successful conclusion of their race with pils, champagne and white wine. After a late night cup of tea at the Lampbrechts' home, Josef took me back to Aalst and bought me some "escargots" at a chip stall in the railway square. But they weren't snails in garlic sauce as I'd expected, but bloody great whelks, and it was some job forcing them down as they were tough and rubbery and almost too big to swallow. To crown it all at 11.40 p.m. we found the hotel in darkness and no amount of banging on the doors and windows, ringing or telephoning could raise anyone. *"We couldn't stir a bloody soul,"* I wrote in my diary.

So I had to sleep at the Lampbrechts. The whelks murdered my stomach. I was at the hotel at 6.45 a.m. for my gear, a 3 mile run, breakfast and the trip home.

Perhaps those rest weeks, 60 to 80 miles, of November had not been low enough for a recovery after my long summer, because I suffered all winter. After Erembodegem I put in weeks of 104½ miles with my left leg beginning to get sore — it was the old hamstring complaint at the top, back of my leg — and 101 miles, this last week being reduced a bit because of Christmas festivities. But I hadn't properly ridden the chest infection and head cold of November.

The entry in my log for the first run for 1969 was: *"Wed. Jan. 1st. M. Ran to work — felt absolutely bloody shattered all the way — probably due to lack of sleep and lack of inspiration."* I was weary all week but still put in 124½ miles.

On the 4th, I was defending my Lancs. Cross-Country title at Witton Park, Blackburn; Friday night saw me going to bed with a cup of Horlicks laced with brandy and I expected I might get beaten this year. Luckily I managed to win, by really forcing myself, with

7th successive Lancashire Cross-Country title.

my legs absolutely dead at the top of the killer hill and having to sprint the last bit to hold off Mike Freary by 6 seconds.

I carried on training, hoping to shake off the bad spell. 121 miles in the next week, then a cross-country race in Antwerp accompanied by two up-and-coming young runners, tall red-haired fellow Lancastrian Andy Holden who had been 5th in the Lancs., and a short-haired, skinny Dave Bedford who had been making a name for himself in the south. My case got temporarily lost at the airport, and I had to train in borrowed kit and Olympic issue, Hush Puppy, boots. My legs felt dead and my heart felt just tired. The race, however, was a success for me, all three of us got up there after the usual blinding rush, accompanied by Polleunis. I'd not met the precocious Bedford before and was amazed when after two laps he turned and said "Should we push it a bit?" "Christ," I thought. "No, hang on a bit, Dave," I said. Only at the very end of the six lap race was I able to forge a lead and win with Andy 2nd and Dave 3rd. Dave was tickled pink, and with his picture in the evening paper and three or four beers in

"C'est moi!" Bedford leads me, Holden and Polleunis.

his belly, he was going round the bar, showing people the picture and shouting, "C'est moi, c'est moi."

110½ miles later was the Inter-Counties at Brighton Race Course. After a very busy week, and a terrible journey there — car, train, tube, train, bus, wander round the sea front at Brighton in the dark on a rainy wild windy night, in frustration a taxi — I found the digs in 12A Mount Square at a quarter to midnight, and shared a room with Peter Goodfellow of the Staffordshire team.

Being the reigning champion I was hoping to do well, and was predicting that Lancashire would have six in the first twelve to easily take the team race. Individually I ran a stupid race with a lot of elementary mistakes. Firstly I set off at the back of the Lancashire pen, right behind the rest and didn't push it at the start which gave me the impossible task of getting through to the leaders, as the track was narrow in parts, and on a ploughed section of the course there was no passing at all. When we finally got on to the race course itself I had to sprint into the wind to catch Mike Freary, and then sit on him for a while in 7th position, then sprint again into the wind to try to get on to the leading group. I almost did it, but I got so knackered that they began to pull away again. That was mistake number two; I should have waited until we were running with the wind.

I slowly caught Alan Blinston, but on the plough he seemed to take his time and Mike Turner and Tim Johnson in front moved away. On the race track I passed Blinston, taking Dick Taylor and Mike Freary with me. With a long run into the wind to the finish I let Dick lead for a while, put in an effort myself, half closed the gap on Turner and Johnston, put Dick back into the lead again, and he let them go. I just sat until almost the end then sprinted home for 5th, only 1 second behind Johnston and 4 seconds behind Turner, whom I had beaten easily in the Lancs. That was mistake number three; I should have sprinted earlier; but really I had just chickened out. Trevor Wright had won the race easily for Yorkshire from Mike Tagg. After the race I didn't feel as if I had run at all. Lancashire did win the team race and easily, with 46 points to Yorkshire's 157 points, with as I had predicted six runners in twelve. Turner 3rd, myself 5th, Freary 7th, Holden 9th, Bob Gregory 10th and Colin Robinson 12th.

Inter-Counties Champions: l. to r., Hill, Holden, Haslam, Freary, Turner, Blakeley, Gregory, Robinson.

It was no consolation for my individual effort; I was very dejected on my way home, and this feeling carried over into the next week's training where I seemed to struggle all week to get in 121 miles. When I got up the morning of the East Lancs. Championships and set off for a five mile run I *"felt like a bloody old man"*. Nevertheless, I had a reasonable run at Woodbank Park, Stockport, was in control all the way to win by 11 seconds from club-mate Eric Haslam. That was my 8th successive senior East Lancashire win, a definite record. I guessed it would be a long time before anyone emulated that. At least 8 years!

I rounded off January with another hard week, 122½ miles, before racing at Mezidon in France, staying at the Blanchets' apartment in Pontoise near Paris for a day before meeting up with Mike Freary and Bob Richardson in Mezidon. Everyone wanted me to win for the fourth time but it wasn't to be. Like an idiot, I ran in bare feet and was slipping all over the place. There was a false start, they weren't called back and we were left standing. The Frenchmen Tijoux and Wadoux ran away and I couldn't even stay with Mike and had to be content, which I wasn't, with 4th place.

Consolation from Jean Wadoux after Mezidon.

It was a cold weekend and a blizzard came on during the night. After lots to drink at the "Bal des Nations", it may have been the snowball fight with the Germans which led to me picking up another sore throat. Through the week, this developed into a bad chest, and then maybe even influenza as my neck got stiff, painful and swollen.

19

Added to this my leg got really sore, the pains spreading to the back of my knee as if the ligaments there were catching on each other and cracking. This got so bad that Thursday I started out to run to work, and had to turn back. I could hardly lift my leg at all. That week my mileage slumped to 64.

Not many people would have run the Northern at Sherdley Park, St. Helens in that condition. It was just stubbornness that got me out; these ailments were not going to stand in my way! It certainly wasn't heroics, although the hero stories in the press made good reading. To add to my difficulties the ground was covered in snow. I ran the race in gloves, scarf and balaclava helmet. There were three laps of three miles and half way round the first lap I was just behind the leading bunch, but as my breathing got worse and worse, they dropped me. As if to finally spite me, a fierce hail storm came on half way round the second lap. My breath was coming in dry moans and I was gritting my teeth with the effort and because of the pain of my leg, but even so, my instincts took me to a sprint to beat Chris Fay for 11th place. I was in a bad way after the race. Bolton won the team race. Hurrah. There were three weeks to go before the National Championships at the Parliament Hill Fields, London.

For three weeks I suffered, ill with my chest and running awkwardly and painfully with my leg and knee. To make it worse the weather was cold and miserable. Snowy and slushy, and my leg injury felt worse trying to push off on slippery ground. The first week I did 65 miles. The second week 89½ miles. The third week, I felt my leg was on the mend, the pains and catchings behind the knee transferring to the top of my leg. I was desperate for fitness and ran 105½ miles. The improvement in that final week was seen in my training log comments:

Tue. A.M. — Leg still in same condition — bad.
Tue. P.M — Felt quite good but my leg is holding me back.
Wed. A.M. — Although my leg was still causing me to run with a limp I felt quite good.
Wed. P.M. — Leg giving me a lot of trouble, especially on the uphill bursts — no co-ordination, ligaments and tendons cracking a lot.
Thur. A.M. — Felt fairly good — leg giving me no pain jogging.
Thur. P.M. — Felt quite good, knee cracked only once or twice.

It was a cold muddy day, muddier than usual, even for Parliament Hill Fields. My mother and dad had travelled down to watch the race, and I borrowed my mother's gloves to run in. I warmed up 3 miles very easily. As the field thundered forward up the hill at the start I was able to get quite well up and be in the mid-30s as we hit the knee-deep patch of mud at 1 mile. On the firm ground after 2 miles I moved through to 10th and downhill, to complete the lap, I was through to 6th.

Up the hill again; but at 4 miles the mud began to take its toll and I fell forward into the deep quagmire as did three others who were with me. Struggling on, at 5 miles, Gerry North caught me and we swapped positions until Gerry Stevens, a comparative novice in top class cross-country, went past me. I went with him, hung on to him through into the last lap, then began to lose ground rapidly, although at 7½ miles, the distance of the International race, I was still 8th. Runners began to file past: North, Freary ("That's me out", I said as he went past), Atkin. A little later Wright of Tipton, Beaver, Alder and finally Rushmer went past. I had given everything I had — no sprint — across the line, 15th. My leg was stiff and sore afterwards.

I had to go to the presentation, as Bolton had won 3rd team medals. Secretly I hoped that perhaps I would be picked for the England team, after all I had been captain the previous four years and we had won on each occasion, and individually I had been 2nd in Tunisia the year before. I'd had an outstanding summer, and a reasonable start to the cross-country season, my only bad run being the Northern, where I was physically in a really bad way. In three weeks I had improved from 11th in the Northern to 15th in the National and, what's more, at 7½ miles — the distance of the International race — I had been in 8th position. Surely the selectors would have had someone at that important 7½ mile point to assess the positions there?

I sat there as the team was announced. The first seven in the senior race — M. Tagg, R. Taylor, T. Wright, M. Turner, R. Richardson, M. Baxter, M. Freary — then incredibly Tim Johnston, who hadn't run because he had 'flu. Hadn't I had bloody 'flu? Andy Holden, winner of the junior race, was the 9th man. Then, just to rub it in, reserves: G. Stevens and D. Atkin.

Not even a bloody reserve! The anger welled up in me. You stupid buggers! You bloody, stupid, amateur, buggers! Someone at 7½? Not bloody likely, you bloody selectors were probably standing in the bloody tent sipping whisky, and popping out only to watch the leaders go past.

At that moment a flame was extinguished in me forever.

I walked out. Before I got the tube, I had a pint of Guinness and a pint of lager in a pub with Arthur Dennis from up the North East and Vince Regan, an Irishman who had recently joined Bolton Harriers. I had a pint of beer outside Euston station. The stupid bloody fools. I drank three pint cans of ale on the train up to Manchester. Who were these idiots anyway? I had a pint of Guinness on Piccadilly station, before I got the train to Romiley. I'd never even heard of some of them. What the hell did they know

21

about cross-country and picking teams? I had two pints of bitter in the Duke of York near home. I don't remember much then; May said I more or less went to bed straight away.

In disappointment I ran 65 miles the next week, then won the Manchester University Cross-Country Championships race for the 12th successive year.

I would show those so called bloody selectors. I put in 96 miles and won the Sutton "7" at a canter, telling jokes and talking for a good while, before winning as I pleased. I ran 103 miles to take me to the Longwood 10 mile road race at Huddersfield, a tough hilly course. It was the same day as the International at Glasgow. On Wednesday I had picked up another sore throat, which quickly spread to my chest, but that wasn't going to hold me back.

A cold day, with an icy wind in parts, and — good! — Dave Atkin was running. The reserve for the England team, but not called upon to travel. I pushed it right from the start, Atkin lasted only about 1½ miles, and that was downhill; I started to move away. I kept up a real pressure, striding out into the wind, and head down up the hills to the finish, to smash my own course record by 1 minute and 32 seconds.

I could have won the bloody International; and I bet those selectors didn't even notice!

My cold lingered on, but I had only two weeks left to the end of my winter season. A road relay at Derby, where I had second fastest leg, and then the A.A.A. Track 10 miles, at Leicester again, on April 5th. On that day I wanted only to win; it would be some sort of a record, 5 successive wins, and I wanted it to be as easy as possible. I hadn't reckoned on the courage of little Ron Grove from Leicester.

It seemed inevitable that there would be a strong wind blowing, this time it was on the first bend. First lap was 73-74; not fast enough for Grove and he was off pulling the field with him. I settled down in 5th place and moved up slowly as the gaps appeared, one by one past Waterhouse, Caine and Lem. John Caine hung on, seemed to start to drop a bit at 2 miles, so I put a lap in, to help him on his way back. It didn't work so I moved out into the second lane. Grove said, "******* hell, lads", moved out too, and shunted Caine into the lead. He lasted one lap before Ron took over again, I followed him through and Caine was quickly dropped. Round and round we went, a hellish wind blowing and me just sitting in letting him do all the work, with never a complaint. I admired him for that and, not being wholly ruthless, I moved alongside him at 5 miles and said, "Well, Ron, you've got ******* guts! Half apiece?" "O.K.", he replied.

During one of my stints, I turned round and said, "Is this all right?" And to my surprise he called back, "You can go a bit faster if you like!" I was trying to relax but not enjoying it, even though the pace was not killing. I made sure that he was leading on the last two laps and as we heard the bell, I sat right on him into the wind on the first bend, poised to make my effort. As we hit the back straight he kicked from the front and I had to really push to catch him and pass him before the final bend. I sensed I was gaining a little as we got to the home straight, but I was flat out and virtually tip-toed up the last 80 yards, no control or co-ordination, the tap was fully on. And it was just enough. A 59.4 seconds last lap, for a win in 47:27.0, a meagre 1.2 seconds ahead. Now I had my self-confidence back.

I realised that I needed a proper rest from heavy training. I just jogged 6 weeks of 35½, 33½, 32½, 43, 64½, and 62 miles.

With my success at 10,000 metres in the Olympics and what I thought was my potential at marathon, I wanted to go for the double in the European Games in September. To do this I would have to run exceptionally well in the A.A.A. Marathon Championship, which was the Maxol Marathon, on July 20th, in Manchester, and the A.A.A. 10,000 metres championships, at White City, on August 1st.

During the rest period, I ran just a couple of road races for the club, and was able to forget about racing and concentrate on all the jobs around the house that needed doing; making shelves, painting, and building terraces for a vegetable garden at the back of the house. I also took this opportunity to have my verucca cut out, perhaps I should say "surgically removed", which was a very painful experience with about twelve excrutiating pain-killing injections around the bony part of my foot, followed by cauterisation with an alarming smell of burning flesh. That left me hobbling painfully for a few days.

At work too, I was trying very hard, for in addition to the day-to-day work , I was to give a lecture on "Deep-dye Viscose Fibres" at the 54th Annual Conference of the Textile Institute, which meant tying in all the loose ends of many series of experiments, mounting samples, drawing graphs and diagrams, having these put on to colour slides, and then writing the script. This kept me occupied nights and weekends, up to flying across to Belfast on May 12th, and travelling first to Dungannon in Northern Ireland, to Stevenson's, part of the Courtaulds Group, meeting up with my manager Stan Ward for talks in the dye-house, and lunch in the quaint wide-street village of Moy, with Harry Stevenson and Bernie Shannon, before journeying on by train to Dublin, checking over the lecture together on the journey.

In Dublin we stayed at the Intercontinental Hotel in Ballsbridge. There I attended lectures, gave my own dissertation fortified with a gin and tonic, went to a fashion show, then O'Donoghue's bar, the Abbey Theatre, the conference dinner, all the time knocking back Guinness, sherry, beer, wine. I didn't realise what a boozy do it would be.

The last night there I couldn't sleep; I'd stayed after the conference dinner drinking beer until they stopped serving, but at 2.00 a.m. my stomach was turning over, so I got up, put on my kit and at 2.30 a.m. headed out in the darkness to the centre of Dublin, crossed the Liffey, ran up to Phoenix Park and back on the south ring road. 7½ miles.

When I got up to go home, the same morning, I felt a complete wreck. I sat in the "Coffee Dock" at the hotel drinking black tea and wondered what I was doing with myself. That was it. From now on I was more or less "on the wagon", nothing stronger than shandy until the European Games were over. And I'd start training tomorrow. The decision was made.

The next week I ran 99 miles and started a new extra session. One lunch time a week, I went up to the 352 yard track at Richmond Street, Ashton-under-Lyne, to run two fast 440's with half-a-mile interval. The fast times I hoped for would give me confidence at the end of any race, and I wanted to be able to do sub-60 seconds for the last quarter-mile of a marathon if ever that was necessary. Marjorie Weldon and Margaret Whitehead, who was now working for me, usually came up to time me.

After the 99 miles was Whit week. We had a holiday from work and went up to the Yorkshire Dales for a farm holiday. We found a really wonderful place, with great food, in Ravenstonedale, not far from Kirkby Stephen, Lower Greenside Farm, kept by Ethel and William Dixon. They had two small daughters, Nora and Valerie, so after our day's outings, Steven and Graham could play games with them. It was fabulous training up there, fresh air, curlews calling, occasionally blue skies; I was finding 9 miles every morning no problem at all and during the day we tripped to all the local castles and to the Lake District, walking, picnicking, sailing on the 'Swan' on Lake Windermere to Ambleside.

It was a good way to complete my second week's training, and I had 7 more weeks to the Maxol Marathon. We returned from the Dales on Friday with a 110½ mile week under my belt, and on Saturday I raced the Pembroke '20'. My first race for 6 weeks, something of a record absence from competition for me.

The Pembroke '20' was easy; I ran with a big group up to 12½ miles, in the end feeling so "bloody bored, and a little worried" at so many people being there, that I took off. Only John Balmer of the local Pembroke club stayed with me, and at the 15 mile point asked me to "take him through". I let him hang on until 18 miles, before I ran away to win by 14 seconds in 1:44.52; my eigth successive win.

My training was really serious now and I followed this race immediately by wins in the Freckleton Half Marathon with a course record of 64:55 and the Notts. '15', 76:17. I didn't race the last two weekends in June but the weeks' mileages that month were 121, 125½, 128½, and 136½. In that last week I slotted in an evening 13:42.8 for

B. PEARSON

The Pembroke '20' was easy.

3 miles win on a sloping grass track at Halifax, running to work in the morning and driving back to work to run home late that same night.

On July 1st, a Tuesday, I had my first major test of the season. I, was selected by the B.A.A.B. to run the 10,000 metres in the World Games in Helsinki. It turned out to be an eventful race. I was with Lachie Stewart, of Glasgow, who was running the 5,000 and 10,000 metres and Gerry Stevens, of Reading, running the steeplechase, with Doug Goodman as team manager. We stayed at the Hotel Valli, away from the centre of Helsinki, and I got £6 10s. 0d. spending money and £2 10s. 0d. expenses, which I thought was "great". Seriously!

The track in the Olympic Stadium at Helsinki was still cinders and, as it had been raining all day, it was pretty soft and lifeless to run on. The track wasn't the only thing that was lifeless, as running from the hotel to the stadium with Lachie I "felt bloody tired". As the race got under way, in the damp evening atmosphere, I found myself last of the 15 starters, but on a windless night it was easy to move through the field as gaps appeared, and by half-way I had run into around 6th or 7th position with three Ethiopians, Nedo Farcic of Yugoslavia, Gaston Roelants and Susuki of Japan in front of me. Suddenly, to my amazement, at the end of the back straight, Gaston ran off the track waving his arm in disgust at the three Ethiopians. I wondered what was going on but soon found out. I looked ahead and saw that as soon as any runner came up on the shoulder of an

Ethiopian he was unceremoniously elbowed or shoulder charged aside. I passed round the outside of first Farcic and then Susuki, striding comfortably now in 4th place with 6½ laps to go.

Entering the home straight with 6 laps to go the third Ethiopian, No. 94, was dropping slightly and I moved to cover the break, knowing that I would have to accelerate quickly to avoid being pushed myself, but as I came alongside he lunged and in fractions of a second I found myself skidding on the rough cinders, flat on my back, to the edge of the third lane, looking up into the floodlights and in pain. "What the bloody hell happened?" I hauled myself to

"I hauled myself to my feet . . ."

my feet and started down the track; Gaston had rejoined the race and signalled with his right hand for me to tuck in behind him as he went through on my inside. I stayed behind him for one lap, then told him to tuck in behind me, and over the next lap we moved up to close the gap on the leading bunch. Suddenly, Farcic was sent hurtling sideways into the third lane. What the hell were they playing at? I was incensed, dived through the other runners, tapped the Ethiopian on his sweat glistening left shoulder and shook my fist in his face. "Do that again and I'll knock you off the ****ing track." I could feel my right shoe was getting wet and squelching a bit, but I daren't look down to see what the problem was.

At the end of the next lap the illuminated lap marker said "2". "Two laps to go? That can't be right," I thought, but the others believed it, and on the back straight Roelants started an effort, taking Susuki and the three Ethiopians with him, expecting to hear the bell for the last lap. I went with them, but as relaxed as possible and not winding myself up for the final lap. Sure enough, the lights were still on "2" when we got in the home straight again. Roelants slowed and threw out both his hands, palms up, questioningly. He was overtaken. I just kept on running until the bell when all three Ethiopians started to move, Degeufu, Masresha and Mamo Wolde. I stayed with them, still not flat out, waiting, waiting. They were lined up three abreast around the last bend. Wolde was dropping but I daren't pass here as I would have to run very wide to avoid being felled, and that would have meant running too much distance. As Wolde tailed off, I darted through on his inside, hit the home straight running diagonally across the track so that I was running very wide, then kicked for home with everything I had, passing the two sprinting Ethiopians, then tying up, with nothing left, to just hang on to win — one of my sweetest victories.

There was no warm down. As I bent over panting, I looked down at my right ankle and felt sick. There were two four inch gashes, from spikes, on the inside of my leg and the back of my achilles tendon; a lot of it was superficial, luckily, but on the inside about two inches was wide open and I could see white which I took to be bone.

Roelants was almost as pleased as I was that I had won. The Ethiopians lodged a complaint that I had been pushing! Not surprisingly this was rejected. I got some antiseptic cream on the wounds temporarily, and at the presentation on the podium, when I received a medal and my prize, a small portable radio, I got a great cheer from the crowd.

DAILY TELEGRAPH

"I looked down . . . and felt sick."

Never one to hold a grudge, I patted Degeufu and Mashresha on their heads and shook hands as they came up for their medals, to the shrill whistles of the disapproving spectators.

I limped off to be examined by two doctors, one American and one Finnish, and the American doctor said the big gash would need stitching, much to my great disappointment and fear. He said, "You won't need a local anaesthetic, the skin will be dead, and anyway I've got a very sharp needle."

"Oh my God."

I lay back on the bench, the sweat pouring off as he worked his way snipping and pulling, and of course the bloody skin wasn't dead at all. When he was finished I was stuck to that PVC covered bench and they had to tear me off it as they lifted me up by my arms.

When I got back to the hotel room, there was a bunch of pink carnations on my table and a little card which said, "To the Great Gentleman".

The following morning I hobbled 3½ miles at 5.30 a.m. I was in so much pain that I felt physically sick. There were 18 days to go before the Maxol Marathon in Manchester, the trial for the European Games team.

The day after that, it took me 50 minutes to "run" 5 miles in the morning and 1 hour 25 minutes to "run" 8 miles home from work. I was feeling knackered and ill. Nevertheless, nothing was going to stand in the way of my preparations. I somehow managed a 7 and a 15 on Saturday, and my 20½ mile run on Sunday. My right foot was swollen and I was still in a good bit of pain. I had to wrap thick bandages around the cuts to stop myself from kicking them, and polythene round the bandages to keep them dry from the muddy country I was running. I went to Ashton-under-Lyne Infirmary for them to look at the stitches and was told that they couldn't come out as the wound was infected. I had to go on a course of antibiotic tablets.

Sometimes I felt dizzy during the day, often I felt knackered. I ran 128½ miles that week, including 59.1 and 56.1 for my two flying lunchtime quarters at the Ashton track, and they took the stitches out on Friday. I stayed on antibiotics for another couple of days.

I was playing around with a special diet. Early in February 1968 I had had a scribbled letter from Martin Hyman about some work that was going on in Sweden with trained athletes, mostly skiers, on a bicycle ergometer which they pedalled at about 75% maximum rate till they could pedal no more (at this rate). The times recorded were mostly between 1½ and 2 hours. Scientists measured the glycogen content, that is the fuel content of the muscles available for easy conversion into energy, and in the beginning it was 2% of wet muscle weight, decreasing to practically zero when they stopped. This was for athletes on a normal diet.

Then they tried various diets and repeated the tests.

First the athletes were fed for four days on a diet high in proteins and fats, but low in carbohydrates. The glycogen content of their muscles went down to less than 1%, and they could cycle for only 1 hour.

When they fed athletes for four days on a diet high in carbohydrates the glycogen content went up to 30% and they could cycle for three hours.

But when a two stage diet was used, even better results were obtained. Athletes were given hard continuous exercise to use up reserves, then kept to a low carbohydrate diet to establish glycogen starvation. Then for two days they were given a high carbohydrate diet, this carbohydrate being converted to glycogen and avidly stored by the muscles. Tests showed that the glycogen content of the muscles increased to 4% and they pedalled the bicycle ergometer for four hours at 75% maximum effort.

Martin ended his letter: "Obviously this is exciting enough to be worth following up. The trouble is the marathon is only fractionally over 2 hours (at the moment) and as distance men are keen on carbohydrate anyway there may be no significant effect."

I filed the letter away in my 1968 file, along with all the bits and pieces from the Mexico Olympics.

But my mind got to thinking, supposing one is running the marathon at near maximum effort and not just 75%. Then, instead of talking one hour, two hours, three hours, we might be talking about 45 minutes, 1½ hours and 2¼ hours, which took us into the realms of marathon performances. Certainly it was well known that things usually got difficult around the 18 mile mark in the 26 mile marathon event and in a top class race this would be around the 1½ hour point. Surely this then must be what was happening. This was the "wall". The muscles had run out of glycogen, they got stiff and tired, the pace dropped, and that was because the body was having to metabolise fats and then maybe even protein, the muscle tissue itself, to get energy; and very inefficiently at that. Now if that point could be delayed up to 2¼ hours . . .

I had forgotten the exact details of Martin's letter; I knew there was something in it about "four days", and in fact for my first tentative trial at "the diet" the low carbohydrate wasn't that low. Sunday through to Wednesday I cut down my carbohydrate intake, having Ryvita and very thin toast instead of bread, a very thin slice of May's fruit cake each day, but still kept on with a banana at work for breakfast, and some potatoes, and a pint of cocoa made with milk last thing at night. Only a couple of times did I feel any odd effects. Monday's evening session was:

"Ran home from work — Navigation Inn, Romiley, Chadkirk — an absolute scorcher of a day — 2x2 min. — 90 secs. interval — 16x30 secs. — 30 secs. interval — 2x2 min. — felt bloody knackered on these — diet? fartlek from Chadkirk. 12 miles."

Tuesday — "Ran home from work — easy running all the way — a bit tired at the end — vest off from Fairfield Station — 7 miles."

Wednesday, the last day of the "low carbohydrate" — "Ran home from work — easy running — felt all right, in fact sprightly at times. 7 miles."

That week I ran 101½ miles. As far as I was concerned my leg was fully recovered and I was ready for the Maxol on Sunday morning. Hopefully, the passport to my first selection for Athens.

The stage was set for a classic race; the Maxol sponsors had a budget of £5,000 for this competition and they were flying in from Japan, Kenji Kimihara, the Mexico Olympic silver medallist, and the tall Yoshiaki Unetani, who had set a new record of 2:13:49 in the famous Boston marathon in April. But most feared of all was Derek Clayton of Australia, who had run an incredible 2:09:36.4 in Fukuoka, Japan, in December 1968, and had topped that with 2:08:33.6 in Antwerp only a few weeks before the Maxol race. Many runners thought him to be invincible.

The competition for British placings would be fierce too, with Bill Adcocks already having run 2:11:07 in Greece this year, and 2:10:47.8 in Japan, December 1968, and Jim Alder with a 2:16:34 clocking this year, a time I had beaten only once, way back in 1964.

However, my training had been methodical and thorough. I had prepared for this race down to the last detail. My hot weather gear was proven; string vest, ultra brief shorts, lightweight shoes with holes punched in for ventilation. My hair was cut short. The special diet was an unknown factor, but it was logical and an attempt to improve my racing. I was leaving nothing to chance.

Sunday, July 20th. I stayed in bed until 9.30 a.m. dozing, reading, then got up and jogged 2 miles on the canal bank. For breakfast I had a bowl of raw rolled oats with sugar and milk, followed by three marmalade butties and a piece of May's fruit cake, swilled down with a pot of tea, finishing about 10.30 a.m. I had a luke-warm bath, soaping my body all over to get rid of any body oils that would prevent me cooling in the race. 11.30 a.m. I had almost a teaspoonful of salt in a pint of blackcurrant juice. I was going to run the race without a drink and wanted to be fully topped up with salt and liquid when the race started at 2.00 p.m.

After that I lay on the spare bed, reading and listening to Beatles' records until 12.25 p.m. when May called me and told me it was time to go. I got my few things together and we went to the car. The bloody thing wouldn't start; the bloody dynamo was knackered or something. We had to push it to get the engine running. What a start! In Manchester, I parked the car at the back of the Town Hall, off St. Peter's Square, left May and the kids, and went to get changed at the Y.M.C.A. It was hot in there. I changed and went outside; it was hot outside too, overcast, hot and muggy. I did about ½ mile warm up in my string vest and gear; I saw Clayton warming up in a full track suit; that surprised me. I met my mother and dad, found May and got a glucose tablet from her in Albert Square where the start was. There were loads of my mates there, crowds wishing me well — the local boy.

Maxol Marathon start. 1 Busch, 2 Kimihara 3 Unetani.

At 2.00 p.m., Sir Matt Busby, chairman of Manchester United Football Club, fired the gun to set the field of 167 long distance specialists on its way. I immediately got up with the leading group and, climbing the gentle rise of Upper Brook Street, all that could be heard was the slap, slap of flat road shoes on black tarmac and the occasional shouts of encouragement from the few spectators on that early part of the course. There was no talking. This was going to be a serious race. Adcocks, Unetani, Jurgen Busch, of East Germany. After 3 miles, at Birchfields Park, Clayton showed up. Well, we were all there now.

At 4½ miles as I strode along Wilbraham Road, following close behind Unetani, I began to feel spots of moisture landing on me. The clouds had turned to rain; I glanced up at the clouds; it wasn't raining at all. I looked ahead and Unetani was throwing off a shower of sweat as he ran along. I switched positions in the group.

Past the 5 mile point and up Princess Parkway, Clayton began putting in short bursts, as if he were testing the field; moving ahead with me following right behind him, then dropping back to the bunch. I hoped that this would give him the impression that I was going well, but I was thinking at that time that both hc and Bill Adcocks were running better than I was as they were running slightly faster on the short downhill stretches.

"Clayton began putting in short bursts."

". . . then dropping back to the bunch."

B. BUTTERWORTH

Above and right:
Clayton (200) and
Adcocks (65) whittling the
field down. Hogan (211),
Kimihara (2), and Alder
try to hang on.

B. BUTTERWORTH

DAILY MIRROR

". . . down to three . . ."

Approaching 10 miles, on Altrincham Road in Wythenshawe, Clayton's bursts had whittled the leaders down to three, himself, Bill Adcocks and me. The sun had finally destroyed the clouds, and our bodies cast short shadows along the road. Just before 10 miles Clayton had a 7 or 8 yard lead and he grabbed for a drink. Bill and I ignored the refreshments, were quickly up to him and I passed him, dodging through the traffic to lead at the 10 mile point in 50:10; only to be quickly caught again by the other two.

The course was a 6 mile run out to a 6 mile loop which was completed twice followed by an 8 mile run out towards Trafford Park and to the Manchester United Club ground at Old Trafford. Along Barlow Moor Road to the start of the second lap Clayton again applied the pressure a couple of times and we dropped Bill,

B. BUTTERWORTH

". . . a couple of times we dropped Bill . . ."

*". . . I sensed
Bill drop again . . ."*

B. BUTTERWORTH

but each time he slowed and each time Bill made contact again. Up Princess Parkway, approaching the Mersey Hotel I sensed Bill drop again by 5 or 6 yards and I took the lead with a sharpish burst to finish off the job, taking Clayton with me, alongside me and finally ahead of me, as I let him lead and tucked right in behind him, slipstreaming the tall heavy Australian. I felt comfortable; yes, I

KEN HEATON

". . . slipstreaming the tall heavy Australian."

35

GERRY CRANHAM

"At 15 miles Clayton grabbed for his drink . . ."

was going quite well, I'd had no trouble up to now. At 15 miles Clayton grabbed for his drink once more, and once more I ignored it. Again I sensed that I had a break and just picked the pace up slightly to worry him and make it more difficult for him to get back. Down the hill at tree-shaded Langley Lane, I was more or less waiting for him to rush back up to me immediately; but he didn't come. He didn't come. Spectators were shouting to me, "50 yards," "60 yards," I couldn't believe it, "100 yards". Bloody hell, could I hang on? I couldn't believe it.

Well, you've got to finish. Relax. Stride out. Hope for the best. This time straight down Barlow Moor Road to Chorlton-cum-Hardy; as I left the lap I suddenly had a bad patch, my legs went tired, my whole body felt fatigued and I panicked, thinking about the 8 miles

GERRY CRANHAM

Jim Hogan cheers me through Chorlton-cum-Hardy.

"A sort of dream state set in."

still to go. The sun was shining; it was hot. Stride out, keep up the pace. I wiped my face with my hand, my chin felt rough; I looked at my hand, it was white salt crusted on my face.

At 20 miles I grabbed a wet sponge, squeezed it over my head, neck, wiped my arms then threw it away. I was refreshed for about a mile; the hotness hit me again after that. I worked out that there should be another sponge at 22½ miles; it was something to look forward to. On round the suburbs of Stretford, the flaming sponge station never came. Oh no! God, I feel so tired, so worried, can I keep going? Clayton must be catching me. A sort of dream state set in. I felt extreme anxiety, worrying about being caught, wanting to stop. I ran past Old Trafford, huge crowds here, cigarette smoke

"I ran past Old Trafford . . ."

GERRY CRANHAM

". . . head back in relief . . ."

drifted my way, ugh! Down into Trafford Park, heading away from the finish. This was sheer murder, a long straight road, I can't see the turn. Where has this gale force wind sprung up from? Still I can't see the turn, I'll never make it. Should I stop and walk? Let Clayton catch me, go with him and try to beat him on the sprint? One foot in front of the other. There's the turn; round; I don't want to look. Clayton will be right there.

   He wasn't. My spirits rose. I got a sponge at 25 miles. Clayton was a long way behind. Keep it going. Keep it going. There are the floodlight gantries of the stadium, nearly home. Frank Morris hands me a pink sponge; cramp almost grabs my legs. Bloody hell, just hold it off. God I'm tired. Turn right, up the little hill, it's hard, hard. Right, to the football ground, into the dark downhill tunnel then back into daylight and round the outside of the grass. Roars, cheers, roars. Someone's catching me, look round, no-one; I thought it was Clayton. The last straight to the narrow tape; my legs wobble a little; head back in relief; I'm through. I'm home. AND I'VE WON!

Hot . . . *work . . .*

DAILY EXPRESS

. . . this marathon lark!

DAILY EXPRESS

1969

Result;

R. Hill	2:13:42 (Personal Best)
Derek Clayton	2:15:40
Jim Alder	2:18:18
Yoshiaki Unetani	2:19:37
Bill Adcocks	2:20:13
John Fewery	2:21:43

First prize was a stainless steel tankard engraved "Maxol Marathon". I had one or two blisters, some stiffness below my calves, but went straight into running to work and back. The A.A.A. 10,000 metres was in 12 days' time. The week after the Maxol I ran 113 miles, the week before the A.A.A.'s 119 miles.

CHAPTER THREE

The A.A.A. 10,000 metre championships held on the black cinder track of White City, London, on Friday, August 1st, was the trial for the European Games. It was a hot humid night with no wind. The pace at the start was slow, but somehow it seemed hard work for me as I stiffened up after 5 laps, my calves becoming painful and not allowing my usual springy stride. Running even-paced, I slowly moved up through the field until I was with the leading group at 5,000 metres. Next thing, Dick Taylor was off. I knew it was going to happen, and I knew I wouldn't respond. I just speeded up a little. Tagg went with Taylor for three laps and then was dropped himself. A big bunch of us were chasing, and with 5 laps to

AAA 10,000m. championship. l. to r. Bedford, Tagg, Wright, Hogan, Caine, Clayton, Hill, Alder.

go I thought there was only Taylor and Tagg ahead. Then I found out that No. 7, in pale blue, running with Tagg, was in the race, he wasn't a lapped runner. He was Matthews or somebody. I shared the work with club-mate Mike Freary, as I wanted to get him into 4th position if possible. I had already made up my mind that I didn't want to run the 10,000 metres in Athens, there was no point as Dick Taylor would surely win the gold medal, and if Mike were 4th, behind me, he would be in the team. We got within 30 yards of Tagg and Matthews at the bell, but I didn't want to sprint for fear of demoralizing Mike, and in fact I almost moved out to let him through. At 200 metres I accelerated a little, closed to 15 yards behind Matthews, and as I hit the straight I decided to go for him. I "kicked past him safely enough without tying up at all".

Result:

1st Dick Taylor	28:27.6
2nd M. Tagg	28:36.4
3rd R. Hill	28:39.2

I told the B.A.A.B. I didn't want the 10,000 metres in the European Games and, after a run-off race, Mike Freary made the team for Athens.

There were now 7 weeks to go before the marathon in Athens. I had a week's "mini-rest" of 95 miles; followed by a week's holiday, a change of training area, in Formby near Southport, where we camped in the garden of May's brother Jack and his wife Marie. That week I covered 113 miles and included a win in an invitation 5,000 metres at St. Helens, 14:00.6, a personal best on the Saturday, and a run for G.B. in the match versus the U.S.A. at White City on Tuesday.

Here I was partnered by Jim Alder and it was a race in which I thought I ran intelligently to get the maximum points for Britain. I had been peeved when in previous races I had had a poor day, and seen my partner take away the opposition and then get outsprinted. I wouldn't do anything so thoughtless. The Americans had a reputation for being poor long distance runners and these two, Ken Moore and Frank Shorter, looked no exception. We let them lead for a couple of laps, then I took over and alternated the lead with Jim, doing 2 laps apiece, to try to burn off the Yanks. On my third stint at the front, Jim started to drop back so, instead of going away, I too dropped back and let the Americans lead. Jim was still struggling so I went into the lead and very gently slowed down the pace, accelerating only when Shorter tried to overtake me, and then, holding the lead, easing down again. Jim recovered his strength and with 6 laps to go actually took the lead, putting in an effort on the back straight of the next lap which failed to dislodge the two Americans. With three laps to go I put in a fast lap, which succeeded

MARK SHEARMAN

G.B. v U.S.A. 10,000m. Moore, Alder, Hill, Shorter.

in dropping Shorter, but left Moore still in contact. I slowed down, gathering myself for the bell, Jim edging into 2nd place, and with its ring I started an effort, not too hard, just dragging Jim along with me. Halfway down the back straight the tall fair haired Moore swooped round Jim and dropped right in behind me. He was to tell me later that he thought he had it "all sewn up here". I kicked into the last bend with 200 metres to go and this is what fooled him, I kicked again, faster, just before the home straight. By the time he looked up I was gone. The result:

1st, R. Hill	29:07.2
2nd, Ken Moore	29:08.8
3rd, Jim Alder	29:13.8
4th, Frank Shorter	29:16.4

From then on it was steady training for five weeks, running hard sessions on Mondays and Wednesdays with my two flying 440's as extra Tuesday lunchtimes, first one usually relaxed in about 59, the second one flat out in around 56 seconds. I ran a 122½ mile week, then with four weeks to go I began to have pains in my left leg again — the hamstring, right at the top, especially after a 28 mile Sunday run in full track suit and anorak. It slowed me down — "leg worse, all down the back of my left thigh — curtailing my stride" — "leg became painful once I'd set off" — but that's all it did. I had no time nor facility for treatment, so I just slowed down. That week I ran 135½ miles. The pains gradually eased away and further weeks of 126 and 111½ miles brought me up to travelling to Athens. All these last five weeks had been done in full track-suit, to give myself heat acclimatisation.

My last race before leaving for Greece was a 3,000 metres invitation at the opening of a new track at Marl Pits, Rawtenstall. It was advertised as an "all-weather" track. I turned up without spikes, but when I found out that in fact, it was a cinder track, I had to borrow Bolton team-mate Keith Baum's spikes and won the race from the front in 8:16.0, my fastest for 6 years. I was in form!

The week before departure I worked like hell at my job, staying there at nights to make sure that I was leaving with a clear conscience, no jobs left undone, and plenty of work for all my assistants.

Saturday, September 13th, we set out for Greece, driving down to Stanstead Airport for the plane to Athens. All year I had been planning this trip for my family. I wanted them near me at this Games, even though it meant spending all the available money we had. And we were helped here by "Jimmy" Green, the founder and managing editor of "Athletics Weekly", who'd secretly allowed one of my boys to travel free with the "Athletics Weekly" party, "In recognition of your services to athletics", which I thought was a marvellous gesture. Jimmy also fiddled it so that I could stay on with the "A.W." party for a few days' holiday after the race with someone else taking my seat on the official team plane back to Britain. My mother and dad were also travelling with the "Athletics Weekly" party.

We were delayed ages at Stanstead, and I had to go out for a three mile run from there in the evening in my jeans and suede walking out shoes. Take off was eventually 9.20 p.m., it was dark and the old Bristol Britannia shook noisily and vibrated as it headed into the air towards Greece. I managed to get an hour's sleep, with Steven, in a bunk at the rear of the plane before we landed at 2.30 a.m. Sunday morning, in fact 3.30 a.m. local time.

Cecil Dale was there to meet me and Bill Adcocks who had travelled with his wife on the same flight, and whilst May and the boys with my mother and dad wearily waited to be taken to their hotel, near the centre of Athens, we were whisked by official car in the opposite direction to the Hotel Cavouri at Vouliagmeni. We were sharing a room with Jim Alder, and Bill had to go and tickle him to wake him. As only Jim could, he hit the roof over this, but soon calmed down and we were all asleep by 4.30 a.m.

The next day, Sunday, we agreed to run together, travelling by car with Frank Read, the B.A.A.B. treasurer, to Marathon, where there is an ornamental wall, near a bridge over a dried river bed, marking the start of the marathon. We were amazed to see that, for a lot of the way, the roads were up. They were actually re-laying the roads for the race. They were going to have to work day and night to get that job finished! I had started the special diet the day before, and this time I cut out all bread and potatoes, sticking to Ryvita, but including a daily handful of nuts and raisins, a piece of cake at night and also at night a pint of cocoa with three tablespoons of Complan. This time I began to feel a little weak.

What with the diet and lack of sleep, that Sunday run gave me a shock. I wanted to do 14 miles, the others 10, so they said that they would join me when I had done 4 miles. After the cool of England, it was a baking 4 miles, and when the other two joined me, fresh, I was all right on the flat for a couple of miles, but when we started to climb, I had to let them go; I deliberately slowed, I was knackered, and it annoyed me that I had put myself at a psychological disadvantage. I wasn't going to bloody well go training with them again. "That's it, lads", I thought as I dripped to a halt at Frank's car.

I wanted everything to go right this time; I wanted every little thing to go in my favour. From then on, every morning, I heard Jim and Bill get up at 8.00 a.m., considerately whispering together, getting ready to go out to run. I was awake all right, but I lay with my eyes closed until they had gone, then I got up, put on my running gear and went out for my own early morning run. I didn't want to appear anti-social.

I left my Maxol Marathon tankard on my chest of drawers, just as a reminder of who had won that race. I drank my cocoa from it every night, and I hoped they would see it and remember.

I was very relaxed and happy there. It was a beautiful hotel, right by the sea and a small sandy beach. Every day, May would bring down Steven and Graham on the No. 16 bus from Athens, the boys would play in the sun, I would sit under a tree in the shade reading. Then in the evening after I had seen them back on to the bus back to the city, I would have my evening meal, read, relax and go to sleep before Jim and Bill got in.

I went to the Karaiskakis Stadium only twice. Once for the hot opening ceremony, with all the teams parading before a capacity crowd, thousands of coloured balloons released into the air, and rockets heading skywards, exploding with a bang

Waiting for the bus back to Athens.

to release parachutes with all the flags of the nations suspended below. Some rockets didn't quite make it, falling prematurely into the arena and into the crowd, and causing pandemonium as they exploded on the ground. The second time was to watch the 10,000 metres final, when in astonishment I watched Dick Taylor lapped, after foolishly warming up for about an hour in full track-suit in that heat, Mike Tagg take a silver medal just behind Jurgen Haase, and Mike Freary was just pipped for the fifth place by Gaston Roelants, both being given the same time. Haase ran 28:41.6. Christ, I could have made a medal after all!

What other athletics I saw was on the T.V. in the hotel. The West German team were also in our hotel, but did not compete, in protest at the banning of 1500 metre runner Jurgen May by the I.A.A.F. because he had represented E. Germany in international competition, before fleeing to W. Germany. It was something of a temptation to see them sunbathing and swimming in the sea; however, common sense prevailed and I didn't want to risk burning my skin or in any way chancing any kind of over-heating before the race, and restricted my ration of vitamin D to that which was obtained in my morning and evening runs up and down the arid coastal paths, and around the quiet hot roads, up in the dry scrub-covered hills inland from Voula. All the runs alone. I heard one night that Jim and Bill had run back all the way from the stadium, and had had a real burn up from the airport. Bloody great!

On Wednesday, I was down to 5 mile runs; Thursday I came on to the high carbohydrate part of the diet: "bags of carbohydrate, rolls, etc., and jam", "steak and chips and a couple of cakes", a chocolate "Aztec" bar in my room at night. Fives on Thursday, fives on Friday, 3½'s on Saturday. No problems. The last thing I saw on T.V. on Saturday night was my old mate John Whetton drive through the ruck up the home straight in the 1500 metres final, to snatch the gold medal.

Sunday, September 21st. Four days before my 31st birthday. I woke up at 8.45 a.m. then just relaxed in bed, resting until 9.30 a.m. Out of bed, I put on my racing shoes and just a pair of shorts and went for an easy run. God, it was hot! 1½ miles was enough. I rinsed my face, went down for breakfast — two pieces of cake and a cup of tea, got a few autographs for one or two people who'd asked me to take their books, and went back to our room. I laid out all my gear carefully, making sure everything was there, and had a lukewarm bath, washing myself well all over. My legs were smooth as I had shaved off all the hairs, as cyclists do, to give an extra cooling effect. And it worked.

At 12.00 o'clock, I went down for lunch: water, a piece of cake, one jam butty and some cereal "Fruhstück Flocken", borrowed from the German team who seemed to be better equipped in that

Posing: Hill, Alder, Molloy, Parody, Adcocks.

47

department than we were. At 12.45 p.m. I collected my gear from our room and a big black old American car took the three of us with the Gibraltar runner, and the tall Mick Molloy of Ireland, down to the training area near the airport. I put my things in a rest room and we went outside to pose for a photograph for the Gibraltar team manager. It was very, very hot. Bloody hell, what were we going to go through later this afternoon? I quickly put the thought out of my head, and went back into the rest room to sit and listen to my cassette player playing Beatles' hits. Everyone looked tense. I swallowed my teaspoonful of salt, dissolved in a small amount of orange juice, in a quick gulp and chased it down slowly with a pint of more dilute orange juice. The coach came for all the competitors; it took us through the centre of Athens and out on to the course; the windows were wide open to let in whatever breeze there was. It was still hot. They had finished relaying the road — thank God for that!

At the start area we filed off the bus and went into a little dressing room, behind the monumental wall, with rows of low hospital type beds. I got one in the far corner and lay down. There were not enough beds by far. I put on my cassette player and some zealous official rushed over and told me to switch it off. "Get stuffed", I said quietly, turning down the soothing sounds of the Beatles until, with my ear close, only I could hear it. I relaxed and almost slept. Later I read a book for a while. 3.30 p.m., time to get ready. I put on my racing gear, brief white shorts, high cut at the sides, and string vest. There were a few murmurs of surprise from the other runners. I went outside.

The skies were now overcast, mercifully shielding us from direct sunlight; but it was still hot, in the 80's, and I just jogged for about 400 metres, to loosen up a little. I'd get plenty of warming up in the 26 miles plus ahead. I repeatedly wet my very short hair and wiped water on my arms and thighs to keep as cool as possible. In the starting area, flagged with rough stones, Greek priests with their long beards and in their black tall hats were praying and chanting. Incense was burning. There were girls in colourful traditional costumes. As it approached 4.00 p.m. the runners congregated, nervously kicking out their legs, jogging on the spot, waiting. We had to take an olive branch from a line of small kids; I took mine, it was tied with a pale blue ribbon, from a fair haired lad who reminded me of Steven and Graham, who were now probably impatiently waiting in the old Panathinaikon Stadium, 26 miles away.

We were called to the line. I swallowed, and tried not to think of the two hours ahead. I put my hands together as if to pray and then remembered that I didn't believe in God. It was up to me. Instead, I kissed the lucky silver ring on my left hand. Both my rings had sticking plaster underneath them, to keep them secure, as I had found in the Maxol Marathon that I lost so much weight that my fingers became thin, and the rings were in danger of slipping off.

At 4.00 p.m. a pistol shot launched us on our journey to Athens. I set off very slowly at the very back. I had no confidence, just an ominous feeling that I was going to have a bad run. But everyone was being cautious in that heat and I began to work through the field towards the front. The press cars were a nuisance here on the narrow roads, they tried to squeeze past the breasted groups of runners, sending up clouds of dust from the unmetalled sides of the roads; V-signs were given, and the crowded vehicles had obscenities shouted at them in several European languages. By 2 miles I was up with the leaders as we turned sharp left off the road and ran to the tomb of the Greek warriors killed in their victorious battle with the Persians. At the steep mound I threw down my olive branch, turned about, ran back to the road, and headed once again towards Athens. The bunch was still a big one — Farcic (Yugoslavia), Akcay

"... headed once again towards Athens." Aktas (688), Molloy (80), Hill (223), Roelants (14), Wagnon (154), Steylen (440).

(Turkey), Roelants (Belgium), Pieren (Belgium), Simon (Hungary), Aktas (Turkey) and Molloy (Ireland) were the ones I could see around me. Almost everyone was wearing white: Roelants with a cap and a very cut away vest, the Turks in their red banded vests looking very brown.

Farcic picked up the pace a couple of times, I went with him, but we dropped back and I wouldn't respond to his repeated signals for me to make a break with him. In the end, probably out of frustration, he went off at quite a speed and deciding not to chase him, I stayed back with the crowd, watching. There were no other takers.

The course climbed a little between 6 and 9 miles; as we got to this stretch the first sponge station was there; Roelants took a sponge and then belted off after Farcic. Again, I didn't respond and was

"Roelants . . . belted off after Farcic."

content to run along with the two Turks and Simon the Hungarian. I felt I was running more or less within myself, but was somehow not

Akcay, Hill, Aktas, Simon.

quite comfortable, and I decided to hit my own slightly faster pace, relying on instinct and experience to know the best speed I could keep without folding.

Just at this point a helicopter descended and hovered about 50 feet above the road. I could see Roelants shake his fist and then I ran into the billows of brown dust, swirling up from the dry fields, which got into my eyes, mouth and on my skin and my vest, which turned brown. I was spitting red-brown dust. The bloody idiots.

I thought I was moving away alone, quietly padding along when a lob of white spit came past me, and to my surprise I found Simon was still there. Relaxing on the downhill and flat bits, gradually I dropped him and looking up I could see that way ahead Roelants had caught Farcic and passed him.

"... gradually I dropped him ..."

After 12 miles the steep hills started, and gradually I too began to pull Farcic back. It wasn't easy climbing in that heat, but he was suffering more than I was, paying the penalty for his impetuosity. I caught him, passed him, and found that he was hanging on. I didn't like it, I wanted to be alone, and his presence just behind me, not running quite stride for stride, made me feel very uncomfortable. I was taking the sponges but no drinks. I felt very relieved when at 15 miles he dropped away. On I pressed, up and up. I knew the hills ended at about 20 miles and, with 6 miles of downhill following, this would be a psychological point in the race for me. On the two times I had been on the course, I had seen the skeleton of a huge oval sign on the skyline to the left of the top of the hill and I had told myself that the race would be over once I got to there.

I was applauded by people all along the route, the small cafés with wooden tables and white tablecloths, people standing there, probably some of them comfortably inebriated on their Sunday afternoon wine, as we sweated up the hills, cutting the bends, looking down at the black road, under the lines of flags and bunting. I could hear applause way behind; probably for Simon. I was second and going as well as I could have hoped. Quickly the clapping got closer and closer. I never look round in a race. Who was coming up? At 17 miles Jim Alder caught me; he ran alongside me; again I felt uncomfortable running in company. I had enough to worry about without someone running there with me, so I said, "Go on, Jim". He took a long sideways look at me, and without having said a word, he went away quite quickly carrying a sponge in each hand.

I had no intention of trying to stay with him. I was going fast enough to know that I would finish. He gained a lead of 30 yards and then stayed this same distance in front of me for about 2 miles. I was thinking, "If I could just keep this going, I've got the bronze medal. A medal, a medal!" We were running on the newly surfaced road now and the tar was melting. Cri-i-i-p, Cri-i-i-p, my shoes went, as I pulled them off the sticky surface. It was hard work. I had to find the tracks on the road where cars, with dust on their wheels had driven, to get some kind of free running.

"I was taking the sponges . . ."

Jim wasn't getting away; in fact I was pulling him back a little, and as I sighted the oval sign and crested the top of the hill, I was only 10 yards behind. I saw him speed up as he went over the top, but I speeded up even more and very quickly went past him. I opened my legs and was flying along, down wide curving boulevards, the tall lamp-posts showing the direction of the curves ahead. For a short while I thought that I had gone too fast as I got a sharp pain across my left shoulder, a sort of stitch, but this disappeared, and all I could think of was pushing on for a silver medal. A white silver medal.

The air was cooling as the light started to fade, and the sponges I was taking I found refreshing, rinsing my mouth then squeezing the water over my head. My string vest was soaked and heavy and hanging way down over my shorts. Number 223.

". . . rinsing my mouth . . ."

There were rose petals, pink mainly, all over the black road in front of me. And one paper cup lying there with a splatter of water. Gaston must be drinking. He must be in trouble. He's going to suffer over this last bit. Someone threw something at me, instinctively I went to catch it, I thought it must be a sponge, but it was a handful of petals. I felt annoyed with myself, I was a fool. Way, way down the long road, as it descended into the taller buildings of the city centre, I could just make out a convoy of cars and vans, red tail lights, flashing red light, flashing amber light. That must be the convoy behind Gaston; well he's a long way ahead as I thought. It was the first time I had seen him, though.

On I pressed, I was getting very tired myself now, but a silver medal. The flatter parts of the roads felt like uphills now, and I was glad to let gravity help me down the slopes, into the narrower streets. Not far to go now before we make a left turn down to the stadium. I kept catching glimpses of the convoy, I was catching Roelants, but I was so tired . . . so tired. For God's sake keep going Gaston, I don't want a bloody battle now, I don't want to make an effort, I don't want to have to chase you. I knew if I got near enough to him that people would expect me to go after him, and I knew that I would have to do it, as it was expected.

With just over a mile to go I could actually see the man now. A way in front; he was turning round; he was worried, but he would get there; he had to, we were nearly home. I was nearly home. There was no hope of winning.

PRESSE SPORTS

". . . he was turning round . . ."

Turn left into the long avenue to the stadium, and a long right hand turn and fairly steep downhill. Move over to the right to cut the bend and cut the distance. Gaston's still on the left. I'm catching him. 30 yards, 20 yards. 1Km to go. I moved over to the left to get right in behind him, to be in a position to attack. I swept down and hit him hard, straight past. I didn't feel a response. I was flying — bloody hell, I was sprinting. But how far to go? I could see some flames in the dusk ahead; beacons; that had to be the entrance to the stadium or . . .

ASSOCIATED PRESS

FIONNBAR CALLANAN

"—the stadium—"   *"—long narrow black track—"*

My heart was pounding; I was feeling sick; physically sick with the effort. Christ, I was going to win. Pushing, pushing, the wind flying against my face — arms pointing left — left — across the middle of the road — a Landrover doing a U-turn almost knocks me down — across the road-steps — bloody steps — careful — pillars — the stadium — long narrow black track — cheers — huge cheers — Oh no! I look round — thank God, it's not Roelants — cheers are louder — I look round again for Gaston — still no-one on the track. I've won! I've won!

ASSOCIATED PRESS

"I've won! I've won!"

The tape. What do I do? What does one do? Bloody hell, I jumped in the air about 2 yards before the tape, then jumped again. I'd done it. My raised fist was clenched. I'd done it! Me! And only me! Take that! Someone touched my arm. "Don't touch me, don't touch me." I felt as though someone had stuck a needle in my arm. Three cups of orange juice. A lap of honour. I saw my family, climbed over the marble wall and up the steps to where they were,

"A lap of honour."

"Roelants congratulated me."

KEYSTONE

"They were overjoyed."

May, Steven and Graham. My mother and dad. They were over-joyed. At one stage in the race my name had disappeared from the leaders' board and my dad had been taken ill and had to leave the stadium. But now he was fine.

Roelants congratulated me. "I won my gold in Tokyo. I am happy for you." Jim Alder was third, "You were due a good run." I went to change. Bill Adocks had had to drop out with trouble with both of his feet, but an ambulance brought him back to the stadium so that

57

ASSOCIATED PRESS

2nd. Roelants 2:17:22.2, 1st. Hill 2:16:47.8, 3rd. Alder 2:19:05.8.

he could congratulate me. My winning time was 2:16:47.8.

I received my gold medal and was proud to hear the National Anthem. We all three victors stood, our arms around each other. Comrades, victors all once more in the battle against "the marathon". Without changing, May came straight back to our hotel,

British medal winners in Athens.

borrowed a dress from our vivacious sprinter Anita Neil and we went to the "Wine Festival". We drank heartily, a couple of glasses with Gaston, walked and talked until the early hours, and when Frank Taylor of The Daily Mirror took us back by taxi to May's hotel, the Hotel Stanley, I was so keyed up I didn't sleep a wink there.

On the beach at Glyfada.

My dad takes off on a leg of the Athletics Weekly road relay,
after the Games.   I ran the fastest leg!!

59

We had five great days in Glyfada, all the family, Stan Bradshaw and his wife Ada from Clayton-le-Moors Harriers, and not forgetting Dennis Clayton, that untiring traveller who this time had cycled to Athens to see me run, and gave Steven and Graham a few happy hours riding them up and down the sea front on his bike. A lot of the time I was in a snappy sort of mood and it took me three days to unwind and relax. At the airport on the way back, John Jewell of the Road Runners Club asked it I would be interested in running the Boston Marathon next year. The Boston! Yes, I certainly would! We flew back the Saturday after the race. At Stanstead Airport some people had to help me push start the car, my battery was flat! See the conquering hero comes! We were soon down to earth, back to reality.

When we finally arrived home the neighbours had put up a big banner: "Well Done, Ron", and hung a huge gold medal in the window. It was really quite embarrassing, but appreciated. As was the pile of letters and telegrams from friends.

I had interviewers, photographers at my home and work. One incident embarrassed me, I can't think of another word to describe it. I was going out for a Sunday 7 miles, the day after we returned, when I passed a group of lads waiting to go playing football, and they just stood and clapped as I went past.

"WELL DONE. RON."

Back to work . . . and my normal washing facilities . . .

DAILY MIRROR

. . . but a rousing reception.

I had plenty of work to do. A new graduate, Arthur Welham, was starting work for me and I was keeping in trim with 2's, 5's and 7's for a race on the Thursday night after we returned. A 30 Km race, which I had asked to be set up at Leverhulme Park, so that I could attempt the World Record.

For once Frank Morris and the Bolton officials really let me down, and I never fully forgave them for the mis-management of the race. Over 1,000 people turned up on a windswept, cold, rainy October night to see what would surely be a new world record. I had studied the pace required and knew if we started with 72 second laps I could do it. I had assembled a good field of mates, who would help me out with the pace all along the line. Andy Holden, Mike Freary, John Jackson, Cyril Leigh, Colin Robinson, Tevor Proctor, Jeff Norman, Frank Maguire, Arthur Walsham, George Brockbank and Stan Clegg. After a full day's work, at 7.30 p.m. we toed the line. It was pouring.

In my training log I wrote, "I have delayed writing about this, I was so sick!" Trevor Proctor and Jeff Norman led for 4 laps, then Mike Freary, who was running 10,000 metres for G.B. against Finland six days later, ran the next 4 laps; the idea was to let me rest by following until no one could take me further, then it would be up to me. After 2 miles Andy Holden took over, and we were moving pretty well despite the conditions and the deteriorating track, recording 29:57 at 10,000 metres, well inside 5 minute miling. At 8 miles we lapped Cyril Leigh and he accelerated to pull us through for a short while, when Andy called, "You're on your own!"

I pressed on. At 10 miles they called 50:55. That couldn't be right, I was way inside 5 minute mile pace. What the hell was going on? For 3 laps I kept screaming at the officials, "Give me the right bloody time." But they could give me no more information. I kept pressing on, surely they would sort it out. I lapped Andy Holden and he led me again up to 20 Km, when a time was announced over the public address system with the comment that I was now 5 seconds outside even paced World Record schedule. This really upset me. How could I be? They had made an absolute bloody balls of it. That was it. "I'm dropping out, Andy." "Don't Ron — keep going." As I thought of the 1,000 or so people who had turned up to watch me, I realised I had to finish it off. Colin Robinson, Cyril Leigh and Andy pulled me through the last stages, but my heart wasn't in it all all. I was covered from head to foot in grit from the flying shoes of those in front of me, and from my own kick back as my legs mechanically hit the mud, pushed off, pulled through and strode on. On the last bend we avoided the rut which was fully six inches deep in water. "Give me a bloody count down," I screamed at the officials, with now less than 6 miles to go. "22 to go." God, 22 laps of misery. I plodded on, miserable, no information was being given out, and I knew I was down to 79 seconds a lap, well outside

B. BUTTERWORTH

". . . I knew I was down to 79 secs. a lap . . ."

World Record pace now. I kept shouting up to Colin and Cyril to slow down, they were going too fast. What was the point of killing myself with no hope of the World Record. 10 laps to go, 9, 8, 7 laps to go. Next time around it was, "4 laps to go." Two laps had disappeared! That was the last straw. What a cock-up! I just plodded to the finish, crossed the line and walked slowly head down, scowling and miserable straight into the dressing room, even though I was mobbed by hundreds of kids. I was covered in black mud, my spikes had worn down from ½ inch to ¼ inch, my legs were stiff and sore.

In the dressing room someone came in and said, "Hard luck, Ron, just 6.8 seconds outside the World Record." I was stunned. Angry. All that work! All that effort! And robbed of the bloody World Record by incompetence. Hell, I could have made up that 6.8 seconds on the last lap alone if someone had told me.

No one came to apologise. I just stood in the shower in all my gear. I couldn't stop shivering and my guts were starting to ache badly. What a bloody balls up.

1969

I couldn't get my spikes off. The laces were tightly saturated and black with grit. All that bloody way. I could have eaten the record. And now it was over. I couldn't go back on the track and re-run the last two laps, it was done. They'd robbed me of the World Record.

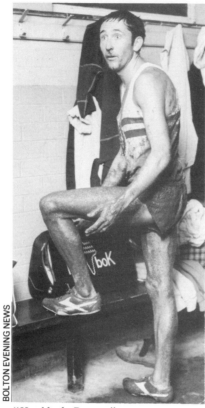

"Hard luck, Ron . . ."
30 Km. 1:32:32.2.

CHAPTER FOUR

For the first time in my career the well established pattern of track and road racing in the summer, cross-country running in the winter, with an active rest taking in the road relays in-between would have to change.

I had been invited to run the classic Fukuoka race in Japan on Sunday, December 7th; so at the time when I would normally be just building up for the Lancs. Cross-country Championship, I had to be at near peak condition.

But first I needed a break after a long and successful summer, marred only by the abortive 30 Km World Record attempt. I dropped down to running 2 miles easy sessions for two weeks of 30 and 40½ miles, then a further two weeks of 2 miles and 5 miles sessions to give 44 and 48½ miles.

What direct energies I diverted from training were instantly taken up in other fields. At work I really pushed myself and also had a week with a colleague from Viscose Sales Development Department, Freddie Daniels, visiting prospective customers in Belgium and Holland, dashing around the country, but always each morning, early, running around the dim cobbled streets of Brussels or along the misty canals of Tilbury.

At home I had to try to get done the jobs that inevitably had been neglected during the periods of hard training; painting the house occupied me for a long time. Painting is a job I hate and to make matters worse I had put a masking tape on the glass of the windows to try to make the job easier and found that the bloody tape wouldn't come off. It took us months of scraping, scratching the glass in the bargain, to get it off.

Every night I listened to Steven do his reading, then I had to read Steven and Graham a story from their comics before they would go to sleep. Every night.

As well as work, there was a civic reception for me, given by the Romiley Council in recognition of my Athens run. It was all pressure, and I eased this pressure almost every night by having a few home-brew shandies to drink, and sometimes a bit of my duty free liquor, which I had accumulated over the years of travelling.

My verucca had come back. It meant another operation to cut it out and this time I had a full anaesthetic, rather than put up with all that painful probing of my foot with a hyperdermic needle. The wound left me limping very badly and was affecting me when I had the first race of my 5 week build-up to Fukuoka. The Suncharm "15", organised by Holmfirth Harriers.

Even though I was not fit, about 6 pounds overweight, I expected a lot of myself and 3rd place behind Bob Ellis, Thames Valley Harriers, and John Newsome, Wakefield, got a "ran a disastrous 15 mile road race" in my diary. My limping run, combined with some heavy cambered roads had caused me to get a huge painful blister on my left foot. The big toe was extremely swollen and "the big toe nail was floating in a massive blister". So much so, that I had to cut a hole in the front of my training shoes, so the painful toe could pop through. Not unnaturally, this led to other blisters where the edges of the hole were rubbing on my foot. I had just started my training, there was little time left, and nothing was going to stop me; even so I wrote in my training log, the following Tuesday "in much pain with various injuries".

I changed to cocoa from home-brew as my nightly beverage, went straight into virtually full training, with hard sessions every Monday, Tuesday and Wednesday nights on the way home from work, and in the dark, rain, and sometimes freezing early snow, I clocked 92½, 118½, 124, and 135 miles before heading out for Japan.

Ten days before I left England I had a smallpox vaccination which didn't do me a lot of good. The day before flying to Japan I felt I needed mileage, and ran 7½ miles in the morning and 20½ miles in

Running to work — through Woodley . . .

. . . to Droylsden.

the afternoon. The next day, Sunday, November 30th, a ten day trip ahead, I left May and the kids, waving from the taxi window as I was driven to Manchester Airport. From there I flew to London, left my bags to arrive, dashed out and got a 285 bus to Feltham Swimming Baths, and met up with Jim Hogan and his protegé, young Welshman Alan Joslyn, for a 10 mile run on the lightly snow-covered roads. I got a 2 shilling fare on the Green Line bus back to Heathrow, collected my luggage, and transferred to Terminal 3 to meet up with my team manager for this trip, Arthur Gold, the B.A.A.B. secretary. I was on the low carbohydrate part of my "special diet", had been since Saturday, and this time I was more careful with it, weeding out even more carbohydrate. There was difficulty with some meals and snacks on the airplane, with me having to scrape out the fillings of sandwiches and throw the bread away.

Getting my two sessions a day in was going to be pretty tricky this time out, and I had to juggle a bit with time changes, taking English time or local time, whichever fitted the right day.

The Boeing 707 of JAL flight 442 to Tokyo was half taken up by cargo, and with me strapped into seat 17A, it took off at 3.35 for Anchorage on the first leg of our journey over the North Pole to the Orient. After an 8½ hour flight to Alaska, we skimmed in to the airport over white tundra and frozen sea with jagged cracked ice. By my watch it was Monday —12.30 a.m. and Arthur arranged with a security cop, in blue uniform with badge and holstered pistol, like someone in fancy dress to my eyes, for me to slip out and run 2 miles out and back on the freezing, slush covered roads, competing with huge gliding ageing American cars.

By the time we landed in Tokyo and transferred by taxi to the Ginza Tokyu Hotel, it was 6.30 in the evening, Japanese time, going dark, and time to change again, de-elevate from room 736, and run 2 miles round and round the block in the teeming streets. Arthur and I had a meal in the Ginza Grill of the hotel, and I retired. I was amazed to get a phone call in my room from Bob Moore. "Bob Moore?" "Yes, Bob Moore who was in Longwood Harriers and used to be at Leeds University." The medic who tried to grow a world record sized rat whilst he was studying. He had been picked to run for Canada. Well his departure from England had done him a lot of good as I remembered him only as a scrubber. He came up for a short chat.

I was awake early on Tuesday morning. The time change. 3.15 a.m. I had a handful of nuts and raisins, two Ryvita with cheese spread, and finished off a really fascinating book, "The Horsemen", by Joseph Kessel. At 6.35 a.m. I was out padding the now quieter streets round the hotel. 4 miles. Pack, breakfast, bus to

Returning from Ohiro Park with Aktas and Akcay.

Haneda airport, Boeing 727, a 2 hour journey down to Fukuoka City on the island of Kyushu. A huge city; I'd never heard of it until its marathon became famous. Press conference, photographs, taxis, grey skies and rain bouncing off the roads — hell, I'd never expected rain here. To the Nishitetsu Hotel, a beautiful new building, with a six foot high Christmas cake, a model of the hotel, in the huge foyer. Piped music everywhere — dining rooms, lifts, bloody bedrooms if you switched to the right (no wrong) channel on the radio. "I'm dreaming of a white Christmas." On December 2nd! Single room, with half bath, No. 856. Unpack and into my running gear, special chauffeur driven cars down to Ohiro Park,

Fukuoka Street.

and training round the lake with willows and pine trees, a long arched footbridge across the middle and misty mountains in the background.

Bob Moore tagged on to me at first, but I didn't want him with me. I had my own personal session to do; I slowed down and let him go. I ran a set of 2, 4 and 6x70 second bursts with 50 second interval in the cold and blustery evening, rain showers occasionally adding to the discomfort. I was on the fourth day of low carbohydrate diet and I could feel it; in my log I wrote, "in real trouble, never been so knackered in all my life — heart, legs, breathing"; and I meant it. I wondered whether it was a reaction from my smallpox vaccination, lack of sleep, the diet, or all three.

The next morning, Wednesday, I ran alone in the park. I was very bad again. I felt sick, my stomach felt sore, my heart was tired. I was crawling at the end. And when I stopped, my arms and neck were aching. I went back to bed for half-an-hour and called Arthur. Arthur was probably the best team manager I ever had. He always had the interest of the runner in mind, was ever prepared with medicines or whatever, and was never too proud to carry my bag whilst I trained! He came along with two aspirins, I ordered a light breakfast, orange juice and coffee only, and throughout the day I recovered.

Thursday morning I woke up at 4.00 a.m. I was on the high carbohydrates today. I had a nougat sweet and a chocolate raspberry cream; I'd bought a quarter pound of each at Woolworth's before travelling out, but couldn't resist another, then another, then another until eventually I had wolfed the whole bloody lot.

69

That day, after I had spent some time on a technical report for work, the athletes went out to see the course, the Turks, Aktas and my old friend Ismail Akcay, the Ethiopians, Mamo Wolde and Bedene, Jeff Julian of New Zealand, Kenny Moore of the U.S.A., who I had beaten in that 10,000 metres at White City, three Mexicans, including Pablo Garrido, an actor, three Koreans and Bob Moore representing Canada. There was another Canadian due in, some guy called Drayton who was supposed to have run 2:12.00, but he hadn't arrived yet. They set us down after the turn-round point of the out and back course, and again, wanting to run my own pace, I waited until everyone else had set off before moving into action in vest and shorts. The sun had come out.

I set off running with no particular intention and quickly passed everyone, picking up Ken Moore along the way, and finding the two Ethiopians coming up to us as we strode freely along the highway, a battery of cameramen behind and alongside and a huge traffic jam behind. Wolde was wearing tracksuit top and gloves at first, but

Training run with Mamo Wolde and Ken Moore.

quickly got rid of the top. I felt I was moving well and at 7 miles Arthur called me the distance and I pulled up. 35½ minutes — not bad for an easy run!

That night I had my first full night's sleep, and was out at two minutes to seven running a big 8 mile loop in the city streets. It was frosty, people were on their way to work, yellow tram cars trundling their way noisily along the lines as I dodged the increasing traffic, gliding along, breath steaming and warm in my gloves.

Later that morning Mr. Shibuya took us by taxi to a religious shrine 40 minutes away; there I got my "fortune" from a slot machine. It forecast "a great success". In the evening I ran 5 miles.

Saturday I ran 2x5s. We had the "opening ceremony" in the hotel and I was introduced first. They had me marked down as a favourite and, in fact, I'd had a "shadow" with me all the time I'd been there, taking pictures of me in training, writing, doing exercises, shopping, and eating. With my initial permission of course; they wanted to run a story on me if I won. After a big dinner I retired to my room,

Shopping with Arthur Gold and Bob Moore.

watching Japanese T.V. for a bit, lots of stations, at least two Samurai Warrior films on, had a bar of chocolate, finished off Ian Fleming's "Casino Royale" and was asleep by 10.00 p.m.

Sit-ups in my room.

71

1969

I slept pretty well and at 7.30 a.m. ran two miles. Race day and it was raining. Kenny Moore was just coming back as I set out. At breakfast Drayton sat opposite me, and said little. Kenny Moore and Bob Moore joined us. I had orange juice, shredded wheat, jam and bread and tea. That was it. I went back to my room and listened to the radio; it was still raining. At 11.00 a.m. I went up to the 11th floor to have my number sewn on my vest. Cloth numbers, I had number 2, white on red, cut down to minimum size. Back to the room, radio again, seemed to be mainly church services, until I got an American football match. Texas 15, Arkansas 14. I had a bath at 11.15 a.m., packed my gear, and went by car down to the stadium. It was still pouring, the track was flooded, and I was reluctant to leave the changing room to go to warm up. Eventually I jogged a bit in my string vest and bikini shorts under a huge umbrella.

The course at Fukuoka is virtually dead-pan flat, the highest point on the course being only 30 feet above the stadium. The start is at the Heiwadai track, then heads out north-east, through the streets, over several bridges, following the edge of the bay all the way, sweeping left on to a narrow peninsula, with the sea in sight, to the turn, then coming back over exactly the same route.

It was miserable and cold waiting for the start; I was in pole position, front row, inside, Mamo Wolde, Olympic champion on my right, standing in 1½ inches of water as the other 78 starters took up their positions.

At 12.30 p.m. we were off, and had three laps of the track to splash through before emerging on to the roads. My legs and shorts

"It was pouring down . . ."

72

got covered in grit and it was like running with sandpaper between my legs at the top. I was about 20th as we left the track and I could see Drayton going into an early lead; there was still a long way to go, so no panic. At 5 Km he was a few seconds ahead and I was running in front of a very big bunch. It was pouring down; my cotton string vest had got very heavy and was flopping about so I tucked it into my shorts. I strode out, feeling quite strong and pulled the group almost up to Drayton. Thinking they would latch on and absorb him into the pack, I dropped back to play the waiting game. But as soon as I went back into the bunch, they let him go. I kept on going as relaxed as I could, cold in the pouring rain. And yet despite the rain crowds lined the route all the way cheering and waving soggy paper flags. Jeff Julian headed the pack for a while, Unetani occasionally went up and pushed the pace along and just after 15 Km, as we turned left and on to the peninsula, Pablo Grarrido had a go at the front.

Drayton was well away as I passed him heading back down the road after the turn and I was getting a little worried as I had let a gap open between myself and the leaders of our little group. Ken Moore came up and said, "How's it going Ron?" Not brilliant," I replied, "but not too bad." As I hit the turn, a tall pyramid bollard with Japanese writing on it, I was with them again, a group of about ten of us and it was still pouring down. There was no need for refreshments but at the first food station I had grabbed a sponge and squeezed it between my legs in an attempt to get rid of some of the grit that was abraiding my skin.

With the thought of heading for home I began to lead the group at my own relaxed pace, until the end of the peninsula when we turned right with 9 miles to go. I looked down the road and decided that catching Drayton would be a hopeless task and lost a little heart. A Japanese runner in cap and dark green vest shot ahead taking Garrido with him, then another Jap passed me and started to chase the other two, but didn't get very far. At 30 Km Garrido had dropped back to me, then slightly behind. I was 4th and just behind the second Japanese runner. I looked down the road again, and still I couldn't see Drayton, just the Jap who was second about 50 or 60 yards ahead. I took stock. We'd never catch Drayton for a start. I could feel a big blister had formed under my right heel and I was having to run on my toes on that foot, which was a bit awkward. O.K. I would sit for a ride with the second Jap whom I had caught by now; sheltered from the wind, save my legs, and go for a bronze. The rain was still hurtling down.

Suddenly Garrido was back with us, and in front of us; we both followed and he was making no impression on the second man in front. With about 4 Km to go the road turned to the left and Garrido

". . . but he was a fighter . . ."

was running wide round the bend. Now this is running extra distance and I could only conclude that he was tired and not thinking. Immediately I cut across and suddenly I was on my own. Encouraged, I started to stride faster. I wondered for a few seconds whether I hadn't gone a bit too early, but quickly and without much trouble I pulled back the white capped Jap who was 2nd. I sat on him. A couple of times I overtook him and tried to get away, but he was a fighter and responded, so I just dropped back and loped with him. He even put a burst in on the final road to the stadium, but I easily covered it and could see that he was shot. Up the short hill to the entrance of the track he began to fold; I went away and even then he tried to hang on, but I had something left and pushed it on the final lap of the track, somewhat surprised to see Drayton only about half a lap up on me. I took 2nd place.

A good strong finish. The diet had worked again. I felt pretty fresh and was in good condition apart from blisters and the blood between my legs from the grit rubbing. My white shorts looked like a butcher's bloody apron.

Drayton, Hill, Tanimura, Garrido

The results:

1.	J. Drayton	2:11:12.8
2.	R. Hill	2:11:54.4
3.	H. Tanimura	2:12:03.4
4.	P. Garrido	2:12:52.8

Another personal best by almost 2 minutes: 2:11 — I was astounded and over the moon with the time.

Back at the hotel I showered, burst my blisters with a safety pin sterilised in aftershave lotion, taped them, and went to a wonderful reception with sea food, Japanese music, two huge ice scultures and we were presented to Princess Chichibu.

The whole race is organised by a newspaper, The Asahi Shimbun, and what a magnificent job they make of it. It really is a classic race which every good marathon runner wants to get to.

Back in Tokyo I spent a couple of hours with my young pen friend of the Tokyo Olympics, Yutaka Sonobe, then went along with Arthur to the house of Mr Aoki, president of the Japanese Amateur Athletic Federation and obviously a wealthy man with his large, new, blue Mercedes parked outside the house. He gave us gifts and we had a marvellous meal Japanese style. I was fine with the raw egg, spring chrysanthemum leaves, burdock root and bean curd, but drew the line when two "fish like a willow leaf" appeared complete with heads and tails, and claimed that an as athlete I had eaten enough. Poor old Arthur, obviously flustered and not wishing to offend, had to try to down everything that was offered.

It was a long journey back and training was tough. I had to do 2 miles at 6.40 a.m. up and down the resounding corridors of Copenhagen airport. The flight couldn't land at Heathrow, was diverted to Amsterdam, then back to Heathrow in the evening. By now I was pretty knackered, but was assured of a flight to Manchester, only to be told at 8.00 p.m. that all flights were cancelled. I got a taxi to Euston. With a stack of luggage I had to get a porter and because I couldn't get through to the Indian, and he insisted that I put my bags down, I just missed a 9.25 p.m. train to Perth which would have given me a connection to Manchester. The next train was 1.00 a.m. and my next training session was 2 miles up and down platform 13. I was in work for 9.00 a.m. the next day.

Despite the battering my body got with travelling, 2 mile sessions for the rest of the week after Fukuoka saw me more or less free from stiffness, and as far as I was concerned I was back in full training. I rounded off the year, two weeks after the marathon, with a return to Erembodegem, in Belgium, for a frozen cross-country race in which Dave Bedford was 2nd and I was 5th. The race was Sunday, Monday night was the laboratory Christmas Party and even 9 pints of bitter didn't stop me staggering into the boiler house to get changed and run the 7 miles home from work, late at night. I got home safely and without incident. Not so my Friday lunchtime training companion Neil Shuttleworth.

He had changed with me and set off home at the same time, but when I ran into work early next morning I noticed that his clothes weren't there. At lunchtime he came up to explain. It seems he had himself run back to his flat in Cheetham Hill, arriving at 1.00 a.m. and buzzing his flat-mate to get into the building. There was no reply so, being more than slightly drunk, he rang all eight other doorbells until a voice told him to "**** off, at that time of the morning". He went out, found a bus shelter, dragged a bench into it, and was just lying down when the police arrived. He said the police couldn't understand him and "tried to make out I was p***ed"; which he obviously was. They moved him on, he set off towards work, got about 2 miles and hailed a taxi. He had no money and had to climb over the works gate at 3.00 a.m. to get some from his clothes, and after paying the taxi driver, Jim Bradley, the stoker, let him sleep on the boilers until 5.00 a.m., gave him a cup of tea and sent him off home on the 6.00 a.m. bus to Manchester. It could only have happened to Neil!

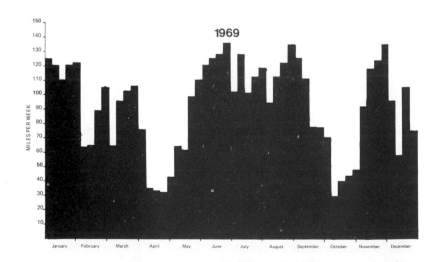

In 1970 I lost what cross-country titles I held. I was sorry in a way, but being dropped from the English team the year before had blunted my enthusiasm for the country. I might even have won the Lancs. at Allerton Park, Liverpool, had I been more aggressive, but after being in the lead I just hung back and then lost it on a hill. Ricky Wilde of Manchester and District Lads' Club Harriers won that race in the snow, and I lost the title after 7 years.

KEN HEATON

Lancashire Cross-Country. Ron Barlow leads Ricky Wilde.

I soldiered on. That week I was awarded the Vaux Silver Tankard for Northern Sportsman of the year, although there seemed to be doubt in some people's minds, and has been ever since, as to whether I was a Northerner, as I had a Cheshire address. If I'm not a Northerner, what am I? Even with the travel up to Sunderland and back for the award I clocked 115 miles that week, but my left knee was giving me a lot of trouble, the ligaments seeming to be catching again behind the knee, and at times my hamstring would get very sore. It was an old injury and I just pressed on, wearing two track-suit bottoms to keep the leg warm.

I had a race in Brasschaat, Belgium, where Gaston Roelants got his revenge over me for Athens; as if I were bothered! and Alan Blinston elbowed me out of 4th place up the home straight. I was feeling tired.

Freary, Blinston, me — Brasschaat.

1970

The next week I ran to and from work only, no detours and I still felt tired. The Inter-Counties race was at Markeaton Park, Derby, and there all I could muster was joint 14th place with Andy Holden. Lancashire won the team title easily, but individually before the race I had felt no nerves and no motivation at all. And yet people shouted to me, and urged me on, with annoyance in their voice because I was down the field. Dick Taylor won the race. For me that day was significant, being the birth of "freedom shorts", one of my original designs. I had started to do some business with a Hyde sports goods manufacturer and he had given me a couple of pairs of shorts to try out. Warming up I had found these slightly restrictive and to give freedom of movement I had ripped the sides of the legs to give a large split. Then they performed well, but looked rather ridiculous and the idea of the wrap-over, the concealed split, was born. And eventually brought to fruition after a few trials.

Without being ill, my chest felt a bit congested all the time, and in the next week I totted up 103½ miles; but things weren't going great. Tuesday morning I felt "knackered and didn't want to get up", Wednesday when I ran 12 miles home I "felt pretty shattered — in fact felt a bloody wreck", and when I got home I was so tired I couldn't eat my tea.

That weekend was the East Lancs. Cross-country championships. When I got up for my 5 mile run in the morning, I "felt shattered and old". After being champion for 8 years, Ricky Wilde relieved me of another title. I was 2nd after being dropped on the hill of Springfield Park, Rochdale. When I went out for 2 miles the next day I was tired all over — "legs, heart, breathing — really down — will need two weeks' rest".

So I had two weeks' emergency rest. 2 mile sessions only, throwing in the Mezidon race again. The Mezidon people in France were determined to get someone to win their race 4 times, the previous best being three which I had equalled, but I couldn't oblige, Noel Tijou and Mike Turner beating me into 3rd place on a course which now included a ploughed field. After the usual booze up at the "Bal des Nations", and a 3.45 a.m. inebriated training session, I was rather the worse for wear. Taking the bus out to the Manchester plane at Heathrow, Joe Mercer, Manchester City F.C. manager and his assistant Malcolm Allison, got on behind me and I said, "Hello, Matt" (Matt Busby). I didn't half feel a fool.

Immediately after the 2 weeks' rest, weeks of 38½, and 35½ miles, I began my training again. I had 10 weeks to prepare for the Boston marathon, and that was important to me. The Road Runners Club had set up an appeal for £200, to send me to Boston, and such had been the response of the road running fraternity, just ordinary runners, putting in their few shillings, that they were confident that the target would be reached.

I got 10th in the Northern Cross-country Championship at Graves Park, Sheffield, won by Trevor Wright, then after three week's training, 116½, 137 and 127 miles, I finished 11th in the National at Blackpool, superbly won again by young Trevor. The "selectors" honoured me with the position of 3rd reserve. Thank you! And to my astonishment put Mike Tagg in the team, even though he had finished 20th but suffering from a heavy cold. My immediate emotion was one of anger; what about me last year? Then I realised that two wrongs don't make a right and perhaps they had learned from their stupidity the previous year. Mike responded to their confidence and won the International that year at Vichy, France.

The National — Blackpool.

"I finished 11th . . ."

79

Bolton Harriers at Blackpool: l. to r., Kenyon, Mayer, Hill, Chapman, Baum, Freary, Ward, Byrne, Swann, Topping, Hopkinson, Eastham.

Well, they could keep their cross-country. I had more important things to think about; in fact the winter was now a drag, trying to stick in 120 - 130 miles a week, with bloody rain, mud, dark, cold, cars cutting in on you on the lonely roads, splashing slush all over you after snow. Conditions that winter were so bad that on two occasions, in snow storms, car drivers stopped to offer me a lift. They looked most surprised when I refused.

After the National there were still seven weeks to go before the Boston and I piled in the training. Wherever I was, nothing would stop me. I had to travel occasionally to give lectures, and to interview prospective Courtaulds employees at Salford University and Bradford University, but I still got out, be it Hyde Park, London, or early morning on Bradford ring road.

Added to which I had jobs to do at night at home, tiling the bathroom, painting, reading with the lads. I hadn't a second to spare. The training was by now a well established routine of running to work in the morning, detours home at night with hard sessions taken from "number stride fartlek," 70 seconds bursts; and 3 x 1 mile, on Monday and Wednesday nights, and the extra track session of 3 miles with two fast quarters thrown in Tuesday lunchtime at the Ashton track. The rest was easy running, and Sunday I did a 20½ miles, with occasionally a 28 miler, and often with Arthur Walsham, a Salford Harrier, for company.

Arthur was a great help to me on these long Sunday runs as, by chatting, the time passed quickly. Alone I was fine for about 1½ hours, then seemed to run out of thoughts. Arthur and I ran the 20's together, on and off, for six years. He was eight years older than I, with an excellent 2:21 marathon to his credit at age 41, and he regularly ran away from me up the huge hill on the Monk's Road, out of Charlesworth!

The weeks totted up 130, 128½, 125, 133 miles, with races on Saturdays always. I regarded these as ultra hard training sessions, short term targets for my training, and always useful experience. I won the Manchester University Championships for the 13th successive year, the Sutton '7' from Alan Blinston and the Longwood '10' from Bob Ellis.

But let no one think it was easy. I wasn't a well oiled machine silkily gliding through all those miles. I was human, I hated the cold and dark, and the wet weather. And the hammering took its toll on my body, my left knee and hamstring were constantly giving me trouble and as a result of favouring the right leg all the time, I developed soreness in that achilles tendon and it thickened alarmingly. For 10 days I found I had blood in my urine, which was pretty worrying; but I didn't complain, I hadn't the time to seek help, I knew what I had to do and got on with it. I learned to live with the aches and pains.

This Easter I did no races, as now I was picking only the competitions that were going to be useful to me.

Three weeks before Boston I eased down to 107 miles, the reason being that I was looking for a good run in the A.A.A. 10 miles track championships, to give me a boost before crossing the Atlantic. I had five successive wins under my belt and thought that I could make it 6, possibly with a new World Record. But it wasn't to be.

The wind at the Leicester track put paid to the record quest and young Trevor Wright dashed my victory hopes. There was no agreement among the runners on pace, therefore I sat in for 5 miles with Ron Grove and Tony Birks leading. Suddenly Trevor jumped into the lead and was off. I responded but could only hang on for just over 1½ laps and, feeling shattered, allowed a small gap to open. After two laps, to my grief, he moved out, thinking I was there to come through and share the pace with him, but when he realised that I had gone his confidence must have risen and he romped away to win in 47:20.2. I slowed until Ron Grove and Welshman, Bernie Plain caught me and outsprinted Ron on the last lap for a 47:35.2 clocking.

Another title gone. Another mild disappointment. But I wasn't really bothered, it was my last A.A.A. '10' win or lose, anyway. In fact on the starting line my emotions were: "here we go, another 40 bloody laps, leading to nowhere". The next day I was out with Arthur Walsham doing a 20½ miles round the Derbyshire hills, and clocked my last big week, 130 miles, before going to Boston.

Physically I had done all I could, all I thought that was essential for a good run out there, and my left leg was now aggravating rather than hurting. I had done my homework, reading Jim Peters' account of the course and the race in his book "In the Long Run", and a book which John Jewell of the Road Runners Club had lent me, Clarence de Mar's "Marathon", published in the U.S.A. in 1937. De Mar, a unique runner, had won the Boston Marathon seven times in all, the first time in 1911 and the last time in 1930! Remarkably, he was running to work and back for training before the 1920's. He was experimenting with diet in 1934 and followed someone called Hauser's principle of an "elimination diet" — one week of living on just fresh fruit and vegetables, except potatoes and bananas (both starchy). He tried the diet several times in 1934. "It was surprising how much faster I could run after each of these weeks of self denial." Well, well! Perhaps I wasn't the first marathon man on "the diet" after all!

CHAPTER FIVE

I knew no Briton had ever won the race, despite us sending across our best. Jim Peters had finished 2nd to the Finn, Karvonen in 1954; Fred Norris, freshly emigrated from England had been 3rd in 1961; and Brian Kilby had been 3rd behind Belgium's Aurele Vandendriessche and U.S.A.'s John Kelly in 1963. The race had the reputation for being the "graveyard of Olympic champions". Not even Abebe Bikila had been able to win, despite 5 weeks acclimatization in the Boston area. I hoped it was going to be a bit kinder to European champions.

From what I had read, the weather could be extreme either way, with tar melting on the roads, or cold rain or even snow. I was going prepared for anything, packing both gloves and string vest; if it were cold I had Fukuoka to look back to and if it were hot I was confident I could handle it after the European and Maxol marathons of 1969.

The Boston course had a reputation for being tough, with the Newton Hills starting at around 17 miles, just before the normal critical point in a marathon, and climaxing at Heartbreak Hill at around 20 miles; I had looked at the times which various people had put up on the course and felt that although it was tough, it could be a fast course. Dave McKenzie of New Zealand had set a record of 2:15:45 in 1968, for Yoshio Unetani to smash the following year with a solo run of 2:13:49.

On Tuesday April 14th, I arose at 6.40 a.m., did a 2 mile run along the canal bank, and set off for Boston, flying first to Heathrow. I had decided to cut the high protein phase of the diet from 5 days to 4 days; in fact it wasn't so much high protein as low carbohydrate. For breakfast I had a two egg omelette with ham and coffee with "Sucron". From Heathrow I was on the B.O.A.C Detroit flight BA.561, which called at Boston and departed Heathrow at 12.50 p.m. Lunch on the plane was lamb cutlet, broccoli, a piece of cheese and an apple. I shunned all bread, potatoes and sweet things. I landed at 7.35 in the evening, which was only 1.35 in the afternoon local time to be met by Jock Semple, Mr Boston Marathon, with a Scots accent absolutely unaltered after almost 20 years in the U.S.A. With him was Dave Williams, a lean bearded, young man who was to be my host, and Jerry Nason, an interesting writer from 'The Boston Globe'. Press, photographs, interviews; this was the V.I.P treatment. Dave ran me in his red Ford Mustang out to his beautiful grey shingled house in Winchester, only about 7 or 8 miles away, but nice and quiet with trees and grass. He lived there with his wife Dolores and daughter Annette and made me really at home, a room of my own and anything I needed by way of food. They had a "German shepherd" dog, which I never saw all the time I was there, and was glad as I found out that German shepherd meant Alsatian, possibly runners' worst enemy amongst dogs. When we arrived I was quickly out, on a sunny afternoon, in vest and shorts, striding along the side walks, under the leafless trees, and feeling fine. Steak, mushrooms and peas for tea, a supper of cocoa/Complan in milk, and I slept well. The next morning, Wednesday, I ran 4 miles and by the time I got back I was shattered; heart, arms, legs. This time I knew, and wrote in my training log: "result of high protein diet". I had half a melon, it was kind of orange coloured and very tasty, a cantaloupe, the first time I had ever tasted one and a ham omelette with regulation two slices of Ryvita for breakfast. I wrote letters and cards, and sat on the back porch in the weak but welcome wintry sunshine until lunch of cold steak, tomato and two Ryvita. In the afternoon Dave got off work and drove me first to Hopkinton, where the start of the race was, then along the course to the 21½ mile point, after the last of the Newton Hills. Peter Lever, an ex-Bolton Harrier, had written to me in England to say the course was easy: downhill all the way to 17 miles, then Newton Hills, then 6 miles down to the finish. It came as a surprise when it wasn't that way at all; from the car it seemed to be hills, up and down, all the way, but the Newton Hills themselves didn't look that bad. In the evening, I did a hard 10 mile session; 2,4 and 6 x 70 second bursts with 50 second interval, with 4 minutes between each set; all this on the roads, Highland Avenue, Fairmount Street, Washington Street. I felt all right, but my legs were weak especially on the hills; the diet. Boneless chicken, asparagus and beans, an orange and a cup of tea. Shopping with the family. Cocoa, Complan and bed at 10.00 p.m.

I slept pretty well again but awoke early on Thursday morning and read a book until I was tired and fell asleep again. When I got up I ran 7 miles and felt quite good; it was sunny again. Two dogs chased me, some kids shouted, "Up two, three, four". Things were the same the world over. Melon, bacon, omelette, fresh orange juice and coffee. It was the last day of the diet. I had a walk into Winchester; blue skies, wooden church with a spire; peaceful. Lunch, cheese, two Ryvita and a glass of water; after, I had a short sleep and trained in the afternoon, 7 miles, in the woods around a nearby reservoir.

I had several telephone calls, interviews, and interest in the race was fantastic, far surpassing anything I had experienced before. The story was building up that this was going to be a real grudge race between myself and Jerome Drayton, after my defeat by him in Fukuoka. But Drayton, who in Toronto, his home city, had been talking about a possible record at Boston this year, with maybe a 2:12, could not be contacted anywhere. I didn't try to stir things up too much, only saying, "I have a score to settle, if I can." "If I can," was significant. I didn't know whether I could beat him. As far as I was concerned, if it happened on the day, it happened, but in my experience, marathons were difficult to predict. I would like to run a fast time but we would have to see. I would like to win, but time was fairly important as I had the selectors to impress with the Commonwealth Games in Edinburgh in July, and Bill Adcocks had already posted a record 2:13:46 win in the Japanese Mainichi Marathon in Otsu, just before I left England.

In all the interviews I made Drayton the favourite, and that was tongue in cheek. I wanted to put as much pressure on him as I could. Personally I was feeling that if I was so close to him in Fukuoka after only 5 weeks' training, here I might do better with 10 weeks' solid training under my belt.

Thursday night I had roast beef, beans and mixed salad. The Williams's had some guests and it was agony watching them tuck into a huge strawberry and cream pie for a sweet. I had my cocoa and Complan at 11.00 p.m. and went to bed.

Friday I was off the diet. I was on high carbohydrate, which virtually meant normal diet plus some extra carbohydrates. I didn't want to neglect the proteins as I felt that they were still necessary for repairing body tissues, keeping the muscles in perfect trim before the race. After a 7 mile run, breakfast was half a melon again, shredded wheat with sugar, egg and bacon, and lunch a ham sandwich and a huge piece of last night's strawberry pie. In the afternoon I watched some amazing colour pictures on T.V. of the splash down of the spacecraft from the aborted Apollo 13 mission. On this first day I supplemented the meals with sweets which I had brought from England, and when I went out to run 7 miles in the afternoon, it wasn't too enjoyable as my digestion was pretty upset. At night, before going into Cambridge to see student riot hit Harvard Square, I stuffed down two helpings of beef stew, fruit tart and ice cream.

Indigestion stayed with me through the night and I had to put on the light to read for an hour about 2.00 a.m. Before breakfast on Saturday morning, Dave drove me to the start of the Newton Hills for a full dress rehearsal. Shaved legs, string vest, bikini shorts, light weight perforated running shoes. I ran 5 miles, and sweated a bit; my verdict was: "hills were pretty tough after all"; but I'd been running 5 minute mile pace without pushing it. Melon, sugar smacks, boiled egg butties and sweet coffee. Lovely. Early afternoon, 4 miles in the woods in full track suit; still a little indigestion but moving fairly well at the end. Cheese and tomato butty for lunch, followed by a bag of sweets, raspberry truffles and nougats, then out shopping to the Mall, pronounced "Mole" — I wondered what the hell they were talking about at first!

Full dress rehearsal on the Newton Hills.

Dave bought some food, and beer; when he bought beer he bought a case! Not like me, two bloody bottles of "Family Ale"; when I saw the way people lived, nice houses, decent reliable cars, not having to skimp with food, etc., it made me wonder where I had gone wrong, or where our system was wrong. The Ph.D., 6 years in industry, champion runner, and practically broke! For dinner we had water melon, chicken in white wine and shallot sauce, creamed potatoes and peas, cake and ice cream.

Sunday morning I got out and ran 4 miles on the roads. Tomorrow was race day. For a few seconds a scary feeling of apprehension and self doubt swept over me. God, would I make it? All those contributions to send me here, my family at home anxiously awaiting the results, the kind treatment from my hosts. I quickly pushed the thought aside. With all my interviews and discussions about marathons, I had developed a technique of almost stepping outside of myself. I could talk about a race, the speed, the time, the pain, the anxiety, without personal involvement. Ron Hill, the "everything else that he was", was talking about Ron Hill the "marathon runner".

Dave and Dolores were perfect hosts and that Sunday we had a day out, no thoughts of the race at all. After cereal, boiled egg butty and peach jam butty we went into Boston to see the historic ship the U.S.S. Constitution, then drove a good way north to a beautiful little village called Rockport. The sun shone from a clear blue sky, I ran 2 miles in my G.B. vest and jeans, and for lunch had a huge chicken salad sandwich followed by apple pie and two sweet coffees in the "Oceania" café run, according to the paper napkin, by Ida and Chip Corliss.

Back in Winchester it was even warm enough, in the late afternoon, to sit out in the back garden, until a photographer came to take a picture of me having breakfast! for next morning's newspaper. Dinner was at 7.00 p.m. The last supper. Hot boiled ham with boiled potatoes, peas and pineapple, lettuce and tomato, Spumoni ice cream, water melon, and finally some "Wine Cheddar". I went to bed just after 10.00 p.m., read until about 10.45 p.m., then fell easily asleep.

Race day, my eyes opened about 6.00 a.m.; I felt quite relaxed; I read a book for about an hour, ate three nougat sweets, then got up and went for a 2 mile run in my racing shoes. How did I feel? Not bad or good, either way. Everyone was still in bed when I got back, so I helped myself to cornflakes, two fairly big jam butties and a cup of tea, which I finished at 8.30 a.m. I went up to my room to lie down for an hour and listen to Beatles music on a record player. At 9.30 a.m. I had a good shower, put sticking plaster on my big toes where I thought I might blister and put talc in my shoes. Downstairs the radio was forecasting an easterly wind of 5 to 10 mph, which meant a bloody head wind, and a high possibility of rain. At 10.00 a.m. I drank a glass of crushed orange juice, jumped into the red Mustang and we departed for the start at Hopkinton.

Surprisingly we were held up on the way, a five mile road race was in progress! We made the gym at Hopkinton, where everyone was changing, at 11.00 a.m. dead. It had started to rain and I realised that I hadn't brought a tracksuit with me.

Inside the gym there were bodies all over the place; a seething mass of humanity, many people rubbing oils and grease into their skin. There was a powerful smell of wintergreen. Dave took me across to a smaller changing room where I casually sat down and gave some interviews, or rather answered newspapermen's questions until Jock Semple shooed them out of the way. This was "Mr Boston Marathon's" big day and by this time he was getting quite excited. People pressured him all the time up to the marathon, and he had a lot of "comedians" to put up with; a typical phone call at his massage room at the Boston Gardens: "Hello? What? How do I know if I got your entry for the marathon? What's your name? Yeah. And where are you calling from? Your house? Goodbye."

This was his day.

With the press out of the way I tried to read a little. Pat McMahon, an Irishman now teaching in the U.S.A., came over to change next to me. Drayton arrived at last, shook hands and said, "Hello." The day before I'd read in one newspaper, "A couple of fly boys from the Commonwealth of Nations are expected to go for the jugular in something of a grudge match in tomorrow's 74th Boston A.A. marathon race." Well, not quite! I slowly changed into my racing gear. I had been given No. 1; I pinned the cut down black number at the top and the bottom, one on the front, one on the back. Drayton was No. 2. I tugged my fawn woollen pullover over my head and at 11.40 a.m. went out to jog around and then down to the start. It was still raining and as I moved down to the line I could smell the wet wool of my pullover. I met three Canadians; Calum Laing, ex-Glasgow University, Bob Moore, the transplanted Yorkshireman, and Peter Lever, a Bolton Harrier like myself, now living in Toronto. "Drayton tried for the 10 mile track World Record two weeks ago," he told me confidentially. "He dropped out after 4 miles." "Oh," I said out loud. "Good news," I said to myself.

There were over 1,000 starters for what one newspaper described as, "America's premier bunion Derby", and I had never witnessed anything like this before. The runners were all shapes and sizes, even women were there, about 10 of them, unofficially and this surprised me. I got to the top ranks, where all the low numbers were. Jock Semple was busy sending all the high numbers to the back ranks in the narrow street. It was cold, the black tarmac shining wet in front of us. I spotted the youthful looking Ken Moore in a white vest lettered "Army" in blue, and blue shorts. I rubbed my hands together to get some warmth. We seemed to be waiting for ages. At last a shot was fired from a pistol high to the left and the field surged forward.

As usual there were two or three clowns who hared off, wanting only to get their pictures in the paper. When the field swept right and on to the main highway they had died and were just a nuisance under the feet of the serious runners. Yellow T-shirt, maroon shorts, No. 2, Jerome Drayton went straight into the lead. I knew I was going to go with him, if I could, but that was as far as I had planned: I wasn't certain how well I was going to run, and only after 4 or 5 miles would I know. I followed at the back of a bunch, Ken Moore, Bob Moore, McMahon, a couple of Japanese runners and a few others. I just hung back watching until after 1 mile Drayton began to move ahead. I accelerated, got in behind him and at 2 miles moved to his shoulder to run stride by stride with him, slowly dropping the others until we were alone at the head of the race. At about 4 miles I felt him drop behind a little and instinctively put the pressure on, effortlessly speeding up the pace. I was away! I couldn't believe it. We hadn't run 5 miles and I'd practically won the bloody race. But — all that way ahead on my own. It was cold, the rain and head wind making it feel colder still. I decided to relax as much as I could, just striding out and running easily.

Shortly after 6 miles, before the first check point at Framingham, 6.3 miles, I heard lone footsteps behind me, slap slapping on the wet roads, they were close as the head wind was blowing the sounds away; I didn't look back but slowed marginally to let whoever it was latch on and his figure reach my field of vision. Wet yellow T-shirt, maroon shorts. "Where have you been all my life?" I joked to Drayton. There was no reply. I was surprised he had come back. Why let go in the first place? This was decidedly odd!

At about 7 miles it began to really hurl it down with rain. My hands were numb with cold. I had to clench them and blow on them to try to warm them up. As I lifted my hands to my mouth my elbow joints felt stiff and achey with the wet chilling wind. But the pace didn't slow, it increased. I stayed right on Drayton's shoulder, head down into the wind. We seemed to go faster and faster. Just once I nearly turned and said, "This is bloody suicide." But instinct told me to keep my mouth shut.

I was getting lots of support from the spectators lining the road, in raincoats and umbrellas. "Come on, Ron." "Come on, Ronnie."

The second checkpoint, Natick, 10.3 miles.

"Come on, Limey." Maybe because I had been in town for a few days and been interviewed they were preferring me. It was nice. I grinned. Mentally. There was an occasional, "Come on, Jerry." Car horns were tooted. That was unusual and I didn't find the blaring horns relaxing at all. In fact a couple of times it made me jump. Neck and neck we ran. "That's the way they called it," I heard someone say. Up and down the hills of the cold shiny strip of tarmac road. "Ron, baby!"

The second checkpoint was at 10.3 miles, Natick. There was a traffic cone on the road. Times given here were insignificant because it was such an unusual distance, 10.3 miles, but I distinctly heard Drayton's coach, Paul Poce, shout to his runner, "The pace is fast; you're running fast and looking good." "Is he?" I thought.

Just after this Drayton faltered a little on a hill! I moved ahead slightly, but thinking of the lonely 16 miles ahead, I slowed and waited for him. "Are you O.K.?" I said. "Yeah, I'm O.K.," he

"On the next hill he faltered again . . ."

snapped back. On the next hill he faltered again and I was away. His footsteps got fainter and fainter. Eventually he cramped badly and had to pull out. I was full of running, especially up the hills. My legs felt powerful. I could drive myself uphill, and on the flat I could stretch out really well, striding heel down, grab the ground, pull it towards me then spring off the toes. I was moving.

"Beautiful," I heard some people saying.

JEFF JOHNSON

"I was away . . ."

I relaxed through Wellesley College at 13.3 miles and on to Woodland Park, 17.3 miles, and the start of the Newton Hills. I deliberately relaxed so that I would have something in hand for the hills. The umbrellas were out, and crowds were lining the course despite the weather. A kid offered me a slice of orange but I needed no refreshment that day.

On to the notorious Newton Hills and again deliberately I relaxed, I wasn't going to kill myself going up here when there were another 6 miles to go once the hills were over. I passed a legless marathoner in a wheelchair, Gene Roberts. "Praise the Lord!" he shouted as I went past. A green helicopter was hovering well above the race.

91

". . . through Wellesley College . . ."

"On to the notorious Newton Hills . . ."

JEFF JOHNSON

". . . and strode up the hills . . ."

I put my head down and strode up the hills with something in hand. I was hearing a commentary on the race on numerous radios held by the spectators. "Half a mile ahead." "Half a mile ahead." Well, don't take any risks — with a lead like that, barring accidents, the race is sewn up. How do they know my lead? Of course! The helicopter.

As I got to the top of the last hill, Heartbreak Hill, a new cry went up. "200 yards ahead." Immediately a wave of fear grabbed me. Two hundred yards? How the hell can half-a-mile lead turn into 200 yards? I didn't believe it until the press bus came alongside me; I was running downhill. Jerry Nason of the "Boston Globe" leaned out of the window and said, "You've got a 200 yard lead." Bloody hell! Who could it be? He must be flying. I quickened the pace.

I heard a Scottish voice shouting, "You're 2 minutes up on the record. Don't let up. You're 26 seconds ahead of O'Reilly and he's coming up on you." Christ! Who the hell's O'Reilly? I'd never heard of him. O'Reilly! I was tiring a bit and my brain kept repeating "Old Mother Riley."

As expected at this stage of the race, and in this situation, fear pumped fuel into my legs. I wasn't going to give this one up without a fight. The last 4 miles were supposed to be flat, but it looked

93

JEFF JOHNSON

Down from the Newton Hills.

JEFF JOHNSON

". . . it looked undulating to me . . ."

Heading for the finish.

undulating to me as I ran through the buildings now, streets lined with people. As I passed Coolidge Corner with 2 miles to go I really put the pressure on, forcing myself to run faster, to that razor's edge where cramp threatened to grab the backs of my thighs. I was listening for applause behind me, the sounds of clapping for the second man; I couldn't hear it. Run carefully, don't lift the legs too high, keep the cramp at bay.

". . . through the buildings now . . ."

JEFF JOHNSON

"Straight down the middle . . ."

JEFF JOHNSON

". . . fist held high in a victory salute . . ."

A right turn, a short hill, a left turn, there was the wide long street to the finish. God, I was going to do it!

Straight down the middle — frowning with the final effort — right fist held high in a victory salute as I crossed the line — a smile of satisfaction. I'd produced the goods. The first Briton to win Boston. Pull up sharp because of all the photographers just past the finish. Jog back down the street. Clap in Eamon O'Reilly — a bearded runner with a green headband, green vest and yellow shorts wearing number 12.

"Pull up sharp . . ."

JEFF JOHNSON

JEFF JOHNSON

Congratulations from Eamonn O'Reilly. Jock Semple looks on.

". . . a laurel wreath on my head . . ."

Back. It's cold, it's cold. I can't stop shivering. A grey blanket. Presentation, Mayor Kevin White puts a laurel wreath on my head and hangs a medal round my neck. What a medal — gold with a diamond in it. Interviews — a microphone shoved under my nose — "I'm just glad that bloody thing's over" . . . "it was a terrible day for a race".

Still shivering — "hot showers?" — into the Prudential Building to a lift — people roped off — clapping — I've never experienced such acclaim before — stand in the hot water until my body stops shaking uncontrollably — Jock Semple gets me to dry off, put my jeans on — clean G.B. vest — the laurel wreath back on my head and the medal back round my neck — more interviews, flanked by O'Reilly and Pat McMahon who was 3rd. My time 2:10:30.1 — Bloody hell — 2:10:30.1 — what a bonus — it's like a dream come true. "I wonder what I'm going to feel like when I stand up?"

"— the laurel wreath back on my head . . ."

Up in the lift to a higher floor for beef stew, but I'm not hungry — more interviews — Dave Williams produces a couple of cans of beer from his bag — fantastic — "Yes, I've been on a special diet. No, I don't want to talk about it; it's a secret. I will say it involves high protein and starts 8 days before the race." Smoke screen. Is it only 3.30 p.m.? It feels more like 6.00 p.m.

John Rodda of the "Guardian" rings from England. "What I would really like to be told is that I can miss the Poly marathon in June, and be selected off this for the Commonwealth Games in Edinburgh in July." Roy Moore, "Daily Mail," phones me from England.

1970

Lots of questions: "How many strides do you think you took?" — "Oh no!" I think to myself.

"Will you run the Boston again?" — "I don't think so; I feel I'd have everything to lose and nothing to gain if I came back."

"How fast do you think you can run?" — "Well, with 2:10:30 on such a miserable day and into a head wind, I feel I have a sub 2:10 inside me."

Finally we got away. Dave's next door neighbour brought round a bottle of Mateus Rosé for us to celebrate, and later we went for a meal to the Hilltop Steak House where we ate in a section called Sioux City; cowboys and Indians! A lot of overweight people in there. By the time I'd eaten a huge salad, I'd precious little room for steak. We were back home by 10.00 p.m. Surprise; my old pal from our 11 and 12 year old schooldays, Roy Langton, rings from Connecticut. I see myself on T.V., in colour! And finally to bed at midnight with some Gatorade and two aspirins.

I slept very little, probably with the excitement of the race. The sheer nervous effort of the competition was something which couldn't be dissipated in a few hours. The 10 week build up I had for the race had worked like a charm. Now I could have a month easy, and there would be 10 weeks left for a build up for the Commonwealth Games marathon in Edinburgh. Provided I didn't have to run the trial.

Tuesday morning, with no sleep in me, I packed early. Dave got my suit from the cleaners and as all week he would not let me pay a cent. The Williams were truly terrific hosts. Jock Semple was at the

Jock Semple, Dolores, Annette and Dave Williams see me off.

100

airport to see me off when Dave got me there for a 10.50 a.m. flight to Atlanta. I was spending another week in the U.S.A. on company business, and it was a marvellous experience for me, seeing the length of the U.S.A. with fresh eyes. With the success of the race, mine was a happy departure. In contrast, the three Japanese runners placed only 2 in the top 100, 17th and 55th, and feeling they had dishonoured their country they shaved off their hair as a penance.

A Courtaulds guy, Winston Sirmans, chauffeured me round Georgia, amongst the red earth and the pine forests, in beautiful weather. Most of my short runs were from the Holiday Inn in Rome, Georgia, but I had one marvellous run on the golf course there, enjoying the hot sunshine, with temperatures in the 80's, and looking in wonder at the beautiful wild flowers and the exotic red cardinal birds.

Alabama.

From Georgia I flew down to Mobile, Alabama, where after one session at the company plant I was left completely alone for the weekend. I soaked up the sun by the deserted hotel swimming pool and arrived in New York the following Monday, as red as a lobster. I had visits to companies in New York City and New Jersey and met up with a Courtaulds friend, Freddie Daniels, who was now working in New York and another acquaintance, Phil Slaney, whom I had known from my days working on a fibre called Spanzelle. Phil treated us to a champagne and beer dinner party at Charlie Brown's in Central Station which rounded off the visit perfectly.

New York.

Nevertheless, I was really glad to get home and see May and Steven and Graham. Arriving from my triumphant marathon victory there was a crowd of none to greet me at Manchester Airport. Graham was home when I got there; his face was swollen, he had mumps.

For a week I stuck to 2 mile runs in the U.S.A., and when I got back continued with 2 milers for a couple of weeks, then a week of 2's and 5's, to give weekly mileages of 29, 32, and 51. My Alabama tan peeled away. Steven caught the mumps too. I didn't race in that time.

On arrival in England I received a letter from Doug Goodman, the England Team Manager for Commonwealth Games:

"Dear Ron,

Re: Commonwealth Games.

I would like to congratulate you on your excellent performance in the Boston Marathon, and as you will agree, it is very difficult for me not to say 'you are selected', but if I were you, I would be very confident that your time in this marathon is good enough. It would be quite phenomenal if many, if any, competitors in the trial do better times.

The Selection Committee does not meet until the C.A.U. Championships, but if I can get a definite decision then I will do so.

In the meantime, I wish you good luck, and all good wishes.

Yours sincerely,

Doug Goodman"

Well — I'd keep my fingers crossed!

CHAPTER SIX

I embarked on my 10 week build up with these words in my training log, after my first 7 mile run: "first steps on the way to attempting Commonwealth Gold — felt O.K. but can expect to feel more tired as the training increases". The method of build-up in my training was to increase the mileage over three weeks to maximum, and also to increase the amount of quality work in the hard sessions gradually, again taking about three weeks to maximum. For instance — 70 second bursts, I did sets of 2-2-2, then 2-4-4, then 2-4-6. Similarly in the session where I ran 2 x 2 minute bursts, then 30 second bursts with 30 second intervals, finishing with 2 more 2 minute bursts, I started with 12 x 30 second efforts, increased it to 16 and eventually to 20. Number stride fartlek started at 45 strides increasing to 50 and finally to 55 strides.

The first week I ran 100 miles. The second week 120 miles. This week was spent mainly in the Yorkshire Dales basing ourselves at the Dixon's Farm at Lower Greenside, Ravenstonedale. The weather wasn't brilliant; cold and cloudy mainly, but the air was fresh and the change was good, and I enjoyed running the windy moors, and jogging the mist quiet lanes of early morning with low cloud waiting to be dispersed. Peewits flapped across the walls and curlews cried far away over the heather. Between training sessions

Lower Greenside Farm, Ravenstonedale.

103

Steven and Graham enjoying the fresh air of the Yorkshire Dales.

With John Whetton after the Plessey Notts. '15'.

again we roamed the castles, Brough, Middleham, Richmond, and Jervaux Abbey, and a couple of evenings May and I slipped out to the Black Swan at Ravenstonedale for a pint or two.

The sudden increase in mileage made my left leg sore, the old hamstring problem which wasn't helped by a sore achilles tendon in the same leg and a painful right knee. I soldiered on, and my first race after two weeks' training was the Pembroke '20'. I was looking for my ninth consecutive win in this race and I only pulled it off after a real battle with John Balmer of the home team and club mate Eric Haslam. With 2 miles to go and with a following wind, Eric pushed ahead and opened a gap of 2 or 3 yards. I couldn't hold him and had given up when suddenly he slowed. Perhaps he didn't realise I had gone, and I wasn't going to let him know, and forced myself past him. When I was about 5 yards ahead I heard him call, "Ron, pull me through." I slowed a little and said to him, "I'll pull you through providing I win." He agreed; I pulled away over the last 400 metres only. The time was 1:45:25. That was my last Pembroke '20'. I wouldn't have to arrange my affairs to prolong that sequence any longer. Two weeks of 128 miles each and I won the Plessey Notts. '15' on a hot sunny day in the midst of a bad chest infection and cold,

1:18:09, a week of 130 miles and I beat Eric Haslam, this time easily, in the Freckleton Half Marathon, 1:06:03; a week of 132 miles and no race but my 28 miles Sunday run round the Derbyshire hills with Arthur Walsham and I managed it easily; it boosted the next week's mileage to 140. My left leg had been giving me a lot of trouble from the foot, to behind the knee, to the hamstring, but at last it was settling down.

The next week I cut down to 108 miles as on Friday night, the end of my week, I was running 10,000m for Britain in a match at White City versus East Germany. It was only two weeks before the Edinburgh marathon, but I felt I could do it and thought the short race would help in sharpening me up.

The race was a little disappointing in a way; but the time was close

BOLTON EVENING NEWS

Rivington Cup 5,000m. Mid-week following Freckleton. 1st. 14:10.0. Here leading Morris and Renshall.

to my best for that distance. My partner was Trevor Wright and he was keyed up to show the selectors they were wrong in leaving him out of the Commonwealth Games team. After a slow first lap Trevor rattled off three 67's, then let the East Germans Eisenberg and Krebs take over. I just hung on until 5,000 metres, in 14:18, when Trevor took off again. This time Eisenberg chased him and left me and Krebs to battle it out for third. In fact Trevor (28:31.6) was outsprinted on the last lap by Eisenberg (28.27.0), and I (28:40.0) did the same for Krebs (28:40.8), after making him do all the work, following right behind him into the wind on the back straight, then coming up to his shoulder and making him run faster with the wind on the home straight.

My breathing hadn't been right. I was usually able to get an occasional deep breath during a race, but this time I was hurting my stomach trying. Even so, I felt I had lost the ability to really hurt myself in a race of this type. On the positive side, I wasn't at all distressed after the race. Saturday morning Trevor and I did a run in Hyde Park with Roger Matthews of Bournemouth, who had been reserve for the previous night's race, and who was in the 10,000 metres team for Edinburgh. He told us as we ran round the Serpentine that he liked to finish off his morning runs with a fast ¾ mile. "Fine," I said, "you go ahead." He didn't know Hyde Park, so I told him to run to the end of the Serpentine, turn left and he would see the park gate leading to Lancaster Gate and the Windsor Hotel where we were staying, on the right. Off he bombed, but instead of staying by the waterside, running under the bridge, he went up on to the bridge and turned left heading at great speed towards the Albert Hall. We shouted as loud as we could, but he didn't hear. Trevor and I had showered, dressed and were having breakfast when he finally staggered in.

We had a slight battle with the team management to allow me to arrive late at the Athletes' Village in Edinburgh. They had stipulated arriving Sunday, 12 days before the race, which seemed crazy to me as it was in Britain. For one thing I preferred to continue training on my home ground for as long as I could, also I didn't want to take more time off work than I needed; I was taking May, Steven and Graham to stay in Edinburgh, which would have been extra expense; and finally there was less chance of boredom the shorter time I spent up there.

I was relieved when Doug Goodman phoned to say I could arrive on Wednesday. On Tuesday I had a short haircut, and at night shaved all the hairs off my legs. Wednesday, I drove up to Edinburgh in our Austin 1100, which was practically dropping to bits, and had to be repaired whilst we were actually in Edinburgh. The repairman cheered me up by advising me to get rid of the car as soon as possible!

It was a none too cheerful departure, as on our way out of Romiley I bought a copy of the Daily Express. I had been interviewed by a reporter, the day before, about the Games, and conversation had turned to professionalism and the fact that certain athletes had to take time off work, without pay, to represent their country. I couldn't believe the sports page headline — "WE SHOULD BE PAID" and some of the text — "His outburst to me as he was packing for departure . . ." Bloody hell! The last thing I wanted was controversy with officialdom before a big race like this; and I should have smelt a rat when a photographer had come round for a picture and asked me to "look angry, look aggressive". Now I knew why. Luckily it blew over and nothing was said, but it put me in a bad mood for the journey.

When we arrived in Edinburgh, May and the lads soon settled in at Mrs. Allison's guest house in Minto Street; my mother and dad were staying there too; I had booked the accommodation in

December last year. When I got to the Games Village, the Pollock Halls of Residence of the University of Edinburgh, to my delight Mike Farrell, an assistant team manager, gave me the key to room No. 401, a single room. Just what I wanted. Here I wouldn't be disturbed. Everything so far had gone according to plan. There was no uncertainty about the continuation of the plan; it was all carefully worked out. The race was on Thursday; I normally raced weekends so I changed the previous Thursday to a Sunday for the purposes of training and worked back from that. I had carefully examined what I had done in the 14 days prior to my 1:36:28 Pembroke '20'; my European Marathon win, my Fukuoka 2:11 marathon, and my Boston marathon win, averaged these out, and virtually had a blueprint for my perfect run up to the race.

I started "the diet" on Thursday, 8 days before the race. There was no problem with food in the village, in fact I can say that the food there was the best I have ever experienced at any games throughout the world, and few 5 star restaurants would surpass the quality and the variety of the food.

I was refining the low carbohydrate stage of "the diet" a little further and taking saccharin in coffee, and the cocoa in the pint of cocoa/Complan mixture, last thing at night was "diabetic cocoa". Details of the diet were leaking out, as I had told Chris Brasher of the 'Observer' about it after my Athens victory and Jim Alder was using a duplicated sheet provided by Chris to guide him through the diet in Edinburgh. One day I saw Jim with the sheet and a huge plate of chips in front of him and I smiled to myself.

The Thursday became Sunday, I ran the first half of the marathon course as a long run, 13 miles, and at night ran 2½ miles across the hills of Holyrood Park because it wasn't really Sunday, and I always ran twice on weekdays.

Friday morning the training plan went slightly wrong as I got lost and instead of doing a projected 7½ miles, I ended up with a 12 and was very tired at the end. In the evening I hit the 7½ mile course I had been looking for, incorporating a couple of miles of the end of the marathon course. I did 3 x approximately 1 mile bursts, and came up with a worry as I had some very sharp pains inside my right knee.

Saturday morning I ran 4 miles and my right knee was hurting a lot. I was very worried. The weather was cold, I was in full track suit, and the pain was a mystery. After that run, I never felt the pain again. It went as suddenly as it came. That afternoon I ran the last 10 miles of the marathon course into a head wind. 2 - 4 - 6 x 70 second bursts. I was absolutely shattered. I could hardly stand up at the end. The diet.

1970

Sunday, the last day of low carbohydrate. I did 2 x 7½ mile runs. My legs were weak, especially on the hills.

Monday I woke up early, had two big bites of chocolate covered Turkish Delight, ran 7½ miles and felt good. In the evening after a day of cereal with bags of sugar, jam butties, sandwiches and biscuits, I ran another 7½ miles and wrote in my log "felt tremendous — having to hold myself back in stretches".

It was very good having the family with me. It prevented me dwelling too much on the race, it was almost like home from home, but as is natural in an atmosphere where top runners are cooped together, the stories were flying around. Drayton had done this session of 400's; Clayton was on form and was going to grind everyone into the ground.

Whichever way you looked at it, with the four fastest ever men in the world running, it was virtually a world championship and it was bound to be a hard and competitive race. I had a map of the course up in my room and was carefully watching the wind every day to see how this could possibly affect my race tactics. That was the mental side of it. The physical side was taken care of, the plan was laid and almost complete, I always trained alone, as at home, so as not to be swayed off course in any way at all.

Six days before the race I "had my last conversation with Jim Alder — he was trying to put the hoodoo on me". Jim, running for Scotland, and in fact defending his marathon title, had told me quite seriously that it was my fifth marathon in 12 months and I should be "due a bad one". I'd heard of him saying this before, "I hope I'm wrong, but you're due a bad one." Now it was me. Being a scientist, I drew a graph of my last four performances, when I got back to my room, and extrapolated to 2:07:45 or 2:10:00 depending on which line I took, that convinced me he was wrong. In fact I did listen to him when I met him again at the Royal Garden Party, two days before the race, but Jim had been on the receiving end on this occasion. He was mad, mad as only Jim can get, because Derek Clayton had said to someone that the marathon was a four man race, Drayton, Adcocks, Clayton and Hill, and when he was asked, "What about Alder?" he replied, "He's got no class." I chuckled to myself as Jim went on about how he would show them.

Another story that came my way two days before the race was that "pharyngitis" was going around. I assumed that this was something like a throat or chest infection, the kind of thing that plagued me often, and when I heard that Bill Adcocks had either got it or had it, and I'd been talking to Bill only that evening, I rushed off to gargle with salt water and get an antiseptic lozenge from the team doctor.

Ready for the Royal Garden Party.

I didn't catch anything. Tuesday I ran a 5 and then a 4, Wednesday a 4, then a 2. The wind still blew hard; looking at the smoke from the stacks of the Portobello power station, it was blowing out to sea and that meant a head wind from the turn. Tactically, a break at 19 miles or just after 22 miles would be on, for at both these places the wind would be across rather than head and both were refreshment stations. I would spurn drink as usual, but if someone with me were to try to take one . . .

The night before the race I went to bed at 10.00 p.m., read a book until 11.00 p.m., then slept well. I woke up around 7.00 a.m. and stayed in bed reading and listening to the radio until 8.00 a.m. I got up and could hear soft wet swishing sounds outside as cars went past. I looked through the curtains. It was raining. I got my kit and tracksuit on and ran 2 miles. I dried myself, dressed and went in for breakfast of porridge with bags of sugar, poached egg, bacon, brown bread with jam, sweet coffee, Multivite tablet, iron tablet, vitamin C tablet, vitamin E capsule. Back to my room; Andy Holden came in to chat for a while, and May came to see me and to wish me luck. I was glad to feel that she was around.

Just before noon I wrote down my hopes for the race: "Wind slight and with us on the way back. Raining all morning. Good

109

conditions. Clayton and Drayton hammering from the start with me running easily with them and Bill Adcocks hanging on. Jim Alder will let us go hoping one or two will blow up. Drayton worries and starts to drop just after the turn. Bill hangs on until the downhill at 20. Big Derek keeps pushing until 22 miles which will be my signal to go, if not before. Time: 2 hours 7 minutes 45.8 seconds."

At 12.30 I went for lunch. A caterer tried to direct me to the mob but I wasn't being directed anywhere today. I said, "I've got a race to run this afternoon and I don't want a load of people talking around me." I ate alone. Two slices of brown bread and marmalade. Salt in orange juice, then orange juice with sugar. Back to my room and I finished off a book about the bull-fighter, El Cordobez, "Or I'll dress you in Mourning". I listened to some Beatles songs on my cassette player. I'd bought a lot of daily papers and was reading these to keep my mind off the race. About 2.45 p.m. Mike Farrell came and told me to get a move on as Holyrood Park, the quickest route to the stadium, was closed because of a Royal Garden Party.

I went downstairs in blue tracksuit, red neckscarf, hat, sunglasses and cassette player slung over my shoulder. I was hiding away from the world. Bill Adcocks, who had been selected on the strength of his 2:13:46 in Japan in April was waiting with our other representative, Don Faircloth, who had won the trial race, the Polytechnic marathon, and his debut at the event, on June 13th with 2:18:15.

We got into an Austin Maxi to be driven by a volunteer driver, an oldish lady, a long way round to the stadium. As we neared the arena, panic, I suddenly realised that I had left my bloody racing shoes in the bedroom. The woman in her confusion missed the only junction that would take us back conveniently. She was a bit annoyed and said, "You wouldn't have missed the shoes if you hadn't got those dark glasses on." This riled me, and I retorted, "I've got 26 miles to run this afternoon; it's my privilege."

We decided to drop Bill and Don at the stadium so they would be safe, then bashed it back to the village, through Holyrood Park, Royal Garden Party or no Royal Garden Party, Mike Farrell getting special permission from three doubtful Scottish cops. Even at the back gate of the village the guard held us up as we explained about the shoes. "Don't make a habit of it," he said as he waved us through. Up to our block, I flew in, up in the lift, grabbed the shoes, down in the lift, into the car and we were off again, explaining our way through the Park. This was truly the way Alf Tupper would have done it! We hit the stadium at 3.30 p.m. The start was at 3.50 p.m. prompt. I was late for everything. Check in. I'd had a glucose tablet at 3.10 p.m., but forgot to take one at 3.45 p.m. and forgot to clean my teeth. I just had time for 6 minutes jog warm up. A final weighing, 9 stone 5 lbs, in my lightweight gear. We were congregating underground, standing on thick coconut matting, looking up to the arena. Clayton looked pale and tense. The men from the 5,000 metres heats came clattering down the steps in their spikes, sweating. When we had put all our things into big polythene bags, we were led up and out on to the wet Tartan track.

It wasn't a big field; 30 runners. We were lined up quickly with England almost on the outside, and Scotland to our left. I noticed that the Welsh team of Dai Davies, Cyril Leigh, and Mike Rowland had been issued with string vests, and Martin Cranny, running for Northern Ireland, had got one for himself. They were catching on! There was no time to dwell on the effort ahead, as the starter called "To your marks". We crouched slightly, then "Bang".

"It was like the start of a 1,500m race."

It was like the start of a 1500 metre race. No leisurely jog, which sometimes precedes the serious part of a marathon, but a fast drive for the inside lane of the track and immediately Derek Clayton set a rapid pace. Quickly Jerome Drayton, Phillip Ndoo of Kenya, an Indian runner and myself were with him. The weather was fairly cool, and as we left the track and hit Portobello Road it was still wet and my shoes were slipping a little. Drayton took the lead here and we all fell in behind him; the air was so humid that I could see my breath coming out. As we turned right on to the long road to the half-way point, Drayton had been joined by Ndoo, the Indian guy seemed to be hanging on and Clayton and myself were just sitting in. By 2½ miles the Indian had gone and I scrutinized the other three runners in our leading group from behind. Drayton was

111

sweating and it was running in streams down the back of his neck. Good; that means he is working hard, or is out of condition. Ndoo looked comfortable and was loping along with a relaxed stride. Clayton looked pale, was sweating a little, but more significantly he was not pushing the pace along as he had threatened.

MARK SHEARMAN

Drayton leads after 3 miles.

Along the flat part of the course we stayed together, and as we approached 5 miles Clayton seemed to be hanging on. 23:31. Clayton began to drop. He said afterwards that he had been amazed by the pace at this point. I was feeling pretty uncomfortable myself, not relaxed, having to force myself slightly to stay there, but imperceptibly the pace slowed, it reached my optimum level, and suddenly things seemed to click and I was running strongly and well. We approached a fairly stiff hill at 6 miles and I was beginning to feel

". . . a fairly stiff hill at 6 miles . . ."

something like I had in Boston. I really forced the pace, the strength in my legs pushing me almost effortlessly up the hill, and I knew I had Drayton and Ndoo hanging on now. I was almost playing with them. At the top of the hill I dropped my hands and waited for them, there was still a long way to go. We ran on to a disused part of the A198 road, then on to the main road again. Once more I was leading and I could feel that the other two were having a job to stay with me.

I decided the time had come to make my effort. Any more fooling about, any more waiting, and I might make a mistake. At 8 miles I slowly began to pull away. Drayton was the first to drop, then Ndoo. I powered on, looking 5 or 6 yards ahead at the road, occasionally glancing up to get my line, trimming the corners, shortening the line between bends. I was fully aware, and relaxing, yet running fast.

10 miles was called, 47:45. That wasn't bad. I felt all right. The other two were still within 10 seconds of me here, but I didn't know this. I didn't look back.

113

There was a boring 1 mile stretch of straight dual carriageway up to 11 miles, then bends and slight ups and downs up to the turn, up a slight slope at the ruins of Redhouse Castle. 1:02:35. It obviously wasn't exactly the half-way point.

The turn.

Round the bollards, and this was the part I wasn't looking forward to, passing the oncoming runners. Now I would know exactly where I was. I had to calculate that the ones behind had to run to the turn too so that my lead would obviously look smaller. I would have to try to look good, fresh, to give no encouragement at all to my pursuers. Drayton looked fairly close; I gave him the thumbs up sign as he went past and said, "Keep it going, Jerry." He waved briefly to me. Jim Alder and Bill Adcocks looked uncomfortably close. I just kept my eyes open, looking alert with not quite a smile on my face. Quickly the others were past too, most of them giving me a shout of encouragement, Jack Foster of New Zealand in his all black strip and Cyril Leigh, a fellow Lancastrian, gave me a big shout. They were gone. Now I knew the real race was ahead.

The twists and turns on the road up to 15 miles were helpful, I could see the big clock ahead; 72:18. It was still fast, but it didn't worry me, I was still slicing away at those sub-5 minute miles.

The roads had dried now; the clouds were breaking, the summer sun was shining through, the afternoon was heating up, and with all the water about from the rain the atmosphere was very humid. Back along the dual carriageway I began to feel a little bit the strain of leading. I was running right in the gutter on some concrete slabs to avoid the fresh chippings on the road which I could feel through the thin soled shoes. It was a little difficult running on this narrow strip.

Looking ahead I could see the white police Jaguar which preceded the race, and the cream and green open topped double-decker press bus, which periodically emitted clouds of blue-grey foul-smelling diesel fumes. I could have done without that. A voice was wafting back occasionally, "Come on, Ronnie boy." I recognised the voice of Jock Semple, Mr Boston Marathon, who was visiting his native Scotland.

Shortly after 16 miles I began to worry. The heat and the pace were beginning to make me feel uncomfortable, and it seemed such an awfully long way to go to the finish. I began to look for Mike Baxter, one of our 5,000 metres boys, and Shaun Lightman, a race walker; they were riding a Landrover and shouting out my lead in terms of time.

The hot humidity was bringing out flies from the wet grass and hedgerows, those little midges that just drift aimlessly in the air. I kept breathing them in and getting them in my eyes. At 17½ miles I took my first sponge, squeezing it over my head and the back of my neck, and immediately I felt better. I consciously tried to relax. I was pretty well alone out there as we were still more or less in the country. On through 19 miles; drinks were offered. I refused, striding relentlessly on to the roundabout at Wallyford Toll, then down the steep hill to 20 miles. I purposely tried to relax on this hill. 1:37:30. This was good; it didn't frighten me, I'd been there before, faster in fact with my 1:36:28 Pembroke '20', but my pursuers were holding me. They were holding my lead to about 1:19, 1:20. Would they now start to eat into that lead?

6 miles to go, there was no doubt about it, I was tired. Could I hang on? I began to worry. An awful sickening worry that tightened my stomach. Could I keep going? I concentrated on the road, on the route; it was flat but I crossed from bend to bend, always on the left hand side of the road as the rules dictated, but always saving the odd yard, the odd foot. There was a feed station at 20½ miles, I ran straight past; I took nothing, my eyes down, searching the road ahead; I passed a whole line of police motor bikes on the road. The policemen were all wearing big gauntlets. There were more people about now, houses, but only occasionally did a shout penetrate my concentration. A woman shouted, "Slow down and wait for Jim Alder." A group of kids, "England — Boooo . . . !" That wasn't necessary. "You're 1 minute 20 seconds ahead." I was still holding them.

Just before 22 miles my legs seemed to go dead. Suddenly I felt I had nothing there. I thought, "How the bloody hell am I going to get back?" I seemed to be running oh so slowly. If I got any worse I would stop. May and Steven and Graham, my mother and dad were waiting at the stadium, they had seen the intermediate times, they must think I'm going to win. How disappointed they will be if I fail now. If I fail.

I looked forward to the press bus, not too far ahead. How nice it would be just to step on and ride back, then go to a bar and line up a couple of pints of cool bitter beer, and knock them back.

The following breeze at the turn seemed to have disappeared. The sun was shining very brightly in my face. Bloody hell, everything was against me. I grabbed two sponges and wet myself all over. Immediately I felt better. My head raised a little and my stride strengthened. I was at the 23½ miles point, familiar ground from some of my training runs. That made it easier still.

I got a white plastic cup of water and poured it over my head. I ruffled my short hair backwards to let the air blow through and cool me as much as possible. I kissed my lucky ring on my left little finger and immediately got cramp in my left elbow through bending it. Christ I was getting into a hell of a state.

Past the Portobello Power Station on the right hand side at 24 miles, I knew the worst was to come, the long uphill road, Portobello Road, to the stadium, but I was beginning to think I could make it.

Turn up Portobello Road.

116

There were crowds of people about now but I don't remember hearing them, my concentration was so intense on moving my limbs and getting myself to the finish. Twinges of cramp grabbed at my groin.

Left turn just before 24½ miles. I heard one voice, Andy Holden's; I didn't see him but I imagined his face and red hair, "Go, Ron. You've got the world's best, go for 2:08." World's best? No, just let me get home. Just let me win. Time's not important. Just win that medal and do the job. Relax, look at the ground and run the hill. Well into the left hand kerb using that as a kind of rail to guide me. I looked for the last refreshment station, 25 miles, just before the crest of the hill. "Water!" I whispered. A white cup was thrust out; I grabbed it and poured it on my head. Fizz, swoosh. Bloody lemonade! Bloody hell. Let's get home. Don't panic. Relax. Nice and easy and you've won it. Thankfully downhill to the stadium. A sharp right turn taken carefully, then run out

"Thankfully downhill . . ."

". . . sharp right turn taken carefully . . ."

117

into the bowl of sound and the silent soft empty red rubber track. I didn't push it. There was a full lap to go. There was such a loud cheer that I looked round a couple of times to make sure that I was still safe, then on the back straight I risked a couple of waves at the crowd; down the home straight; and on to the tape with my fist raised high. "Take that, take that!" I said to myself.

THE SCOTSMAN

"Take that!" 2:09:28.

Waving to my family,
after the race.

Result:

1. R. Hill (England)   2:09:28
2. J. Alder (Scotland)   2:12:04
3. D. Faircloth (England)   2:12:19
4. J. Foster (New Zealand)   2:14:44

Two post-race quotes:

Bob Moore (Canada) 14th (2:20:47): "I caught Clayton at 12 miles and said, 'What happened?' 'The pace is suicide,' he replied, 'we'll wind 'em in'."

Derek Clayton (Australia) (DNF): "I caught Drayton and we ran together. Just before 18 miles I said, 'There's not much point in carrying on, we're not going to win this one; let's stop and have an orange juice.' Drayton replied, muttering, 'I've got to keep going, I've got to keep going.' Finally we agreed to drop out. Drayton sat on the kerbside and started to cry."

The thrill of winning was nothing like that I had felt in Athens, rather the sentiment I had was of a job completed successfully. Even the time of 2:09:28 didn't impress me. Only slowly over months and years did I become proud of the 2:09.

A fascinating sequel to the race was that Alf Tupper, my early 1950's hero of the Rover comic, sadly now in strip cartoon form, in a comic called the 'Victor', also ran the marathon race in the Commonwealth Games in Edinburgh. He was unable to make the England team through injury, but reaching peak fitness he was nominated as the sole representative of Tristan da Cunha, a tiny island in the South Atlantic! Fortified by a big bag of chips at the half way stage he passed two runners on the track to win in a new British record time!

4   *" Tupper's eating chips in the middle of the race!"*

There's great news for all boys on Page 13!

Three happy finishers.
Jim Alder (2:12:04), me (2:09:28) and Don Faircloth (2:12:19).

Looking at our congratulatory telegrams.

Within a week I was back in full training. I seemed to recover quickly and the only thing that troubled me was a sore and swollen right knee. But that didn't stop me, and after three weeks the pains had gone away. I had three objectives left for the year. Firstly a 30 Km World Record attempt at Crystal Palace on September 5th, which I had been instrumental in setting up. That gave me 5 weeks of training, and three weeks later I had a race in Canada, a 12 miler at the Springbank Road Races in London, Ontario, where I was scheduled to meet Jerome Drayton again. Nine weeks after that, on December 6th, I was running the Fukuoka marathon once more. After Edinburgh I felt I could tackle anything.

The winds of change and uncertainty were blowing through the laboratory at Droylsden. There was talk of economies, redundancies, and not two weeks after winning the Edinburgh marathon, my manager had me in his office offering me jobs in Swansea, the centre of Manchester, with our Viscose Sales Development Department, or at Samuel Heap's dyehouse at Rochdale. Christ! Just when I was beginning to put it all together in my running. I told him I definitely wanted to stay at Droylsden. My training routine of running to work and back was exactly right, and with the European Championships in 1971 and the Olympics in 1972, I didn't want to risk changing my routine.

All this left me feeling insecure and I found it difficult to project ahead to where I was going with Courtaulds. I certainly didn't want a job as a dyehouse manager, where I would be tied down rigidldy to a career with little or no opportunity for time off, and with the very vague thought in the back of my mind of an escape route, I started a small spare time business. I was to learn a lot from this — the hard way!

The business I started was mail-order retailing of running clothing and later running shoes. I was specializing in the action cut "freedom shorts" which I had designed and were being made by a local manufacturer in Hyde.

With mail-order I could work from home, and we stored our stock in the loft. But it began to mean extra work for both May and I at nights. Everything we made, for years, was ploughed back into the business. It wasn't intended as a great money making venture — just that escape route. However I put everything on a legal footing by becoming Ron Hill Sports Limited. To do this and remain an amateur I had to give an undertaking that all the money in the business was my own. That is, no-one else was using my name to make money. Not that we couldn't have used some extra money. We had just had gas fired central heating installed with a hire-purchase agreement, and the bloody 1100 car was now dropping to bits. Brakes failing, engine almost falling out, the sills rotting, bodywork needing welding all round. What a champion — gold medals certainly didn't help financially, and sometimes I felt it worked the other way, though why it should I was at a loss to understand.

I continued to work hard at my job, as my conscience indicated I should, and I took on an extra duty of fortnightly visits to a huge company weaving shed at Skelmersdale, where I worked with their design and development department in preparing and dyeing new cloths to a range of different colours to show off the samples to best advantage.

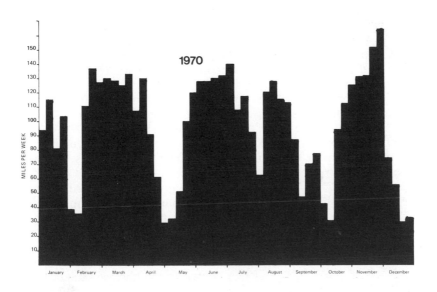

123

CHAPTER SEVEN

The five weeks' training up to the 30 Km race ran: 102½, 128, 115½, 113 and 87½ miles.

Towards the end of it I was feeling a little tired, but I easily won a half-marathon, from Barry Watson, in a small town in Belgium called Geraardsbergen, though the effort had felt hard. I did "the diet" for the 30 Km race, but it turned out to be a race where nothing went right. I stayed the night at Crystal Palace and raced on September 5th. I went down to the track to start a short warm up, and we were suddenly called to the start. The organisers had moved the event forward by 8 minutes and no one had bothered to tell me. I had just eaten two glucose tablets.

A good field had been invited: Gaston Roelants, Tim Johnston who had broken this World Record in 1964 with 1:32:34.6, Jim Alder another previous record holder with 1:34:01.8 in 1964, Mike Turner, Gerry North, Barry Watson, Ron Grove and Bob Richardson. We were attacking Jim Hogan's World mark of 1:32:25.4. As I went to the line I didn't feel like running at all.

The early pace was brisk as the lesser runners did the work over the first 5 Km for the "contenders". After that Roelants, Alder,

DAILY MIRROR

"... annoyed and humiliated ..."

Johnston, Turner and myself did 2 lap stints apiece. At 10 Km I was hanging on and opted out of the pace making; my legs were going great but I had a nauseous sickness in my stomach, which I could only pin down to the glucose tablets and it was making running difficult. Jim Alder sensed I was in trouble and at about 8 miles stuck in 5 laps, averaging just under 71 seconds which disposed of both myself and Roelants, who eventually dropped out. I plodded on, pulling both Alder and Johnston back in the later stages, but all I could get was an unhappy 3rd. Jim smashed the world record again with a 1:31:30.4, Tim was 2nd with

1:31:56.4, whilst I too beat the old record clocking 1:32:17.0. I was annoyed and humiliated at being able to only virtually jog round in front of a big crowd, including my parents, whom I could hear shouting, in a race which had been put on for my benefit.

It was time for a "mini-rest" as I didn't want to fail in Canada in three weeks' time. I ran 47½, 70½, 77½ miles, most of it easy running before tackling the 12 miles at Springbank, London, Ontario. What a marvellous trip it was; one that will live in our memories forever, people were so generous with us.

May, Steven, Graham and I flew out to Toronto on Tuesday. We were met there by Peter Lever, ex-Bolton Harrier, who fed us until Dave Prokop, the race organiser, arrived to take us to the Holiday Inn in downtown London. There we stayed for a week, me training, attending a couple of running "teach-ins" and interviews. Nobody had told Steven and Graham about the effects of time differences and when May and I awoke the first morning, they said that they had been out, through the sliding doors into the enclosed central garden area, playing football "in the middle of the night" in their pyjamas. We never heard them, and God knows whether they disturbed anyone else.

We met Dr. Bill McInnis, a charming gentleman, and a runner member of the organising committee who hired a car for us during our stay there. We were also introduced to Bill Johnstone, a good hearted, generous building contractor who lent us his country cottage on Lake Huron for a week's "away from it all" holiday after the race. On September 25th they took us all for a meal at the local golf club and to my complete surprise produced a huge birthday cake — it was my 32nd birthday.

The relaxation did me good. It was the fall; the leaves on the trees were turning to autumn colours. As a family we walked in Victoria Park and the boys knocked down conkers from the horse-chestnut trees. The only competition for these rich brown nuts in Canada were the half-tame grey squirrels which kept us amused for hours. We drove to Port Stanley, a ghostly shuttered holiday resort; to the Fanshaw Dam; we picnicked and strolled. I only hoped I would do well in the race.

I seemed to be able to raise my game in foreign races, and this was no exception. The weather was cool with sunny periods and my main opposition was Jerome Drayton of Detroit who was learning fast and had got himself a string vest for this race; I expected him to be very tough over this distance. The course record holder was also in the race, Boston Marathon winner Amby Burfoot of Connecticut, who had set a time of 58:23.0 in 1968.

From start to finish I got a lot of support from Northern Englanders — I could tell by their accents, and even from Boltonians — "C'mon Bolton!" But this time Drayton had his own vociferous following of friends and on every one of the four laps I heard, "Beautiful, Jerry, beautiful", "You're looking good, Jerry", "Remember, Jerry, number one, number one!" The course consists of 4 laps of just under 3 miles with a sharpish hill just after the start, a long downhill and flat bottom half, in the river valley of Springbank Park, then a long drag up towards the finish.

Introduction to the crowd before the start.

The start was fast and after half a lap Drayton and I went out on our own. As we passed the crowds, clapping and cheering at the end of one lap, a time of "12:41" was called. I knew it should have been 13:41, but even so that was very fast, and instead of being satisfied with that pace, I decided to try to intimidate Drayton by going even faster, and I put in a burst. He came with me, but as we wound our way to the top of Zoo Hill I edged away slightly. I relaxed coming off the hill, let him catch me, only to gain another 5 yards by nimble

". . . I put in a burst . . ."

". . . and take the lead."

". . . he headed me . . ."

". . . he put in a surge . . ."

turning on a left hand hairpin bend at the bottom of the lap. Again I eased fractionally to let him catch me and take the lead. I didn't mind if he headed me into the slight wind on this section of the course; but after the long drag up to the end of the second lap I was feeling a bit rough as my breathing was not coming too well. 27:35. Even so, I got slightly ahead again up Zoo Hill and this time made him work to catch me. The pace must have eased fractionally on the 3rd lap, for suddenly I began to feel relaxed. I pushed a little up Zoo Hill for the last time, just to make him worry, but with 2 miles to go he put in a surge, which had me alert, but it only lasted about 50

". . . I kicked, and won . . ."

yards and from then on we ran stride for stride along the river and through the trees, turning left for the uphill run for home. I was getting more and more confident, the adrenalin beginning to build up for the coup when, with 600 yards to go, he spoke to me. "Do you want to run in together, or race?" Immediately I felt a sorrow; to run in together was alien to my philosophy of racing; but in the same thought I knew I had won. "We'd better make a race of it," I said, and then, "I'll forget you said that!"

With 300 yards to go I kicked, and won by 15 seconds in 55:34.6, 3 minutes inside the old record. I'd produced the goods. I could relax and enjoy it now.

I met a lot of people I had known in the old days in England. Martin Walmsley, a crack miler in my early University track days, now working with Labatt's Brewery in London, Ontario; Bill Hopkins, a Manchester University cross-country runner; "Issy", Isabel, John Whetton's girlfriend at University. We were so glad to see them again. It is great to have these friends in far flung places and indeed the support of strangers. When back in England, I received the following letter from London, Ontario:

"Dear Ron Hill,

I saw you in the race last Sunday in the Park. My daddy gave a great shout, 'C'mon Ron Hill'. I thought he was a bit crazy but he said he was just giving you a bit more ' 'couragement'. Ron Hill, I think you are a very good runner. I came from England too.

Love from,

Alexander Gordon, 4 years old
(belonging to the Junior Jet Club)"

The day after the race Dave Prokop took us to see Niagara Falls; the day after that we followed Bill Johnstone, in our hire car, to his wooden holiday cottage, complete with central heating, at Bright's Grove on Lake Huron. On the way we picked up a large basket of

". . . a big soft bull mastiff called Judd . . ."

tomatoes, a basket of grapes, two baskets of apples and two dozen eggs, and after making us hamburgers on his outdoor barbecue, he left us with a bottle of whisky and a crate of beer to have ourselves to ourselves for 6 days. We befriended a big soft bull mastiff called Judd, and were happy together, returning to England on Wednesday, October 7th.

About to say goodbye to Dr. Bill McInnis at his house.

Autumn and winter were approaching and my last objective for the year was the Fukuoka marathon in Japan on December 6th. Two weeks of 42½ and 31 miles I regarded as enough rest before tackling the build up for Japan. For three weeks I increased my mileage and the amount of quality work in my training; 94½, 112½, 125½ miles.

I wondered what would happen if I went beyond my 120 - 130 miles per week. Would I reach another plane of fitness and capability? I had to find out; therefore, week by week I slipped in a third session of 6½ miles in my lunch break at work. Easy running,

Sep. 19th. Hollingworth Road Relay — bringing Bolton home first.

*Lancashire Road Relay, Oct. 17th.
Sitting on Ron Barlow, then handing
over to Mike Chapman of Bolton's
winning team.*

usually with Neil Shuttleworth. I did fairly well in a road relay race, and ran close to my personal best in the Waterloo Road Race with a 37:32 clocking for fifth place. But I was never really happy. A lot of the time I felt slightly fatigued and towards the end of this increased training stint I seemed to be doing nothing but changing in and out of running gear.

The whole mood wasn't helped by the weather; it rained a hell of a lot that winter and training continually in the wet and dark became depressing.

Remarks from my training log read: *"Wed. Nov. 11th, E. Ran home from work — Nav. — Wern. — Rom. — Chad. — rained from start to finish — miserable — 'no. stride fartlek' up to 55 and down x 2 — felt tired and weary and bloody well fed up of running."*

My mileage went 131, 132, 152 and 164 miles. 164 miles, my highest ever and the last big week before tapering down for the Fukuoka. That week is described from my log again:

Sat. Nov. 21st, M.   *7 miles easy running — slight hangover.*
Sat. Nov. 21st, A.   *13½ miles — felt pretty tired when I set off.*

1970

Sun. Nov. 22nd, M.	*20½ miles — pace seemed to be reasonable.*
Sun. Nov. 22nd, A.	*5 miles — felt all right apart from strange feelings — twinges in both achilles tendons.*
Mon. Nov. 23rd, M.	*7 miles — raining.*
Mon. Nov. 23rd, Lun.	*6½ miles — felt pretty tired.*
Mon. Nov. 23rd, E.	*10 miles —shattered.*
Tue. Nov. 24th, M.	*8 miles — felt a bit tired.*
Tue. Nov. 24th, Lun.	*6½ miles — a bit weary.*
Tue. Nov. 24th, E.	*9 miles — moving pretty well for a change.*
Wed. Nov. 25th, M.	*8 miles — easy running.*
Wed. Nov. 25th, Lun.	*6½ miles — didn't feel too bad.*
Wed. Nov. 25th, E:	*12 miles — felt pretty well.*
Thu. Nov. 26th, M:	*8 miles — a bit stiff when I got up.*
Thu. Nov. 26th, Lun.	*6½ miles — felt all right.*
Thu. Nov. 26th, E.	*8 miles — not bad.*
Fri. Nov. 27th M.	*8 miles — a little bit tired at 6.40 a.m.*
Fri. Nov. 27th Lun.	*7 miles — faster than usual with work pressing.*
Fri. Nov. 27th E.	*7 miles — felt pretty tired at the end.*

My companion on the trip to Japan was Bill Adcocks, and Cecil Dale came as team manager. We travelled JAL via Moscow and stayed a night at the luxurious "Otani" Hotel in Tokyo, where we met up with Jack Foster (New Zealand) and Ken Moore (U.S.A.) and trained together.

Cecil Dale, me, Bill Adcocks.   *In Japan.*

132

We moved on to Fukuoka, the station Plaza Hotel, and John Farrington (Australia) joined our English speaking group. Two Russian runners were there, Volkov and Velikorodnik, with a team manager, and at first were all seriousness and frowns until jolly Cecil Dale got to them every day, communicating in pidgin German until, breaking down the barriers he had them laughing and then saying, "Good morning."

I went on "the diet", got a sore throat and generally didn't feel like a race at all. Two hours before the start I wrote in my log: "After a long hard season I don't feel in perfect condition. What do I expect? I don't know;

Pre-race run with Jack Foster.

it's a matter of approaching the race with an open mind. What the race will produce will be a surprise package no matter what happens, a kind of lucky dip. I can't really guess what time will

High carbohydrate with Jack Foster and Ken Moore.

133

win the race or who. I've run 2:10 and 2:09 this year, both under difficult conditions but with fast competition for the first 10 and 7 to 8 miles respectively and being in good condition for both. Last year here, with only 5 weeks training, but fresh, and under pretty difficult conditions I got 2:11:54. It could be 2:10, but I'll probably hang back (tentative plan for the start) and in this case I expect 2:12. We shall see."

Fukuoka — the start.

It was much worse than 2:12.

A bright cold day greeted the runners as we lined up on the track. I had warmed up 1 mile and didn't feel bouncy at all. I set off in the bunch and Ken Moore said to me as we circled the track, "My, you're actually restraining yourself." John Farrington took an early lead, but it wasn't long before Unetani started to do the work. I kept dropping behind the bunch and for 10 Km I had Maxol winner Usami behind me. I was moving reasonably well until about 10 miles, when strangely my legs began to stiffen and before the turn was reached I had lost contact with the leaders. I was beaten, and just watched helplessly as they streamed away from me. I tried to hold my form, hoping that an energy boost would pull me through at the end, but I just continued to lose ground.

I passed two runners just before the turn, and just after caught a Japanese runner, white vested with a red stripe. We stayed together for about 11 miles, passing another Japanese, in black, then Tanimura, third last year, who had blown up. At 23½ miles I left my companion and plodded after one more little Japanese runner,

134

catching him just before the stadium. He was unbelievable, running along slapping his sides as if to say "Giddy up", hitting himself like a jockey would whip a horse at the end of a race. I passed him and finished an undistressed 9th in 2:15:27. God, I hadn't believed I would ever go so slowly again.

". . . 9th in 2:15:27 . . ."

Usami became the first Japanese runner to win the race with a time of 2:10:37.8. Ken Moore was 2nd, 2:11:35.8; Unetani 3rd, 2:12:12. Jack Foster ran a superb race for a New Zealand record of 2:12:17.8 with John Farrington 5th, 2:12:58.4. Bill Adcocks made magnificent comeback with 2:13;32 for 6th place.

I was bloody fed up. I'd had enough long distance racing for a while, it was time for a rest. Back home I dropped down to 2 mile runs, and enjoyed the Christmas festivities. My last run of 1970 was:

"Thur. Dec. 31st. E. Two mile road course opp. — easy running — not too pleasant with four pints inside me — sloshed on my last run of the year. 2 mls."

The first run of 1971 was not much better:

"Fri. Jan. 1st. M. 2 mile road course 7.40 a.m. — very frosty — felt grim after last night's drinking until 2.00 a.m. — drunk still on the first run of the year. 2 mls."

With my last two cross-country titles gone last year, the Lancs. and the East Lancs., my compulsion to run these events disappeared and on the first Saturday of 1971, I did something that a few years before would have been impossible . . . I went to watch the Lancashire Cross-Country Championships at Springfield Park, Rochdale, and saw club-mate Mike Freary win his first Lancashire title.

I was still resting. That week I got a sore throat which as usual spread into a chest infection; but it didn't matter, I was only doing 2's anyway. My weight that week went up to 9 stone 12½ pounds, probably my heaviest ever. I finished the "rest" off with a 50 mile week and decided that I'd had enough of the easy life and would have to get training again and become once more an "iron man".

After only one week of running to work and back I finished 14th in a grim and muddy "Cinque Mulini" — 5 Windmills Race, near Milan, Italy. That wasn't bad in an international field. Mike Freary was less than half a minute ahead in 6th place; the awards were poor though, and we both got "a bloody cake!" for a prize. But my enthusiasm was fired a little. I began to look for speed.

Another week of running to work and back, and on Friday morning I suddenly found the run to work easy. I had clicked. I had often found this. Starting a build up, the runs to work would seem a drag for two or three weeks, then suddenly, one morning, it came easily. I clocked 104½ miles, ran 20½ miles on Sunday with Arthur Walsham, then picked up another sore throat which within 24 hours became a bad chest.

I felt weak and miserable, but it didn't stop me running. 13 miles on the Saturday, another 20½ miles with Arthur Walsham in wind, rain and cold on the Sunday. That week I ran 114 miles, and travelled to Normandy. The Mezidon people were still trying to get me to win for a fourth time. This year they even changed the course, putting in some hills across the valley from the stadium. They thought that as an Englishman I would like hills and the course would suit me better. The continentals didn't like hills; unfortunately for me, John Caine, one of my team-mates, liked hills better than I did. During the race my position fluctuated from first to sixth; after each ascent I made up ground on the rushing downhill run, but with the illness in my legs I lost ground each time we climbed, eventually finishing 20 seconds behind Caine, and outsprinting Frenchman, Le Chevalier, on the track. He knew about my sprint, and let me through on the inside! Club-mate, Eric Haslam was fourth.

Trying so hard to win took it out of me. In the next week I felt very, very weary. *"Tuesday E. — 7½ miles — was feeling very rough — and quite ill at present with a cold and a bad chest. Thursday M. — 7 miles — ran to work — practically crawling — short stride — stiff in the joints — still a bad cold and a bad chest making me feel low."* Added to this, first Graham and then Steven caught scarlet fever.

I should never have run in the Northern Counties Cross-Country Championships at Witton Park, Blackburn. In the morning I ran

7½ miles, recording in my training log: *"chest so tender I could hardly bear to cough — chest aching too — felt weak physically — thought I was going to collapse a couple of times — couldn't eat anything when I got back".*

I also wrote in my diary: *"didn't want to run in the afternoon, in fact felt like going to bed for a blanket rest for 3 days".* But I had promised Bolton Harriers that I would turn out. The best I could manage was 26th, after starting right at the back and dying on the hills each time. 9 miles of murder and I couldn't raise a sprint at the end.

"Bolton won . . ."

Bolton won the championship from Bingley with Sale Harriers 3rd.

A mere cold and chest infection were not going to beat me. Next day I was out with Arthur Walsham, running the Derbyshire hills, 20½ miles — "felt weak and dare not cough again — could hardly talk at first — weakened on the hills — and towards the end was just plodding — it was murder". I stuck to my training plan and introduced my 2 x 440 yards track session on Tuesday lunchtime. 121 miles I covered that week. My sinuses became blocked and I had headaches.

With no race that weekend I ran 13 miles Saturday and 20½ on Sunday, after having stayed in bed until 11.30 a.m., my longest lie in for years and years. I felt a lot better than the previous Sunday and began to perk up only to find that Friday morning I woke up with another sore throat. During that morning my throat and neck got worse and for my lunchtime session at work I ran only 3 instead of 7 miles — "at last I have given in — did only 3 miles (part with Neil) — felt stiff, aching and tired — I can say 'cheerio' to my National chances next week". Nevertheless, I clocked another 121 miles that week and helped Bolton win the Manchester Athletic Club Cross-Country relay at Heaton Park on Saturday afternoon.

This time the infection climaxed quickly and I was soon over the tender lungs stage and coughing up phlegm, which as far as I was concerned was the road to recovery. Perhaps if I eased down, I might not run too badly in the National. I tapered off to 78 miles that week.

I had decided to travel towards Norwich on Friday night so that I wouldn't be tired from driving, and left home at 2.30 in the afternoon. The exhaust of my car had started to blow and I hadn't gone 10 miles when the noise became unbearable. There was nothing for it but to turn back to Stockport and get a new one fitted. A bitterly cold wind was blowing and it started to snow. I had to hang around a draughty exhaust repair shop until 5.00 p.m. before I could depart once more. Just beyond Newark, I stopped for chips and two fish, then drove on to Swaffham; I tried a hotel there, they said they were full. I drove on and tried a hotel in Dereham, they said they were full too. How could they be full on a Friday night? Perhaps it was my unconventional dress, a long maxi overcoat and a red scarf knotted around my neck. I was furious, and beginning to despair, when I caught sight of "The Swan" guest house. I knocked, the Irish landlady had a room and Peter Griffiths, a Tipton Harrier, and a couple of his mates were staying there too.

When I woke up on Saturday morning I had yet another sore throat. I had a diabolical race on the frozen course. I warmed up wearing sun glasses and a scarf, hiding from the world. It was windy and bitterly cold. I was crazy and ran in a string vest. After only 400 yards the course bottlenecked through a farm gateway. Two of our Bolton runners were taken to hospital after the race with spike wounds. I was miles behind and found it almost impossible to work through. On one ploughed section it was virtually impossible to pass. Some spectators were calling out positions, 65th I heard after one lap. Over the second lap I moved up to about 50th, then I couldn't go any further forward. I seemed to be flat out and was not making any headway, running downhill was getting to be as hard as running uphill. At 7 miles the group I was with started to move ahead of me; I had blown up; people of all shapes and sizes started to pass me. The harder I tried the slower I seemed to go, I was ashamed at not being able to hang on. I remember Barry Watson passing me on some plough, shouting a word of encouragement, then spiking me on my left foot. On to grass land; I was really trying hard. On the last section of plough two or three others passed me. I wanted desperately to stay in the first hundred. A thin bespectacled runner went past — long hair, pale white and spotty. I couldn't stay with him. God, how can he be beating me? I tried to speed up as we turned left towards the finish. The finish banner became hazy; I veered over to the left instead of running straight forward; I was on the edge of collapse. It was over. A small brass disc was thrust into my hand. As the queue of finishers stumbled along I glanced down at it. Number 82. I almost burst into tears, but took a grip of myself. I thought I must have been really ill or something. I was sad about my condition.

For the record Dave Bedford had won the race easily in 47:04

with Welshman Mal Thomas 2nd, 47:44, and Trevor Wright, my Northern successor, 3rd, 47:58.

To look at another side of the race; one of the North Eastern runners told me later about a club-mate, on the coach back home, talking about his big battle with Ron Hill in the National; how with half a mile to go he was with me and wondering whether to make his effort then or wait and kick with 200 to go! It was no contest.

I was depressed and dropped back to 2's and 3's for a week then built up to 101 again; but unbelievably, another sore throat, my sixth since December. I tried to train through it again with a 107½ mile week, but by Thursday I was writing "felt tired — no spring and yet haven't trained properly for ages", and Friday "no enthusiasm for running at the moment — will have to take stock and re-think — probably need a rest".

April 9th. Salford '7½'. With George Lawson and Denis Hopkinson.
Eventually I was 5th.

And rest I did. Through the end of March and April I cut my mileage to 88, 56, 42, 60 and 80 miles. Weekends I still ran in road relays for Bolton, but I regarded these as good training sessions, and in road races I evolved a technique for taking the pressure off myself by starting right at the back of the field and working through, thus avoiding head to head confrontations with the accompanying physical and mental pressures.

In May I started to build again. I had six weeks to go before the Maxol Marathon on June 13th, and this was the trial for the European Games in Helsinki. I had tried to avoid this trial by writing to the B.A.A.B. asking to be excused on the grounds that the European Games were only 9 weeks after the trials and a hard marathon such a short time before the Championships would surely take the edge off my performance. Surely they could allow one exception? That would still leave two places open, and I had proved myself competitively over the last two years. Arthur Gold rang me with his answer. Everyone must run the trial. After all, I wasn't that much better than anyone else.

Bloody hell! Not that much better? Only 2½ minutes if you looked at the Commonwealth Games result.

On long reflection, perhaps the selectors were looking at my disastrous 2:15 in Fukuoka. But that was after experimenting with higher than usual mileage. Perhaps they were looking at my winter's performances. But surely I had been ill all winter; I'd had a go when most people would have been laid up in bed. I had no coach to put my case, no-one to lobby for me with the selectors. I'd have to run the trial.

But it annoyed me to have my abilities doubted now that I had proved them. I'm certain the stars in other countries would have had more consideration. I couldn't help seeing what is perhaps a typically British sort of attitude towards success: if you see a man at the top, try to knock him down.

It is also apparent when we consider winners and improving standards. The cry has always been "look after the up-and-coming athletes, give them financial assistance, give them trips for experience", when the attitude should be "we have a star, let's try to keep him up there, let's try to help him improve". Perhaps the right attitudes are coming now, but they have been a long time in arriving; meanwhile other countries have been helping and honouring their champions.

MANCHESTER EVENING NEWS

Training for the Maxol Marathon. My two flying 440's at Ashton track, lunchtime. Here having been paced by Neil Shuttleworth, my two laboratory assistants Margaret Whitehead and Marjorie Welden time us.

CHAPTER EIGHT

The first two of my six weeks build-up, I was on a company management training course near Kenilworth, but that didn't stop me doing my running morning and lunchtimes, when other course members were lying in bed or supping their halves of beer. I clocked 110 miles the first week and finished 2nd in the Longwood '10' at the weekend to Mike Baxter. The second week I logged 118½ miles, and on Saturday had a disastrous 10,000 metres in the Northern championships at Cleckheaton. I felt tired and sick in the race and recorded 30:24.6 behind Mike Freary's 28:53.8. Fortunately I had the hilly Rossendale Half-marathon the next day. I set off at the back, worked through and caught the leaders at 2 miles, before the long climb to the 5 mile point. By the time we had reached 5 miles there were only three of us in it, John Calvert (Blackburn Harriers), Stan Clegg (Salford Harriers) and myself. Here, John put in a hard burst that had me knackered and feeling sick, but I just managed to hang on and in fact leave him on the steep downhill sections after 6½ miles. On a tough climb into the wind, after the left turn at the 'Bull and Butcher' pub, I tired badly and John caught me again as we started the long descent into Rawtenstall. I started to recover. Around the 9 mile point I casually asked a spectator how far we had run, and John said later the tone of my voice finished him off. I moved away to win by 54 seconds in 1:07:06, a new course record.

This was my last race before the Maxol marathon, and it had given me the vital confidence I needed. I clocked in 132½ miles that week, which included on Thursday a 12 mile run to work and a 23 mile run home.

I wanted to make sure of this long run as at the weekend we were off to Majorca, the whole family of us, for our annual holiday. We stayed at the once small village of C'An Picafort at the newly built Hotel Tonga. It was a cheap holiday as it was out of season. In those two weeks I ran 275½ miles. It was delightful to relax! Our mail-order business had been building up and putting pressure on both May and I, as orders had to go out promptly, and I had to do all my work on it at night. It was great to feel the sun on my back and I ran most of the time without a vest.

I am a great believer in sun-tans. A bronzed skin not only is healthy, the body gets its full supply of vitamin D from the action of sunlight on the skin, but it looks good too, both to the wearer and the opposition! I trained round a 2 mile woodland circuit near the hotel, on the sandy side tracks through the fields and on the roads.

141

PAUL LIVESEY

Racing John Calvert in the Rossendale ½ Marathon.

The locally available maps were infuriating as some of the roads either did not exist or disappeared into swampland. A couple of times I followed tracks which suddenly disappeared under water. Bloody frogs leapt to left and right, plop, plop, plop and when I got up to my calves in warm water and could see no further ahead, I had to turn back and squelch my way home on the main roads.

It was a happy time with all of us together. The kids found friends and occasionally we would all do a little run together.

Returning to England, I had to wrap up somewhat in the cold June weather, as I ran through the low carbohydrate part of "the diet" and tapered down for the Maxol.

Saturday, the day before the race, I thought about my chances and summed it up: "Not sure how this Maxol race is going to go at all. Have felt pretty shattered Thursday and especially yesterday, but it could possibly be that I have eaten a hell of a lot on those two days. Today I've tried to cut back my food, but I'm still tempted into eating a lot of biscuits and cake. Everything could go wrong and I would miss the European Championships, but it doesn't seem to worry

Graham, May and Steven in C'An Picafort.

me too much. I don't want to run the Maxol at all. I'm just going to go in for the race and see how it goes. I don't want a hard race, yet I'd hate to hang around and be left as I was in Fukuoka. If I feel like moving, and I'm going easy, I probably will. We'll see."

The start was at 10.00 a.m., so I had to get up with the alarm at 6.50 a.m., with time for a 1 mile jog on the canal bank, followed by porridge, one marmalade butty and a cup of sugarless, milkless tea. We got down to the Manchester Y.M.C.A. by 9.25 a.m.

The weather was cloudy and cool with little wind. I jogged about ¾ mile warm up and felt O.K. No nervousness. I stood on the front line; my mother and dad were there, my Uncle Harry and Aunty Ethel. When the gun released the 200 odd runners, I got immediately near the front to keep an eye on the field. I seemed to be moving pretty well. Don Faircloth took an early lead, and John Newsome, the Wakefield runner, chased him, but by 2 miles we had pulled him in and at 3 miles I began to think, "Why take it easy and use up energy running slowly, when I can relax better at a faster pace?"

I side-stepped the leaders, clicked into gear, and strode to the front. John Newsome was the only taker and after a couple of miles I relaxed a bit and Jim Alder pulled a big group through to join us up Princess Parkway. I was feeling great and on all the short uphill sections kept putting in bursts to break the field up and upset the other runners. Each time they came back to me. At the top of the

Parkway, turning left towards Sharston, it came on pouring down; cooling rain, making running that more efficient, that much easier.

I dropped to the back of the group to let Jim Alder make the pace for a while. He seemed confident. I went up front again, pushing the pace, and running on the pavement as we crossed the River Mersey at Northenden to let an ambulance through, sirens wailing. I could hear footsteps on the wet road behind me, heavy footfalls matching my own stride for stride. That would be Trevor Wright, like me wearing a light string vest; quieter quicker footsteps, that was

Plain, Hill, Wright.

B. BUTTERWORTH

Bernie Plain in the red vest of Wales. I didn't need to look round.

Left on to Barlow Moor Road. "Jim Alder's 10 yards down," someone called. I turned the screws and speeded up the pace. Hit him where it hurts. Trevor and Bernie stayed with me. It still rained. My paper number 17 became sodden and dropped off.

Right up to 15 miles I towed these two round and until suddenly the quicker footsteps began to die away. I didn't look round; Bernie had gone. We hit Palatine Road for the second time and Trevor was beginning to move alongside. "Plain's 50 yards down." There were just the two of us now.

Trevor touched his side. "How are you?" I said. "Great," he replied, "just my vest is a bit tight." "Well if you feel that good," I thought, "you can do some leading." I slowed fractionally so that he could get ahead. I wanted to put some pressure on him. I knew how pressure could hurt in a marathon, and this was his debut. At 16½ miles a man came alongside on a bike and to my astonishment handed Trevor a note. "From Joe," he said, then dropped back. Joe Lancaster, the journalist, who had a keen professional interest in my career and whom I had given lifts many times to and from races, was now Trevor's coach. Trevor read the note, half handed it to me, thought better of it, and threw it away. I don't know to this day what the note said, all I knew was that this kind of assistance was strictly against the rules; but it didn't rattle me.

I ran with and behind Trevor through 20 miles, and although I wasn't moving too badly, just a bit of stiffness creeping in, I was getting a little bit worried. Trevor was showing no signs of slowing up. We turned right after Longford Park in Stretford, towards Old Trafford; I was talking to him, giving him directions as I knew the course, telling him to bear left then right to cut the corners where we could. Suddenly, just after the right turn, at about 22 miles, he said, "Go on, Ron."

"I ran with . . . Trevor . . ."

145

". . . and behind Trevor . . ."

"What's up?" I asked.

"My legs have gone," he gasped.

"What the hell do you think mine are like?" I retorted. "A bloody sprinter's?"

Into Old Trafford.

On the short, sharp, humpback bridge at 22½ miles I got ahead, but decided to wait for him and run together. Past Old Trafford cricket ground, I talked to him; the slightly slower pace had allowed me to recover well and I encouraged him and told him how much further there was to go. Not far. Not far. We could see the tall gantries and floodlights of Manchester United's football ground. As we passed the entrance to the ground for the 2 miles out and back loop into Trafford Park I just said to him "O.K.?"

"Yes, go on, Ron," he said, and I strode away.

146

I found it easy for the end of a marathon, just a slight cramp in my arms near the end. I finished smiling with plenty left, 2:12:39. Selectors take note. I need inspiration to run great marathons and you have just stolen some of that inspiration for the European Games by making me prove myself in the trial!

"I finished . . . with plenty left, 2:12:39."

Trevor ran the fastest marathon debut of all time, 2:13:27, with Jurgen Busch of East Germany third, 2:14:03, Jeff Julian, New Zealand, 4th, 2:15:19 and Colin Kirkham, Coventry Godiva Harriers, setting a personal best of 2:15:21 in 5th place. My Sunday morning training partner, Arthur Walsham, was first veteran home, 9 days short of his 41st birthday in a magnificent 2:21:38.

I didn't go to the post-race dinner. I hadn't wanted any part of the race. I'd done what I had to do, so we cleared off home and had roast beef and salad. That night I slept without any trouble, unusual after a marathon race.

What did I do now? There were only 9 weeks to go before the European Games Marathon race in Helsinki. No time for a decent recovery and build up. I decided I would have to train right through to Helsinki. 3's — 5's — by the end of the week I was up to 7½'s, but stiffness was persisting and I realised I would need a week's decent rest to recover properly, but first I had entered the half-marathon at Freckleton near Blackpool.

On my way to my parents' house at Blackpool on Friday night, our car started to make some strange noises and I just managed to get off the M61 motorway before the engine seized up. After long waiting in the rainy night, I had to be towed to a garage and my Uncle Harry's son Peter came to pick us up and take us on to our destination. The bloody car had to be left and that was more money for repairs.

In the race the next evening, for fun, I set off right at the back and ran dead last for the first lap of the track. By 5 miles I was through to 2nd clocking 24:25 and it took me another 2½ miles to drop John Balmer, Pembroke A.C., and catch young John Fewery, the Preston man running for the home team, Blackpool and Fylde A.C. I just stayed with him then until one mile to go, and ran away to win by 12 seonds with 65:25. I was very stiff at the end.

The next week I eased to 2's and 3's all week to notch up 42½ miles. That weekend there was a Sunday race, the YMCA 20Km road race in Manchester. I thought it would be a good start to my training build up for Helsinki, but it turned out to be truly one of the toughest races of my life.

There were some fast runners in this race, and at noon under cloudy skies after rain, we strode off over the first grass and I went straight to the front of the pack as we left the big field and hit the road. Chris Fay of Blackburn soon joined me and I let him get ahead and start pushing the pace. Slowly the runners who had been surprised by the fast start closed the gap and latched on to us leaders. Steve Edmunds (Sale Harriers), Ricky Wilde (Manchester and District Lads' Club Harriers), Cyril Leigh (Salford Harriers) and Mike Freary my Bolton club-mate. A couple of times I pushed ahead, but I couldn't get away. In Sale, at the 5 mile point Mike was having a go up front. 23 minutes 18 seconds; I thought it had been fast! Leigh, then Edmunds, dropped away. One after the other we all hit the lead and tried to burn each other off. It was very competitive. Ricky Wilde faded away. At one stage we almost got Freary, but he just managed to hang on and in the end proved to be the strongest. At 7 miles it was my turn to force myself to stay in contact, tiredness was flooding through my body, I was trying to stride to keep within that vital yard of the other two, but any second I expected to cross the razor's edge and give in. I couldn't hang on much longer. At 8 miles Fay, slowly, slipped back. Mike was charging on and I kept telling myself to go on for just a bit longer. Just that bit further. Up Princess Parkway, heading towards home, I was following Mike, any minute now I would go, even though the pace was dropping imperceptibly. I would try to hang on until 10 miles and get a decent time, then Mike could go on alone. Left down

YMCA 20K. Fay, Edmunds, Hill, Leigh.

MIKE BRETT

by Southern Cemetery; there the 10 mile marksman called out 46:25. "Christ," I said to myself.

Mike tried a couple of efforts and I stretched myself to go with him; my thoughts now were that the longer I could hang on, the less distance would I have to run alone in my desperately tired state. Suddenly Mike spoke. "How far to go?" he asked. "About 1½ miles," I replied. A few seconds later he said, "Go on, Ron, take it."

Was I relieved and surprised. I could win this now. "Stick

149

together," I said. There was no way I could speed up in my knack-ered state. There were two or three little hills before the finish, which I was dreading, so I said to Mike, "Relax, up the hills, take it nice and easy." But it was for my sake not his; and the pace didn't really drop much at all, but he had given in.

On the last road to the playing fields, he said again, "Go on." I tried, but only gained about 20 yards. I daren't go any faster until I could see the finish line; and when I tried to sprint with 300 yards to go, my legs felt like they were going to buckle. I crossed the line with 58:07, a course record, with Mike 58:14. No one has been near these times since. In my training log I wrote: "Moral: hang on as long as you can and keep your mouth shut."

Anxious to build up mileage I went out and did another 3 miles in the evening. My legs were stiff.

The following morning, Monday, I stepped out of the porch to start my 5 miles morning run and I almost fell down. My right leg sort of collapsed under me. "That's strange," I thought. I ran my 5 miles, the leg felt funny at the back at the top. I ran 103 miles that week and when all my accumulated stiffness had disappeared I was left with a painful right leg.

The next week I ran 124 miles as planned, with speed sessions at night and the flying 2 x 440 yards Tuesday lunchtime (59.7 and 57.4). My right leg got worse, there was no drive from it, the pains were spreading the full length of my hamstring, and the ligaments behind my knee were catching and cracking.

The Games were so close now, I couldn't go back on my plans. I clocked in 129 miles, and ran a negative 4th place, 14:18.0, 5,000 metres at the Rivington Cup meeting in Bolton. Sunday I ran 21½ miles from my parents' house at Blackpool with Andy Holden. Both legs were beginning to get stiff and tired; I was forced to modify my training and just run to work and back, 7½ miles each way, to total 122½ miles.

The last week in July I spent training in the Yorkshire Dales. This week was sponsored by "The Champions Fund" whose secretary was Ron Pickering, the coach and T.V. commentator. Did I train! The runs I did were almost suicidal.

We stayed in a caravan, sited by a stream near a 400-year-old farmhouse, Cravenholme, below the site of the Roman Fort at Bainbridge. It was let to us by Mrs. Scarr. The first day there I found a morning run which took me on tracks, up on to the moors, a climb of 1,000 feet until I hit another track which brought me left round by farms and back into Bainbridge. It took me just over 1¼ hours. It was too much; yet, having done it once, I wasn't going to give in and find a shorter course; I ran it every morning! In the afternoon I ran

Caravan at Cravenholme.

11, 13, or 15½ miles. Some comments from my training log describe the terrain: "over-reached myself a bit, the hills were enormous — absolutely knackered at the end" — "some of the hills are killers".

It was hard work. My right knee was cracking and my right ankle swelled. To take my mind off the fatigue and pain I took to counting the number of different species of wild flowers I could see on a run. Friday I counted 37 species. One day after my morning run, I took my lucky ring, the silver one I had bought in Mexico, off the little finger of my left hand and put it on the bonnet of the car to have a swill in cold water. It caught my nose if I didn't remove it. I forgot I'd taken it off. It was only half way through the day out that I noticed I wasn't wearing it. That night we searched the grass, the gravel track and a few hundred yards of road to no avail — I never saw it again.

Saturday morning, on my last 10 mile morning run, I pushed it a little and got my time down to 1 hour 4½ minutes. Saturday afternoon I ran a 13 mile fartlek session and the backs of my legs were so sore that I couldn't get out of breath on the bursts. I'd run 146 miles that week. I only hoped it would show dividends.

The week before travelling to Helsinki, my right leg was restricting my stride and had me really worried; I reduced my runs to 7½ miles to work and back, gave myself heat treatment and rubbed Algipan into the sore part. 125 miles.

The British Team flew to Helsinki in a noisy old Vanguard. The supporters and "tourists" left an hour later, and landed about the same time as us. At the Athletes' Village of Otaniemi, I shared a room with my marathon team mates, Trevor Wright and Colin Kirkham. The food wasn't brilliant and right from the start I had

151

stomach trouble. Constant stomach ache, wind and diarrhœa. Colin had brought his own apples and big fruit cake baked by his wife Anne, which he kept on the floor by the side of his bed. But he wasn't spared the guts trouble; it hit him badly right in the middle of the marathon; and Trevor was really bad with sickness and diarrhœa in the week before the race.

I asked the team doctor for some Streptotriad. Pink pills which had worked for the teams in the previous Games I had been to; but *he* didn't believe in it. Bloody great!

The first night there I was so bad I sat on the toilet until 2.30 a.m. and read the Daily Telegraph from cover to cover.

My right leg continued to trouble me, but was easing slightly with the lighter mileage. I went on "the diet" and was very methodical about the low carbohydrate four days. On Tuesday afternoon, the third day of the low carbohydrate stage, I did a session of 2-4-6 x 70 seconds bursts with 50 seconds interval, over the last part of the marathon course and the now synthetic track of the Helsinki Olympic Stadium, and ran myself into a state of acute distress which I had never experienced before. I was almost outside of myself observing what was going on. The last set of 6 on the track was so trying that I was finishing the efforts moaning "Oh no! Oh no!", and starting them talking loudly to myself, saying, "Go on, go on." I was in such a bad way after the session that it was a big effort to prevent myself from bursting into tears.

Time passed quite well; the British runners were a good crowd even if they did tend to use our room as a lounge. I met some old friends. Ismail Akcay, the Turkish runner, who I had been sending details of training schedules to, gave me a lovely embroidered suede jerkin for May. Robert and Denise Blanchet of the Mezidon race were both there as officials of the French team.

By Friday — the race was on Sunday, August 9th — my stomach had stopped aching but I still had the "runs" and regularly had to dive into the bushes while training. There was definitely some bug going around. Andy Holden, who was running in the steeplechase, told me he had been sick twice on the day of his competition. Hardly preparation for the championships for him, or for me. Trevor Wright became so bad I didn't see how he was going to run at all.

Race day morning was cool and overcast. At 9.00 a.m. I walked down to the training track, just below our room and jogged 8 laps. I felt O.K. There was a medical at 10.00 a.m. so I had to rush to the dining hall to breakfast on English cornflakes (there had been so many complaints from the athletes that the team officials had to fly in supplies of cereal and fruit from England), marmalade butties and a cup of tea. The medical involved giving a urine sample, electro-cardiograph, blood pressure and listen to the chest. I was O.K.

At 1.00 p.m. I brewed a cup of tea in our room and had a couple more marmalade butties. The race was scheduled for 3.40 p.m. At 1.40 p.m. I had a teaspoonful of salt in concentrated orange juice swilled down by a pint of orange juice with fructose. Outside it came on absolutely throwing it down; it was looking good for the marathon.

At 2.30 p.m. Rab Foreman, the Scottish official "in charge" of the marathon runners, took us down to a waiting car. I was wrapped up; track-suit, anorak, scarf, cap, sun-glasses and my cassette player with soothing Beatles music. The roads to the stadium were awash from the rain; cars were spraying up huge fountains of water.

As we reached the changing rooms, my guts started playing up. I rushed for the toilet. The bloody "runs". I had to go three times in the hour before the start. I'd thought a lot about the race in the previous days and there was only one man I feared, Roelants. I was toying with the idea of going from the gun; but now, my bowels in this condition, it would be impossible. I would have to start carefully so as not to upset them. What a bloody blow!

We were called to the starting pens under the stands. It was crowded there. I took off my tracksuit and sat down, nervously smoothing my shaven legs, stroking them. At last they called us out; out into the huge noisy bowl and on to the wet, empty red track. I walked over to the steeplechase water jump and put cold water on my hair, then on my arms and legs. They called us over to the start line. 52 runners: some pale, some sun-tanned. "Good luck, Trev," "Good luck, Colin — have a good 'un." I kissed my wedding ring on the line.

"CRACK!" We were off; the runners, mainly in white, surged forward. Someone fell, I gave him a hand up and leisurely set off round the track. I was next to last out of the stadium, after a lap and a half, nice and easy. It didn't matter, nobody important jumped the field, only Pat McMahon, over from the States to represent Ireland, sprinted off. Down the hill and right on to the main road. I felt good and quickly threaded my way through the runners, who hadn't really started to breathe hard, until after only 1 mile I was in the leading bunch, with McMahon in white about 100 yards ahead. The fool. Nobody bothered to chase him. By 5 km we had almost caught him.

The course was more or less undulating, but climbing overall out, and descending coming back. I was feeling bouncy, and putting in enthusiastic bursts, then dropping back into the bunch. This was fairly negative running but I had to be careful. Everyone else was being careful. By 10 km we were well out into the country, but I was looking only at the black road and the other competitors, just hoping it would come right.

One or two people chanced their arm, bursting to the front because it felt easy in the group, then dropping back when they could take no further responsibility for the pace. Father Paddy Coyle went up; then the swarthy Aktas from Turkey had a go; Toth from Hungary put in a few hundred metres. But none of this signalled danger. Wright and Roelants were steady in the bunch. At 11 miles (every English mile was marked as well as the kilometres), my left leg began to stiffen and get sore at the top. Left leg? The bloody legacy of favouring that leg in training all the time to take pressure off my right leg. It was just plain tired. Stone me! I was feeling it this early on! I was beginning to get worried, especially as there was such a big group of runners still together. This was most unusual.

At 20 km Roelants had had enough of hanging around. We had just climbed a long hill and were striding down towards the turn at Klaukkala, when he cleared out. Trevor turned to me and said, "Roelants is going." "It's too early for me," I said, and Trevor went off after him.

When they had got about 10 metres ahead, Lismont, Roelants' Belgian team-mate, came up alongside, pale and sweating, forcing along with his ungainly stride, arms protruding. He elbowed me in the ribs a couple of times, unintentionally, looked very carefully at me, then scuttled off after the two leaders.

I wasn't feeling anything like I had in Boston, Edinburgh or at the Maxol, my legs weren't striding as they should have done, but I should have tried to hang on to them. Instead, I was a coward, I took the easy way out; I said to myself, "Roelants will come back, Trevor will come back with him and as for Lismont, he has no chance." I was hoping that nursing my effort carefully would get me through, as in Athens. But what effort? The early pace hadn't been hard enough to hurt anybody. even Colin Kirkham came up to me at the turn. I was having a bad run.

Colin and I ran together, followed by a couple of Finns, and I was so down that I let him lead me at about 25 km whilst I took a breather behind him. I took over again for a while, but I had always found it easier to follow and tried to shunt him into the lead again. However, he wasn't going fast enough for me.

Suddenly at 30 km I woke up. "What the hell am I doing here?" I said to myself. At 31 km I took a sponge and immediately felt better. I could see Roelants was slowly coming back, having been left by the other two. I pushed on. At 22 miles I passed Gaston, crossing to his side of the road but this time patting him on the back as I overtook, "Allez, Gaston."

He latched on to me for a short distance. Then fell back. Right! Now let's set about catching Trevor. Bodily I was running well; it was just that both my legs were sore, my right one at the top in the injured hamstring and the left one was stiffened up completely below the knee. That calf was solid. I was limping on that side.

I started to catch Trevor and was only 28 seconds behind at 40 km, but I realised then that unless he had an accident I wouldn't do it. "Oh, why couldn't there be another 3 miles to go instead of 1 mile," I thought. It was the only marathon I have run where I was wishing for more distance. The physical restrictions due to my injuries had ekcd out my energy supplies and I still had some left. If only I could have used them.

"I wasn't distressed . . ."

Disappointed, I slowed a bit, apart from the limp, easily climbing the short hill to the stadium. Stan Bradshaw was there cheering loudly and looking pleased. But I wasn't pleased; I waved my arms as if to say "Rubbish." I ran on to the track. I wasn't distressed and at that moment I actually felt fresh. And angry.

Trevor, looking grim eyed, was on the line to congratulate me. I was annoyed and walked straight off the track to the changing room. I couldn't be bothered to shower or change. I put my track suit on, and took my special drink out of my bag — gin/orange squash/aspirin/vitamin C. I drained the lot. The reporters were there. I had to admit, "I ran it like an idiot," but had I any choice? I had one thing to say, "If Britain wants a gold medal in the Munich Olympics next year, the selectors had better forget about a trial for me!"

I went out for the victory ceremony. Lajos Mecser of Hungary was just finishing. I saw the final times, K. Lismont (Belgium) 2:13:09. Bloody hell! 2:13 had won the gold! 2:13 in perfect condi-

"Trevor looking grim-eyed . . ."

tions. And I'd run 2:12 in the flaming trials! Tevor had clocked 2:13:59.6. Myself 2:14:34.8. Colin Kirkham, completely out after the race due to stomach trouble, was fourth with 2:16:22.0.

I limped across the wet grass, my left leg was solid. First Lismont, looking pale and haggard, climbed the rostrum for his gold medal; he raised both arms and waved to the crowd. Then Trevor, he waved too.

"Third, Ron Hill." I stepped up, head bowed. I'd nothing to bloody wave about. The Belgian official, hanging the medal round my neck, said in English that he was sorry for my disappointment. The Belgian National Anthem played. I stood to attention, there was a lump in my throat, I was close to tears. I couldn't believe it. The end of a year's preparation and struggle and I was beaten. I was the best man in the field and had finished third. How cruel could life be?

As I said to the Press boys, "That bronze medal was only marginally better than a kick up the backside."

I walked back to the changing rooms. Suddenly stomach pain creased me. I was in agony and couldn't do anything about it. The doctor gave me two codeine tablets, but it continued. There was supposed to be a car back, but Rab couldn't find the driver. Blow it, I would get the bus back. The pains were killing me, and I started to sweat like hell; outside two Frenchmen began to carry me; even then I had to stop once and bend double over the bonnet of a car, the rain in globules on the blue paintwork close to my face. I got on a coach and for 10 minutes was twisting this way and that for relief. Finally and quickly the pain drained away and a wave of relief swept over my body.

I stayed up most of the night drinking beer. I knew I wouldn't sleep. I knew the following day I would be depressed. And I was.

I really blamed the selectors for losing me that gold medal. If I hadn't run that trial I wouldn't have got that injured leg, and I would have been full of inspiration for the European Championships. No — not selectors — how could they be selectors? They didn't select anything. All they did was bloody well rubber stamp the first three in the trial. But I blamed "Them", whoever they were. I blamed the system; I blamed British running.

British running had had me. From now on I was only going to run abroad. And the next 12 months I was going to dedicate to winning the Olympic Gold in Munich. My commitment was total, as was the commitment of my family.

For five weeks after Helsinki, I kept in light training; 60-70 miles per week. Two weeks after Helsinki I had my first race — abroad! I won again the half-marathon in Geraardsbergen, this time by over 2 minutes. I had more trouble getting the prize back than winning the race. It was a tumble drier, which I managed to get on the plane O.K., but it took a mighty effort to hoist the 35Kg box on to the roof rack of my car at Manchester Airport!

I expected my leg to get better quickly on this reduced mileage, but when it was still sore three weeks after the marathon I went to see a physiotherapist in Manchester. This wasn't my usual way, I normally eased and let things get better themselves, but this injury was persistent, and with Munich next year, I could afford no risks. Freddie Griffiths examined me and said that I had probably torn the hamstring at its origin, where it joins on to the bone at the pelvis, after the YMCA 20Km and it had caused severe internal haemorrhage. He put me on a course of heat treatment.

I received an invitation, through the B.A.A.B., to run in Munich in a pre-Olympic marathon, on the course which was going to be used in the actual Games.

It was impossible for me to race another 26 miler, only four weeks after the European, but I wanted to see that course and told the Board this. I wanted to go and produce a report on the course for the benefit of myself and British marathon runners. I don't think that it had occurred to our officials to send someone to see the course, and I could get no one to agree to sponsor this inspection, although Arthur Gold recommended it. Amazingly, a

The Japanese filmed me training.

compromise was reached whereby I had to travel out there as though I were going to run in the race and then use "your native wit to make the best of the situation that you can".

That meant travelling to Munich with Bob Dobson, a 50Km walker and "failing" the medical examination due to a bad leg. I can tell you I felt very, very guilty about it, and rather angry that this was the best Britain could do. The Japanese had five runners, three coaches and two doctors there for the marathon and they were backed by a Japanese T.V. film crew. They even filmed me training, following me in a car round and round a car park.

I ran the course slowly, the morning of the pre-Olympic race; it was flat, there were one or two rough places underfoot in the Nymphenburg Park and the English Gardens, but it looked fast. Usami, from Japan, won the competition in 2:15:52, with Kimihara second. Under the conditions I thought they should have run 2:10:00 and Usami admitted "weather good". I said to him jokingly, but seriously to myself, "This year you win. Next year, me win!"

A week later I declared a month's rest and the last half of September and the first half of October ran weeks of 31, 37½, 46½ and 62½ miles. I enjoyed myself in this period, eating out at lunchtime occasionally and having a couple of pints. With work I was out quite a lot, liaising closely on the Deep-dye Viscose project, often with Joe Whitehead of the Sales Development Department in Manchester, and also with Jack Ibbotson the head of Suncourt Shirtings and his team, and Gordon Richardson in the Design Department at Skelmersdale. I was always well received, because of my running fame, by personnel at all levels of customer firms we visited, but it didn't seem to be appreciated as a spin off to my running activities in my own division.

At home my work load was increasing; the mail order business was expanding. May helped out a lot there. We were having to store more stock in the loft, where I put down some rough boards on the joists and installed a crude light. We also stored the stock under the the floor boards. We had found a huge sloping space under the floor, as our house was on a hill, and by enlarging the trap door we could utilise this space for storing running shoes, home made beer and my stock of duty free spirits which had peaked and was now dwindling due to more frequent imbibing.

In mid-October, when I did start back into training, it was only gently, around the 75 miles mark for three weeks. My right leg still wasn't healed. The ligaments behind my knee kept catching and cracking, and I had restricted movement in that leg. I developed a style dragging that leg a little. One morning, feeling full of beans, I went to hurdle a fence, couldn't get my leg up as far as I thought, and went crashing over. I didn't do any permanent physical damage, but I never jumped that fence again.

Training began to get a bit depressing as it was dark both going to work and coming home, and as such had to be all on the roads. There seemed to be more traffic on the roads each winter; more fumes and longer times to wait when crossing streets.

Simmons, Rose and me, on the way to Bolbec, France.

". . . I finished like a drowned rat, 7th."

1971

My first race of that winter session was in Bolbec in France. It was a train and sea journey with Jack Davies as team manager and young Nick Rose and Tony Simmons as team-mates. As usual the hospitality was superb. I stayed with the Bentot family on Rue Emil Zola. My race was rubbish. Nick and Tony blasted off on a rainy; muddy day, and I finished like a drowned rat, 7th. Well, I'd done no real training for months, what did I expect?

I went to watch and train at races in England, but that was mainly to sell gear and to keep people guessing as to what I was up to. I had my plans and had detailed them to the British Board with a request to be selected for Munich without a trial. The letter read;

"Would the British Board please select me for the Marathon race in the Olympic Games in Munich now, in order that I may get on with the training I have planned to give me the maximum opportunity of winning the gold medal in that race? The several points I wish to present to you in support of my case, I list below, not specifically in any order of importance.

1. *The successful pattern of training I have evolved over the years I feel is unique amongst marathon runners. This involves a series of peaks, averaging about three per year, followed by "rests". My usual "rest" is about four weeks averaging 40 miles per week and my ideal build-up to a peak occupies a period of 10 weeks. I have recently plotted a histogram of my weekly mileage since 1967 in order to take a realistic view of my past experience and this "ideal build-up" is confirmed.*

   Examining my recent history of marathon running the following statistics are of interest:

   1969   *7 weeks "rest"; 9 weeks build-up Maxol Marathon, 1st, 2 Hours 13m 42s (personal best). Unable to rest, 9 weeks continued training, European Marathon, Athens, 1st, 2 hours 16m 47s. I consider that I was very fortunate to have won this latter race as I was well past my best. 5 weeks "rest", 5 weeks build-up, Fukuoka, 2nd, 2 hours 11m 54s (personal best).*

   1970   *2 weeks "rest" following a semi-rest during cross country season, 10 weeks build-up, Boston Marathon, 1st, 2 hours 10m 30s (personal best).*

   4 weeks "rest" (and no trial); 10 weeks build-up, Commonwealth Marathon, 1st, 2 hours 9m 28s (personal best). Rather foolishly I did not rest after this. 3 weeks "semi-rest", 2 weeks "rest", 8 weeks build-up, experimenting with 3 times a day training and high mileage (experiment failed). Fukuoka, 9th, 2 hours 15m 27s.

   1971   *Moderate training only through winter, 3 weeks "rest", 7 weeks build-up, Maxol Marathon, 1st, 2 hours 12m 39s (with no great effort), 2 weeks "semi-rest", 7 weeks continuous training, European Marathon, Helsinki, 3rd, 2 hours 14m 34s.*

   This last race was disastrous for me as I knew I was the best man in the field and yet I did not win. However, having overcome my despondency I am treating the defeat as a blessing in disguise as it made me more determined for Munich, and in fact I have no fear of the distance as my last three races have not been distressing. But, I do not want a repeat of this year and my plea becomes the more important as I now learn that the trial for Munich will be held on July 2nd, just 10 weeks before the big race and at a time when I hope to be just starting my build-up.

2. *I know that the all-round standard in Britain is very high, but it can be argued that this is a reason for letting our best man "off the hook" as for most people once the*

160

trial race is over, a large measure of inspiration has gone, and the feeling is "I've made it", when this is not the case at all. Usually there is not enough left for the really big race, and this is borne out by the fact that we go to the big games, often with the best people on paper (because of the high level of competition) but never achieve the gold of Olympic 10,000m and marathon races.

3. One other important point in my case is the special diet which I adopt pre-race; this does not appear to work the second time around at such intervals of 9 or 10 weeks and here a tremendous advantage is lost.

4. What is there to gain by selecting me for Munich now? A gold medal which I think I have a damn good chance of winning.

5. What is there to lose? It means virtually that the 3rd string would have been left out, assuming that I failed absolutely miserably, and it is not often that 3rd strings win gold medals. I know that in certain events there are surprise medals, which could not have been predicted 1 year in advance, e.g., Andy Carter, but these are not precluded by selecting one man as there are still two places available.

6. What other things can be gained by my selection at this stage? The following things spring to mind:

   (a)   I can ask my company for more generous consideration with time off for training.

   (b)   I can seek some financial aid from a sponsor or fund to help me with diet and travel for training etc.

   (c)   I can plan my holidays (training) and train with confidence.

7. I maintain that if the authorities have confidence in a man and he is treated like a champion, he will act like a champion and rise to the occasion.

8. Well over 90% of the people who have spoken to me after Helsinki say that I should have been allowed to race without a trial, therefore public opinion would be behind my selection now. Obviously, there would be an outcry from certain marathon runners, but this is only to be expected. However, it is I who can win that gold medal.

9. Certain other countries tend to select well in advance. Lismont (Belgium) is now selected for Munich. The two Russians who ran in Fukuoka (1970 Dec) did not feature in the Russian trial, yet they ran in Helsinki and only the winner of the trial went. These Russians had been groomed as had Gammoudi in the past, and Roelants and Vaatainen and Busch of E. Germany.

10. You may have noticed that most top marathon runners do not last long. Bikila was an exception and he raced infrequently. The others have been more or less specialist marathon men and I am convinced that you can become marathon "punch drunk". These people usually retire or deteriorate rapidly. I have been around a long time and have kept improving by careful planning of training and not too much marathon racing. I would prefer not to race marathon at all before Munich and start fresh and ready for my big effort. The Japanese ran their last marathon on March 11th and they know something about marathon running!

11. Ever since Tokyo (1964) when I failed miserably, I have trained twice a day and once on Sunday and I have never once missed a session. This is the dedication I have to offer. I am not asking for a free trip to Munich — I've been to Munich, I've run in the Olympics — all I'm asking for is the best chance to win a gold medal which is almost mine.

12. Examine my record in recent major races and games:

    Mexico 10,000m — 7th
    Athens Marathon — 1st
    Boston Marathon — 1st
    Edinburgh Marathon — 1st
    Helsinki Marathon — 3rd

My worst non-winning time was 2:15:27 in Fukuoka (after unsuitable training) and such are my standards that I consider this time pitiful. In the last 3 years I have never let Britain down and I have been consistent. Please select me now and give me the chance to gain Britain her first Olympic Marathon Gold.

My plans for the coming year are as follows:

Winter to March 18th, averaging about 80 miles per week, concentrating on speed (I want to be the fastest man in the marathon field) and short fast cross-country races on the continent.

March 18th to April 15th, "Rest", i.e., 40 miles per week.

April 15th to June 4th. Build-up training to get speed, fitness and endurance again.

June 4th to July 1st. "Rest" — 40 miles per week.

July 1st to September 9th. Final build-up to Munich.

I am very willing to come down to London and present my case personally and naturally I will undergo any medical examination it is thought to be necessary. Fitness tests at appropriate times would be represented by my racing records. Obviously, if for some reason things were not proceeding according to plan a definite selection would be cancelled.

Allow me this chance, a chance which athletes in other countries are getting, and I'll produce the goods.

I know the selection committee will give this careful consideration and I look forward to receiving their decision as soon as possible".

Part of this argument was not relevant when the date of the trials was changed at a Long Distance Running Conference at Crystal Palace, part of the Munich programme. To the amusement of Harold Wilson, Parliamentary Leader of the Opposition, Bill Adcocks and I objected loudly when Arthur Gold gave out the official date of the marathon trial, July 2nd, as part of his list of fixtures for 1972. We challenged his consultants on this date, the Road Runners Club, and declared that the most important people, the top marathon runners, had not been asked. Eventually, after agreement with the Maxol Marathon organisers the date was changed to June 4th.

CHAPTER NINE

On the Saturday of that weekend I watched an International Cross-Country race at Parliament Hill fields, whilst training there in spikes. I replaced a couple of worn out spikes on my shoes, but couldn't find a full set of new ones, therefore I put the longer new ones on the inside part of the shoe. I knew it might throw my foot over on to the outside a little, but I thought that on soft ground it wouldn't make much difference. I ran 12 miles in all.

Early on Sunday morning I ran 17½ miles with Don Faircloth. Or rather I started off with Don as with 3 miles to go he dropped me completely. My legs felt like lead. What did I expect without hard training? With good mileage that weekend I totalled 100½ miles for the week; I needed to, as I had a race in Stabroek, Belgium, the next weekend. But it wasn't lack of fitness that eventually worried me there. My training log tells the story well:

Tuesday 30th November, M.   *Ran to work — easy running all the way — felt pretty good although I had a bad pain at the back outside of my heel.*
Wednesday, 1st December, M.   *Hobbling on my bad right heel — very painful.*
Wednesday, 1st December, E.   *Right heel worse still.*
Thursday, 2nd December, M.   *Heel really painful, virtually hobbling for 3 miles.*
Thursday, 2nd December, E.   *Heel the worst it had been — felt sick with the pain.*

I never pulled out of races. On Saturday I went to Stabroek, tried the course and found it terrible. It was rough and bumpy grass which made the pain worse. On Sunday, race morning, I had the ankle strapped up, tried it out in spikes, but towards the end of 6 miles I was almost vomiting with the pain.

After a lot of discussion I decided the only thing I could try was a painkilling injection, which I had never had before, and Bob Wezenbeek, the race organiser, fixed up to have this done. I was staying with a couple called Jean and Joele, and whilst I was waiting wrote letters to Japan, apologising for not being able to run in Fukuoka, and to my brother Jeffrey, who was now a soldier and on peace keeping duties with the United Nations in Cyprus.

The doctor came at 2.30 p.m. He said something about a sheath of muscles from the ankle radiating down the side of the heel which would be easily damaged by imbalance — those bloody spikes — and he gave me two injections of Xylocaine. I couldn't believe it. It was like magic. Instantly the pain had gone. I could jump on my toes, run on the spot and feel no discomfort at all. Wow!

I jogged to the course and warmed up. The start was a shambles. As with numerous Belgian races, we had to wait for a signal from

"Veteran, Michel Bernard passed me . . ."

the T.V. people that the programme producer was ready to shoot the race live. Meanwhile, the runners had crept at least 50 metres up the course before they bolted away. It was one small lap and four big laps and although I got left badly at the start, by the end of the second big lap I was through to 7th with three runners lined up in front of me to pass. Suddenly I started to get pain on the *inside* of my right foot, which rapidly got worse and worse until I was limping whilst I was running. Veteran, Michel Bernard passed me on the fourth and final lap; I couldn't hang on, and even had to try to sprint up the home straight to hold 8th. The pain killer quickly lost its effectiveness. It was the last one I ever had. Now I could hardly walk, let alone run. It brought home to me that pain was a danger signal, a warning by the body that things were going wrong. If you cancelled those signals, gagged the warnings, untold damage could be done.

That night when I arrived back at Manchester Airport, I looked so bad that a stewardess asked me if I wanted a wheelchair!

For three days I was down to 1 mile "sessions", twice a day.

Monday morning it took me 15 minutes to "run" 1 mile. I was in absolute agony every time I lost concentration and tried to run normally. Similarly in the evening I "was in very great pain". My whole ankle was largely swollen and the foot could bear no weight at all. Tuesday morning I recorded 9/10ths of Monday's pain. Wednesday morning's hobble recorded 8/10ths of the original pain. Progress! Wednesday night I was, "not having to hop quite so much but still only levering on my right leg". Thursday I did 2 x 2's, Friday 2 x 3's with the second 3 miles accompanied by Neil Shuttleworth up at the Ashton track — "15 laps — after 6 we did alternate laps in which I tried some efforts — doesn't look as if it will get better quickly". But I had faith that it would get better.

I read the result of the Fukuoka marathon in Japan; 1st Frank Shorter, (U.S.A.) 2:12:50, 2nd Usami (Japan) 2:13:22.8, 3rd Jack Foster (New Zealand) 2:13:42.4. In my diary I wrote, "Great! Shorter is banging in the marathons, U.S.A. Championships — Pan American Games — now Fukuoka — he still couldn't beat my this year's best on an easy course. I wonder where Derek Clayton was? Usami second on his own midin and in 2:13 only — ties in with his poor time in Munich — and he has to run again in March — that should see him off!"

"Although my right root is pretty bad, so bad that it can only get better — I feel that the way is opening to my victory (in Munich). Even the injury is a help, I'm strengthening my left leg — my weak one!"

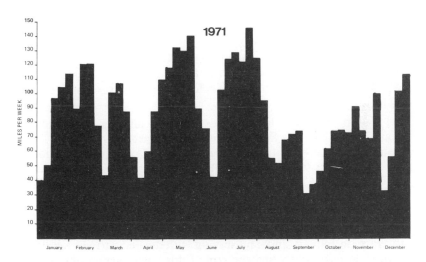

My dad had a great faith in herbal remedies; I remembered he'd always used "nip-bone" for his football injuries, so I tried it myself for four days, soaking my foot in hot water containing the leaves, then strapping the strained leaves next to the injured heel with a crepe bandage. It gradually improved. After a 33 mile week of hobbling I was up to 4 miles by Saturday. I had to pull a sheep out of the canal on that morning run. The stupid beast jumped into the water as I ran towards it near my turn back point. When I did turn back I saw it had clambered out but, lo and behold, the bloody thing leapt back in again as I returned. Mid December was hardly the time for paddling about the "cut", so I grabbed it by the wool, hoisted it out and shooed it off in the opposite direction. By Wednesday I was "running" to work, 73 minutes for 7½ miles, and it came down to 67 minutes on Thursday, 62 minutes on Friday, a gratifying experience and from 56½ miles that week I went 102 and 113½ miles to the finish of 1971. "End of a pretty unsuccessful year — on the whole a failure — but lessons learned I think."

1972. This was the year. And it started off well. Back in November I'd had a letter from No. 10, Downing Street. It read:

"Sir,

The Prime Minister has asked me to inform you, in strict confidence, that he has it in mind, on the occasion of the forthcoming list of New Year Honours, to submit your name to the Queen with a recommendation that Her Majesty may be graciously pleased to approve that you be appointed a Member of the Order of the British Empire (M.B.E.).

Before doing so, the Prime Minister would be glad to be assured that this would be agreeable to you. I would be grateful if you would let me know by completing the enclosed form and sending it to me by return of post".

I couldn't believe it. In my successful years, nothing. In my failure year — this. But, the Prime Minister might change his mind. That would be too cruel; but, you never know. So I kept quiet and didn't say anything or tell anyone about it. Sure enough, on New Year's Day, a Saturday, in the list under M.B.E., was "Ronald Hill, for services to athletics".

I celebrated my M.B.E. with a race in the 11th International Cross of Ninove in Belgium, going out on New Year's Day 1972 for the race on January 2nd, and staying with the de Schrijver family. I turned in fairly early and the son, Eddie, who was acting as my interpreter showed me to my bedroom. I asked him for the "bathroom" and down we went to a toilet next to the house, just outside the back door. He followed me back up again and I could see him flicking through the dictionary in a puzzled way. Finally he found a word, shrugged his shoulders and said, "Do you still want a bucket, or anything?" He must have been looking up "chamberpot", and I wondered if my secret of Hannut, years previously, had somehow leaked out (if you will forgive the pun).

In the race, won easily by Gaston Roelants from Willie Polleunis, I was 11th after another disastrous start; but although my injured foot had been restricting my stride, it had stood up to the test well. Now I could get down to some serious training.

I had piles of congratulatory letters and telegrams on my M.B.E. — friends, clubs, and club athletes, colleagues at work, the Company's directors. I was very, very proud. My manager at work called me into his office to "formally" congratulate me on my award. He asked me how did one get an honour like that. I didn't know. He knew a bloke in his Rotary Club who seemed to get one for selling the most insurance in his company. That put me in my place!

11th in Ninove.

I clocked in 103½ miles the week after Ninove and ran gentle fartlek on Monday, Tuesday, Wednesday with 3 x 1 miles fast on Thursday. I didn't race the next weekend and therefore ran 13½ miles Saturday afternoon and my first 20½ of the year on Sunday.

My mileage climbed to 119 but on Thursday and Friday that week I ran easily as I had two races in Belgium that weekend. A Mr. Gabriel Pauwels, of Lokeren, had been arranging races for me in Belgium. I don't know why, but he had. He must have been getting worried by my poor runs in Stabroek and Ninove, and this weekend I was running in his own race in Lokeren, near the Dutch border. I flew from Manchester to Brussels on Friday evening and Gabriel drove me in his Hillman Minx to his home. He was married with four young children and they made me feel very much at home. That night I made a start on my autobiography with a "tentative fifteen minutes"! He need not have worried too much about my form as my foot was now better and my training was paying off. Before the race at Gabriel's house I read in the French magazine, "Miroir d'Athletisme" that Lismont, the European Marathon Champion, had spent some time at altitude in St. Moritz before

167

Helsinki. So — though I hadn't rated him as a danger, he had obviously been taking things seriously. And as usual, had had handed to him the chance to do altitude training, where as usual, us Britons had had nowt.

Lismont was the official starter of the Lokeren race, and although he wasn't naturally the talkative type, he said that he thought that Frank Shorter would be a danger in Munich. "He is fast", he said. I looked at him and smiled. "I am going to win there", I said.

On a cold but dry Saturday afternoon, in spite of my usually poor start I won the Lokeren race and I almost had the feeling that the early leaders were waiting for me to do it, as they kept looking over their shoulders, a thing I never did in a race. Towards the end of the competition, after having overtaken everyone else, and with one small lap to go I let the second man overtake me so that I could be in a better position to strike. He speeded up all the way home, but not enough to get away, and as we turned into the last sandy field I kicked for home. There was no response from my Belgian rival, de Beck. I'd won and I was pleased. My sprint was back.

". . . I won the Lokeren race . . ."

On Sunday, Gabriel drove me to Lommel, for another cross-country race, about 8Km as in Lokeren, and six laps; whereas the Lokeren course was on paths, the Lommel course was over rough country, sandy scrub and grassland, and someone said that they had included three extra hills per lap to make it worse for me! After three laps there were only two of us up there, Johan Janssens and

Lommel — ". . . there were only two of us up there . . ."

myself. We ran side by side on the fourth lap until near the end where there was a stiff cold head wind blowing and I shunted him into the lead. It was more difficult running tucked in behind as I couldn't see my footing on the rough ground, and Janssens began to move away. The start of each lap was on the local track and as we hit this with two laps to go I was 4 or 5 metres down and thought I'd had it as my legs were beginning to seize up. The smooth relaxed running on the track gave me just enough seconds to relax and recover and pass him as we started the rough again. I wanted a clear view of the ground ahead; I knew how tough it was following. He hung on for a full lap, but on the last I sensed a gap forming and encouraged and realising I might win the race without sprint, which would have been almost impossible with my legs being the way they were, I ran faster. It worked and I won by over 6 seconds.

After dinner with Mr. Houdemaeker, the club treasurer, an English couple who lived in Lommel, John and Valerie Cummins, drove me to Brussels, Zaventem Airport. I was messing about so much buying a ticket for Geraardsbergen, two weeks later and getting my "duty free", that I didn't notice the time passing and suddenly realised I was cutting it too fine. I sprinted for Gate 5 only to find that they had just closed the airplane door and wouldn't re-open it. I rushed round to a London plane. That was full. I dashed to information; could they re-route me via Paris,

Amsterdam or Zurich? Nothing doing. It was only 8.00 p.m. and I was stranded. The boat? No, I was no better off on that.

What a carry on! I knew May would be worried stiff. We weren't on the telephone, so there was no way of contacting her and in the bargain I had no front door keys so she would probably be waiting up all night wondering what had happened to me. By 9.30 p.m. the huge airport departure area was empty, the last plane had gone. I read a book as long as I could, until at 1.15 a.m., "parched as a bloody bull frog", I curled up under my maxi-overcoat, on some seats, and tried to sleep.

I got the early morning London plane, changed to Manchester, and drove home for 10.00 a.m. May's friend Elsie, from across the back was in; I could see May was upset, her eyes were red from crying and she had been up all night. I would have to be more careful in future. I packed her off to bed, went for a 3 mile run, and then had an hour myself.

I went up to the school to reassure the boys. Steven, the eldest, was watching at the yard railings for me. "Hi-ya dad, where've you been?", he said as I gave him his bar of chocolate and packet of chewing gum. I asked him to take me to Graham who was inside having his school dinner. I couldn't see him at first, he was at the far end of the hall. Suddenly I saw him running towards me, smiling; he never said a word.

This incident, worrying as it must have been for my family, did not halt my rigid schedule of events. After a week's hard training I was turning out in Wingene, Belgium, for another short sprint round narrow forest trails, accompanied this time by an official English team under manager Jack Davies. Trevor Wright and Mike Tagg were running with/against me, and Jim Alder for Scotland stayed with us in the house of Mr. Van Caneyt, sharing a room with myself. Jim was an arch rival for this summer; I would give nothing away to him. The sets of exercises I did everyday, forward bends to touch my toes, sit-ups and lying down, legs over the back of my head, to stretch my hamstrings, I did in secret, in the shower room, so that Jim wouldn't see them and copy them. Jim was playing it canny too; we were both travelling to Puerto Rico the next weekend for a half-marathon and he told me that he was only going on the condition that myself or Trevor Wright or Don Faircloth were going. He didn't want to risk doing the wrong thing.

A handsome German with long black hair also roomed at Mr. Van Caneyt's; Lutz Philipp. I was to race him more seriously in the summer. Short cross-country races were the speciality of that great Belgian champion Gaston Roelants. He had the ability to sprint away at the start, avoiding trouble and the obstacles of slower runners, and keep going. He easily won Wingene with Lutz Philipp second, Trevor Wright third, Jim Alder fifth, Tagg eleventh and me thirteenth. I wasn't too disappointed as it had been a really high class field.

Whilst I was in Wingene, I dreamt that I had lost a third European Championship Marathon, the one after Helsinki, but there were no more details than that. Running was undoubtedly on my mind.

I wanted everything to go perfectly for Munich and to this end I was planning ahead as carefully as I could. I'd read about altitude and its beneficial effects on running at sea level through increasing the number of red blood corpuscles, and I wanted to use it myself, sometime in the spring or early summer, and then before the Olympics themselves.

I was adamant that my family would have to be involved in these time periods, otherwise I would risk making May ill, unwanted disharmony in our marriage, and over the Olympic preparation and competition weeks, the loss of form I'd had when I'd been away for a long time. I explained all this in an interview with Frank Taylor of 'The Daily Mirror', saying that "the best results are reached when a man or woman can reproduce his natural home life environment during the course of competition". I was disappointed and angry when the headline appeared, "Sex as usual — it's first in the medal race".

May was beginning to get depressed at this early stage with all my weekends away, the only saving graces were the good prizes I won in Belgium, and I had to cancel a solo trip to Turkey to train at altitude, as we were heading for some sort of crisis.

Holiday brochures were scrutinized looking for places at altitude to train in Austria or Switzerland. But things were so expensive that finally we decided to go for sunshine instead and aim for two weeks in Spain, after the Maxol Marathon and prior to my build up for Munich. My request for pre-selection was still with the B.A.A.B., but I knew their attitudes, and held out little hope.

These training trips were all going to cost money, which I didn't have, especially the three weeks in St. Moritz just before Munich. I was quite adamant, if May, Steven and Graham didn't go, I stayed at home too. It was going to take sponsorship — cash — and I tried a lot of people to see if I could get it — unsuccessfully.

The Maxol people I though would be a good bet; after all I'd won the race and set the record twice, but at the time the matter was raised the story appeared in the "Daily Mail" headed, "Hill plans to boycott Maxol", and that saw off my request. A polite refusal was all I got.

On January 24th I had a letter from Arthur Gold:

1972

"Your request . . . . . "select me now" — submitted to Selection Sub-Committee — full meeting of the Board the following day confirmed the Sub Committee's recommendation that it would not be possible to nominate any athlete to represent Great Britain in Munich at this early stage".

I more or less expected it, but it depressed me; back in the same boat!

But it wasn't going to stop me.

Another week's hard training and I was back in Belgium, Cross de Geraardsbergen, accompanied by "Sunday Times" sports writer Norman Harris, a friend and runner himself, who was doing a piece on me for the Sunday Times colour supplement. It was a freezing weekend, so cold in fact that at the Oudenberg Hotel I slept in a pair of May's old tights, running vest, long sleeved vest and tracksuit top.

We did a lot of talking. Norman was fascinated by the fact that we didn't have a telephone at home, in fact I didn't even put a number on our door. I didn't see the need for a telephone. Outside work and running, I valued my privacy. A chance remark which he printed landed me in trouble with my employers: "People can phone me at work or write, nothing is that important". Obviously I didn't mean that I encouraged people to phone me at work, or gave the number out freely. However, it came right down the chain of command from a director, until it reached poor little me, that remarks like that might lead to complaints from the shareholders!

Geraardsbergen.

172

The race course was dead pan flat, on an old airfield, and frozen solid. I warmed up in my huge black Henry VIII cap, the "casquette", I wore that year to try to develop some sort of image, and on the white hoar-frosted, bumpy ground, finished second to speedster Emile Puttemans, with De Hertoghe and Herman Mignon, two Olympic 1500 metre runners, behind me. Poor old Norman Harris was lapped, but did better than any other athletic sportswriter could have done, with the possible exception of Chris Brasher.

After a couple of beers in the converted airplane cafe, I picked a small vacuum jug for my prize and flew back to Manchester. Temperatures were sub-zero there and my car wouldn't start. The bloody thing. There was no option but a taxi, I couldn't mess about, I was off to Puerto Rico the next day.

The San Blas Half-marathon is an event I would always like to return to. The only problem for me is the race itself. The course is a killer. For my first time though, I was very excited. The Caribbean, sunshine in the middle of winter.

As I was getting up to run 2 miles, then prepare to meet my taxi, Graham, my seven year old son, said, "You're always going away, aren't you Daddy?" I replied, "Aye, but it's the last time for a long while". My plane from Manchester to London was delayed by fog, and there were delays at London too, sufficient to allow me to do 2½ miles in my jeans and racing shoes, clutching my passport and ticket, the rest of my gear being guarded by team manager, George Tolley.

The T.W.A. flight to New York was on a 747, Jumbo Jet, entered from ground level. I was amazed by the size of the thing, it was higher than a house. We were seated near the back of the huge plane where, once in the air, there seemed to be a lot of movement. Jim Alder, my team mate, didn't like the turbulance at all; when we hit one patch, just as we were being served lunch, he hid his head in his hands and I was killing myself laughing at him until a three second flash of panic as the monster plane bounced and trays and cups flew all over the place. It was one of the few times I have been frightened in a plane, but who wouldn't wonder at the magnitude of the forces that could toss around such a gigantic machine like a piece of straw.

We were behind schedule all along and from J. F. K. airport I took Jimmy into downtown New York and we surprise-visited Freddie Daniels, my Courtaulds colleague and his wife, Ruth, in Churchill Apartments, near the United Nations building. It was 1.00 a.m. English time when the Eastern flight took off for San Juan.

A man from the race organisation was there with his son to meet us at the airport and to take us by car over the mountains to Coamo, the venue for the race. As we left the city a sign was flashing on a building — "5.50" the time, then "73 degrees F" the temperature. Dawn was breaking, and I resisted sleep as we rode the twisty mountain roads, looking at the trees, fields, mountain peaks, rows of tobacco, huts, red blossom on the bushes; it was like Jamaica, like Mexico, marvellous!

After something less than two hours we entered a populated area, pulled off the main road, past an old Spanish Church and town square, halting at a cafe, "Los Muchachos". I thought we were stopping for a cup of coffee; instead we had arrived! I couldn't believe it; this small village was where the world famous San Blas Half-marathon was held? This was Coamo? Past winners had been Gaston Roelants of Belgium, Jerome Drayton of Canada, Alvara Mejia of Colombia and Rafael Perez of Costa Rica. This year there were teams from Ethiopia including Olympic marathon champion Mamo Wolde, Kenya, Germany, Belgium, two Finns, Lasse Viren and Seppo Tuominen, John Farrington of Australia, Neil Cusack, Ireland and runners from Canada, U.S.A., Mexico and all over South America. There were reputed to be half a million spectators on race day, which climaxed the end of the fete week to the patron saint, San Blas. How could this sleepy little place put on such an event?

Outside things were just beginning to wake up, cocks were crowing; the locals were rousing, and we were nodding off. Deposited at a building-materials yard on Boldarioty Street, we climbed the stone stairs to an apartment and finding two single beds in one room, Jim and I crashed out.

We slept only a couple of hours, then went out for a first run in the hot sun; naturally just in shorts. The apartment was on the course, about 300 metres from the finish in front of the church, and we jogged back down or rather up and down the route, marvelling at the leathery black flattened carcasses of 8 inch toads on the road.

There were lots of hills on the course and after two or three days we both had stiffness in the fronts of our thighs. Our stay there was memorable. The apartment belonged to Frank Pagdin who was manager of a garment knitting plant in town. He was a legend; all the English speaking teams and a few others used his house as unofficial race H.Q., and British teams boarded with him every year. It was the best kind of place for a stay for me; Frank made me so welcome that I started to cook and eat all my meals there rather than go to the restaurant, and when he was free he took me sight-seeing on the island so that for once I felt I had done justice to a place I had visited.

In addition we had a quiet bearded youth called Joe to drive us about, and after school hours, two young girls were there to act as guides and help us with any translation from Spanish which was necessary.

Coamo — with a group of local runners.

I enjoyed the hot weather and the tropical scenery. There were natural hot springs nearby at Los Banos, a ruined hotel which once upon a time must have been a magnificent building, which Jim and I could stand in up to our necks to ease the stiffness in our thighs. For a week I enjoyed too the friendliness of the people and the gentle pace of life. Whenever I hear cocks crowing, I think of Coamo; they crow there pretty well all day — and all night.

Los Banos.

As I hinted before, the only drawback of the trip is the race. Perhaps I exaggerate a little, after all that is why we were there; nevertheless the route is a very, very tough one. It starts well out of town on the mountain road towards San Juan, and drops gently and smoothly for around 3 miles until a bridge over an almost dry river bed just outside town. Expectedly the pace on this section is hard. After the bridge there is a tough sharp climb into town, part of this is one in four at least, then a flat and gently down section for another 2 miles. A steep curving drop to another river bridge leads to a climb, steep at first, but which never seems to flatten out. Right turn after about 7½ miles and the real work begins on the "mountain". This time the road ascends gently and then gets harder and harder, twisting back and forth through trees until a crest with four miles still to run. The work isn't over, but at least there is time for a breather before the switch backs which end with only 1Km to go. 1Km curving gently to the right, then straight down the main street towards the white towered seventeenth century church whose entrance is flanked by two huge dark green yew trees.

To add to the difficulty it is usually very hot. 1972 was usual; the temperature was in the 80's and the yellow and black school bus took us up the winding road to a white line which said, "START".

I didn't bother to warm up, I was warm enough, and got left in a mad scramble of sprinting young kids and locals as the race got under way. I had deliberately started at the back and this was a mistake as the leading bunch opened up a gap I was naver able to close. There were lines of people in front of me, and I picked them off one after the other, and didn't see Jum until the middle of town after the steep uphill at about the 3½ mile point. "I'm having a bad one", he snapped as I went past. I was too knackered to reply, but I thought to myself that I wasn't having a great one either! The crowds were out in force, many had been there since early morning. They were throwing water, offering ice, and three hose pipes were in operation at various spots on the course. I found they were more than a little partisan.

A Mexican, Gaspar, was just in front of me for a lot of the way, and whereas he was offered cups of water by certain groups of the crowd, they were withdrawn for me. As we turned right up the hill, Gaspar was moving away. I just put my head down and ran. I passed the Kenyan, Phillip Ndoo, and was pulling back Tuominen and Neil Cusack, who had been dropped by the leaders, until the really steep bits when the heat took its toll and they pulled away again.

I thought I would go from the top of the mountain. I didn't. The only other guy I passed was Cusack, who had blown up with just under 2 miles to go. No matter how hard I tried I couldn't catch

San Blas ½ Marathon — 7th.

Gaspar as we threaded our way down the final street with just a narrow corridor betwcen the sea of spectators almost filling the roadway. I was 7th in 1:06:17, 8 seconds behind Gaspar and one position in front of Jim Alder. Victor Mora (Colombia) had flown round the course in a new record time of 1:04:22, 25 seconds ahead of Mamo Wolde.

Jim was furious. As we threaded our way back through the crowds back to Frank's apartment, he complained that he had only just got going by the end of the race! It was too late then! We stood on the balcony and watched the runners coming in. Dick Woods, Frank's knitting mechanic, with 5/6th of a bottle of Bacardi inside him, "a load on" — as he called it — was giving a running commentary. The race didn't end until after more than 2½ hours, when out of the gloom, surrounded by jogging spectators and huge motorcycles, trotted "the barber". He was 66 years old and traditionally the crowds stayed to cheer him as he came in, the "lantern rouge" of a really great race.

The race and the travelling left me pretty weary and I put in an easy week to counteract this before a final month of training to the end of my winter. This would terminate with the Manchester University cross-country championships on February 26th, the National at Sutton Coldfield, where I had won the title four years previously on March 4th, and the John Oultram 10 mile road race on March 11th.

1972

The easy week was 68, then I started to train. Life wasn't that easy, training hard, working hard all day and then working a lot of the night on the mail order sports goods business. The pressure was getting to May too, as stocks steadily built up and the amounts of money spent got higher and higher. Neither of us had experienced signing cheques for hundreds of pounds on a regular basis, and May was worried about the house burning down without any insurance, or even a ceiling collapsing with the weight of shoes in the loft. At times the atomsphere became very strained.

The atmosphere wasn't helped when eight days after the Puerto Rican race I ran home from work to be confronted with May holding two Valentine cards from Coamo. It was all entirely innocent, but took some explaining away.

My 1100 car practically fell to pieces. The garage offered me £10 scrap value; I had to accept it. Happily for me I was able to buy a good second hand car from one of the dye-stuffs firms I worked with, and I purchased a Triumph 1300 for £325 which was "book" value to that company, but well below market value. I had some good friends in the trade.

As the nights lightened I stuck in 127 miles and 131 miles. In the M.U.C.C.C. Championships at Wythenshawe park I broke my course record of 29:45 set in 1965 by 2 seconds, clocking laps of 9:42, 10:03 and 9:48, dropping first Colin Taylor, and only at the end Paul Carey. The day after, of my 20½ mile run, I noted in my diary — "On the run, near the end when I was tired, I felt that the Olympics were almost becoming too much for me, even at that early stage".

Nevertheless, that record made me think of the English Cross-Country team again, especially with the race on a course that had suited me before, and I trained hard — 128 miles.

March 4th started out fine and I drove to Birmingham with hope in my heart. The course was about 1½ miles from the school where everyone was changing. I jogged down with Andy Holden and just as we got there it came on raining. I warmed up in spikes, another 1½ miles and suddenly a downpour started which left everyone completely soaked and cold. Whereas in 1968 I had started with other internationals over on the far right, this year I had to stick to the rules and I shivered on the line in pen 86, way over on the left, frozen and waiting for the "boom" and the mad dash down to the right hand bend at the bottom of the first straight. My start was poor, I was in the middle of the ruck, and by the time I got to the bend I was having to run in gorse bushes just to keep moving. As we reached the stream for the first time I was literally marking time in a solid mass of runners as the field bunched at the obstacle. I got on the outside of the wide column of runners, but it was almost impossible to make ground as there was nowhere there firm enough to run, just boggy, soggy ditches and potholes. Through a wood I moved up well, then we spilled on to a swamp in which the ground seemed to be moving under my feet, through another stream and up the hill on to firmer ground. I was still freezing in a long sleeved shirt with a vest on top, and not thinking straight. I got through to about 50th position as we completed a lap and there was someone ringing a bell. Alan Spence from Bingley, in his blue and white striped vest, was right beside me. "Is this the last lap?", I asked. "Aye!", he replied.

The rain continued to hurtle down and at times was mixed with snow.

The National — Sutton Coldfield.

We had been running into a headwind which made me feel even colder, and I felt very despondent as I couldn't see myself getting up to the first 9 in only one more lap. I moved through a little more easily as I could see my footing a bit better; towards the end of the lap I heard 36th, and gathered myself for the final sprint as I crested the hill and hit firmer footing. I lengthened my stride, I was passing people 1 - 2 - 3-4-5. "Oh No!" The bloody idiot was still there ringing his bell. I could have wrapped it round his bloody ear-hole. There was still another lap to go!

I stayed calm and looked on the positive side. I could still catch a lot more in 3½ miles. I passed Roy Fowler, that wasn't bad. I respected Roy a lot; I overtook Keith Boyden. I was moving forward, but still hadn't got warm. I felt pains on my wrists like electric shocks as the ends of my sodden sleeves slapped wet upon my bare skin. On the very boggy section, I was moving over from one side of the track to the other to try to find a shallower rut, when I went headlong, full length on my left hand side into a ditch full of peaty brown water. My only feeling was one of shock from the cold. I scrambled up, but felt nearly paralysed. I couldn't get going again. I had runners lined up in front of me, waiting to be overtaken, but my whole body was numb. I stumbled along and the figures in front moved away. It was getting dark. It was snowing now and raining. People began to pass me, but I couldn't be bothered. I dropped from 29th to 53rd by the end.

In the finish pens people were moaning and crying. I felt sick. I couldn't move. My mother and dad were there but couldn't help me. I thought of the journey back to the school, I could never make it. I couldn't run it. I had no will power. Luckily one of my club mates flagged down the Mayoral car which was just leaving, told them who I was and got me a lift back to the changing rooms.

Even there I was so bad I couldn't get dressed. I was shuddering uncontrollably. I couldn't hold a cup of hot coffee in my hands, they were shaking so badly. Only after half an hour, propped by a radiator did I come round. John Rodda, of The Guardian, asked me about the race. "I'll never run the National again", I said, and meant it then.

I trained one more week, 88 miles, and ran 3rd in the John Oultram '10' behind Colin Roberts, City of Stoke and Harry Leeming, Derby and County. My 49:49 on a tough course wasn't too bad, considering I only arrived 5 minutes before the start, which they held for a couple of minutes whilst I got changed, and I set off right at the back. I was pleased to beat several people who had beaten me at Sutton Coldfield the week before. That was looking on the positive side. It was the closing of a somewhat indifferent winter season, the commencement of a four week "rest" period.

As usual I ran more or less 2 mile sessions for a fortnight, then 2's and 5's for another fortnight, some of this in heavy Army & Navy Store shoes, rather like boots. It was an attempt to slowly strengthen my legs in general, and hamstrings in particular. I still competed as this was part of my training, and I always tried to sell a bit of gear afterwards, shorts and running shoes, to help the business along. However, the race after my first week's rest had to be unofficial as when I arrived at the start of the Sutton '7' in St. Helens I found that Bolton Harriers hadn't entered me in the race. It was usual for the club to enter a block of runners as a team, but this time my name wasn't there. This incident was the start of a loosening of loyalty towards the harriers for me. Norman Ashcroft, the Secretary would not accept any late entries, so I ran unofficially and would have been 5th had I crossed the finish line, despite being shot by an air rifle half way through the race. I felt a sharp stinging blow on my right thigh as I rounded a corner; realised what had happened, but not wanting to break the rhythm I could only shake a fist in the direction I thought the shot had come from.

That same weekend Gaston Roelants won the International Cross-Country Championships held at Cambridge. The Daily Telegraph on Tuesday revealed Gaston's plans for Munich; he was already in the Belgian team for the marathon: "Today Roelants leaves for Tunisia for a training holiday followed by a month's altitude work in St. Moritz. The Belgian will spend most of July in Mexico."

Christ! What were we up against?

Some variety of training routes were introduced. The third week of the "rest" I spent at Cranfield College in Bedfordshire on a "Marketing Course for Scientists". It was a fairly high level course, and I was amused at the thought that had to go into filling the personal details on the application form when we came to the line "position". I was told to put "sub-section leader". In fact in my 8 years at Courtaulds I hadn't moved from "senior research chemist"; now unofficially I was leader of a sub-section, or perhaps a sub-standard section leader? It was windy and wet as I trudged around the country lanes.

It was windy and wet too in the Isle of Man, where I spent my last week's "rest". I thought variety would do me good, especially if we had some Easter sunshine. Luck didn't seem to be with me this year. The whole family of us travelled to Douglas on Good Friday, driving to Liverpool, parking the car after waking up the Irish car park attendant, and catching the 11.00 a.m. steamer across the Irish Sea. There were a lot of other runners aboard heading for the Manx Easter Festival of Athletics (or Drinking — depending on your motivation), including our friend Andy Holden, now studying to be a dentist at Birmingham University, but for this weekend representing a fictitious team "Stirling Strollers".

181

We stayed in a boarding house, "Braeside", at 24 Victoria Road, about half a mile back from the sea front at Douglas, presided over by Mrs Hickey. The four of us were crowded together in room number 1 on the first floor and until Monday the rest of the "digs" were full of student runners.

Brian Whitehead of the Manx Amateur Athletic Club had arranged a tiny subsidy for our trip and I was happy to race three times in three days. It was all pretty light hearted. I got 6th in the road race on Good Friday evening, the day we arrived. I would have done better had I known where the finish was, but the weather was poor, an eerie mist covered the island and I couldn't see the grandstand of the T T motorbike course until we were over the finish, otherwise I could have outsprinted Hinton and Leeming of Derby.

On Saturday I pulled Bolton through from 22nd to 9th on the second leg of the sea front, four stage relay recording fourth fastest time, and in the Easter Sunday Fell Race starting from near the Highland Pub, in pouring rain, I struggled up the hillside and then hurtled down the stony track and the slippery grass fields, falling once on the approach to a wall and just dipped out Trevor Proctor of Rochdale Harriers for 6th place after a terrific sprint in the last field. It was so close that I didn't know who had got the decision until the presentation in the Athol Hotel that night. When I went up for my

prize, I had to down my pint in one, by popular request of the drunken crowd. I barely managed it: there was just room; I'd had six pints in the "Dogs' Home" beforehand.

Making the most of the rest of our stay, in the face of the chilly wet weather, we played football on the beach, collected shells, visited the castles of Peel and Castletown, the splendid Laxey Wheel, the gale swept top of Snaefell, the forlorn deserted beach at Ramsey.

Mrs Hickey looked after us well, and even lent us her red Viva, bless her heart, so that we didn't have to use the buses or electric train and the boys really took to her dachshund, pro-

Graham, Steven, May — Castletown.

nounced "dashhound" by us, Johan.

Predictably the sun shone long and warm on our departure day.

In Douglas I had bought a new lucky silver ring, to replace the Mexican one which I lost in Bainbridge the year before. When I got to work I got Keith the engineer, to cut it into identical thin rings, one I gave May to wear, the other I wore myself on the little finger of my left hand. That was superstition taken care of for Munich.

The relaxation month was now over. It was time to begin my eight week build up to the Manchester Maxol Marathon on June 4th. During that month I had picked up three important pieces of information about my Munich rivals; firstly, Usami had won the Japanese Marathon trial from Unetani and Kimihara, in the slow time of 2:20. My conclusion was that if they were running so slowly they would be no danger whatever the conditions. Secondly, Roelants was intending to run 40 miles a day in training. Great! He would kill himself. Thirdly, Trevor Wright was injured and would have to have four months off. This was tragic for Trevor, who I liked a lot; but it made my task easier, both for getting on the team and for winning the gold medal in Munich.

With mother and dad. Receiving my MBE at Buckingham Palace.

183

CHAPTER TEN

The weekend I started my training, I got a kick in the teeth from my own club, and it was in our own production too, the Egerton Road Relay at Bolton. I arrived there, fresh from my quite reasonable exploits in the Isle of Man, considering I had been resting. Getting changed in the old Sunday School Hall I was chatting to the Blackburn lads, John Calvert and his friends, and they were saying that they were going to give us a run today. I joked back that the only danger to the 'A' team today would be our 'B' team. What I didn't know, was that Jack Haslam, the team manager, had put me in the 'B' team! Nobody had the guts to tell me, and it was only when I went for my number that the news was broken. I was flabbergasted and extremely annoyed. Bloody hell! On my way to becoming an Olympic Champion and in the 'B' team!

They didn't even tell me who I was taking over from, and I waited on the take-over line, looking in vain for a Bolton man to touch my hand, when Norman Ward came jogging back up the course and told me he had been the first leg runner for the 'B' team and I should have gone ages ago. I was so exasperated, I just swore, "******* hell", which is unusual for me in public. I pulled 12 or 13 runners back, and had a good leg even though obviously I didn't get a correct time. The crack between me and the harriers was widening.

Blackpool Memorial Relay — fastest Bolton runner.

My first week I put in 100 miles exactly, Tuesday and Thursday I ran to work and back in the very heavy shoes. Wednesday I started my once a week lunchtime 2 x 440 yards sessions, 61.8 and 59.7, which was promising.

The Blackpool Memorial Relay was my next race. This time I ran in the second team by *my* choice, just to show them. I strode out on the second leg, moving up 5 positions from 10th to 5th and was chuffed to record second fastest time of the day, beating all Bolton's first team. With a long 21½ mile run on Sunday at Blackpool, I pushed the next week's miles up to 121½. Don Faircloth and his wife, Sue, stayed with us at the weekend. I ran a rather forced fifth fastest leg in the Manchester and District L.C.H. Road Relay at Kersall, Salford, and on Sunday, Don and I ran the Maxol course with a group of local lads, Steve Edmunds, George Brockbank, Sam Hardicker and Ricky Wilde, most of the way. We trotted a fairly easy 2:41 for the full course minus the lap of Old Trafford Football Ground.

Start — training on the Maxol course.

I had a map of the Munich course on my spare bedroom wall, and I showed this to Don, taking care to take down my training plan beforehand; I wasn't giving any secrets away just yet. It wasn't intentional, in fact he may not have noticed, but I had marked on the map my hoped for time at each 5Km checkpoint. The figures at the finish were 2:07:50.

The state of my legs on that pre-Maxol run, I watched carefully, My left leg had been cracking a lot in training and I could feel my hamstring a little at the top. In the next week my right leg started to crack too. Not that it was too painful, but there was obviously something wrong.

On Monday I dreamt about the Marathon trial. It was on some strange yet familiar course I couldn't pinpoint. Moving well at first I began to slip back and when I had dropped to 4th position I realised that I could do nothing about it and I was running slowly and couldn't speed up . . . .

Wednesday night my legs were cracking a hell of a lot on the way home from work. I suspected it was the unaccustomed strain from the very heavy shoes, so I asked May to take the laces out of them, put the laces on one side (no point wasting things), and throw the shoes in the dustbin. I clocked 122½ miles that week.

The weekend of April 29/30 I was going to jog the Three Peaks race for training. Saturday morning I ran 7½ miles, in the afternoon 13½ miles. Out of the blue an Italian TV film crew turned up for a pre-Olympic feature; Paulo the director, Tony the cameraman and Barbara the organiser. Well, the Italians at least knew who was in with a chance in Munich. They didn't have to wait for any bloody trials!

I told them about the Three Peaks race and I think they were fascinated by what they saw on the Sunday, way up in the wild Yorkshire Dales, as Jeff Norman defeated all opposition in the cold, rainy conditions, to complete a hat trick of wins in this event. Incredibly, his time of 2:36:27 was exactly one second slower than his record of a year before.

I personally only wanted to train and stood behind after the gun had gone to make certain I was last out of the field behind the Hill Inn, at Chapel-le-Dale, wearing a yellow wet weather jacket, a white peaked cap, and just as an experiment, suede spikes. I passed a large number of the 232 starters as I trotted to the rocky top of Ingleborough, where the rain was now pouring down onto the miserable racers. I was around the 70th position and passed another 20 on the long gentle drop into Horton-in-Ribblesdale as I trotted easily along, speaking to the runners as I quietly overtook them. My dad was waiting in Horton to give me an electrolyte drink which I gulped down before jogging off to Penyghent. I overtook another 10 people just before the very big climb and some of those, Peter Walkington, Paul Livesey and Roger Grimshaw re-passed me as I took it as easily as I could up the steep final ascent. It was difficult running down steep hills as the smooth backs on the soles of the spikes gave me no grip and no braking action, and three more people passed me on the way down. I wasn't worried, I pulled a Mars bar out of my pocket, peeled it and started to eat it. That was easier said than done as the chocolate kept solidifying in my mouth with the rush of cold, cold air as I tried to breathe and chew at the same time. The next thing I knew, I slipped down, got the Mars bar muddy, and after another two mouthfuls of unsuccessful chomping, I had to throw it away and concentrate on running. I passed Peter Walkington, to his loud commentary about 1½ miles before Ribbleshead, where I paused for another drink before jogging on towards Whernside, which had always been a killer for me. "25th", someone called. Well, well!

People who had gone off too fast were dying now. On the tracks to the wild terrain of Whernside, I passed Trevor Proctor and Dave Makin; climbing a couple of walls I felt twinges of cramp on the insides of my thighs and I thoroughly expected to die climbing this last peak. It was a stretched queue going up to the top, and I was moving up to it. First club mate Kenny Mayer on the lower slopes, and almost at the very top, Welsh Cross-Country International, Dai Davies. As a reward for climbing so easily, the weather threw down a violent hail storm for me.

I slithered and slipped down the steep bits on the descent, where my spikes were totally ineffective, and jogged in for 13th position. As a bonus I had done 2 hours 59 minutes, my fastest time ever. Five weeks to the trial; this was a good omen.

I got in 124 miles that week, some of these miles at altitude in Switzerland. I discovered that a group of athletes was going out to St. Moritz for altitude familiarisation, but only those athletes who had not been to altitude before were invited. Altitude training prior to a major competition was the "in" thing. It was supposed to raise the number of red corpuscles in the blood, the body's natural reaction to the lower oxygen of higher regions, and hence make the transport of oxygen easier and that much better at sea level. I realised that many of my adversaries in Munich would be getting this training, indeed many of them had it in-built as they were natives of high altitude countries, Ethiopia, Kenya, Mexico etc. I was determined to somehow get May and the boys out there when the time came and take advantage of Britain's plans of pre-Munich altitude training in St. Moritz. But I wanted to know at first hand whether St. Moritz had sufficient flat areas for training. I put my case to the B.A.A.B. and was invited to join the expedition and the report on the suitability for long distance training.

We arrived in St. Moritz on Tuesday. I shared a room with 10,000 metre man Roger Matthews. Trevor Wright was there too, and it was sad to see him hobbling round with a damaged arch on one foot, and an achilles injury to his other leg.

It was a beautiful and inspiring place to run, mountains in the background, fresh air (what air there was), pine forests, the lake. Friday I ran 16 miles, Saturday 14 miles, feeling knackered, and I returned to England Saturday afternoon. I was running the

1972

Michelin 15Km at Newcastle-under-Lyme on Sunday; it was a bit much to hope that two days at altitude would have any effect, but you never know.

It was raining and cool. Ideal conditions for a fast road race. I warmed up 2 miles and didn't feel too bad. The start wasn't the flat-out mad dash that you sometimes get, yet I couldn't go with them. I had intended to lead the first two miles, but after two laps of the field it was all I could do to get on to the back of the leading bunch, so I change my mind and sat in. At the first hill I was dropped. People who I expected to slaughter just ran away. 25:11 at 5 miles; I though I would catch up on the downhill, but I was just as bad. I got a huge stitch right across my shoulder, and eventually Alan Dean caught me — an 800 metre runner! We ran the last 1½ miles together and finished joint 7th. I was a worried man. What had gone wrong? Return from altitude? Lack of sleep? Travelling?

Whatever it was it made me feel low. Having missed my Sunday long run, I did it on Monday instead. 23 miles in a big loop round the Derbyshire hills to home from work. I wrote in my log: "Pretty miserable, was tired at the end". I didn't pick up Tuesday or Wednesday. My right knee was cracking all the time and Wednesday I wrote in my diary, "felt knackered all day — hope it's the training 120 miles per week and not old age or bad form. Worried about the Maxol".

I had to live through this. I had my plan and there was no wavering. 129 miles that week, and the Rossendale half marathon that Sunday. I didn't ease even before a race like that. Saturday morning 7½ miles, Saturday afternoon 7 miles. Sunday morning "Woke up feeling knackered — headache and legs and body felt stiff and tired", 5 miles. Sunday afternoon race. My training log describes the race.

"1½ miles warm up with Arthur Walsham on the track — set off down and relaxed — Cyril Leigh and John Calvert broke and got a maximum lead of 50 yards — waved to John Balmer and George Brockbank — after about 1½ miles Brockbank and I pulled away — into a slight head wind — after 2½ miles we weren't making much impression so I piled on the pressure (relaxed) — got them at about 3½ to 4 miles — sat on them up into the wind —near the top Cyril put in some ineffective bursts — I felt like I was jogging — we turned at 5 miles (26:20) — immediately John and I broke — really sprinting — up the first hill John started moaning in his breathing — then I broke away — streaming down the hills — charging up the hills — still, about 1 mile past the 'Bull and Butcher' I was only about 50 yards up (according to bystanders) about 7 miles — at 10 miles I had pulled further away (50:20) — I felt like I had only run 7 miles! — just strode down the slope and then pushed up the final hill — 65:53. Course Record".

Five weeks into training there had been transition and I had clicked at last. My whole attitude changed, I felt I was moving well. I did my Sunday run on Monday evening, and was out for 3 hours and 34 minutes, running from Droylsden, taking in those tough Derbyshire Hills for a 27 mile detour home. All this put my week's mileage total at 134½. I had no more races before the Maxol, and didn't need any. I was confident that my form was back; all I had to do was complete my training.

My left achilles tendon and my right knee felt as though they were on a knife edge, but I was almost ready to start tapering down and they held out. 13 days before the trial race I had a very short hair cut. When I got home I looked in the mirror; my appearance was mean, moustache, thin, drawn face. "Jim Alder will appreciate that", I thought. That night I dreamt that I missed the start of the Maxol which in my dream was being run at 9.00 o'clock at night, over a course I had dreamt about before, starting in Accrington, the town where I was born. I had to go in a car to get my racing gear, and realised I was going to be late. I desparately tried to think of somehow trying to catch the time-keepers still on the start line, and to get them to send me off with a a ten-minute deficit . . .

Twelve days before the race I fell on the pavement on the way to work and took a big chunk out of my left hand and skinned my leg. It was painful, and took a long time to heal, but it was just another minor obstacle. 9 days before the Maxol I heard that Bill Adcocks was out of the race with injury. Calf problems. Well, that made my job a little easier.

129 miles that week, and it was into the final stages. On Saturday, the day before I started the "diet", I seemed to be subconsciously stocking up on food, my body jibbing at the carbohydrate starvation to come. This time I cut out even more carbohydrate. The more refined the "diet", the better it would work, I thought.

Instead of having a night-cap of sweetened drinking chocolate with Complan, Casilan and milk, I cut it the first day to unsweetened cocoa, Casilan and half a pint of milk, and the second day to unsweetened cocoa, Casilan, water and saccharin — a thoroughly revolting mixture.

It was bad enough training without carbohydrate, but the weather was atrocious to boot. Monday night I had a head wind and rain all the way home. In a field at the bottom of Mill Lane, about 1½ miles from home, a black dog came for me, snarling and barking, the fur on its back standing up. I slowed down and raised my hand as if to threaten the dog with a stone, an action which often scares dogs away. The next thing I knew its owner had dashed across and was going beserk, screaming obscenities at me and threatening to break every bone in my body if I touched his dog. "It won't touch you", he said, which is a classic. The dog was inches away from my legs, teeth bared, snarling viciously.

I realised I was dealing with some sort of mad man and when I got a safe few yards away, I turned and issued my threat. "I'll report you and your dog to the police if it touches me". After that, whenever I saw this pair, the little owner always slipped a lead on the dog before it could mount another assault.

As far as dogs are concerned it is always the runner that is in the wrong. I remember once running home from Droylsden when we lived in Fallowfield; I had just passed Fairfield railway station and was just heading for an open bit of land when an Alsatian dog came hurtling towards me; the alarmed cries of its owner didn't slow the dog one iota, and the thing leapt into the air at me. I just managed to duck and turn to avoid the snap of the jaws as the beast sailed past. By this time the owner had fumbled a whistle from his pocket and managed to halt his pet before it mounted a second attack. Then he laid in to me. "What the bloody hell do you think you're doing running like that? You ought to have more sense. That's an ex-police dog!" There was no answer to that.

Tuesday night the diet really took effect. I ran 11 mles and was absolutely exhausted, especially when it came to any hills. That night I dreamt about a party. It was partly in Accrington Grammar School. There were trifles and lovely sweet cakes; I was going round picking them out. One in particular I remember, a jam pasty, lovely red jam in puff pastry . . .

Wednesday I barely plodded to work and back.

Thursday I really piled in the carbohydrates. Someone came from Radio Manchester to interview me. I got him to buy me lunch; pork pie, chocolate eclair, strawberry tart with fresh cream.

By Saturday I felt much better, though my last 2 mile run at lunch time didn't feel that great. I looked back through my training log at the last two marathons I had run, and saw that I had been feeling really good on that session previously. It worried me a bit; on the other hand it rather took the pressure off me to plan a leading race. I would have to go in and play it by ear.

It was 11.35 p.m. when I got to bed; I didn't have a brilliant sleep and felt little like getting up when the alarm went at 7.00 a.m. I dragged myself out, put on my running gear, and jogged a mile along the canal. It had rained but was fine now. Birds were singing.

A bowl of raw oats with milk and sugar, a marmalade butty with a cup of tea took me to 9.00 a.m. I was going to have to hurry as the start was 10.00 a.m. It looked fairly cool, so I downed only half a teaspoonful of salt, and half a pint of orange juice; then we bombed it in the car down to Central Station Car Park, near the Y.M.C.A., the changing rooms, in Manchester, When we stopped Steven said, "That's the scariest journey I've had with you, dad!" I changed quickly, I was a bit nervous through being late and pinned the large, stiff, awkward number well down on my string vest to prevent my diaphragm getting a chill. Number 175. I trotted downstairs and out into St. Peter's Square. The start had been changed from Albert Square because of a veteran car rally. The sun was shining now, I jogged and strode about ¾ mile for a warm up, finishing in the square with the bobbing colourful mass of runners.

It was a real international race. The West Germans were using this race as a trial for the Olympics and had sent over 19 runners; the Spaniards too had sent their top four for a selection race. Besides that, athletes from Austria, Canada, Finland, Greece, New Zealand, Holland, Portugal, South Africa and Sweden were all running. All the press previews tipped me as a certainty to be the first British athlete to book his ticket for Munich. Why the hell couldn't the selectors see it the same way? Even now with Trevor Wright and Bill Adcocks injured I still had to run and one official was quoted in the press as saying: "There will be no second chances. The British team of three to go to Munich will be announced after the result of the race is known".

On the line people chatted nervously. Don Faircloth came up, shook hands and wished me luck. I was surprised to see Bill Adcocks in his racing gear on the line. Despite injury he was going to start. As the man said, "No second chances". I was standing next to a black South African. Bill nodded towards him, "I see he's been sunbathing round Romiley".

I said, "Hey Bill, I think Jim Alder's locked in a toilet in the Y.M.C.A.".

Quick witted, Bill replied, "Aye, it's locked from the inside. He told me that if he doesn't make this team he will cry for three days". The pressure, training and work had really got to Jim and he was reported to be on tranquillizers after he had finished one race shaking all over.

The clock on the town hall began to chime its build up to 10.00 a.m. It was time. Time we were away. We stood in the square facing away from the Midland Hotel, still for a moment, then on the stroke of 10.00 surging forward.

I set off down the field. The Spaniards went straight into the lead, but I was content to lope along in the 20's, feeling relaxed, keeping an eye on the front runners. At 2 miles a runner with red shorts, a red vest trimmed with white and white cap went to the front and gained five yards on the field. With these colours I thought it must be Bernie Plain in his Welsh strip; that could be dangerous, I increased my pace, rounded the other runners and caught him. It wasn't Plain; it was number 4, Ristimaki from Finland. The rest of the bunch had followed me up and we closed together.

Running with the Spaniards.   *". . . I dropped to the side . . ."*

Suddenly at 3 miles, an English runner, with even less sense than hopes of winning, shot into the lead and increased the pace until it was uncomfortably fast. This broke the field up until at 5 miles I was only aware of two Spaniards in their national vests of red with two yellow bands and a third Spaniard, Haro, in a turquoise vest together with Ricky Wilde of Manchester, wearing a red singlet with "Nos Galan" on the front, Bernie Plain who in fact was wearing a white vest and a pair of white freedom shorts with two green stripes, and the little Finn, No. 4.

Haro kept treading on my heels, so I dropped to the side of the bunch to avoid him and be in a position to cover any breaks. The unwise leading Englishman was finished and dropped by 6 miles. No. 4 kept surging ahead, but it was nothing dangerous, and at 11Km he grabbed for a drink and practically stopped.

The sun was out and it was proving to be an uncomfortable day. I just snatched a sponge and squeezed it over my head, then pushing the pace, hoping to take advantage of the break in rhythm, I took the lead. But it wasn't positive enough and the Finn soon caught me, bringing Ricky Wilde and the rest of the group with him.

My left foot was beginning to hurt on the outside where the thin kangaroo leather upper of my racing shoe was bulging over and making contact with the rough road surface; I could feel a long blister developing.

At 10 miles I was leading and Haro was treading on my heels again, through running too close. Annoyed, I pulled sharply to the side and waved him past, I saw the Finn was still with us as also was Wilde and Plain. Immediately the pace began to drop, and as I knew that I could run faster and still be comfortable I swept into the lead again, striding long. An old mate of mine, Dave Makin, was close by on a bike. "Bernie Plain's struggling", he said quietly. I speeded up a tiny bit; Haro began to drop; Bernie made an effort to get back, with Ricky Wilde running alongside him. At 12½ miles, running up Princess Parkway, I had a 3 yard lead; I'd almost broken the contact. Suddenly Bernie Plain fell back, I could tell this as his footsteps disappeared from hearing; this made me push a little harder, until Ricky Wilde's footsteps too died away behind me. My spirits lifted, my stride lengthened even further; at the top of the Parkway, at the left turn, people were shouting that I had 80 to 100 yards lead.

I thought to myself, "I've won it, I've won it". I took stock of how I felt. I was good. Admittedly I'd had a worrying moment between 11 and 12 miles when my right leg seemed to go dead, but it had recovered and I settled down to run as relaxed as I could.

Dave Makin was close by again on the bike, "Lutz Philipp's coming through like a bomb", he said. I had time to reflect. "Well, I'm going pretty fast", I thought, "If he's going faster than I am, he is going to pay for it later. He's got no known marathon form and running so fast in the middle of a race should be disastrous".

The messages kept coming from spectators and sure enough at 16 miles, just after some traffic had got in my way, he caught me, and passed me. Not a word was spoken. I watched his back; string vest — people soon catch on — and I made no attempt to stay with him. My pace I knew from instinct was dead right to get me through to the end in my best time. I thought he'd blow.

His lead over me stretched only to 20 yards, then the gap stayed. For 2 miles he ran his pace, I ran mine; and they were identical until at 18 miles I sensed that he was coming back. I got pretty close to him; I think he heard me, because he suddenly shot off again. Nevertheless, at 20 miles, with a time of under 1 hour 39 minutes, his lead was only 10 yards. I took stock of myself again; my left foot

"His lead over me . . ."

". . . stretched only to 20 yards . . ."

was hurting pretty badly, but it was only surface pain; there was no hurting in my thighs and I felt still pretty relaxed.

He ran 10 yards ahead for another couple of miles until suddenly I was upon him at 22 miles. I could have gone past, but this was only a trial, a selection race, the big one was still to come. In any case, he was a spent force now. I decided to shadow him, but this lasted only about ½ mile. On a very short, sharp hill over a railway line, I dropped him; but holding myself in check, I waited for him and slowed down to run with him.

Side by side we passed Old Trafford football ground, the final finish, for the aggravating 3 mile run, out and back, into Trafford Park. As we ran along the grim, black industrial estate he said, "I think we run together". That was all right by me. A man stood at the turn point, with a car beyond. Lutz thought the car was the turn and ran on. He was soon shouted back and I waited for him before we started off back together. I thought I had it in the bag.

DAILY EXPRESS

"... I was upon him ..."

"Side by side we passed Old Trafford football ground ..."

My legs were beginning to hurt a little, and I turned to him and asked, "O.K.?" He didn't reply. I saw the following runners coming towards us; we were in no danger of being caught. Approaching the right turn to the short hill to the football ground, about 600 yards to go, he spoke. I thought I heard him say, "First I want to be", which I took to be, "I want to be first", and whilst my reactions were scrambling — "Why does he need to win — what cheek — I've been waiting for you", my sub-conscious corrected my first interpretation to what he really said, "First I want a beer!" I almost laughed.

Up the final hill our pace increased in unison. Panic. Twinges of cramp almost grabbing the backs of my thighs. We turned right again into the concrete paved approaches to the back of the stands. I didn't see the point of a sprint. I knew whoever got into the narrow black tunnel first, would win, and for some reason I let him go first. He carried his momentum of the downhill tunnel on to the cinder path around the green turf and sped away. I knew I wouldn't catch him, and left the gap at about 10 yards.

Just before the tape he stopped, waited until I had almost caught him, stretching out his hand to shake mine before breaking through just ahead of me. A great sporting gesture.

DAILY EXPRESS

". . . he stopped, waited . . ."   *The victor.*

His time was 2:12:50, a personal best by quite a margin. I was given 2:12:51. Behind us Bill Adcocks had tried bravely until his legs had given out at 16 miles, and Jim Alder, as fit as he'd ever been, had been forced to drop out with blisters at 15 miles. A surprise 3rd in the race overall was Scotland's Don Macgregor in 2:15:06, winning his way to the Olympics together with Colin Kirkham who was 4th in 2:15:17.

I tried to analyse my defeat positively. Firstly I probably could have won if I'd gon past Philipp at 22 miles or attacked anywhere in the last 4 miles. Secondly, my time on a pretty warm day was only 12 seconds slower than the previous year's race which was run under pretty near perfect conditions; and thirdly, perhaps I wouldn't be labelled the favourite and would encounter less pressure before the Olympic race.

At the presentation, I sold a few pairs of freedom shorts and T-shirts I'd had printed with Japanese lettering. I had to keep the business going even though I had just run 26 miles. But I wasn't that tired anyway. Afterwards I drove all of us home together with Neil Shuttleworth who was looking after Steven and Graham whilst May and I took a train back to Manchester for the official dinner at the Grand Hotel.

I sat between the Finns and the South Africans. The meal was good but the speeches were long winded. Towards the end David Warren of Maxol asked me to get up and speak. I did. I'd had a few glasses of wine and didn't pull any punches when I said that people expected us to do well in the Olympics, moaned when we failed to provide the medals, and yet were not willing to do anything about it. I spoke of how the athletes of some other nations had greater advantages with regard to sponsorship, whereas our athletes got nothing. I said I wouldn't be going for altitude training unless someone was able to help me financially to have May and the lads with me.

It was useful to be able to do this in front of the assembled dignitaries and journalists, and the response was immediate. Maxol promised to donate the £100 that was left in their budget, and John Rodda of The Guardian bought me a pint and told me he would look favourably on an application for a £60 grant from the Montague Trust Fund towards a recuperation trip to the sunshine of Spain. Shortly afterwards the Mayor of Bolton, Alderman Alan Clarke, set up a special fund to help my Olympic preparation. Stan Ward, my manager at work, said that Courtaulds might be willing to help, and in fact they came up with £200 in addition to the extra time off for altitude training.

Arthur Walsham, who had Don MacGregor staying with him, gave us a lift home; at least, to the 'Spread Eagle', where I had three pints of bitter, then finished off some home-made beer at our house with Neil. I was pretty sloshed by the time I got to bed at 11.45 p.m., but it hadn't been a bad day's work!

197

1972

The first part of my preparation for the Munich marathon was a month's rest. Naturally, I ran twice a day, but I ran weeks of only 53, 31½, 41½ and 42 miles. I was determined to get as much variety as I could into my training, and two weeks of that month were spent near Marbella, in Southern Spain, on a Cosmos tour to the Hotel Pinomar. The family of us shared a small bungalow away from the main hotel, and it was magnificent, lying in the sun for most of the day and just doing short runs, mainly in the heavily scented, wild foothills away from the sea. Whether I was feeling the pressure, or was determined to completely unwind, I was drinking a bottle of wine nearly every day, plus beer and spirits. As they say in Lancashire, I certainly "supped some stuff".

Even so far away, I was able to be tracked down. We were eating lunch in the hotel dining room, the Wednesday before we came home, tuna salad and Milan rice, when I was paged. A phone call from London. In my diary I wrote "eventually they found on the lines who wanted me — some bloke called John Schlesinger (his assistant actually) — wanted to know if I could do a film for them (or chat about it) — on Monday — told him I had a BBC interview". How was I to know it was Schlesinger, the famous film director? I was a bit annoyed that my privacy had been disturbed.

I started my final ten week build-up to the marathon on July 1st. It was two weeks longer than usual and three of those weeks would be spent training at altitude, which was another departure from my normal training; but I hoped that this extra work would lead to an extra special performance.

I cut out drinking, except for Saturday night when I usually had home brew shandies. I bumped the mileage up fairly quickly, with two hard sessions a week, usually 70 second bursts with 50 second intervals, or 30 second bursts with 30 second interval sandwiched between two sets of 2 minute bursts with 90 second intervals on Monday, with my "number stride fartlek" session on Wednesdays. I threw in the two fast 440's as an extra session Tuesday lunchtime. In both types of hard session, I built up the number of repetitions or bursts from a low number to maximum after 5 weeks. On July 1st, following my four weeks rest, I won the Winsford 7 mile road race on a hot day; a good omen. A week and 103½ miles later I was 6th in the YMCA 20K at Manchester. "What happened?", the journalists asked. The training was obviously tiring me at first.

I did worse 118½ miles and another week later, in a special 10 mile road race at Crystal Palace, London. I travelled down on the day of the race with Bolton clubmate, Peter Lever, and sat out in the hot sun all afternoon chatting to him and Don Faircloth and watching the AAA 10,000 metre championship. Dave Bedford, who the night before had won the 5,000 metres in a new European Record time of 13:17.2, just .6 seconds outside Ron Clarke's World Record, was fantastic, reeling off 66's and 67's in the scorching heat to win in 27:52.8, a time which only he and Ron Clarke had ever bettered.

Lachie Stewart of Scotland was second in the race in 28:38.8, thus qualifying for Munich as did Dave Holt who was 4th behind Jos Hermens of the Netherlands in 28:42.0. Dave's qualification was remarkable as the field had been so big for the 10,000 metres that the officials had split it into two races, and they were trying to force Dave to run in the 'B' race. However, he stood on the line for the 'A' race and wouldn't budge. His persistence was rewarded.

By the time the special road race came on I was thoroughly baked by the sun and felt little incentive to push myself over 10 miles of the hilly car race circuit. I was overheated before even a mile of the race was covered and trailed in 7th out of only 10 starters to no applause, even though the announcer did broadcast that I was running considerably under distance! Kind of him!

The next day, BBC filmed me during my 20½ mile Sunday run and interviewed me afterwards. That week I ran 125 miles, and my right leg was beginning to twinge a little.

A muddy 5,000m — Bolton.

199

1972

July 22nd, I ran a muddy 5,000 metres at the Rivington Cup meeting, clocking 14:18.8 behind Mike Tagg and Mike Freary. I was quite pleased with that and set off for Keswick in the Lake District for a weekend change of training scene. Sunday I ran a 19½ mile run round Bassenthwaite Lake, starting out with some of the Keswick AC lads. I was back for work Monday morning.

The next week saw 122 miles and twinges in my left leg. These miles were made harder by the fact that May had a boil, where it was very painful to have a boil, and had to stay in bed for a couple of days which left me cooking for the kids and cleaning up after them. They were incredibly untidy. On Thursday an ABC (USA) film crew had arrived from Munich to film me at work and then at home in the evening, which was bloody inconvenient. After it all, they had the cheek to give me £1 "to cover the electricity". Wednesday night I had to go to a BBC studio in Manchester to appear in a programme called, "The Succeeders", with Brian Hall of Liverpool Football Club. During the show it came out that I had never missed a day's training since 1964 and I said that I thought that the Olympic Gold Medal was mine, I had earned it. The interviewer then asked me what happened if I didn't win the Gold medal and I replied, "Well, it's another four years training to Montreal". That flabbergasted him.

Thursday night I had to appear at the Empress Club, Bolton, which was giving up its takings on that night to boost my Olympic fund. There I met Mr. Vessey who was in charge of the feed stations in the last Maxol, and who had suggested the fund to the Mayor of Bolton. I was grateful to him. Sunday night we drove up to Buckden, a little village in the Yorkshire Dales. There, George Bottomley, who owned a dye house in Huddersfield, had a lovely cottage and he was lending it to us for the weekend. At nearby Ripon, I ran a 10 mile road race and outsprinted Steve Kenyon, my Bolton club mate to finish second in 49:46. Mike Freary had white-washed both of us with a 48:33, but I was happy with my run and the next day ran a 24½ mile course over

5,000m — Crystal Palace.

the moorland tracks to Bainbridge and back.

My last race before going to altitude was a 5,000 metres at Crystal Palace. I was now in full training and ran 131 miles that week. My two x 440's I got down to 58.7 and 57.1, and there were five weeks to go. John Schlesinger and his crew duly arrived and filmed me extensively at work and at home. He was one of 8 internationally famous film directors doing a section of the official Olympic film to be called "Visions of Eight", and his segment would be on the marathon and me. In the 5,000 metres I got 4th, 14:05.4, not bad with five weeks to go before the big one. Schlesinger finished shooting the next day, with a lot of film of me running my Sunday 20½ miles through the tough but beautiful Derbyshire hills around Marple Bridge, Charlesworth, Glossop and Broadbottom. My mother and dad had spent the weekend at our house; I wouldn't see them again until after Munich. As they left, my dad shook my hand and said, "Don't let anyone get in front". My mother kissed me. We weren't normally given to showing affection in that way. I knew they dearly wanted me to succeed. The last seven days before travelling to St. Moritz, my sixth week of training, I clocked up 122 miles. I was beginning to feel tired, my legs were starting to get sore right at the top of the hamstring. That week's lunchtime session I did 4 x 220's instead of 2 x 440's and clocked 27 seconds for each of them.

Family portrait — before leaving for altitude.

CHAPTER ELEVEN

The Mayor of Bolton's fund had been successful and had exceeded the £500 target, which meant that May, Steven and Graham could be with me during my three weeks' training at around 5,500

feet in St. Moritz. We got the 9.45 a.m. plane out of Manchester for Zurich, the 1.36 p.m. train to Chur, then the 3.30 p.m. postal bus over the mountains to Chamfer, just down the valley from St. Moritz. The British altitude contingent was staying at the 'Eurotel' — a very sploosh place where I was sharing room 223 with Don Macgregor. May and the kids, who were on a privately organised trip, had to make do with a dirty, noisy dump, right on the main road.

My second night there I had a dream. I was back home and it was sometime after the Games. I had finished sixth in the marathon and suddenly it dawned on me that it was all over and there was no going back. I almost cried in my sleep. With only putting in a couple of 2's on the day we travelled, that first week was a short week, a meagre 94 miles. I did my 2 x 400's at the track and was surprised with 56.0 and a 57.0. I had arrived in pretty good condition, but was finding it tough going, especially in the mornings and on the hills. To add confusion to the situation, two doctors on the team were advising that we should spend time, and train, at 8,000

2 x 400's — 56.0 and 57.0

feet to get maxium benefit; as I wrote in my diary, "in fact, get stuck up a bloody mountain". Most of the time the weather was poor too. Cold, rain, occasionally snow, and at times I wondered what the hell I was doing up there freezing, as preparation for the cauldron of Munich. No-one had told me to expect such cold.

But we settled into a routine, training, walking and the boys took to Don, even though Graham did call him "specky four eyes", and they played a lot and swam with Andy Holden. When there was occasionally a decent day, we picnicked in the woods, where the boys lit a fire and roasted sausages. My diet was good and I stuck to my own routine as closely as possible, even taking to our room two raw eggs and milk, which I drank before training in the morning.

After a week there, I did my first long run, 21 miles, more or less out and back, round to Pontresina, and up the Val Roseg. Of coming back down the Val Roseg I wrote, "should have felt relaxed here, but was tired and cold". It was the start of a big week, 132 miles, and it was killing me. I daren't let up, I had to have faith in my plans and I was praying it would all come right in the end. My 2 x 400's were slower, 59.9 and 56.5, "felt weak, fairly satisfied". Wednesday my two sessions were:

". . . the weather was poor . . ."

". . . the boys lit a fire . . ."

203

August 23rd. M.	**7½ miles course — with sweat shirt and anorak — very easy running — had to be as I felt absolutely knackered — no energy at all — legs lifeless on the hills — only felt a little bit better at the end.** **7½**
August 23rd. E.	**Paths to St. Moritz — Lej da Staz - Pontresina — down to main road by paths — up through Celerina — St. Moritz — path to Champfer — raining all the way — felt knackered again — n.s.f. up to 55 and down to x 2 (from the last climb) — full track suit and anorak with hood up.** **12½**

I planned to cut my mileage in the morning and cut out the hills after this week.

Thurs. Aug. 24th M.	**7½ mile course — almost didn't go, felt so knackered — took it very, very easily — bright and sunny but cold in the woods — sweat shirt on.** **7½**

Sunday, August 27th. I started my last 6 days at altitude with a 21 mile run round by Pontresina, up the Val Roseg and then over the Fuorcla Surlej. In vest and shorts I had 35 minutes of solid climbing which took me 2,000 feet past amazed parties of climbers, fully togged up, and as I jogged past the cafe at the Fuorcla Surlej summit, I got a rousing cheer. The views were inspiring but unfortunately not energizing. My 400's that week slowed to 59.8 and 57.6 "disappointing but not surprising considering the state of my legs". With the advice of the doctors at the back of my mind I managed to get a run at Corviglia, a small beautiful lake with a sawdust track all the

Corviglia.

way round, reached by mountain railway and a short walk. There were beautiful wild flowers up there, just below the snow line.

With most of the British Olympic contingent gone, or going, on Monday, the vice-director of the Eurotel, Giarmi Barraré, let May and the lads come in and stay in room 323. He said their original place was one of the worst "doss (he didn't us that word exactly — it was stronger!)-houses" in Switzerland. In the Eurotel, served by three young waiters from Bolton, it almost home from home!

Don Macgregor departing with Sheila Carey, Joyce Smith and family.

On Wednesday, Don MacGregor left for Munich, by coach, with the canoeists. He'd had enough of hanging around St. Moritz; he was fed up. Brendan Foster, Ian Stewart and John Kirkbride left by car with Harry Wilson the coach, and Dr. Ray Watson, a physiologist. We were the last there, each day climbing the mountain railway

Brendan Foster, Ian Stewart, John Kirkbride depart.

CHRIS SMITH

Final training at Corviglia.

to Corviglia, looking for marmots amongst the rocks, all of us running round the lake, and returning to the hotel, spinning out the last few days before parting and my final departure for the big race.

Friday I switched to light shoes in an attempt to save my legs more.

Saturday was good-bye time, seven days before the race. Harry Wilson and Ray Watson came back up from Munich in their special car to ferry me back. May was going back to Zurich, then home with the boys. At the final farewell Graham said, "I'll give daddy a kiss now, in the room". I waved to them as the VW van pulled out heading for the mountain pass and then for Zurich. It was raining.

Harry and Ray didn't waste any time getting to Munich and Ray was touching 110 mph on the autobahn. We didn't stop for lunch; I had raw ham, cheese and an apple in the car, I was on the no carbohydrate part of the diet. Someone had said that at altitude, the glycogen content of the muscles can go down by 30%; I daren't think about that; I had to do what I had to do.

The weather changed from wet to dry. As we hit Munich I saw long flags, lime-green, white, turquoise, striking and unusual. Ray hared the car to the Olympic Village, through a gate, without showing a pass, into a depressingly dark underground car park. I had arrived. We found Area 10, got a lift to the seventh floor, flat 73. Miraculously I had a room of my own; a bottle green wardrobe and cupboards, a bed; sparse but adequate. Steve Hollings, the steeplechaser, was next door, and Ian Stewart with Don Macgregor next door to that. Cecil Dale told me I had to go to the Administration Building and there I was photographed and given a lime green plastic pass with my photo and safety pin attachment. It was numbered 1-7F. I did 15 minutes' running round the village and called at the Tiger hospitality shop for a chat with Mr. Kitami and Yoshi Hikita of the Tiger shoe company. They gave me three pairs of training shoes. At 8.00 p.m. I had dinner with Don; four small tough pork chops, salad, cheese, two cups of tea. Back at the room I got a batch of letters and telegrams. I felt a bit depressed. Went to sleep by 11.20 p.m.

Sunday, September 3rd. *Got up at 7.25 a.m. . . . ran 7 miles easy with Ian Stewart, a little bit of stiffness below my calves . . . fried boiled ham and boiled egg for breakfast . . . organised a small table in my room as a desk . . . lunch at 11.55 a.m. with Dave Bedford, his final tonight . . . had tomato and lettuce — kept putting packets of sugar on this instead of salt and wondering why it wasn't getting saltier — cheese and a slice of Ryvita . . . sat on the balcony and wrote a letter to May . . . an old acquaintance Till Luft from the Manchester University Athletic Club Freiburg trip in 1963, came up to see me . . . later Don and Ian came out to sit in the sun and Jack Foster and Terry Manners of New Zealand joined us . . . 3.00 p.m. ran 8 miles, some of it on the course — 5+5+6 minute efforts with 3 minutes interval, managed them O.K. but had some guts ache on the intervals . . . went to the stadium to watch the 10,000 metres with Don . . . very crowded getting back . . . had dinner alone, beef, lettuce and tomato, chicken, broccoli, cheese, brought back two cups of milk for my cocoa/Casilan . . . Denis Clayton turned up, chatted and gave him a pile of fruit and a bottle of lemonade . . . chatted to coach Wilf Paish about arrangements for the marathon . . . bed at 10.40 p.m. . . . read until 11.30 p.m. . . . took me a long, long time to get to sleep . . . kept thinking about the race, working out strategies for the finish if I was with, say, Frank Shorter . . . get the lead, push along the back straight — kick at 200 metres then finally kick off the bend right up to the finish — then if it were Lutz Philipp, get the inside and hit the tunnel first — my heart was palpitating like hell as I thought about it!*

On the balcony, in the sun, with Ian Stewart.

1972

Monday, September 4th. *Woke up at 7.30 a.m., read a book until 8.00 a.m., shaved, ran 5 miles, a bit heavy and lethargic from the diet, no problems with my legs . . . breakfast at 9.15 a.m. . . . scrambled egg and ham . . . wrote postcards . . . lunch at 12.00, sat with the walker Phil Embleton, had two trays of tuna fish, lettuce and tomato . . . back at 1.00 p.m. . . . sat on the balcony outside our rooms . . . chatted to Tim Johnston, his achilles is a mess from all the operations . . . very hot in the sun . . . shaved my moustache off . . . got Ian to take before and after pictures . . . had my hair cut very short . . . Lynn Davies and Mike Bull fooling about in the barbers . . . had to force the girl to make it very short "praktisch" . . . she got the message . . . didn't recognise myself when I looked in the mirror . . . got a car to take me to the course, ten miles from the finish at the time I expected to be there in the race . . . cool but surface of roads in the "Gardens" terrible . . . freshly laid loose chippings, murder on the feet in racing shoes, 2-4-7 x 70 seconds burst, seemed to be moving pretty well . . . dinner at 6.15 p.m. with Don, roast beef, roast pork, beans, tomato, chicken, three cheeses, Gorgonzola, Camembert, and fromage aux fines herbs, lots of tea and couple of cups of coffee . . . back to room, had mineral water and an orange . . . writing and reading, bed at 11.00 p.m. . . . read for a while, couldn't get to sleep . . . 12.30 a.m. loads of noise from upstairs, bumping of beds and banging on the floor . . . one of the heavy discus throwers drunk . . . still not asleep at 2.30 a.m., bloody annoyed!*

Tuesday, September 5th. *Got up at 8.00 a.m. felt bog-eyed . . . ran 7 miles in the heat, knackered, just putting one leg in front of the other, arms felt very tired too . . . scrambled egg and pepper and ham with tea for breakfast . . . back to room, shaved the hairs off my legs . . . sat in the sun and wrote a few postcards . . . sweating like hell . . . Ismail Akcay came up and gave me a present. Norman Harris dropped by for a chat . . . lunch at 12.15 p.m. with Don and Dave Bedford, olives, lettuce and some meat or other, can't remember with "diet" getting to my mind . . . there was a story of some shooting . . . Arab guerillas had shot two Israelis and had about 20 hostages . . . rumours flying of the Games being postponed 24 hours . . . that would affect the diet . . . back to the room, wrote more postcards, Dave Bedford there, we listened to his tape recorder . . . went for a car at 3.00 p.m. . . . tried out my silver shorts . . . ran 7 miles of the course up to 15 km point with Don and Dave, was really tired, very hot indeed, sweating a lot, had to keep slowing the pace down, had to climb over a gate to the Nymphenburg Park, Don really struggled over this . . . strict security on the gates, shower, washed two slips, bought a complete set of Olympic stamps and they cost me over £2 . . . dinner at 6.00 p.m., fish, sprouts, roast beef and salad, four different cheeses, tea, coffee and orange . . . talk still of 24 hour postponement . . . saw Frank Shorter, said we were going to propose that the marathon should be kept at Saturday but put back to 5.00 p.m. . . . asked Danny McDaid and the three New Zealanders to do the same . . . saw Ken Moore with his wife on way out . . . told him the same thing . . . back to the quarters . . . "diet" playing havoc with me, didn't feel like doing a thing . . . read a bit, talked to Don . . . rumours still going . . . a notice on our board said the Games may start again at 1.00 or 2.00 p.m. tomorrow . . . we didn't know what to do about the "diet" . . . wandered down to the shops, met Ismail Akcay, he said he'd been to the doctor's and Clayton was in there . . . and "Usami was no good" . . . that cheered me up a bit . . . walked slowly back to the rooms still wondering about the diet, I couldn't face another day without carbohydrate . . . coach John Le Masurier came in at 10.00 p.m. and said there would definitely be no competition tomorrow . . . the story flashed that the hostages had been released (in fact they hadn't, and were killed at Furstenfeldbruck airport), but there was a memorial service at 10.00 a.m. tomorrow . . . Craig Sharp, a canoeing coach, advised me to come off the "diet" tomorrow, so I got my chocolate ready, Mars bars and things I had been hoarding . . . wrote up my training log and diary . . . stayed up and read until just after 12.00 midnight.*

Wednesday, September 6th. *12.01 a.m. It was now Wednesday, I couldn't wait any longer, had a box of muslei and can of pears all mixed up with fructose and milk in my pint Maxol tankard . . . had three pieces of chocolate . . . went to sleep at 12.30 a.m. . . . woke gain at 5.30 a.m. . . . had a Mars bar, slept again until 6.30 a.m. . . . got up to go for a run, there were two notices on the bulletin board, the first said, "The Competitions would start again at 1.00 p.m. or 2.00 p.m.", the second, timed at 12.30 a.m. said, "The Competitions would carry on as normal. The Israelis have been freed and the Arabs dispersed" . . . ran 7 miles, felt O.K. in snatches but got tired towards the end*

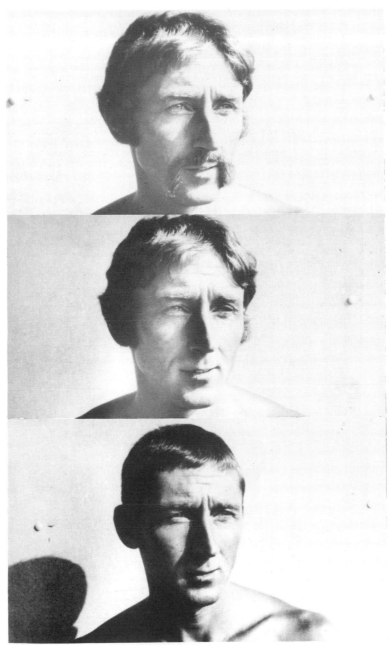

". . . got Ian to take before and after pictures . . ."

. . . as I turned a bloke in his pyjamas was telling someone else that a bomb had been thrown into the room with the Israeli hostages . . . breakfast at 8.00 a.m., cornflakes, scrambled egg on toast and four sausages, coffees with fructose. 10.00 a.m., at the Memorial Service at the Stadium Avery Brundage announced that there would be a day of mourning, everything would be put back a day . . . so we'll have to see how the "diet" works now. 12.10 p.m. lunch, soup, steak butty, cake, two orange juices, two cokes, ice cream, felt really full, nearly sick . . . had a sleep on the balcony . . . Denis Clayton showed up later on, gave him some food and things . . . had two Mars bars . . . it rained . . . 4.50 p.m. ran 5 miles with Don — pace built up to be quite fast, didn't feel brilliant again, legs a little bit sore on top of my thighs, near the bones, sweating a bit again, ran into the stadium just to try it . . . 6.20 p.m., dinner, turkey, corn, broccoli, potatoes, cake, honey, peaches and ice cream . . . up to the room with Don, had coffee, cake and grapes, listened to music and chatted . . . posted a card, met Arthur Gold on the way back, he said that a chap from Courtaulds had tried to contact me . . . I had to phone him tomorrow . . . wrote my diary for 10.45 p.m., cleaned my teeth, went to bed, started reading, 'The Grapes of Wrath', by John Steinbeck, I'd been saving this book for years for now . . . I slept pretty well.

Thursday, September 7th. Got up at 8.00 a.m., a 7 mile easy run, felt O.K. at the start felt lousy after 3 miles, began to feel better as I got nearer the camp, inside of my thighs were still a bit sore on the bone . . . breakfast with Steve Hollings and Don, muesli, jam and bread, coffee . . . phoned Mr. Stenz of Courtaulds, arranged to meet him at Gate 7 at 12.30 p.m. . . . back to room, shaved, tidied up a bit . . . got some stamps off Dave Bedford's fan mail, he had some strange letters, one from Bournemouth asking him to go and stay and sleep in a room with her son for an unlimited period of time; another from a bird in the U.S.A. with a song inviting him to the mountains! . . . 12.00 noon, lunched with Don, beef butty, cake, fruit salad and ice cream . . . met Mr. Stenz at 12.35 p.m., he had a "Good Luck" card which June Witty, editor of Courtaulds company newspaper, had been organising. I could see it being an embarrassing flop with just six or seven names; Mr. Stenz gave me a book full of signatures from practically all the people in Courtaulds, over 17,500 in total; I was truly amazed . . . photographs, said "Cheerio" . . . went to the Olympic Park Hotel to talk with John Schlesinger's people, Jim Clark and Drummond Challice, about filming, panic messages would have to be sent to the various camera men around the course to cancel my description of longish hair and moustache . . . watched the 5,000

17,500 signatures.

metres heats on T.V. . . . ran 5 miles at 4.30 p.m., feeling a bit tired, hot and sultry, sweated like hell . . . wrote a card to May . . . dinner, fish fingers, green beans and chips, cake, fruit salad and ice cream, yoghurt, cake, coffee . . . back to room, reading, writing . . . had a bath at 9.30 p.m. and massaged my legs . . . cocoa/Complan with water (I had forgotten milk) and a teaspoonful of honey . . . writing . . . bed at 11.30 p.m., reading until 11.45 p.m. . . . quite a bit of noise but I was soon away and slept quite well.

Friday, September 8th. *Put a top cover on the bed sometime in the morning, slept very well then until 8.45 a.m. . . . got up and felt pretty shattered, did only 2½ miles, my legs were pretty sore again . . . breakfast with Steve, cornflakes, scrambled egg on toast, banana on toast, two cups of coffee, enjoyed it . . . went for medical at 10.10 a.m., Cecil flapping because I was ten minutes late . . . to the stadium, found the first aid room . . . had I had throat infections or 'flu lately? — examined my teeth and the roof of my mouth, checked my breathing and blood pressure, that was it . . . left Cecil and Don to take the car back; Colin Kirkham, his usual quiet self, went off in the opposite direction to get some pictures, I went to the upper levels of the stadium to get some first day covers for people at work . . . bus back to the grey, crowded, prison-like village . . . film people*

". . . the grey, crowded, prison-like village . . ."

there, took me reading my book, asked me questions about the Israeli tragedy . . . walked over to lunch at 12.10 p.m. with Don, they filmed us doing that, Arthur the cameraman pushed a few people about, but banged into a lamp post for punishment . . . had boiled ham and lettuce butty, yoghurt and cake, orange juice . . . back to the room, had an apple, moved mattress outside to rest in the sun, bloody warm again, read papers, Harold Wilson had demanded that the team be brought home! . . . John Jewell and his wife came up to talk to us . . . Cec. came out for a sleep . . . Bicourt came to read the papers . . . played Ian Stewart's tape recorder . . . 3.00 p.m. tea and half a bar of chocolate . . . had a nice letter from May and wrote her another card . . . 4.25 p.m. had a pint of DW4 electrolyte drink . . . 5.05 p.m. ran 3 miles around by the finish of the course, legs still sore and I'm a bit worried now . . . 5.50 p.m. dinner, piece of pork, chips, peas, corn, piece of cake, two biscuits . . . back to block . . . decided to see one of the physios about my legs, waited ages reading a book. Veda said Ted or Bill was coming back soon. 7.45 p.m. — no one had come so Veda brought one of the team doctors in , he examined my legs . . . the thought suddenly struck me that the only different thing I had been doing was wearing those new soft spongy shoes; that was it! How bloody simple! Veda massaged my legs and I was out at 8.00 p.m. . . . wrote my diary, had tea and an apple, had a hot bath and massaged my legs again . . . had cocoa/Complan, bed and read until 10.40 p.m. . . . took a while to get to sleep, but I was quite relaxed . . . slept pretty well.

1972

Saturday, September 9th. *Up at 9.00 a.m. after a good sleep . . . went down and had a good massage from Bill Shillibeer . . . did only a 1½ mile run, felt O.K. in racing shoes, problem with my legs pretty well gone now . . . 9.50 a.m. breakfast, cornflakes, scrambled eggs on toast and tea . . . back to my room, read for a while . . . another massage from Bill at 12.00 noon . . . another 1½ mile run, felt O.K., in fact felt quite sprightly for a change and no pains in my legs . . . lunch, soup and toast, cake, fruit salad and ice cream . . . back to room, stayed in all the time, today overcast and cooler than of late, wonder what it will be like tomorrow? I'll be bloody glad to get the race over with . . . 3.00 p.m. cup of tea and some chocolate . . . watched a bit of T.V. at 5.00 p.m. . . . took some pictures from the top floor . . . 6.00 p.m., dinner, posted the card to May, who I am missing, on the way . . . read some papers, B.O.A. had refused extra security, I'd heard rumours that the I.R.A. had threatened to blow up our block . . . veal, chips, beans, cake and ice cream, tea, Don came to join me . . . back to room, reading, crossword, Wilf Paish came in, I told him I wanted a sponge, he said he would get one for me (he cut up a pillow), Don got one too, told Wilf to tell Colin so that we wouldn't psyche him out at the start . . . had a bit of chocolate with pear liqueur, but not too much . . . Don brought in some sheets with all the marathon competitors on, Dave Bedford dropped in for a chat . . . when he had gone Ian Stewart, then Brendan Foster, then Colin Kirkham came in for a talk, Brendan said that Donal Walsh, an Irish marathon runner, had told him that there were about thirty I.R.A. people in Munich (they had already disrupted the cycle race) and that they would blow up our block tomorrow night (Brendan had also heard that a gang of them were intending to jump on me from ambush in the English Gardens during the race; luckily he kept that to himself), we all agreed to go and spend tomorrow night at the four bedroomed flat of a friend of Ian Stewart . . . hell, they call this sport? . . . got them all out at 10.30 p.m. . . . wrote my diary for 10.50 p.m., read for a while, put the light out at 11.20 p.m. . . . slept pretty well.*

CHAPTER TWELVE

Sunday, September 10th.

I see a crack of daylight.

The curtains are drawn and it is still dark in my room. I pull my arm out from under the warm blanket and look at my yellow fibre-glass watch which I bought in Switzerland. The dial is luminous and the fingers point to 8.30 a.m.

So this is it. September 10th 1972; a day late, but this is it. A thousand miles away in Blackpool, May and the kids are getting up and saying, "This is the day." My mother and father too.

I lie for a couple of minutes relaxed. Yes, I've slept pretty well, which is good. My left hand throws back the bedclothes. I swing out of bed and go to the window. I pull back the heavier curtains which keep out the daylight, part the net curtains and peer out over the balcony at the rows of buildings, then the sky. Grey; everything is grey. The apartments and the sky. The weather is dull; well that's a consolation at least we haven't got the hot sun of the last few days, but the weather hasn't broken as predicted by the forecast.

I put on a slip and switch on my cassette player. Steve Hollings is next door but he won't mind the pop music as his event is over. I am going for a short run to waken up and loosen up. I find my light-weight silver racing shoes and carefully put them on for a final try out. They haven't been worn much as they are a bit fragile. They were made at the last minute and I've sewn them up in places to reinforce them. They feel good.

I slip on my silver running shorts, again for a final try out. These are pretty spectacular but I'll just have to stand the inquisitive stares and raised eyebrows. Let them look; everything counts in this race. I know the silver Lurex string vest is O.K. so I leave that off and put on a purple and yellow nylon vest. My green identity card set in plastic is on the table and I fasten this with a safety pin low down on my vest and tuck it into my shorts. I don't want to get held up outside the village today.

After the usual long wait I go down to the ground floor by lift and go to the physiotherapist's room where Bill Shillibeer gives my legs a final massage. After it I feel O.K. and the trouble I've had earlier in the week with pains on the insides of my thighs, the results of having trained in some foreign shoes I had been given, has now gone. Through the two sets of doors, down past the armed guard at the entrance to our block, I check my watch and jog off to gate 7. I don't look at anybody in case they are staring at my gear. Outside the gate I turn left into Lerchenauer Strasse and run against the flow of people already making their way towards the Olympic stadium. I run on the cycle path and keep checking the watch. At 4 minutes I turn back. I'm thinking, "How do I feel?" no stiffness in my legs, fairly fresh in body as a whole, breathing all right; yet I don't feel as bouncy or springy as I have felt before some marathons. Perhaps its because it's fairly warm. Perhaps it's nerves, it sometimes happens like that. On the way back I put in a few fast bursts to stretch my legs and again still do not feel too bouncy.

Back in the room I don't bother to shave and have just a perfunctory swill in cold water. Donny (MacGregor) has had his breakfast. I see him as I leave the bathroom. "Morning, Jock!" I'm trying to be funny, I know he doesn't like that name. I dress in my navy corduroy jeans I got given in Belgium by Herr Pauwels, and green shirt. From a tin on my table I pour out a pile of pills into my hand and select one red Super Plenamin, one brown Boots Iron Tonic tablet and one white vitamin C tablet. I drop these inside my shirt pocket. I nearly forget my breakfast ticket, switch off my cassette player and head over to the restaurant. Alone.

When I meet a team mate he says, "All the best this afternoon, Ron." They look at me like I was a condemned man. The marathon. As if it were some bloody mysterious and deadly event.

As usual there are crowds of people about in the village and I thread my way through them trying not to look at anyone. On the way to the cafeteria building I nip into the information centre and pick up today's athletics programme. It's green with a blue motif of a runner. 10.15 a.m. They are still serving breakfast. I walk carefully up the steps to the top dining room conserving energy and reducing the risks of injury. I could see the headline "Top Marathon Runner Breaks Leg". I hand in my ticket to the uniformed attendant. They love those uniforms, the Germans. Inside I head across to the self-service counters and pick up a box of cornflakes and a carton of milk and four slices of the bread which they are using to make toast. It's the only decent bread for making jam butties. It's pretty quiet. I put a plastic cup of black tea on my tray and then find a spot on my own.

I start on the cornflakes, making sure it's sugar I put on them and not bloody salt. I'd been caught out earlier when I was on my low carbohydrate diet. The packets were so similar. I open up the programme in front of me and turn the pages until I reach page 8. This is headed "Marathon". 15.00 h. Final. It looks like the list of runners has been seeded for their position on the start line and I work through the runners selecting the danger men and assessing their possibilities. Each runner produces his card from the computer which is my brain. Usami, Akio, Japan; No. 2 on the start line, a good and tough runner, carrying the hopes of Japan, but he has run a lot of marathons in the last eighteen months and his times have got slower and slower. Philipp, Lutz, West Germany; he beat me in the British Trial, the Maxol marathon in Manchester, but I think that was his run of the year. He didn't seem to rest after it and produced some pretty poor 10,000 metres times. I don't think he will be a danger. Lismont, Karel, Belgium; the winner of the European Marathon championship in Helsinki last year, where I was third. That was a bloody lucky race for him; I was injured, the standard of the field was not that great and his winning time was nothing special under those cool conditions. I don't expect to see him anywhere near at the end. Moore, Kenneth, U.S.A.; Kenny was joint first in the U.S.A. trial in a time of 2.15 odd but ran in with Frank Shorter and therefore was obviously not fully extended. Even so, their trial only being nine weeks ago should make him still tired from that race. Hill, Ronald, Great Britain; that's me! The 2:09:28.0 looks good in the list, the second fastest time ever. Clayton, Derek, Australia; the world's fastest marathon runner with 2:08:33.6. Now he could be a danger. Although he has had a lot of injury problems in the last four years he still managed the world's best time of 1971 with me third on that list and he has been lying pretty low this year, reportedly conserving his energies for the Olympic Marathon. He will have to be watched.

Foster, Jack, New Zealand; another great runner for his age — must be 40 by now, but I don't think he will be in the medals; but I hope he is well up there as he is a pal of mine. Roelants, Gaston, Belgium; Gaston has been doing some fantastic mileage in the last year and has spent, according to all accounts, about two months at altitude at St. Moritz. I would like to write off Gaston as he has never run a fast marathon yet and he must have left a lot of his natural ability on the trails and tracks of St. Moritz, but Gaston is always a danger. Shorter, Frank, U.S.A.; Frank has a very good record although he has never broken 2 hrs. 12 mins. yet and he should be fairly tired after running the heat and the final of the 10,000 metres. Clayton does not think he is a natural marathon runner as his leg action is too high.

This list has obviously been seeded as all the top men are at the head of the list. I begin to gloss over the rest pretty quickly with just a flash of recognition here and there. I know most of them, but some better than others. 19, Kirkham, Colin — one of ours. 24, Akcay, Ismail, Turkey; fourth in Mexico, we write regularly. 31, Perez, Carlos, Spain; the sociable little Spaniard who played with our kids in Athens. 44, Bachelor, Jack, U.S.A. Big Jack, bloody big. Almost

1972

at the end, 67 and 68, Mejia, Alvaro, and Mora, Victor, both of Colombia. Their "personal record" column is blank, but I know that Mejia has won the Boston Marathon and Mora could be a surprise, he won the San Blas Half-Marathon in Coamo, Puerto Rico, in February where I was 7th. The last name on the list raises a smile, Medaui, Shag Mousa, Sudan.

A shiver of nerves goes through my stomach and I close the programme. My opinion of the race is unchanged; myself, Clayton, Roelants, Shorter and maybe Usami will be in at the kill but all being well I will be away by then. I finish off my now soggy cornflakes, make the jam butty and eat it, washing it down with black unsweetened tea. I want to eat more, probably through nerves, but resist and pick up the two slices of bread I haven't eaten, wrap them up in a polythene bag and carry them back to my room for my lunch.

Just outside the restaurant I meet Mohamed Gammoudi, of Tunisia, who wishes me all the best for this afternoon "J'espere pour toi cette apres-midi." He puts his arm round me. "Thanks," I say and head back to our block. I've been a bit surprised at how many people have said they would like to see me win this race. Naftali Temu of Kenya, an old friend and rival — well hardly rival, I don't think I have ever beaten him — said that he hoped I would win, and so did Victor Mora.

When I get back up to the room I feel somehow a lot happier and I put on my cassette player. I don't want to lie about so I start to pack one of my suitcases with the things I know I won't need again. Books, training shoes, dirty shirts, towels, left over nuts and dried fruit. We go back on Tuesday and I'm doing some shopping tomorrow; I need to get some packing out of the way. I have my window open to keep the room cool; it's still not sunny but the day is heating up. I remember my sponge. I wanted this to use immediately before the race to keep cool. I fill mine with water, put it in a polythene bag and place it in the fridge in the refreshment room next to the door to our flat. I remind Donny to do the same.

At 12.30 I have my second jam butty and a cup of tea — glucose and lemon tea, dispensed in the refreshment room. With the last meal inside me I go to the bathroom, have a thorough shave, then a lukewarm shower. There is no curtain, as the bathroom was obviously not finished, and water splashes on the floor; I don't bother as tidiness in our flat has now got to take second place to the preparation before the race. I soap myself thoroughly all over, head, under my arms, chest and legs, then rinse off completely. I half dry myself, return to my room, close the door and put on only a slip so that I stay cool all over. I gather my racing gear together and the other things I will need after the race go into my Olympic Airways

216

bag which we got at the European Games in Athens. Dry shoes, a clean vest and slip, my gold metallic shorts which I will wear on the rostrum, if I win. I hesitate here a little; it may be bad luck to anticipate, but I roll them up in a towel and stuff them in the bag. I pin my numbers on my vest, stick a small number on my shorts as requested and a larger number on my track suit. Number 289. I mix up a drink made from orange and salt and drink some from my stainless steel Maxol tankard, then I have another ½ pint. These will make sure that my reservoirs of fluid are fully topped up. We are due out at 1.50 p.m.; 10 mins. to go! I sit on the bed and write on my left hand MAY, STEVEN and GRAHAM, and underneath MOTHER and FATHER. These may give me motivation if it gets hard at the end and perhaps a little bit extra. Right, nearly time to leave. I quickly put on my racing shoes, racing slip, silver shorts and vest, my dark blue GBR track suit with red trim and my sun glasses, these latter so that I am protected from the outside world. I clip the Beatles' "Abbey Road" into my cassette player, turn up the volume, sling it over my shoulder, collect my refrigerated sponge, and leave for the stadium.

Donny is ready, Colin Kirkham is standing by the lift, quiet as usual; we are all quiet today, and Dick McCoglan, the official in charge of us today, takes us down in the lift to the basement where a car is waiting for us. We go first to the exit gate, get out, walk through, get into another car and drive to the stadium. There, we go into the labyrinth beneath the stands. We can't find the bloody changing rooms! And after a half mile hike we go to the physio-

The stadium.

therapists' rooms near the indoor warm-up area where Ted Chappell and Bill Shillibeer have a room. Most of the other competitors are congregating in this area, so we go into the massage room and I lie flat on the bench.

There is an elaborate and ridiculous system of reporting and Wilf Paish has clocked in for us at the first call. I look at my watch, 2.25 p.m. I will start to warm up about 2.40. Marathon runners are coming in and out of our room to use the toilets. There is tension in the air and no-one seems too friendly.

At 2.30 p.m. Dick comes in and says we have to go for the final reporting. I go outside and turn left to the top of a long rubber covered corridor. There are tables there and they are giving out green plastic bags (for our gear) and asking runners to strip off and go through to the stadium. I start to get annoyed; this is ridiculous, half an hour to go and we have to take off our track suits and hang around. That buggers my warm up. Dick tells me to take it easy. I go back, use the toilet, strip off my track suit, put it in a plastic bag, leave my other stuff with Ted Chappell and jog out carrying my sponge in one hand and the green bag in the other. I curse the organisers, they obviously haven't consulted anybody who knows about marathon running. I dump the bag with the piles of others and follow the tail enders down the corridor presumably towards the stadium. I emerge in the entrance tunnel where it is relatively dark and cool. I can see the crowds outside and the buzz of the spectators' voices penetrates the darkened cave of the tunnel. I just start to jog nervously around on the concrete slope as a warm up when the voice comes "All marathon runners on to the track, please." Hell no! What are they playing at? What the hell are we supposed to do out there for 15 minutes in front of that lot and with no protection from the heat? I become quite agitated. They can wait. Roelants trots by; he looks grim and doesn't speak. I ignore this, we are all tensed up.

I delay as long as I can then jog out after everyone else on to the red rubber track. It is beautiful and feels like warm velvet. I run slowly round the track clockwise away from the amazing transparent tent roof to the start of our race on the back straight. There are a few whistles on account of my gear but there is no escape from the anonymous wall of human faces. It's a trap. I hear a few shouts "Come on Ronnie boy", but up in the crowd I can pick no one out from the sea of faces. Just a couple of big Union Jacks waving. I wave, I put up my left fist and shake it. Perhaps I should save that until after the race.

There are two clocks on opposite sides of the stadium. They don't seem to agree, perhaps it is the angle I view them at. "Christ, it's warm out here." I jog a little on the synthetic track, in and out of the

"I lie down on the grass . . ."

other runners and occasionally dip into my polythene bag and wipe water all over my hair and arms and legs. I offer some to Ismail but he smiles and shakes his head. Perhaps I should be resting. I lie down on the grass for about three minutes. The cool green blades of grass under my body and the sky above are the only natural things in this god-awful place. The film men arrive, Christ, they must get this bloody shot. John Schlesinger directs them. I try to ignore them. My heart is beating pretty hard. Hell, I can't relax, so I get up and just now an official points to the start line.

They are reading the runners' names out. I'm on the front line, "Clayton" they call. "Hill," an official points to a white curved line on the red rubber track. I walk up and look at Derek in his white vest with the green and gold kangaroo badge of Australia. He isn't looking my way but I say quietly, 'Hi.' "Shorter." Up comes Frank in his white cut-away vest with U.S.A. in red, white and blue splashed on the front and navy-blue shorts. No. 1014. I look up at him and we nod slightly at each other. "Kimihara," "Wolde." The others are called up and I keep looking at the clock.

With one minute to go they are lined up, and I step out on to the grass in front of the ranks, deliberately squeezing the rest of the water from the sponge over my head for a final cooling down, and drop it on to the ground. There is a gasp from the crowd. I step back into line and notice Victor Mora has picked up the sponge and is

219

". . . one minute to go . . ."

". . . squeezing . . . the sponge over my head . . ."

rubbing it on his arms and legs. I glance at the clock again. 3 p.m. As Donny said, "Commonly known as the hottest part of the day." Bloody organisation! I look at the ground. I am nervous, my stomach turns over. The crowd is silent. The runners are silent. "Auf die plätze!" Tense. Bang. We are off.

Somewhat reluctantly I push my body into motion around the first bend, we have two laps of the track and then exit for the roads around Munich. The noise of the crowd rises to a crescendo. My mouth gets dry almost immediately and I do not feel comfortable. I glance round to see where everyone is; all the runners are doing the same. I spot the tall ones immediately, Clayton, Shorter, Lutz Philipp. Some idiot jumps into the lead and sets what I think is a fast pace. I just keep up near the front, looking at the running clock as we pass the start for the second time. 2 minutes 30 seconds — Hell, it feels a lot faster than that.

"Bang. We are off."

Perhaps it is just nerves. We leave the stadium via the tunnel on which there is a slight incline; it feels hard work up here and I lose a few places which I quickly regain on the flat outside. We cross the autobahn by a narrow bridge and an electric van filled with photographers is leading us now, but too close. Just after the bridge we have a short right turn up a dirt hill and the electric car has difficulty making it; it forms an obstruction and throws up clouds of dust. Shorter, right up its backside, gives a vigorous hysterical V sign into the telephoto lenses of the cameramen riding it. I think, "What a cock-up."

221

The van clears out quickly and we run on narrow black asphalt paths with the Olympic village on the right. Some other nurk takes the lead and Usami goes with him. He's an unknown, so I don't bother. I think it is amusing that Usami goes, almost as if he has had his instructions to go up no matter who it is that leads. Clayton is close, Shorter and Jack Foster. We swing left, down a ramp through some new buildings and Usami and his leader are caught. My legs are feeling dead and it is uncomfortably warm. We run down Pelkovenstrasse about 400 metres and left into Hanauerstrasse before turning right into the wide Wintrichring. I follow the blue lines to orientate myself on the wide road. There is a blue line round the whole of the course. Usami and Clayton are more or less just in front and crowds line the road on both sides. I think I see blonde-haired Rita Ridley but then I hear an Australian voice shouting "Come on Derek" and I realise it's Rita's twin sister Iris, who married the Australian runner Tony Cook. I still feel bad, I'm not relaxed and my legs feel they are swollen, like balloons and I have to throw each leg forward to maintain speed rather than just flowing along. I am worried, I don't understand it, I should be clicking about now.

The other runners are sweating. I inspect Usami's neck under his white peak cap and his shoulders and arms; he's sweating. Clayton too. I look down at my own arms and they are dry. My breathing is O.K. but my legs feel knackered. O.K., O.K. — just press on.

At 5 kilometres I look up at the board to get a time — 15 mins. 51 secs. Subtract 30 secs; 15:21. Hell, we're way outside the 5 minute mile pace which is slow for the early part of the race and I'm feeling rough. This means the time is going to be way outside 2:11 allowing for slowing down at the end. Clayton is pulling away and Usami is going with him as we follow the blue line over to the left hand side of the road. 2 yards, 5 yards, 10 yards, Christ, this is it, I can't hang on. I feel desperate, but I have to control myself.

Right; I ignore them and hit my own relaxed, but maximum pace. At Maria-Ward Platz I follow Clayton and Usami into Allacher Strasse, a very wide street with a slight incline up to a bridge over a railway line. As I pull myself up the hill Jack Foster eases past. I am surprised that he is wearing all black gear, especially in the heat. Then the three Americans pass me, Shorter, Moore and Bachelor in echelon, all tall, white vests and navy shorts. Oh hell! this can't be true. Clayton is 15 yards up when we turn left into Halderberger-strasse with its thankfully narrower road and little suburban houses and gardens on either side. Still people line the pavements but cheers have now turned to polite clapping. The nightmare intensifies as two Ethiopians pass me, one is Mamo Wolde, now Lismont, now Roelants, now two Finns. They spread right out across the narrow road and I try to hang on to them but I feel awful. I realise that I am nowhere near in control of the race as I ought to be. I'm just following, hanging on and hoping.

I cut all the corners I can see as I observe that the other runners in front are not doing this. I must use everything that I know and gain every yard that I can. The leaders turn sharp left into Nusshaher Strasse which is narrower still and lined with trees; it is cooler here and we are heading towards the Nymphenberg Park. The road surface is a little bit rough and I am watching where I put my feet.

I glance up and see that the field has concertinaed. Christ, Clayton has slowed up! Perhaps he's over-heated. I maintain my pace and rapidly move through the field to Clayton's side as Usami doesn't seem to know what to do and no one else is taking the initiative. I wonder if everyone else has been feeling the pace. My spirits rise and I accordingly push up the pace slightly; they are now following me in a big bunch. I hear a Liverpool accent, "Christ, it's slow." Out of the corner of my left eye I see a shape in black with a very low arm action and a slight forward lean; it's Jack Foster. Half a minute later, the same voice says "This is bloody slow," and I think to myself "Oh no! any minute now someone is going to blast off." So I am not running well after all.

But I still lead out of the lane into a right turn, then a left sweep down under a railway bridge where the road is very rough again, then round and up and right across two main roads to the top of the Nymphenberg Park. This very slight uphill sorts me out and I feel lethargic again. As we pass through the old brick walls of the park and the high spiked gates which Dave Bedford and I had to help Donny over earlier in the week when we had found them locked, I begin to falter and Clayton goes ahead again just after 10 kilometres. 31 mins. 15 secs. I don't feel like concentrating but I do the sum. Take away 16 minutes, 15:15 and add nine seconds, 15:26, well the pace has speeded up a bit but this is meaningless as the bunch is overtaking me again. The surface in the park is bloody awful to say the least. It's like a yellow brown sandy gravel and they claim to have bound it together with resin or something but in fact it's smooth in some parts and loose in others. I'm looking ahead through the runners for the first feed station. I intend to take a sponge here to cool me down and to take one at every other station possible. I will create my own rainy conditions.

The course straightens out and there is the feed station ahead on the right hand side. The leaders speed up momentarily to get into a position to grab their bottles. I slacken off a little to keep out of trouble as I am heading for the last tables where the sponges are. I

almost collide with Shorter. He pauses at the first table which holds
the numbered individual bottles of the competitors then runs on
empty handed shouting, "Some bitch pinched my soda!" I grab a
pink sponge from the table, thank God it is a fully loaded one, and
squeeze it over my head, then the rest of it over the back of my neck.

". . . squeeze it over my head . . ."

Hell, I don't feel refreshed, I feel a lot heavier and instead of the
increase of pace I expect, I see the others going further and further
away as if in a nightmare. The other Ethiopian is about 20 yards in
front and he has missed his drink. In a little panicky voice he shouts
"Mamo, Mamo" to his comrade who is 30 yards in front of him and
carrying his own plastic bottle. But Mamo does not hear.

The badly surfaced path twists and turns through the park and the
little brown Ethiopian in the dark green vest and yellow shorts is the
only runner I can see. I just keep going as fast as I can. Across a little
bridge over a stream and the Schloss is ahead. Quite a few people
are here and they are held back from the course by ropes. Right turn
under an archway, across a courtyard, over a cobble stretch a bit
painful to my feet in their thin shoes, sharp left turn then along into
a short street with high buildings on either side. This street curves
right ahead, I can't see anyone. My God, I am running on my own. I
make the turn and there's a refreshment station; Hell that was
quick! I grab another sponge and douse my head, the back of my
neck and wipe my arms. There's a little moisture left in it for my
legs, and I sponge the fronts of my bare thighs and throw the sponge
down.

". . . the back of my neck . . ."

I look up ahead and past the Ethiopian; I see the black figure of Jack Foster not far away. Clayton seems to have been dropped and is coming back. The rest are in a bunch. Well there's hope yet, I just have to keep going, the diet may help over the last few miles. It may give me an advantage.

I push along the wide Maria-Ward Strasse and keep my eyes focused on the ground about 5 yards in front. I'm trying to relax, I am on my own and I'm consciously concentrating on getting the best out of myself even though it's not going right. I use the road, cut the corners. I'm at Maria-Ward Platz again and the course does an acute right turn into Nederlinger Strasse, which bears left into Baldurstrasse. I notice the spot where the car had waited for Dave Bedford and Donny and me on Tuesday. A soldier driving us had been asleep, Christ, that had been a hard session, the last day of the difficult part of the diet and stinking hot. My legs had been drained of energy and I was sweating like a pig in vest and shorts, but there was Dave running in a track suit. Bloody hell, I don't feel any better now. I pass the 15 kilometre check point, I see figures but they don't register and are meaningless, it's position not time that counts today.

Turn right, over a small stretch of cobbles and I recognise the Dante stadium where they held the mini Olympics last year and there is a long straight stretch here. I look up far ahead and there is a lone figure in a white vest and dark shorts, well in the lead. I can't see who it is but I guess that it is Shorter; he must not have been able to hang around any longer at that pace. It suddenly hits me: *I'm not going to win this race.*

225

All that preparation, training, travelling, careful eating, no boozing, special equipment, special diet gone on an inexplicable day like this. Oh no! This was going to have been my day and look at me trailing like a flaming invalid near the back. I don't feel like going on but I know I have to. I know I have to finish. I've got more than half of the race to go with no incentive, but I will never drop out. I'll finish as well up as I can, so bloody well get on with it.

At the end of Dante Strasse more cobbles hurt my feet as I turn right again and follow the tree-lined canal straight down to the Nymphenberg Schloss. This is a difficult part with the road being so straight and me being alone. One of the small electric cars drives in front of me and for an instant I feel cut off from the rest of the race, the way ahead has been blocked. But I'm so far away it doesn't matter. They're wasting their time anyway filming a failure. The other runners I can see some way ahead are on the right hand side of the road, I'm running on the left. I try to use the electric car as a pace-maker but I can't get nearer to the Ethiopian who is next in front of me.

At the bottom of the road I'm in open ground and on cobbles again; there's a sponge station on the right hand side of the left hand bend and I nip across, grab a sponge as quickly and efficiently as possible, then head directly for the next corner and into more built up streets. I shower myself with the sponge and take a bite on it to cleanse my mouth.

"I shower myself with the sponge . . ."

This time it does refresh me a bit. I'm doing all I can to make the passage home easier. The streets look like side streets and I know we are near the 20 kilometre point and a little park with a lovely

". . . the road twisting and turning . . ."

smooth dark road. At 20 km I look at the board, 1 hour 02 mins. 41 secs.; it doesn't mean a thing. There are few people in this park and with the road twisting and turning I keep losing sight of the Ethiopian, but I think I am catching him. At the exit of the park there's a feed station, the Ethiopian loses about 10 seconds here,

". . . every time I catch him he sprints away."

fiddling with his bottle and I almost catch him, but not quite. Thank God, I've got someone to latch on to though, but in the next half mile, in built up streets, every time I catch him he sprints away. Why the hell doesn't he settle down? By using the road better I catch and pass him and he hangs on. Together we turn right, over more cobbles, at Rot-Kreuz Platz into Donnersberger Strasse.

I can see someone up ahead, just jogging; no, he's walking. The first casualty. Christ, it's Gaston, and he's putting on his usual show, holding his left side. I rapidly catch him and say as I go past "Il faut finir, Gaston." I can afford to be generous with my breath at this point as I am out of it. I don't expect to see him again.

At the end of the street there is a left turn, we run under a motorway bridge and left into Marsstrasse, which circles right and puts us left on to Pappenheimstrasse then right on to Brienner Strasse. We seem to be running straight across the very centre of Munich now and it's a long drag. The Ethiopian is running with me and I don't attempt to get away, I am happy to use him. We cross

"The Ethiopian is running with me . . ."

several cobble squares and I search into the distance for the other runners. I can see the white figure of Clayton, well up at the front. He must be coming again. Jack's moved further away. The next in front of us looks like Dave McKenzie, small, long red hair, white vest. Well there's someone in sight.

Lots of people are lining the route now. It's embarrassing. My small figure running pitifully and without honour on the wide area of road between huge historic buildings and monuments. Occasionally someone shouts "Come on, Britain," sometimes in a tone that is complaining. But naturally. I feel sorry.

The electric cars keep popping up to film me and just after 25 km as we cross the road to the left hand side, avoiding the tram lines and spending as little time on the painful cobbles as possible, the little Ethiopian gets inspired by this attention or something and literally sprints away. I can't hang on to that, so I am on my own again.

I make the left turn into Odeon Platz and look up Ludwigstrasse. It's like something out of a Canaletto. Wide with tall regular buildings on either side. I cross immediately to the right to take a sponge, and run up the blue line, unfalteringly marking the course but not always taking the shortest route. I stick to this line here for orientation in such a wide road. There are crowds and crowds of people on either side of the black macadam but they do not shout; they don't know who we are, they are mostly getting a free look at an Olympic event and waiting for the West German runners. They clap as I pass.

Christ, I can hear clapping behind me. Someone else must be catching me, but I don't look round. He's coming up fast.

The interval between rounds of applause gets smaller and smaller and as he draws alongside to my left I see it is Kimihara, his eyes fixed in front and his short legs pattering away at a hell of a lick. I move in right behind the Jap and try to hang on in the hope of

"... it is Kimihara ..."

229

getting nearer to the Ethiopian and McKenzie; Christ, it's like a bloody sprint. I stay there for about 100 yards then my breathing becomes hard and my legs start to hurt, I'm in oxygen debt. Oh, let him go! Another minor defeat . . . so that's another one in front. What the hell. If he keeps that pace going he will get in the first three. Oh, if only I were fresh enough to go with him. At Professor-Huber Platz there is a fountain, and the course jinks down a side street, then runs in a long arc along Königinstrasse. The big park, the English Gardens is on the left with iron railings and green trees and big houses are on the right. Kimihara is already passing McKenzie and I feel like I'm almost walking.

Immediately I enter the English Gardens the road surface changes from smooth asphalt to rough stony track. It hurts my feet and I curse the organisers again, amazed that they have allowed this to remain in the condition that it is in. It's like slotting the back straight of the old White City cinder track at its worst into the synthetic track at the Olympic stadium. How would the track men like that? I calculate that there's less than 10 miles to go and try to reassure myself that this isn't too bad; but I know it's no good. At best I know I'm heading for home, and once I leave the Gardens I'm on familiar ground.

On one straight stretch up between the trees I can still see the Ethiopian and further ahead McKenzie; so they aren't getting away, and miraculously no-one else is passing me. I can't look up again as I have to concentrate on where I'm putting my feet on this disastrous surface.

About ¾ of a mile later the track changes to a rough tarmac which will be the surface right to the end of the Gardens. It looks like it's been laid by hand, it's bumpy with steep cambers in parts and surfaced with small sharp stones. We had complained bitterly about this throughout the week and asked for protests to be made. They said that they had swept it, but at our last inspection it looked like they had sent a mechanical sweeper with a drunken driver over the road, once, to ease their consciences. At the sides of the track it was sometimes 3 in. deep in small stones which gave no purchase and made running very inefficient especially as on a twisting course the runners run from edge to edge taking the inside of the bends to decrease distance. Our subsequent protests had obviously been ignored because it's just the bloody same. So it's a case of head down and cut as much corner as possible.

Just before 30 km I turn a corner and there is the Ethiopian just in front. It's a surprise. He's right there in the middle of the track and practically walking. This time he offers no resistance as I pass him.

The course bears right then swings left under a motorway and then back on to the park road. I catch a glimpse of another runner up ahead, red hair, it's McKenzie, and I'm catching him fast. Christ, this is going to be two passed in less than a mile. I cut all the corners and catch the red-head.

I'm going to say some encouraging remark and look for the face of the New Zealander who I've met with Jack Foster in the village, but it isn't him! I don't know who it is and I'm startled. Hell, scrubbers in front of me now. The unknown warrior hangs on for about 50 yards then the crunch of his shoes on the loose stones slowly dies away. Passing two runners encourages me and although my legs are getting quite tired and my feet are hurting I push myself to try to stride out and consolidate the gains I've just made. Another feed station; I sponge down and feel fresher, the temperature of the day is dropping as it approaches evening and in the trees it's cool. I'm still heading up the park on the snake-like track and I spot another white figure through the trees and surprised again, I keep looking ahead to see who it is. White vest, white shorts, short legs and a white cap. It's Usami; he's blown. My brain chuckles though

". . . I keep looking ahead . . ."

there's nothing funny in his situation, or mine. I watch him as I close in. His head is back a little and he is running slap bang in the middle of the road with no attempt to cut the corners whatsoever. Well, he's a goner. I cross diagonally from the inside of one bend to the next and catch him quickly. As I draw alongside I catch hold of his left hand in my right and shake it, and I say "Good luck, Akio." His eyes are glazed and he half smiles. I leave him.

My pace seems to take up some urgency now. Is it the cooler weather or is it the adrenalin pumping again at having passed three runners?

Just before the top of the park I see another white form disappear round a corner. There's another sponge station and another cleansing cover of cooling water; they seem to come so quickly it's a delight. I turn the corner and see no-one, nor round the next corner. It looked like Clayton, but I can't see anyone now. But, yes, there he is! Big Derek; and he's finally cracked too. I'm going to beat him, but he won't care. It takes me a long time to get with him and this part of the road is the worst being rough and with such big slopes at the sides that I have to run in the centre. It can't be far now to the end of the park. I push and push until I catch the tall Australian. I draw up on his left hand side. He isn't hanging about but he looks knackered. His face is permanently twisted in pain, probably mental and physical. I say to him "Finish it off, Derek. Keep it going." I try to run ahead, but pull away only very slowly. Someone on the grass on the left hand side of the road is crouching holding a stop watch and he shouts in a foreign accent "Go, Hill, you are three minutes down." I turn and shout back to Clayton "Derek, he wants us to bloody well sprint." Derek shouts back, "What?" so I repeat, "He wants us to sprint," but I judge that he probably doesn't find it funny and just try to get away.

"The smooth road feels great . . ."

We have just passed the 35 km point, which is four miles to go. I try to assess how I feel. Well, I will finish but I will have to be careful I haven't taken too much out with passing those four.

There is a human barrier across the road ahead and I look up to see a marshal pointing me right. I'm out of the park and I'm on home ground at last. I've rehearsed this last part and run on it so many times in the last week and memorised it that I feel I'm nearly there.

The smooth road feels great after the grit and gravel of the Gardens, and I drive my legs forward and left into Osterwaldstrasse.

"It's not Bacheler . . ."

There's another runner about 50 yards ahead and he's coming up to a feed station. White string vest, dark blue shorts, could be Bacheler, he's tall. I can't believe my luck with another one to aim at and I'm almost beginning to enjoy it. He stops at the feed station and I'm on him and past him as he messes about picking up a drink and starting up again. It's not Bacheler, it must be one of the Finns. It's a bit disappointing to pass him without being able to use him, but I'm not grumbling. There's a right turn, up a slight hill, a left turn, down a short street then another right turn on to a long road that leads to "The Hill" and the stadium. First this road bears left and I look up to see a group of familiar trees, I drift over to the left hand side and once round the bend look ahead to a square where the road does another jinks. I can see well ahead now and there's another runner about 100 yards away. He's very tall, white vest, navy blue shorts. It must be Bacheler; I might or might not catch him. Crowds are lining the route again, applauding as I pass. Very polite. I've just taken a sponge and feel that I will finish all right and am settling into a nice rhythm when I think I hear some applause behind. Yes. It must be for the Finn. Another 100 yards further on the time between my clapping and the clapping behind diminishes and I think "What the hell is going on?" I glance round and get the shock of my life; there, head on one side, black rimmed spectacles, grimacing face, it's MacGregor. I think "Bloody hell fire, it's Don and I thought I was

". . . it's MacGregor."

moving through." I panic a bit. Hell, what if he should beat me? He can't, I can't let him. I push my pace as hard as I can in the hope of dropping and demoralising him. I run across Bonner Platz like I'm bloody well sprinting and I can see "The Hill" now, and I know the Stadium is near it, but I know that there is a fair way to go yet. I cross Belgradstrasse and Donny has moved closer still. Oh Jesus, my legs are shattered and he's still catching me, it can't be true. What do I do? I look round and sure enough he's still there. Right! I signal with my left hand for him to come alongside and I slow up infinitesimally to let him do so, but not too much. If I can get him to over-exert himself so much the better. I don't know whether I think this or whether it's just an automatic tactic after years of running. We lock in psychologically, and the pace seems to pick up even more, but it isn't me that's speeding it up.

In no time at all we catch Bacheler and pass him. One, two! And we are flying across up to the last new road before cutting through "The Hill". I can see Jack Foster now about 60 yards in front and ahead of him Kimihara but I'm not interested. No. I don't think I'm going to make it. I keep glancing at Donny. He's ungainly but Christ he's travelling, he's like a man possessed. I daren't let him beat me; if he does I'll be the second best Briton. I can't have that. 40 km — I see the clock, 2:09 odd. 2:09 odd! And over a mile to go. Pathetic! Over a mile to go! My legs are stiffening up now and becoming painful. Both legs especially at the tops of the hamstrings. Two old injuries playing up. I can feel my heart straining, hurting and bouncing around like a rubber butterfly inside my chest. Donny won't let up, and I won't let him go. I try to keep him just one quarter stride ahead so I'm not inducing him to go faster, and am fastening myself to him with a piece of invisible steel rope, which won't break. I hope.

"I try to keep him just one quarter stride ahead . . ."

Head across right, cut the corner, I'm on the outside on this bend, I have got to run a yard further and the precious effort is almost enough to finish me. He still seems fresh. I mustn't think about slowing; I've got to hang on.

Jack's closer. I'm on the inside of the bend. Jack's on the outside, he must be tired, he's not thinking. I am, my eyes are wide, all my

1972

concentration is focused on beating Don. I have to. I must. My mouth is wide open dragging air down into my stinging lungs. There's a sponge station on the right. Bugger it. Keep going.

The stadium, the lights. My memory dictates: a right hand bend, round the outside of the stadium, slightly downhill, under a foot-bridge, slight uphill. I'm on the outside now so I drop in almost half behind Don to cut down the radius of the bend and save half a yard, a foot, an inch, anything. It is a slight uphill, but it's like a bloody mountain. There's the tunnel. Downhill. Get right behind him. Christ, he's going faster. Right on to the red synthetic track and a bowl of light.

I hear no sound. I see hurdles on my left, black and white, and I shunt Donny into the lead for the last lap around the track. My right

"... I shunt Donny into the lead for the last lap ..."

leg is beginning to cramp up behind the thigh, it feels tight, painful. Oh, God, please don't let it happen. We are on the back straight and Donny is moving aside, no hurdles, we cut in, use the track. He's moving out to let me in. What the hell for? Gentleman? British? I'm going harder still and start to sprint with 200 metres to go. I'm looking at the shadows on the track. I can see only one. I still see only one as I hit the home straight. I glance back, Donny is 8 yards down, I'm going to do it and I keep on sprinting down the mile long straight and across the line. It's over.

"It's over."

I ache in my stomach, my guts, my legs, my hopes. There are no tears. Just an intense and sickening disappointment.

DESPAIR

1972

RESULT
1. Frank Shorter (U.S.A.) 2:12:20.
2. Karel Lismont (Belgium) 2:14:32.
3. Mamo Wolde (Ethiopia) 2:15:09.
4. Ken Moore (U.S.A.) 2:15:40.
5. Kenji Kimihara (Japan) 2:16:27.
6. Ron Hill (Great Britain) 2:16:31.
7. Don MacGregor (Great Britain) 2:16:35.
8. Jack Foster (New Zealand) 2:16:57.

CHAPTER THIRTEEN

Life would never be the same; but it had to go on.

Mon. Sept. 11th M.   *1½ mile jog in full track suit — it was bloody cold today and raining slightly.*   *1½ mls.*

Mon. Sept. 11th E.   *15 minutes jogging with Steve Hollings — mainly on grass — stiffness not too bad. 2 mls.*

Tues. Sept. 12th M.   *Could only manage 1 mile easy running — one bloke cleaning the grass said, "Olympiad fertig." — gave him the V sign.*   *1 ml.*

We returned home Tuesday, me via Euston station, where I dumped my bags on the platform and ran my second session of the day, fully clothed, 2 miles out to Regents Park and back. I stopped, sweating at a pub outside the station for my first pint of English beer for a month.

I tried to start my car to go to work on Wednesday, the battery was flat. When I eventually got there there was a big banner outside the lab. which said, "Welcome back Ron." They had baked me a huge icing cake and on it was written, "Tokyo, Mexico, Munich — Ron Hill", plus the five Olympic rings. Mr. Ward gave a speech and said, "Courtaulds will continue to support Ron in his running — I think." I got them to add the word "Montreal" to the cake in felt-tip pen; I thanked everyone for their support and apologized to everyone for not winning. I felt very depressed.

"Mr. Ward gave a speech . . ."

Nine days after the Munich race I dreamt that I won the Olympic marathon in a time of 2 hours 14 minutes. It wasn't Munich, it was somewhere quiet, without all the crowds and a morning start. After the race it was found that we had missed a bend in the course and we had to re-run it in the afternoon. I won it again; this time in 2 hours 13 minutes!

I started drinking a fair bit at nights, home brewed beer and my considerable stock of duty free spirits, and for six or seven weeks I smoked a bit too, just out of defiance to a way of life that had cruelly rejected my efforts.

Two weeks after Munich May and I were guests of honour at Clayton-le-Moors Harriers Jubilee Dinner (the club had been formed in 1922) held at the Coronation Hotel near Gisburn. We stayed the night with Harry Smith, a recent convert to running, and his wife Sylvia who lived in Barnoldswick with their daughters, Shaun and Shirley-Ann. From being complete strangers, Harry and Sylvia became two of our best friends. They were down-to-earth, honest Lancashire folk like ourselves. The dinner went off boozily and magnificently. As well as the local runners, many like Stan Bradshaw and Billy Hill from my own early days with Clayton, they had managed to get Bob Beecroft. He still looked youthful, and was a wealthy man now, but he was overweight, smoked and didn't run at all anymore. Despite my recent disastrous performance, I knew whose shoes I preferred to be in!

Clayton-le-Moors Harriers Jubilee Dinner. Stan Bradshaw on my right, Bob Beecroft on my left, Harry Smith top right.

At the beginning of October, Dave Prokop flew me over to Canada for the Springbank Road Races and I stayed in London, Ontario, with Bill Johnstone and his family. I finished 25 seconds down on Frank Shorter and over a minute up on Karel Lismont. I stayed on in Canada, and flew to Montreal to do some technical

Springbank — leading Karel Lismont.

Springbank — 2nd to Frank Shorter.

service work with Courtaulds for four days. I stayed at the Montreal Airport Hilton, which doesn't cater for pauperous pedestrians, and I had to dice with huge cars every time I staggered out for a 2 mile run. I was hosted in Montreal by Clive Knee, a Courtaulds man who like myself had been educated at Accrington Grammar School, and hadn't lost a bit of his Lancashire accent. I think I started him off on a belated running career. I worked hard there, but welcomed the chance of seeing the city which would put on the Olympics in 1976; and I "supped some stuff". A couple of times I had to have a scotch before breakfast to get me on my feet!

241

1972

For the rest of the year my training had no direction; my mileage yo-yoed between 60 and 90 miles per week, I raced in local races, I even won a couple like the K & M 15 miler at Holmfirth, clocking a surprising 75:08, but there was little enthusiasm or hope. I declined an invitation to the Fukuoka marathon. Even on reduced mileage, the training wasn't easy and at the end of November I wrote up one training session:

Mon. Nov. 27th E. *Ran home from work — tried to run fast from 2 miles to 6 miles — was pretty tired — not breathing too well and heart felt tired, as if the altitude training had adversely and permanently affected it.* *7 mls.*

Work progressed in a routine way. I had a new graduate assistant, Peter Newton, so I was able to take on further responsibilities and with Arthur Welham took on technical service for "arachne" fabrics, produced by one of Courtaulds' subsidiaries. This was in addition to my technical service and development work on deep-dye viscose fibres which continued to bring me into contact with friends in other divisions.

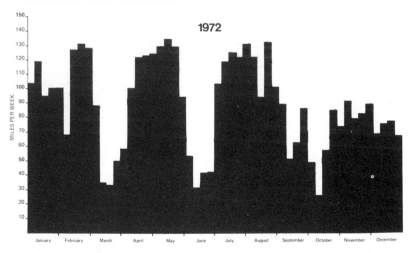

At home we had started looking for another, bigger house. Normally at night I spent an hour or two up a ladder in the freezing loft getting orders together and working on my mail-order running gear business. The rest of the night was spent drinking. I drank so much that it produced the following entry in my diary, following the beery lab. Christmas party and a further session in the King's Head: "went and got changed, Neil followed me, he was in a state of collapse — ran home at 11.45 p.m., did progressive fartlek on the way — left leg pretty sore — was running better than last year — probably because in the last week (in fact since the trauma of Munich) I had a lot of practice in boozing — Bob Charlesworth and Margaret stopped at the Travellers Call to see if I was O.K. — I said, "I've never felt worse — but I'll make it" — got in at 12.45 a.m. — had to knock on the door — May let me in — then there was a row."

After an alcoholic Christmas at home and an equally alcoholic New Year with John and Sheila Briggs at the restaurant they were running at Wrea Green near Blackpool, I tried to gather resolution. By the end of January I was up to 100 miles a week and by mid-February 116 miles a week, bringing cross-country results of 10th in the Lancashire, 5th in the East Lancs. and 11th in the Northern; but

"... 5th in the East Lancs. ..."

"... 11th in the Northern ..."

243

my body wasn't responding and I was feeling tired all the time, especially around my heart. Towards the end of February:

Wed. Feb. 21st. Lun. EMERGENCY REST. Decided on the run to work that more training would do harm — experience from the past — must have been altitude/Olympics — did 3 miles — still felt very tired — weary — lethargic — drained — rather like training at St. Moritz.   *3 mls.*

Just over a week later I finished 30th in the National Cross Country Championships at Parliament Hill Fields and Bolton had second team only 6 points behind Gateshead. Through the whole of March I averaged about 35 miles a week; and carried on drinking a lot and feeling depressed.

On this complete lack of training I went to run the Classical Marathon in Athens, Greece. I needed the break and could do with another look at the course to help me with the autobiography I was determined to get restarted. I enjoyed the trip and the social drinking with a Canadian, Rich Pyne, a Finn, Paavo Hyvonen and Danny McDaid from Ireland. Most of the time the weather was marvellous but on race day we had rain and thick slippery red clay washed off the fields across the road. Colin Kirkham won the race by nearly 2½ minutes from Kimihara, Japan, with 2:16:29, Paavo was 3rd, Doug Schmenk from the U.S.A. was 4th and I was 5th in 2:21:29 just ahead of my old pal, Ismail Akcay of Turkey.

Greece — Paavo Hyvonen, me, and Rich Pyne.

I ticked over until the end of April to try for a good one in the 'Three Peaks', on the "diet". Unluckily I had to run a leg in the National Road Relay at Derby the day before, which was a complete waste of time as Bolton were right at the back. Despite this, on

National Road Relay — Derby.

Sunday I got 7th place in glorious weather and clocked 2:47:04, a personal best time. The day after the race my left foot was sore, near the heel, and gave me a lot of trouble.

May 5th. Egerton Road Relay.   Handing over to Tony Byrne — Bolton won!

Following that race, for the first three weeks of May I tried another build-up and averaged 110 miles a week with interval work and my Tuesday lunchtime sessions of 2 x 440's. This, combined with happenings in other areas of my life, was too much and I had to rest again. I had been having discussions on a new job in Technical Marketing which with my name and experience would have been ideal, and in fact I'd been to Courtaulds' Head Office in Hanover

Square a couple of times to discuss it and to agree a salary, but this seemed to be dying a death. I was given a rise in salary to £3,200, representing about 7%, one of the lowest rises in the lab. that I could find out about. Really encouraging! My athletics was doing great for me; I don't think!

We found a new house; a three bedroomed detached in Gee Cross, Hyde. We moved from Green Lane on May 21st; on May 24th we were driving through France to Spain in the Triumph 1300

". . . we were driving through France . . ."

which was continually overheating. That week I dropped to 53 miles. We were on a camping holiday, on a shoe-string. We had only a six foot hike tent with us, which May and I slept in; Steven and Graham had to sleep on the seats of the car. Nevertheless it was a holiday to remember; we visited Zarous, south of San Sebastian on the Basque coast, where I made contact with a running "aficionado" Jozé Salegui, who owned a bar there. I trained a couple of days in the hills, and once on the beach with the Spanish runner, Maiz. Before we moved on, Jozé treated us to a marvellous meal in his cellar, preceded for me by a few glasses of vino tinto. In the cellar were hundreds of dusty bottles containing a low alcohol cider, produced locally by an 80-year-old man, which we drank with the meal of Basque omelette and steaks grilled over a charcoal fire accompanied by lettuce and raw onion. We talked and enjoyed the good food. Graham, who was nearly eight years old, would have nothing but crisps and Coke.

We drove over to Saluo, on the Mediterranean coast, camping at Lerida on the way, where on a morning training session off the main roads I almost ran into a snake on a dyke. It was green, about three feet long with the front foot erect, poised, seemingly ready to strike. I wasn't arguing, stopping abruptly with an obscenity and running back rapidly to take my chances with cars on the road rather than with reptiles.

When we got rained off at Saluo, I drove towards France, stopping fairly briefly to be fined heavily by the Guardia for arguably crossing the end of a continuous white line across the road, "no overtaking"; passing through the snows of Andorra and on up to Chartres for a couple of days running round before hovercrafting back from Calais to Ramsgate.

After the holiday I tried another build-up through June, 55, 99½, 106, and 95½ miles, with a few track races thrown in. My left foot was painful again, but I was getting fit. On July 1st I got 5th in the Y.M.C.A. 20 Km road race in the time of 60:54, behind Mike Tagg's 60:34, which was very encouraging, and the following

Y.M.C.A. 20K: l. to r., Leeming, Pratt, Domleo, me, Tagg.

weekend I ran the Winsford '7' on the Saturday, winning in a course record time of 31:55, and on Sunday broke the record in the tough Hyde '8' Road Race, with 39:04, beating Alan Blinston by 15 seconds. The Hyde race was one of those occasions I felt I could have run all day; all the power was there, I just had to turn on the tap and the speed increased. I hadn't felt like that in a long time. It was back!

I was now in a position to make my long term plans. I wanted to defend my title in the Commonwealth Games in New Zealand at the end of January 1974. Although I was best Briton in Munich, despite problems, I guessed I would have to run another bloody trial, and that would be the Harlow marathon on October 27th; I needed an eight week build-up to that race, preceded by a four week "rest" commencing August 5th. After the Winsford/Hyde weekend I had only two more races before the "rest"; the Szeged Marathon in Hungary on July 21st and the Lattrig Fell Race at Keswick on August 5th; I averaged about 95 miles a week through this period.

The Szeged race was a quick trip, flying to Budapest on Friday, being driven to Szeged, a majestic old city in southern Hungary, on Saturday morning, racing on Saturday evening, getting back to England on Sunday. I enjoyed almost every minute of it. The race started at 6.00 in the evening. As the weather was hot, the pace was easy and I felt I was only jogging until out in the country Gyula Toth, the Hungarian champion, put in some hard running between 10 and 15 Km.

Szeged ". . . the pace was easy . . ."

". . . "Tempo good" . . ."

We dropped everyone else and by the turn — it was an out and back course — Toth himself was struggling. I kept waiting for him; he kept saying, "Tempo good". It got dark, which made it uneasy running on the none-too-level road surface without street lights, and I began to get alarmed as I started to feel sick at 30 Km. How ironic it would have been for mc to lose to Toth after having waitcd for him for so long. Justice was dune; I left him as we entered the city with just over 1 Km to go and just held off vomiting until I had crossed the line in 2:23:02 and dashed into some nearby bushes. I enjoyed the honest Hungarian hospitality after the race and that of the East Germans as we drank champagne and beer into the early hours.

Although the Lattrig Fell Face on August 5th was something entirely different with its very steep final ascent through the pines and over short sheep-croppcd grass followed by a jarring precipitous descent, I made the prizes in third place behind specialists Harry Walker and Dave Cannon.

For once summer stayed late in England and I enjoyed my "rest". Two weeks at 37 and 57½ miles brought some freshness back. After the first week I was still able to manage a 49:28 10 miles at Worsley for 4th place only 10 seconds behind the winner Alan Blinston with Steve Kenyon second and Steve Edmunds third. After the second week I easily won a grass 5,000 metres in 14:48.7 at the Ashbourne Show on the Saturday, and the next day got 8th place in the

"Weets" Fell Race at Barnoldswick, organised by our friends Harry and Sylvia Smith.

A third week of 65½ miles and May and I were flying out to Belgium for the half-marathon at Geraardsbergen. This time August Daneels had found me a place to stay, the other side of the hill, the thatched Oudenberghof — a lovely restaurant run by Alphonse and Alphonsine. We soon realised that it wasn't in fact a hotel and Alphonse and his wife had given up their bedroom for us. I finished 2nd in the 5 lap evening race, over a new course to the north of the town and starting outside the railway station. The winner by 59 seconds was Gaston Roelants, a runner I always regarded as superior to me over anything below the marathon distance. He was a very versatile man and held an exhibition of over 90 of his oil paintings to coincide with the race. A long way behind me was fellow Englishman Barry Watson. We had a great night after, at the Oudenberghof, knocking back Pils and Trappist beers.

My mother and dad were looking after Steven and Graham in Blackpool and we were free for another week. On Sunday Jozef Lampbrechts, from the cross-country race in Erembodegem, picked us up and took us to his home to stay a couple of days with him, his wife and his daughter Magda. Belgium seemed so different in summer. Jozef toured us a little; to Gazbeek Castle, near which we sampled red Kriek beer, made from cherries; to Aalst for a meal of "moules frites", a huge bowl of mussels each, together with tasty chips the Belgians so adore; and to a restaurant, the "Scheldoord", by a wide misty river, which specialised in eels; I had mine in a tomato sauce; May had hers fried.

DAGBLAD TUBANTIA

Me and May in Enschede.

From Erembodegem, we journeyed by train to Enschede, for the famous marathon in which I had finished 2nd to the Japanese, Mifune, in 1967. I was reluctant to admit that I was only there for a jog, at the end of a short holiday. They were looking for "names" for the race, and it would be experience for me. But after 4 weeks' rest, what could I expect?

Steve Kenyon and Vince Regan had travelled over from Bolton to run the race too, and I said I would run with Steve and try to help him out. Facilities at Enschede are excellent and I had a massage to my legs, in preference to a warm-up. The field looked strong with a number of internationals, including Ziegler and John Vitale of the U.S.A. The weather was scorching.

At the 1.30 p.m. start from the Diekman track I started leisurely, some dust rising from the cinder surface, and slowly pulled Steve through over the cobbled streets surrounding the stadium until we joined the leading bunch. By 5 Km I found myself at the front, but moved aside to let someone else take the pace. We bobbed along in a fluctuating group until suddenly, at 10 Km Donal Walsh of

"We bobbed along in a fluctuating group . . ."

Ireland, wearing number 5 on his green string vest, shot off into the lead and built a huge gap. Well, there was nothing I wanted to do about that; in any case we were running into a head wind. I stayed behind in the main bunch which included Jim Alder (Scotland), Eric Austin (England), Vitale (U.S.A.), Stawiarz (Poland), Mladek (Czechoslovakia), Jonsson and Harkansson (Sweden) and, of course, Steve.

It was a day for sponges. As we approached 20 Km, sweaty runners veered to the right to grab into the buckets at the water station. Steve grabbed and missed and with a groan ran on. I was already five yards past when I saw he hadn't got one, so I ran back, picked out a juicy wet sponge, and sprinted down the road to hand it to him with a, "Be a bit more bloody careful next time." I could afford to be generous as I knew I wasn't going to win. I hadn't even bothered to cut my hair, and was putting on a show with my silver Olympic mesh vest and Union Jack shorts.

Approaching the turn, the crowds were out and loud applause is usually the signal for someone to speed up. First of all it was Eric Austin who cleared off, under the motorway bridge and through the winding cobbled streets of Haaksbergen. Walsh as he passed us on his return journey was miles ahead. Turning at the half marathon marker, the clock showed 1:09; this must have been another signal as Jim Alder, Jonsson and Stawiarz picked up the pace and cleared out. They gained about 10 yards, and as though a magnet was drawing me towards them I slowly began to pull away from Steve; I looked around for him; he was obviously faltering, so with a relaxed effort I eased up to the three in front of me. A couple of kilometres later the Pole faltered too. I overtook him and slotted in behind Jim and Jonsson.

Between 25 and 30 Km, the Swede dropped back, and looking up the road I could see the green figure of Walsh coming back a little. I turned to Jim and said, "You could win this!" He didn't reply immediately. Then just after 30 Km he said, "My body feels O.K.,

"... I felt relaxed ..."

but my legs have gone." He disappeared out of view, out of earshot, and I plodded along at the same pace with the Swede about 20 yards behind me for a while, then passed the exhausted Walsh.

Christ, I had the bloody lead, even though I had slowed with Jim, I felt relaxed and from the sounds of the clapping behind, I was moving away. I just looked at the road, cut the corners and relaxed. It got harder and harder as the stadium approached, but it was mainly a mental effort. My legs didn't get sore, my hamstrings were O.K. I had no cramp. As I turned right for the slight rise to the back of the stadium I risked a glance back down the road. There was no-one in sight! I smiled to myself, slowed down a bit more and relaxed through the crowds, into the short tunnel and on to the black track for the envelope of cheers, right fist raised high and a grin as I broke the tape. I'd bloody won it!

1.   R. Hill — 2:18:05
2.   H. Jonsson — 2:19:05
3.   J. Alder — 2:20:41

"I'd bloody won it!"

On the victory rostrum I received a small silver plated cup, a huge laurel wreath around my neck, and after the anthem an official approached me holding a portable television. Hell, I'd won the telly too! I'd forgotten all about that. As always, nowhere in the race had I thought about the prize; winning, or if not, doing as well as I could had been the motivation, and afterwards the satisfaction. Prizes were a bonus.

Well, well, well. Winning the Enschede at the end of a rest period, on an average of only 56 miles a week. And in 2:18:06, on a hot day, and with very little effort. It made me think. Yes! It made me think that 120 to 130 miles per week perhaps weren't absolutely necessary for good marathon performances.

CHAPTER FOURTEEN

I now had my ideal 8 weeks to build up for the Harlow marathon on October 27th. This was the A.A.A. Championship race, and also the trials for the Commonwealth Games to be held in Christchurch, New Zealand, at the end of January, early February.

The mileage I built up gradually; 80½, 89, 93, 94½, then just topping the 100 for two weeks — 100, 103½, before my taper down week of 74½ miles. Almost all of it was very easy running, probably not much under 7 minutes per mile pace; and it included two speed sessions a week, starting on the third week, with 16 x 70 second bursts with 50 seconds jog interval on the way home from work on Mondays, and my "number stride fartlek" session building up to 55 and down, two sets on Wednesdays.

Before Enschede, I'd had some problems with my left heel being sore; it hadn't bothered me in that marathon itself, but it troubled me occasionally later, especially after a track race at Witton Park, the "Mr Whippy" 5,000 metres, when the morning after the race I could hardly walk at all. This 5,000 metres gave me some problems and led to a headline in the 'Daily Telegraph': "The Loneliness of Ron Hill". I drove all the way to Blackburn on Tuesday night and thought it looked a bit quiet when I got there; no wonder — I was a day early. Annoyed, I trained there, went home and drove back the next evening vowing to claim double petrol money for my troubles. I had a good race, 2nd in 14:22.4 to Ricky Wilde but imagine my disbelief when, despite it being an invitation race, I was told, "No prize and no expenses".

After almost five weeks of training I got a sore throat and cold; but still ran in the Commonwealth Games 10,000 metres trial at Crystal Palace on October 6th. I finished a pathetic 17th; lapped in a thunderstorm by the three placers, Black, Simmons and Ford. This had me worried. What if this had been the marathon trial? As usual, a formality now, I'd asked if I could be excused the trial on the grounds that I'd been the first Briton home in the Olympics despite having a bad run, and two marathon wins in Szeged and Enschede without being anywhere near fit. As usual, a formality now, I was turned down.

But ridiculously the selectors had put out a statement that the first three in the trial would go to Christchurch. Thinking about the chance of a cold or illness on the day, I asked the England team manager for Christchurch why they had been so rigid; they could have said they would select three runners primarily on the results of the trial, but bearing in mind any other circumstances. Would they definitely pick the first three. He said, "Yes."

"O.K.," I said, "what if I am leading the field by a mile, get knocked down by a bicycle following the race, pick myself up and limp in fourth?" "You'd be out of the team," he replied.

The blood rushed to my head, making my ears tingle and my hair bristle. Such was my anger, that all I could muster was, "Well, I can't argue against that," meaning that I would be wasting my time.

The hard race, and it always hurts more when you're having a bad day on an unwell body, left me a tired feeling, especially in my heart, but as the marathon trial approached two reasonable performances in the Lancashire Road Relay at Southport over 3 miles and the National Road Relay Championship, a 3½ mile lap, at Keele University, helping Bolton Harriers to victory, brought my confidence up.

The day of the Keele run I started on the low carbohydrate phase of the "diet" and by Wednesday I was weary and exhausted in training, especially on the uphills. To add to the misery and the worry, I picked up a sore throat.

The mesh vest becomes commercial for Ron Hill Sports Ltd.

GORDON ENTWISTLE

Lancashire Road Relay — Southport.

To blunt the increased confidence of racing well, I had a real downer at work. Ten days before the trial the manager of the lab called me into his office to discuss the fact that a section leader was leaving Droylsden, hence, creating a vacancy. I had seniority over any other candidate, experience with quite a large staff and number of projects, and happy relationships with other divisions in Courtaulds; so it looked good to me.

Five days later Marjorie, one of my junior lab assistants, came to me and said, "Tony Sutton's got the section leader's job." I couldn't believe it; a junior knew before even I did. I stormed into the manager's office and told him that I thought it was bloody poor he hadn't been able to tell me to my face. He didn't seem to think that there was much wrong there, so I asked him how he would have felt if he'd been considered for a major promotion and *I'd* come in to tell *him* he hadn't got it. He may have seen the point.

The Wednesday before the trial my sore throat spread to my chest. I stayed at the Saxon Inn at Harlow Thursday night, for B.B.C. filming on Friday, and Friday night I had a difficult night's sleep as my throat was irritated and I had to keep swallowing all the time. The morning of the race I ran 1½ miles. In my training log I wrote, "throat and sinus possibly worst it's been all week — otherwise legs fine".

A clear, bright, cold day provided ideal conditions for the marathon as some guy called Woodward hared through the first of the two laps of the track in 70 seconds. I set off slowly, there was a long way to go, and was 60 yards behind the leader as we headed out on to the roads.

Very gradually I passed runner after runner, still mentally examining myself, unsure of how I was going to perform. I was sweating at 4 miles; unusual in the cold weather; my throat felt dry and burning, a symptom that I was a bit ill. At 4½ miles I drew up to the leading group led by Don Faircloth. I was surprised, as I hadn't expected to get up there until more like 10 miles. I looked who was in the bunch — Kirkham, Leeming, Boyden, Tagg, Edmunds, Simmons, Johnston, and three unknowns. Unknowns worried me a

"... the bunch ..." Hurd (281), Kirkham (53), Hill (26), Thompson (partly hidden), Johnston (157), Leeming.

bit — what the hell were they doing up there? One of these was Mick Hurd, a good runner whose results I'd read in Athletics Weekly, but never actually seen.

By 11 miles I was drifting up to the lead and occasionally had to tell Faircloth and Hurd to cut the corners and use the road. Shortly after 11 miles, Harry Leeming fell down. There was a momentary scuffle and a few leaps to avoid the tumbling figure and I winced at the thought of white skin on the rough chippings on the road at that particular point; but on we ran, less one.

At 16 miles we had completed one small loop and one big lap and there was a big lap remaining. As we started on this, I grabbed a sponge and squeezed it on my head. I wished I hadn't; it was too cold and my hands felt frozen and uncomfortable for a long way. Otherwise I was cruising along. At 17 miles Don Faircloth suddenly dived off into the bushes; I didn't see him again; and at 18 miles up a longish hill through parkland, one of the unknowns in a yellow vest put in a long burst. "Who the bloody hell's that?" I thought, responding with an equal increase in speed, but only for about 400 yards when I thought, "Hey, this is a marathon, I'll see you later," and let him get away. I could hear the heavy footfalls of Colin Kirkham drawing closer, clop, clop, as he tried to catch me; from the sounds I heard, he only got within 5 or 10 yards and after 20 miles the sounds of his footsteps grew quickly fainter. I could see the yellow vested unknown about 150 yards up front and could hear the cries of, "C'mon, Ian." "Ian who?" I thought.

At 22 miles I was comfortably second. "I only need to qualify," I told myself. I had just passed a big round-about, and looked back in curiosity to see Colin Kirkham making the left hand turn; I waved my hand high to him. This was easy. I was having a good time.

A few yards down the road I passed someone I took to be the unknown's coach who said, "Give our man a tow when you pass him."

I didn't bloody well pass him; in fact he increased his lead over me at the end. I ran through the tape, undistressed, my two hands held out palm up in a silent disappointed question"Why did you make me run a trial again?" and jogged easily a lap of the track for a warm down.

That unknown? Ian Thompson, Luton A.C., 1st, 2:12:40; R. Hill, 2nd, 2:13:22; C. Kirkham, 3rd, 2:15:25.

Well, I had my Commonwealth Games place and an easy 2:13:22. I was back!

Training for the Christchurch marathon hardly needed thinking about. Four weeks rest, and a steady nine weeks build-up would see me in top form, although it seemed unusual to be peaking for a marathon at the end of January.

Selection for England brought added conflict at work. I was fed-up enough to write of the lab., "Bloody cheesed off with the place," before I was told that I may have to consider taking some of my holidays for the time in New Zealand. I gave my point of view, that it was hard on my family to take away *their* holidays for me to represent my country, and we were supposed to have an agreement on the "Big Games". That view was considered, and I was told that I *had* to take a week of my holiday entitlement. I was furious and wrote in my diary, "I've finished with Courtaulds now."

During my "rest" I averaged 50 miles per week, easy running. Half way through, I ran the Waterloo Road Race and had a pretty scarey experience there. Unfitness had caught up with me quickly, and I was having to push it very hard to stay with the leaders Steve Kenyon and Laurie Reilly of Sale Harriers. I was still third at the roundabout with just over a mile to go, but getting pretty tired and holding my head back to gulp down air. Just as we swung right, my heart seemed to stop beating and my head felt like it was swelling. I thought I would collapse, eased up to 6th, but ran through it to finally outsprint Tony Byrne for 5th place. Even the next day my heart felt peculiar.

I ran a couple of cross-country races in the Red Rose League; I regarded these as excellent training for the marathon. Running is running, whatever the surface, and I could never push myself as hard in training sessions as I could in a race. One race I didn't quite make however, was the Harry Whitehurst Memorial race in Sheffield. We set off in good time but by mistake I got on the Barnsley road and had to turn back. Hitting Sheffield, we got hopelessly held up in football match traffic; and once free of all this I couldn't find Graves Park; as usual. Just as we pulled up at the pavilion, after a round tour of the city, I heard the bang of a gun and knew I had just missed the start; I could have cried, but did a ten mile training run instead.

The job I made of my next race was not much better. I flew to Belgium, to Erembodegem, with a new Bolton clubmate, John Harrison. It was a typical Belgian start, elbows, in the rain, the field creeping forward before the gun over the muddy tangled grass, then a mad dash. After only 100 metres there was a left turn and a bottle neck; half-a-dozen runners fell down, I had to walk, hands held forward, pushed from behind, whilst the leaders raced away. I never got used to those Continental starts. Eventually I finished 11th, John 15th.

The highlight of the trip was a visit to Remy's new house. Remy was the town's fire-chief but his business was wholesaling beers and wines. He liked a drink himself; to say the least. We had visited him in the summer, when he lived in the centre of the town in one of those old Belgian rows of houses with tall doors, facing right on to the street. The new house was next door to his warehouse, not far from the cross-country course, and Remy gave me a full case of French wines to bring back, each a different variety.

On and off since April, possibly since the Three Peaks race, my left foot, especially the heel, had been sore. Sometimes it was worse than others; occasionally it was so sore I could hardly stand when I got out of bed; but that hadn't prevented me from putting in some good performances, especially the 2:13:22 at Harlow, so I was just grinning and bearing it.

Christmas came up with a full complement of training, but I was still able to make merry and just suffer one or two extra long hangovery runs. The lab. party went off with a bigger bang than usual for me. I think someone had doctored my beer with spirits. In the 'King's Head', after the festivities in the works canteen were over. I couldn't even sup a full pint. Neil Shuttleworth "ran" home with me that night. It took 1½ hours to travel the six miles and I had to force myself to run 30 strides, then stagger 30 strides; I fell down once and kept colliding with garden walls. I got up in the middle of the night to go to the toilet. It was dark and I screwed up my eyes to see the time on my watch. I was sure it said 2.30 a.m., but it couldn't have done because when I finally surfaced in the morning I discovered that somehow on the way home I had smashed the watch glass and there was only one bent finger left on the face! Happy days!

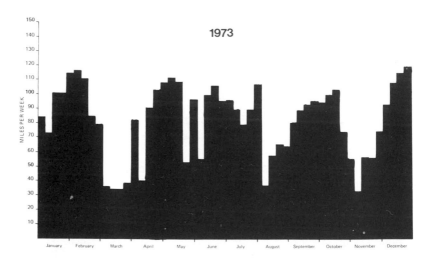

Christmas itself didn't go off without incident. On December 23rd we had a new shag carpet fitted in the lounge. The night after, Christmas Eve, I was fixing a Christmas tree in the far corner of the room when I found the carpet deep in water. The fitter had knocked a nail right into a central heating pipe. Water was gently jetting out. Have you ever tried to find a plumber on Christmas Eve? Thankfully, a good Samaritan by the name of Jim Clee, a craftsman in Gee Cross, answered our phone call and with the agreement of his wife, came up, drained the whole system, dug up the pipe, and replaced the punctured section. Neil came and stayed over Christmas and trained with me for three days, but my foot wasn't much fun:

Fri. Dec. 28th M.   *7½ mile course — easy running (10.00 a.m.) — not too bad but left foot is extremely sore now — stress fracture?*   *7½ mls.*

The pain wasn't stopping me training; I was clocking around 115 miles a week, but combined with cold, wet weather and the dark it was making me pretty miserable. Also the whole country was in the throes of an oil crisis and at work there was no heating. The sunshine of New Zealand and some physiotherapy out there would surely cure my troubles?

My position in the Christchurch Commonwealth Games marathon was a shock beyond my worst nightmares.

The journey out was very long; thank God it was a Boeing 747; and it was tricky fitting in my twice a day training:

Thur. Jan. 10th M.   *BAHRAIN — jog round the airport lounge with Brendan Foster, Tony Simmons, Dave Black and Colin Kirkham — 17-18 mins. — foot got sore at the end — right leg cracking a bit.*   *2½ mls.*

Fri. Jan. 11th M.   *SINGAPORE — had to jog round a very confined space in the airport lounge — wouldn't let us out at all. P.M. of Japan arriving — 14 mins. with Colin Kirkham — warm — sweating a good bit.*   *2 mls.*

Fri. Jan. 11th N.   *MELBOURNE — 2 miles in a long, shiny-tiled corridor with a little bit of carpet and downhill at the end.*   *2 mls.*

A Maori band rattled our senses as we climbed out of the jet and on to coaches to the Games Village, the University of Canterbury's Halls of Residence at 11 a.m., just east of the city centre. Our block was on the perimeter of the campus. I was on the third floor, room 53, shared with Colin Kirkham, the bunk above me, and Ian Thompson top bunk opposite, Tony Simmons below. Colin's wife, Ann, was in Christchurch too, and I didn't see much of Colin. In fact, in the whole three weeks before the race I never saw him run once. Ian kept very much to himself and hardly ever said a word.

The Games Village.

Tony palled around with the 5,000/10,000 boys and my mate most of the time was Steve Hollings, the steeplechaser.

It was the coldest New Zealand summer for about 35 years, race day was good for the marathon men. Training went well for me out there, apart from my heel, and the fourth day after arrival I clocked 57.5 and 57.2 for my two x 400's, on a grass track. I had treatment on my heel, ultrasonic, massage, heel pads, butazolidene tablets, and was almost personally looked after by Dr. Frank Newton, an ex-Manchester University Cross-Country Club man; but no-one seemed to know the exact problem, or best treatment, and it didn't improve.

My training sessions were planned exactly. The race was on Thursday, January 31st; I called that a "Sunday", calculated back over seven day cycles, and two weeks before the race I ran 20 miles on the marathon course; I felt so good that I was having to hold myself back.

I had one race 12 days before the marathon, a 5,000 metres down at Timaru. I ran only about 14:40, and wasn't too worried about that as I had been roasting in the sun right up to the race, but I was surprised when I couldn't flatten "wee Donnie" MacGregor on the sprint and we dead-heated. He says he thought he beat me, but I reckon I "dipped" him at the line!

The day following Timaru, I had my one major sight-seeing trip of the visit. It was a Sunday, a genuine Sunday. I had met a bloke called John Mills who I had known as a constant supporter of Sutton

Touring — Ian Thompson, me, John Mills, Steve Hollings.

Harriers and a regular spectator at U.K. races in the 60's, and who had emigrated to New Zealand, in fact to Christchurch. He offered to drive me in his VW Beetle to see Mt. Cooke. Naturally Steve Hollings came along and I invited Ian Thompson as he seemed to be on his own all the time. We were up at 5.40 a.m.; Ian and I went out for a run:

Sun. Jan. 29th M: 5 mile course with Ian Thompson — foot extremely sore at first — then picked up later — pace picked up too!   5 mls.

It was a marvellous drive; cloudless skies all the way, some tarmac roads, some dusty dirt roads, around Lake Tekapo, a beautiful blue-green colour, and Lake Pukaki, to climb for a beautiful view of the rugged snow covered peaks.

On the way back we had another run with Steve joining us. Immediately the pace seemed too fast for my sore foot, so I stopped to pretend to tie a shoe lace, let them gallop away, and then ran at my own pace for 5 miles.

By the time race day approached, I was getting pretty homesick, and the regular letters from May only seemed to make things worse, especially the little notes from Steven, now 10 years old, and Graham, eight: "Good Luck, Love Graham   XXXXX"

"I have just started to do the dishes for twopence a week. P.S. Wish you good luck. Love Steven   XXXXX".

I wanted to get the race over with and get back home. I was ready

Old mates reunite — John Farrington, me, Jack Foster, John Robinson, Terry Manners.

My weight was down. The day before the race my pulse was a low 42. I wrote the following "reflections":

I felt O.K. when I went out in the morning. At lunchtime I went out in just shorts, the sky was clear blue and the sun belted down. I felt like my legs were swollen with glycogen, almost like balloons. I felt really good, stepping high and wanted to jump to head leaves and put in little bursts. The only problem I've had has been preventing myself from eating too much and suffering the effects.

Yesterday I came in the room and Ian Thompson was shaving the hairs off his legs with a safety razor. It doesn't take him long to learn.

I gave my legs a final polish at the front with my shaver.

Today was hot, reaching 30 deg. C and it was still hot at 5.00 p.m. But at 6.45 p.m. it had clouded over and there was a blustery wind blowing which would give more or less a following wind on the way out in the race. This suggests that if I feel all right I should go out and run my own race completely and forget about the wind on the way back.

Farrington (Australia) thinks Drayton (Canada) will be a tiger. Drayton has been quiet and pretty surly. He doesn't mix. He runs with no vest. He looked a bit stiff legged when I saw him at 6.00 p.m.

Armstrong (Canada) seems to have trained himself into the deck. Seems to run a bit with a limp. Trains hard in the morning — even this morning! — round the little track on the grass on the route to the dining room.

Colin Kirkham has been elusive. I haven't seen him run once. He is doing the "diet" for the first time.

Ian is on the "diet". Studies a lot.

MacGregor seems ebullient but seems a bit stiff-legged lately.

I don't know what to expect. Apart from my painful foot, I've never felt better before a race!

The 1973 Commonwealth rankings were: John Farrington (Australia) 2:11:12; Derek Clayton (Australia) 2:12:07; Ian Thompson (England) 2:12:40; Ron Hill (England) 2:13:22.

Race day was cool. I jogged 1½ miles in the morning. felt O.K., and spent most of the time in our room until at 3.30 p.m. we left for the stadium at Queen Elizabeth II Park by special car. On the grass outside I ran a gentle half-mile in my special gold coloured lightweight racing shoes. Stan Bradshaw was there to wish me luck. How did I feel? I felt all right.

I had given Ian Thompson one of the special mesh marathon vests I was having made; but I myself was going one better with a backless, halter neck style, giving complete exposure to the skin at the back. My latest creation! Union Jack shorts completed my costume. I certainly stood out; but the gear was right and I wouldn't be around on the course too long.

The referee kept us under strict supervision before we went out on to the red synthetic track and we each had to have a red line

Ian Thompson (22), Jack Foster (59), Terry Manners (51), Bernie Plain (16).

drawn on our numbers, presumably to prevent a repeat of the incident in Munich where an imposter preceded Frank Shorter into the stadium and through the finish.

From the start the pace was fast; ignoring two hares who shot round the track and out of the stadium, Ian Thompson got right up there leading a big bunch of runners. I was just on the back of the pack at 5 Km, 15:12, and feeling it was perhaps too rapid a pace I eased back a little and by 10 Km I was 10 seconds adrift in 30:25. Still, quite fast, and many if not all of them up there must surely die. I was running with Malcolm Thomas (Wales) and we hit a good pace passing the first of the dropped runners, Brian Armstrong and Don MacGregor.

I felt full in my stomach and at 15 Km began to feel unrelaxed, strained and to make things worse, Thomas started to move away from me. At 17 Km my foot started to hurt. I expected that; and I expected the excitement of the competition would remove the pain from my consciousness. But footsteps . . . and Don MacGregor had passed me. "On you go, Donnie." Hopefully I would settle, come right and start to motor again. At 11 miles I passed Derek Clayton and pressed on towards the turn.

Blimey, Ian Thompson had a good lead coming down the other side of the dead straight Memorial Avenue, and Jack Foster was well out on his own chasing him. Bloody hell! Jack at 41!

My foot was getting more sore, another Australian, Brenton Norman, was just behind me at the turn and to crown it all I started to have guts trouble and had to leave the road and dive into a garage for a quick pit stop.

I got into action again to find Derek Clayton back in front of me. Suddenly at 15 miles he ran off the road and stopped. "Keep it going, Derek," I called. "No, no, Hilly," he replied, "I'm finished."

Now I was on my own and the pain in my foot was getting more and more severe; I tried running on my toes on that foot, any way to lessen the hurt; it wouldn't go, I could do nothing to avoid it.

As I limped into Hagley Park, a red vested runner, Cowell, of the Isle of Man passed me. This was a nightmare. At 17½ miles a black runner strode past. Disaster. Disaster.

On the windy road by the River Avon I saw a runner on the grass between the road and the water, bending to touch his toes; it was Drayton. I shouted up to him, "C'mon, Jerry, get back on the bloody road and finish this off." "C'mon, run with me," I ordered We ran together, making terse conversation between 21 and 23 miles, and Mike Teer from Northern Ireland passed us. Mike took nearly 3 minutes out of me in the last 3 miles.

I was hardly running now, I was limping so badly, and told

Drayton to go on and leave me. He could finish easily now. Slowly I dropped behind and plodded on sad, embarrassed, in my flash gear. Polite claps, and from one group, "Go on you Pommie bastard." I saw red.

"... in my flash gear."

"Down the lonely road ..."

Down the lonely road and left turn into the stadium. The event had finished ages ago. For me it was a matter of stubbornly completing the distance, it was no longer a race. I limped over the line. I could hardly stand. Ted Chappell lent me a shoulder and I walked awkwardly towards the tunnel. Just before going down I glanced at the illuminated score board: "Ian Thompson, England, 2:09:12." Not only had he taken my title, I thought bitterly, he had got my record as well.

1974

1. I. Thompson (England) 2:09:12
2. J. Foster (New Zealand) 2:11:18.6
3. R. Mabuza (Swaziland) 2:12:54.4
4. T. Manners (New Zealand) 2:12:58.6
   :
18. R. Hill (England) 2:30:24.2

Friday my ankle swelled up like a balloon.

Fri. Feb. 1st M.   *Did a half-mile very limping jog on the grass*
track — was really bad — foot killing me and
swollen.   ½ *mile*

Frank Newton took me to hospital to have my foot X-rayed. Nothing was broken but there was a shadowy spur projection from the heelbone, towards the front of my foot.

Fri. Feb. 1st A.   *NEW BRIGHTON BEACH — hobbled and*
jogged about 1 mile on the water's edge in bare
feet — the walk back was really painful.
1 mile

I remember standing on the beach at the end of the one mile jog, head aching and sick with pain, thinking, "How the hell am I going to get back there?"

There was a final bitter pill to swallow, on landing in London; unluckily I got off the plane just behind Ian Thompson, and the cameras were all flashing at him.

Trevor Wright was there to meet his wife, Rosemary. He held out his hand and said to me, "I'll congratulate you, if no-one else will."

It was a painful start to what was to be a painful year in more ways than one.

CHAPTER FIFTEEN

For many people I suppose it would have seemed the end. Failure in the race plus a cripplingly painful injury. For me it was an obstacle. I would never retire. I would stop running the day I died. And as far as International competition was concerned, I would stay at the top as long as I could. I never wanted to reach a stage in my life where I would look back and say, "If only I'd . . ." I was going to do it, and what I didn't achieve wouldn't be through lack of trying.

Optimistically I looked ahead. The European Championships in Rome were early in September, and the trial for the places in the marathon team would take place on June 15th, the Polytechnic Marathon now on the roads around Windsor.

There was no doubt about "resting" after Christchurch; it was enforced, I just couldn't run. For five miserable winter weeks all I could do were limping one mile sessions on surfaces where I could see where my foot was going down. Anything more awkward and I nearly passed out with pain. I used these "runs" as a barometer of progress; the barometer stayed permanently low for nearly five weeks. I wrote in my training log:

"Foot sore as usual" — "foot sore" — "foot not good" — "foot as bad as ever" — "foot sore but better than three weeks ago" — "foot pretty sore".

I was puzzled by this lack of improvement.

I started to cycle to and from work to maintain some level of fitness, but after the beginning of March I decided I'd had enough of 1 mile sessions, my weight was up to 9 stone 12½ pounds, and I commenced running some 2's and 3's for three weeks, a couple of times throwing in long runs of 5 miles. There was a marginal change for the better; "foot improving," I wrote.

Sun. Mar. 17th M.   *2½ mile course — easy running — tried a couple of bursts — was very unfit — heel still sore, but bloody murder when I first got up. 2½ mls.*

"Heel static" — "foot reasonably comfortable" — "foot mediocre", my log continued.

My first race, 8 weeks after Christchurch was the Burtonwood Road Relay. Politely I was given a place in the Bolton 'B' team, and struggled round with an unfamiliar breathlessness and uncontrollable legs which I suppose is called "unfitness". I clocked 19:01 for 101st fastest time out of 220 runners, but that day began the real road to complete recovery. I'd been having regular treatment from a physiotherapist in Ashton-under-Lyne, Alan Bonnelle, micro-wave, interferontiometer and infra-red, and indeed continued this for another six weeks, but all of it produced no dramatic healing.

After the race, standing getting changed in the school before getting my running gear out to sell, one of my club mates, Denis Leigh said, "What's been up with you?" I described all the symptoms, and he said, "Oh! I had that. I went up to Bolton Infirmary, they built me a big arch support and almost straight away afterwards the heel got better." The theory was that tendons run from the heel bone, over the arch to the front of the foot. If the arch flattens the tendons become taut and can begin to tear off the bottom of the heel, leading to pain and in prolonged and severe cases ossification at the tear, forming a heel "spur". Now, if the arch is supported, the tendon can relax and start to mend.

As soon as I got home I built up a big arch support for my left shoe. The next day when I went out to run — "foot felt reasonably comfortable". That week I started to run to work and back and clocked up 55 miles. The next week I ran 72½ miles and with a careful run in the Rivington Pike Fell race, produced 18:42 and 16th place. I was pleased. There were still 9 weeks to go to the Poly marathon. I reckoned I could do it. I had my hair cut very short and shaved off my moustache; I looked a right idiot, but I was determined to make that team.

After two more weeks of 71½ and 87 miles, I tackled the 'Three Peaks' and sadly that gave me another setback. It was a wild and windy day, snowing on the tops and misty. I just wanted to train, was well wrapped up complete with wet top, and set off dead last out of the field to enjoy passing and chatting with people. At the 2nd checkpoint in Horton-in-Ribblesdale I was about 60th and took a cup of Accolade from my dad. I held my position over Penyghent but, being unsure of my foot and running rather awkwardly, fell on the steeply descending rocky track, cutting my left hand and some-how numbing the whole of my right side. Two runners helped me to my feet and I continued more slowly and carefully. On the road to Ribblehead I moved through to 50th, threw my gloves to my dad and headed for the last peak. I died on Whernside. As I hit the first rise I got a grabbing cramp on the insides of both thighs, started to walk and never ran again until after the summit. On the final slopes I was on all fours, kneeling and stopping frequently in freezing snow and dense mist. Runners crawled past me; one gave me two lemon flavoured glucose tablets which I gobbled down. My foot had grown so sore that even after the summit I had no running left in me and I was continually passed down the hill until I thankfully stepped over the finish line 125th.

I got over the exhaustion of that day within a week and the following Sunday took 20th place in the Michelin 15 Km road race at Stoke-on-Trent. I was delighted with that. However, two days later I got up out of bed to feel terrible pains down my right side. I could hardly run, I felt as though I was winded and was literally gasping with the pain. I couldn't cough, laugh, sniff, or breathe deeply. If I did I got a huge spasm of intense pain across my ribs and back. I went up to Ashton Hospital, an Indian or Pakistani doctor examined me, and told me to come back in a week if there was no improvement. Marvellous! I took the law into my own hands, went into the physiotherapy department, armed with Alan Bonnelle's name and a nurse there said I'd probably cracked a rib, and strapped up my chest.

I had to hold myself ultra-steady when training to and from work, but my thighs and knees started to hurt because of the weird style I was adopting. Naturally both my stride and breathing were affected in the Altrincham '10' that weekend. All I could produce was 20th place in 51:18, 4 minutes behind winner Mike Baxter. Gradually the problem cleared, and I trained 105½ and 116 miles weeks. We decided on a simple camping holiday that year, starting with a couple of races, the Newport '15' on May 25th, and the Yeovil '10' on May 27th, and then spending two weeks in Cornwall to get some heat training in case it turned hot on the day of the "Poly".

We sold the dark turquoise Triumph 1,500, which we could not stop overheating, and bought a brown Ford Granada automatic, again at "book value", from a dyestuffs company. This made driving with a family of four a lot easier.

Friday night we drove down to Newport in Wales and stayed with the mother and father of Bob Sercombe, a good Welsh road runner. I took Bob out for a five mile run in the morning and in the afternoon he ran away from me in the 15 mile road race clocking 73:18, with Atkinson (Cardiff) 2nd. I had a comfortable race, joining Cavin Woodward in 3rd place at 6½ miles. We went through 10 miles in 49:48 and with the Yeovil '10' only two days later, I was content to sit on him and wait for the sprint. I was so easy as we approached the finish and the adrenalin started to flow as we came to the school gates. As soon as we turned I would go. I was right behind him. We turned left, I was ready to pounce . . . and someone said, "That's it, well done Cavin." The race was over; the gates were the finish and I thought we would have at least 50 yards to go once we turned. Always check you know exactly where the finish is before you start a race!

Motoring south we camped at the hamlet of Littleton Pannell and the next day via Stonehenge and Camelot we drove to Yeovil where

". . . we camped at . . . Littleton Pannell . . ."

Tom and June Barber were our hosts for a couple of days. It was a hot day for the 10 mile road race organised by local man John Flatters and I was happy to hang back before taking the lead at 2½ miles, striding away along the quiet roads, amidst leafy hedgerows, and banks of wild flowers to win by over a minute from Popel of Westbury in 50:38.

Unfortunately that was the end of my heat acclimatization. We

"We 'did' Lands End . . ."

drove to St. Ives and camped in what would have been great training country with cliff paths, lanes and hills, deserted tin mine buildings adding an exciting eeriness to the landscape. But wind, rain, cold and drunken yobboes returning to the camp site late at night spoiled it all.

We switched to the other side of the peninsula. A quiet site at Praa Sands. Equally good for training, but equally cold. On Sunday, after listening to the foghorns of ships in the English Channel penetrating the cold grey mist outside our tent, we decided to move. Perhaps inland we would catch the sun. We "did" Lands End to say we had been there, we couldn't see much, headed toward Torquay still with bad weather and finally voted to return home, bombing it all the way back to Gee Cross.

Heat acclimatization would have been useful as the day of the "Poly" turned out hot. I took Steve Kenyon down Friday night, and we stayed at a bed and breakfast in Windsor. In spite of my setbacks I was as prepared as I could be. I'd been on the diet until Thursday and had no present injuries.

The start was at 2.15 p.m. and the skies were cloudless, the sun beating down. I decided to be cautious, but Usami and another Japanese runner, Hamada, rushed off down the Long Walk, completely ignoring the heat. A second large group of runners formed behind these two, and a hundred yards further back I ran with a smaller group, running carefully up the hills to try to save energy and stay cool. I was sweating a lot. Gradually runners dropped off the front bunch and, with Keith Angus and Steve Kenyon striding like dual shadows behind me, I picked them off. I took a sponge at 8 miles. We were pulling the main bunch back. Between 9 and 10 miles Steve complained, "My foot." I looked down and saw blood on his shoes. He dropped out. At 11 miles I took another sponge; Angus was still with me and we had almost caught the big pack ahead. At about 12½ miles we latched on to the tail end, and I was looking forward to sitting in for a while. I was feeling good.

Just as I settled in at the back, Lesse of East Germany put in a burst and broke up the whole group. Bob Sercombe went off the back as did I, and we struggled on with Jim Alder just in front. I was looking for a refreshing sponge at 14 miles; I expected it; at 14 there was nothing. Psychologically it was a terrible blow, especially as the bunch was moving away, and involuntarily I slowed. Jim began to move away, then Bob Sercombe passed me and left me helpless. Now alone, I began to suffer; at 16 miles even my arms were getting tired and I honestly didn't know how I was going to finish. I plodded on. Never since the 1968 marathon trial had I taken a drink in a race, but at 18 miles I grabbed a carton of orange juice with a straw and

273

snatched up a sponge. I was desperate. With the water on my body and the fluid inside me I immediately began to pick up the pace and moved through steadily until the end, passing Jim Alder at 21 miles, Hamada a little further on, Colin Kirkham, who looked dead, at 25 miles, and finally Tim Johnston with a sprint on the track. At the end I was full of power; no cramp, no stiffness.

Only two places on the British team were going. After all my personally futile campaigning for exemption from trials, they had picked Ian Thompson for Rome in advance. Usami had won the race brilliantly in 2:15:16 with Bernie Plain (Cardiff) 2nd in 2:18:32; that was one place gone. 3rd was Lesse (G.D.R.) 2:18:44; 4th Bob Sercombe 2:19:52; 5th Keith Angus 2:20:20; myself 6th 2:21:36.

Controversially, Bob Sercombe and Colin Kirkham in 8th position were disqualified for allegedly cutting corners. That would have given me 3rd in the A.A.A. championships, but I refused to go up for my prize and medal. Everyone had had to cut corners at some stage in the race.

There might be a chance of being selected for Rome on that run, I thought; after all I had a good record, I had only just recovered from a bad injury which in Christchurch had led to my only finish time outside 2 hours 30 minutes, a cracked rib had delayed my return to form and I was obviously improving all the time. Surely they wouldn't take a runner to the European with a personal best of only 2:19:52, with all due respect to Bob Sercombe?

I had momentarily forgotten that in the marathon the selectors didn't select; how could they without the relevant recent and historic information on all top runners' performances? They merely rubber stamped the results of the trial.

It was the first time I'd been out of a major Games team since 1962. I had to come to terms with that.

The Montreal Olympics were a long way ahead. 1976. I would make the team there; meanwhile, there was really no point in making any short term plans for training; I would just live from race to race, the next notable one being a return to Szeged in Hungary on July 20th, five weeks ahead. In between I trained around 75 miles a week, raced locally, trying hard, getting nowhere, and becoming very depressed with running. Two weeks after the "Poly" I raced the Y.M.C.A. 20 Km road race, I was 6th and my race account states: "set off determined to win" and finishes: "heart felt knackered after slowing — fluttering a bit — the run was an awful shock to me — I feel that I'm more of less finished — if that's all I can do for 20 Km (61:51), what about marathon? — just nothing there — not flowing, no spring of years ago — just graft — nothing from the word go — this could be it at 35 years old."

Exactly one year after my two record breaking runs at the Winsford '7', Saturday and the Hyde '8', Sunday, I ran the double again. Winsford I was 2nd to Ricky Wilde with 32:30, 30 seconds slower than the year before, and Hyde, I was 4th, 2 min. 35 seconds slower than previously with 41:39. I was tired, weary, and troubled with lower back pain; so the week before Szeged I tapered down to only 51½ miles.

The trip was the rather ludicrous one runner plus team manager situation. There was some kind of rule about it. Very often the team

Hyde '8' — 4th.

manager was superfluous to requirement, occasionally a downright nuisance. For instance on this occasion my manager was a retired school master. We jetted to Budapest and after a night in the Spartaka sports club where we had to share a room, we went south by bus with the other international runners, Swiss, East Germans, Czechs, stopping halfway at Kecskenet for strong coffee. We were staying at the grand Tisza Hotel again, but this year we were given a shared room. I collared the bearded young Tomash, one of our interpreters and told him I wanted single rooms. He fixed it and two keys were placed on the counter of reception. I picked up one, 207, and set out to find the room; up two broad flights of mirrored stairs, up again a further two flights to the second floor, turn right, to the end of the corridor, right again and way down the end of that corridor, on the left, was 207. I let myself in. Bloody hell! No bathroom or shower or toilet as I'd had last year. I was sometimes bad with my guts after a hard distance race and a toilet in the room was a big advantage; also I liked to soak in a hot bath after the race. Anyway, hiking miles backwards and forwards to the room before the race wasn't going to do me much good either.

I dumped my bag and went downstairs. The team manager was there and I told him the whole tale. Do you know what his reaction was? He laughed and said, "Oh! I've got a smashing room, just round the corner here, with bathroom, toilet, the lot. Luck of the draw," he said. I was flabbergasted.

1974

The sun was casting long shadows across the cobbled boulevards in Szeged as we lined up for the 6.00 p.m. start. It would be dark when we finished. My stomach was trembling with nerves, I kicked my legs out restlessly, anxious to be on the way. There was no obvious reason for such tension; it was just another international race. But perhaps subconsciously I wanted to run a really good time to show the so-called selectors they were wrong in not picking me for Rome.

When the gun went, I shot straight into the lead. Around the wide streets and then through the narrow corridor between all the market stalls alongside the twin spired church and out on to the open road, I felt I was moving well and fast. There was only one set of footsteps behind me. That would be Gyula Toth. I strode down the country roads, 5 Km in 15:20, 10 Km in 31:00. I took a sponge, I was really motoring; 15 Km in 46:45, still the footsteps were behind me; I couldn't shake off my pursuer. Then, hell! He started to come alongside! The hard fast pace was starting to get to me; my legs were getting tired. If only I could get away, I knew my spirit would be lifted. Just before 20 Km the figure right beside me started to move ahead and pull away. I looked hard at him. It wasn't Toth. I had a shock. It was the Swiss guy. Who the hell was he? The Swiss didn't have any marathon runners. Why hadn't I taken more note of his best time and other details before the race?

As he pulled away my legs buckled a bit, and I dropped rapidly. At 25 Km, Judid, our personal interpreter, called to me that I was 40 seconds down. I tried to relax. At 30 Km he was 70 seconds up. "About 7½ miles to go on my own," I thought. I was counting off the kilometres written on the stones at the sides of the road as they passed. By 35 Km it was dark, I was resigned to 2nd, and just pushed on. The Hungarian crowds standing by the route were showering me with rose petals, peering in the gloom at my number and chanting, "Hoy-ra, hoy-ra."

Half way to the 40 Km point, I glanced up the long dark road, and just caught a glimpse of the Swiss guy in the headlamps of the convoy of cars following him. It looked like he was coming back. Sure enough, the red tail lights of his entourage were coming closer and closer, he was dropping. I piled on the pace, some kind of hunter instinct releasing from within me energy which I thought had long been exhausted. Just after 40 Km I caught him, passed quickly and pushed on over the long bridge and into the square for the finish. I pushed it at the end. One of the luckiest races of my career. I'd won! The time 2:19:27.8, to Bob Sercombe's 2:19:51 in the "Poly". That would make the "selectors" think . . . maybe.

The mystery Swiss was Hans Daehler and he hung on to 2nd with

2:20:09 in front of Gyula Toth, 2:24:25.

During the next week at work my manager called me in to talk about my career prospects, which he had been discussing with the director of Research Division. In May I'd had a salary rise from £3,200 to £3,500. I did a bit of investigating and found out that amongst senior staff cash wise it was the joint worst rise in the whole lab. Christ! Ph.D., M.B.E., ten years' experience in industry and that's all I was getting. I felt bitter about it, especially when I knew that contemporaries younger than I, with nowhere near the same

Szeged — Daehler, Hill, Toth.

credentials, were getting £1,000 a year more, plus a car. No, I was no blue-eyed boy.

I was asked if I would be willing to move elsewhere, Liverpool, Leicester; I repeated that I wished to stay at Droylsden. I said I was sure there was scope for a job in marketing and development of fibres and fabrics for sportswear. I was made for a job like that, even head office were passing enquiries in this field to me.

A few days later I got a letter from the Research Director which in a friendly and diplomatic way said that opportunities for any *further* advancement at Droylsden were limited. I hadn't progressed anyway from senior research chemist except perhaps to an unofficial "sub-section leader". The letter continued that opportunities for moves outside Droylsden would become progressively fewer as time went on.

Ron Hill Sports Limited had been started as a life-line in 1970. It was progressing well and business was building up. We were selling shorts, shoes and a whole range of athletic gear by mail order, and orders were coming from abroad, Yugoslavia, New Zealand, U.S.A. and Canada. We were just starting to import the NIKE brand of running shoes from the U.S.A. May helped a lot with packing the orders and taking them to the post office in Gee Cross and I found that I was spending more and more time at night working on the business. We had regular callers for shoes, Andy

Etchells and his brother Martin, Dave Whaite, Stuart Keech, Ken Hodkinson and of course Arthur Walsham all gave us valuable custom. We also had a couple of friends including Harry Smith working for us as agents.

We didn't take a penny out of the takings, ploughing everything back into the purchase of stock to give a more comprehensive and prompt service. The business was my life-line, and I was almost ready to grab it.

My next marathon would be the Kosice classic on October 6th. The organisers had been at Szeged and badly wanted me to go. The B.A.A.B. had selected Keith Angus and myself as consolation for missing Rome.

I had three days "rest" after Szeged, and I needed it. My lower back was getting more and more sore through August which just made some of my unaccountably bad racing performances worse. During the "rest", I just didn't recover my usual freshness. After two weeks I ran Bob Midwood's Barnsley '6' and unbelievably finished somewhere in the 70's after being pulled through from the 80's by Keith Boyden. I had no idea what was wrong and it was embarrassing after the local papers had given me a tremendous build-up. "Theere 'e is!" people shouted, spotting my number in the crowd, way, way down.

The week after that I ran Harry Smith's "Weets" Fell race at Barnoldswick. I was 16th. *"I'm in really bad form at the moment but I don't know why — struggling when it comes to any sort of speed."* I'd just done my first week of eight weeks' training for Kosice, 82 miles. My back got so sore that I was sleeping on the floor to try to get it right, and I had to take aspirin before I set out for work in the morning. The week after "Weets" May and I drove to Dover and got the ferry to Ostend. Steve Kenyon and Vince Regan followed us by car and we were running as a Bolton Harriers team in the half-marathon of Geraardsbergen. We stayed the night at Sports Centre Blosse, found only with extreme difficulty, and after a run in the morning, during which I got chased out of a graveyard — it was the quietest place around — we drove on to race Augustin Daneel's Jubilee 10th half-marathon. They had made a special effort this year with teams from Poland, Spain and Great Britain in addition to the top Belgian road runners. Belgium had one, two and three with Gaston Roelants, Jose Revijn and Rik Schoofs, Steve was 4th and myself 10th just in front of Willy Polleunis. I suffered. My back was killing me; every time I turned a corner I had pains, and on the last lap I sniffed once and got such a spasm of pain down the whole of my back I thought it was going to stop me.

Alphonse and Alphonsine kindly looked after us again at the

Us, Alphonse and Alphonsine and family — Oudenberghof.

Oudenberghof. May and I were in Europe for a week's camping before a 10 mile road race in Breda, Holland and Alphonse advised us to go to the Ardennes, more specifically La Roche. After a night out and a meal of eels with old friend Jozef Lampbrecht and his wife of Erembodegem, we drove to La Roche.

La Roche.

It was a beautiful place and the running would have been magnificent amongst the hills and pine trees if it hadn't been for the frustrating and tearful pain of my back which seemed to get worse. I had hoped that camping and sleeping on hard ground would improve it, but it wasn't so. By a great co-incidence Herman Mignon and his wife arrived at the same camp site in La Roche. Herman was a Belgian Olympic 1500 metre runner who lived in Geraardsbergen and had supped a few beers with us at the Oudenberghof after the half-marathon. We didn't run together but drank a few more ales.

279

From La Roche we drove to Maasluis in Holland to find Ad Bouwens who had invited me to Breda. After locating him, we were conducted to s'Gravenzande and the house of a young Dutch runner Jacques Valentin, whom I had met briefly at the Barnsley '6'. He was the son of a market gardener; they had tomatoes and grapes in the greenhouses at that time and leeks in a small field. Jacques' sister, Ine, another runner, gave up her room for May and I to sleep.

The "Bouvigneloop" over "10 Engelse Mijl" was even more of a disaster than the half-marathon in Belgium. My name was plastered all over the posters and although I couldn't really expect to do well with such a painful back injury, I still took it personally. Conditions were windless, raining slightly but warm and humid, the course flat and mainly roads through and around a forest. I was hanging on to the leaders in oxygen debt and having trouble with my breathing until just after 10 Km when I took a right angle bend and seemed to twist my spine, sending pains right through my back: "last two laps were murder — almost collapsed towards the end of the last lap — staggering about — after the race I was really in a bad way — sweating and only just able to stand." I'd placed 6th in 51:28. Dutchman, Henk Kalf was the winner in 49:20. The Breda race was on the last day of August.

When we got home I put two planks under the mattress at my side of the double bed. Steven started at Hyde Grammar School. On Wednesday, September 4th I was 30th in the Linotype '5' — "heart knackered". I ran 65 miles that week, a mini rest, with my *"back still bad — shuffling"*. Sunday, September 8th I ran the Notts '10', gaining, if you could call it that, 6th in 52:21 — "back had held up but was feeling unfit". Colin Kirkham won in 49:07. After the race I sold a bit of gear then dashed back home to watch the final day of the European championships from Rome, including the marathon: *"cup of tea, meat butty, parkin — did some sports business work between races and had red wine before tea — saw Thompson win the marathon easily — disappointed at not being there"*. The results of the Rome race were:

1.   Ian Thompson (G.B.) 2:13:18.8
2.   Eckhard Lesse (E. Germany) 2:14:57.4
3.   Gaston Roelants (Belgium) 2:16:29.6
4.   Bernard Plain (G.B.) 2:18:02.2
14.   R. Sercombe (G.B.) 2:27:13.0

The next week I trained 101 miles. The planks did the trick, my back went O.K., but my right knee was sore. On September 14th I ran the Harold Doggett Handicap Chase at Boggart Hole Clough, Manchester. I think I was handicapped on reputation rather than

Family portrait — Blackpool, with mother and dad.

form and was off five seconds ahead of scratch man Stan Curran, an up and coming young runner from Salford, who quickly passed me. Encouragingly I got 4th fastest time over the tough 6 mile course.

I went into full training, 121 miles bringing a 50:19 Nuneaton '10' on September 21st: *"best 10 for a while!"*

On 24th September, the day before my 36th birthday, I made a jump for my "life-line". There had been talk of redundancies at the Droylsden lab. and I offered myself as the first in the queue, adding that they could forget about the marketing job, I was no longer interested.

Another big week of 125½ miles and I got 6th in the Chris Vose '7', 35:17. That weekend I started "the diet" and a taper down to Kosice.

Rain, rain, rain. It never stopped all the time we were in Kosice. It was nothing like I had imagined, but my thoughts were most certainly coloured by the miserable, wet, cold weather.

Keith Angus, team manager Mike Rawson and myself flew first to Prague, sitting on the plane opposite Ivan Mauger the speedway

281

champion whom I'd met at a car "Race of Champions" at Oulton Park. From Prague we boarded a prop. plane for Kosice via Bratislava, in company with an Irish team of Brendan O'Shea and Dick Hodgens and also Hans Daehler of Switzerland. After a long wait in Bratislava, it was announced that due to bad weather we wouldn't be able to land at Kosice and therefore we were going to another airport. That was Papra-Tatry where as we got out of the plane there was a beautiful view of a grey snow-capped mountain range in the distance with a bank of clouds whipped along the slopes and piling over each other.

Kosice.

Another wait, a bus to the railway station and another wait. I took Keith along to a hotel, told them who we were, and asked if we could change somewhere for a run. We stumbled around the dimly lit, pot-holed streets for 20 minutes, changed back, returned to the station, had goulash and a doughnut, and watched some of the locals getting seriously stoned in the station bar. When we finally chugged into Kosice railway station at 8.45 p.m. we were met by rain and a welcoming committee, and we were each given a red carnation wrapped in cellophane. Buses took us to the Hotel Slovan where I was happily surprised to meet two old mates, Jack Foster from New Zealand and John Farrington from Australia. It was the 50th anniversary of the marathon. Also there was Ismail Akcay of Turkey and Dutchman Henk Kalf who had beaten me in the Breda 10 miler. This was going to be some race.

There were even two Americans, Steve Hoag and a friend, Scott Sundquist, who was about to marry a Czech girl he called "Hanna the banana", and who kept muttering things about the Bermuda Triangle. It rained all the next day. I was asked to lay a wreath of pine branches and red carnations on the tomb of the founder of the race which I solemnly did in a quiet dripping tree-shadowed grave-yard. We went to see the course afterwards — it looked reasonably flat but with about 7 miles dead straight stretch to the turn, which would be boring, especially on the way back.

Race day it poured. I warmed up about half a mile with a wild Belgian, Walter Van Renterghem. Despite the conditions I wore only my featherweight mesh vest and Union Jack shorts, my only gesture to the weather being a pair of light cotton gloves. We all stood miserable and shivering on the flooded, muddy cinder track until at 1.00 p.m. a pistol crack sent the huge field splashing round the almost deserted stadium. For me it was to be an event of 50% exciting powerful running and 50% shocking misery.

I got a poor start; I moved to the outside lanes to try to avoid the churning mud and the grit thrown up from the feet of the other athletes; as a result of this I was at least 80 metres down on the trio of Truppel (E. Germany), Jack Foster and John Farrington as we left the arena.

Once on the wet tarmac, I hit my stride and began to work through the various groups. I caught the leaders at just about 5 Km and heard the time: 14:54. I was going well and decided not to sit in with them, and strode past. Jack Foster said something about "Another Boston", and I pulled away. Only John Farrington gave pursuit, but by 10 Km I had dropped him clocking 29.54. This was fast but I felt like doing it and decided to continue with this uninhibited pace. You never know what you can do unless you try! 15 Km went by: 45:00 dead. There was a slight following wind; it didn't feel strong and shouldn't be much trouble on the way back, I simply felt powerful and good. 20 Km was 60:13 and I hit the turn in

". . . I hit the turn in under 1 hour 3 minutes."

283

under 1 hour 3 minutes. Eagerly looking up the road for the pursuing runners I had a good lead and I was prepared for a harder run home; I put my head down and pushed into the wind and rain. Jack gave me a shout as he went past and later I saw Keith Angus sheltering in a big group of runners, way behind me. You didn't win races hanging back like that, I thought.

It began to feel tough; I glanced up and could see horizons way ahead on the slightly uphill road in the direction of Kosice. Well, it was tough, but I expected the others to suffer just as much and I would go still further away and win easily. I reasoned that once I hit 25 Km, with just over 10 miles to go, I would be O.K.

I passed 25 Km and suddenly I heard footsteps on the wet road: Truppel was there beside me, then past; I couldn't stay with him even though I tucked in right behind him; I just didn't seem to get any shelter. Then Jack Foster came up, "C'mon Lancs.," he said. I tried to get behind him, but he quickly moved away. My strides were becoming short and the two in front were moving away swiftly; so I thought, "Well, 3rd, that's not too bad."

The rain began to come down harder, and all at once I really began to suffer. I can't remember a lot after that. It seemed to be an age, running up that cold, wet road. Runners began to come past me rapidly, in file, quick fire. Almost literally they left me standing, but almost every one of them to a man gave me some word of encouragement in their native tongue.

My strides became almost nothing. I wanted to walk. All I could think about was a hot bath; jumping into a tub of hot water to take away this awful pain I was suffering. My jaw cramped up, some muscle under my chin just froze, and I had to let my mouth fall permanently open to breathe. My arms went rigid with the cold, locked at the elbows. It was a nightmare; I couldn't escape it. As it rained harder I moaned audibly, "Oh no! Oh no!" Instinct and pig-headedness just kept me going, pushing, pushing, towards the finish. Almost there, I passed a poor little Japanese runner Kimio Ohtsuka, he looked only half conscious and was staggering about the road. I was locked into gear, like a robot, and chugged on to the track, ankle deep in water to cross the line and end it all.

It was the first time in my life I had welcomed a blanket from the helpers at the finish.

Bloody Keith Angus had won it! 2:20:09, with Truppel second, 2:20:13, and another East German I'd never heard of before, Cierpinski, 3rd in 2:20:28. Jack Foster had dropped from 2nd with a mile to go to 18th. I ended up 28th — 2:28:30.

Back home there was enough of early Autumn left for us to rush out and gather blackberries and elderberries to brew home-made wine.

CHAPTER SIXTEEN

Early on October 16th 1974 I grabbed my life-line; I handed in my resignation by letter. It was late afternoon next day when I was asked "Did I want to talk about it?" I did and said I wouldn't stay for an extra £1,000 a year. Yes, I had another job, but I wouldn't divulge what I was doing. I was hoping they would pay me up and tell me to get out immediately. But — it was not to be. I would have to serve my full six months' notice. "Would I be willing to do any odd jobs that turned up?" What choice had I? I just had to stick it out, before going "on my own" with only what I could withdraw of my pension contributions to enable us to live, whilst hopefully I could boost the business enough to pay us a wage.

In a way it was a load off my mind, and for a while my running responded. After a couple of weeks of 60 miles I trained hard for a month until the Canadian Cross-Country Championships, in between taking 4th in the Gale Fell race, 24:41, 3rd in the K & M '15', 1:15:51 (passing 10 miles in 49:09) and 2nd in a Red Rose

". . . 3rd in the K. & M. '15' . . ."

285

cross-country league race at Rochdale.

Al Pedlar, whom I didn't know from Adam, contacted me from Canada and asked whether I could get Tony Simmons for the two of us to run in the Canadian Cross-Country Championships at Brock University, St. Catherine's, Ontario. Tony said yes and the B.A.A.B. agreed to let us go without a team manager. Tony finished 2nd to Neil Cusack of Ireland, and I struggled for 15th. What was more important about that trip was that I met up with Peter Lever, a Bolton Harrier now living in Canada and his wife, Kim, and Pete put me on to a marathon to be held on November 30th in Maryland, U.S.A.

With Tony Simmons and Al Pedlar — Canada.

Hardly had I got back to England when I received a telephone call from Baltimore, a gentleman named Hy Levasseur and the invitation for the Maryland Marathon was clinched. Somebody was interested in me, and had faith in my abilities if the British selectors hadn't. In the middle of the fortnight between Canada and Maryland I breezed the Brampton to Carlisle '10', taking 41 seconds out of Steve Edmunds, Sale Harriers, in the last two miles to break the course record with 46:40.

I was ready for Maryland. I went on "the diet", and flew out of Manchester, Wednesday before the Sunday race. In New York I switched to Allegheny Airlines and was in Baltimore by 5.30 p.m. local time. Hy Levasseur, a tall handsome guy wearing a yellow and green striped rugby shirt, strode into the airport foyer, introduced himself and drove me in his red sports car to the other side of Baltimore, the Hunt Valley Inn. What a beautiful place that was. I had a magnificent double room to myself; it was like being in dreamland. Before leaving England I had decided to stay on British time and that meant being anti-social, going to bed very early and getting up in the dark at around 4.00 a.m. local time. It was nice to run those quiet rolling hills around Cockeysville in the still, starlit, frosty pre-dawn. British time gave me a couple of problems; firstly someone rang my room when I was asleep to ask how they could enter the race, and then the next night the phone rang at 2.30 a.m. my time, for a guy to say he was a fan of mine from Boston 1970. I cancelled all calls after that.

Training at the Maryland Marathon — with Frank Shorter a "speaker" at the event.

I was kept very busy with a press conference, radio shows, Hy's Keep-Fit TV Show, visiting the "Gentleman's Gentleman" barber shop to thank the people there for sponsoring my trip over to the race, and looking at the course. I would have called the out and back route moderately hilly as we climbed the six lane highway to about the 7 mile point. Thereabouts, the course goes on to a narrow winding road with trees and big wooden houses until it sort of falls

287

off the edge of an escarpment with a steeply descending rush. Then it is beautifully scenic running through trees along Loch Raven Drive with Loch Raven itself adding to the charm for the last couple of miles to the turn-round point.

On the way back the severity of the hill back up the escarpment really impressed me. I enquired as to its name; Satyr Hill it was called, and it started at 18 miles on the way back. It was almost a wall atop "the wall".

Things went perfectly for me in the race. The parents of Kathy Switzer, a very prominent American woman marathoner, took me to the start which was scheduled for 10.30 a.m. outside the Memorial Stadium, and dead on time, under the sponsorship of W.B.A.L. Radio 11 and the Maryland Fitness Commission, 635 runners pushed off up the slight hill on to the 26 mile 385 yard journey out and back. It was a clear cold morning; I had covered my arms and legs with "Radian B" linament and was wearing gloves. I was going to sit with the group and play a waiting game, but after 1 mile I found myself in the lead and striding well. It was early but I decided to go and in no time at all the footsteps behind me were out of earshot.

I had a good, good day. When I hit the turn and headed back for the finish I saw that I had a reasonably good lead and thankfully, unlike Kosice, I stayed there. As I ran into the bulk of the field heading towards the turn, I was genuinely surprised at the amount of support the other runners gave to me, a total stranger. Or was I?

"I had a good, good day."

Winning the Maryland Marathon.

They cheered, clapped, raised their clenched fists in a salute and shouted — "Looking good, Ron" — "Way to go, Ron" — slapping my hands as I passed them going the other way. I'd never experienced anything like it and I was moved.

Satyr Hill presented little problem; just a slight hardening of the muscles at 21 miles. Then all the way home, Joe Holland, one of the race directors called out my running time — "1 hour 49 minutes" — "2 hours 2 minutes". I thought I might dip under 2:17 but most of the last three-quarter mile was uphill and I finally broke the tape in 2:17:23. Exactly seven minutes in front of the second man, Ron Kurrle of Long Beach, California. My biggest winning margin ever.

289

1974

I was happy and reckoned my performance was worth 2:12 on a flat course. It was the best organised marathon race I had ever been in. After swift radio interviews in front of the crowd on the dais, I walked to Eastern High School across the road to change. There was soap and towel and hot shower for everyone who finished, followed by a free meal of beef stew, sandwich and beer.

When the impressive presentations were finished, I celebrated. First at race-starter Victor Frenkil's house, Baccardis and Coke and oyster vol-au-vents for me, and later at the house of Les Kinion and his wife, Joyce. Les, of the Baltimore R.R.C., had designed the course! It was in the very informal surroundings of his party that I first met some of the road runners from Baltimore and New York; Mike Sabino and Fred Lebow are names I filed away in my diary with addresses.

Monday I cadged a car lift from lady marathon runner Nina Kuscik with her three kids for a five hour drive through pouring rain to Kennedy Airport just in time to catch my plane to Manchester.

December's confident rest of 50 odd miles each week I enjoyed. I was back in business.

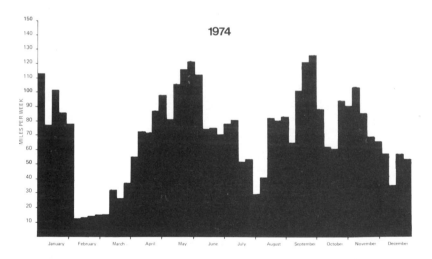

My notice with Courtaulds was due to run out on March 7th 1975; then I would be free. Meanwhile, I was kept well occupied with responsibilities at least as great as any I had had previously, liaising between the Northern Weaving Division, Marks and Spencer, and company dyehouses and printworks on the production of co-ordinating ranges of garments, backing this up with technical information and recommendations from the laboratory.

Through January I ran around 80 miles a week with fairly indifferent results. I returned to the Mezidon cross-country race alone, no official team had been invited, but only managed 7th place. Yearly, I was slipping down the list, and frustratingly the winner, Rault, who absolutely streaked away with the race was 39 years old — three years older than myself. Even the "Bal des Nations" in the evening lost its flavour; rowdy, few runners, no air of celebration. Another chapter was closed.

A bad chest and cold hampered my running in the East Lancs. Cross-Country Championships and I plodded round Springfield Park, Rochdale to finish 6th, over a minute behind Frank Briscoe.

6th in the East Lancs. Cross-Country Champs.

I dearly wanted to run well in the National Cross-Country Championships at Luton on March 1st and had dreams of maybe making the England team again. I stepped up my mileage to 100 miles a week for the first fortnight of February, but my hopes were blunted when I had an awful day in the Northern Championships at Towneley Park, Burnley, and finished down in the 20's. And worse, mid-race, some guy with glasses from Leeds, I could hear his supporters urging him on, passed me. I recorded — "felt ashamed that a duffer like that should be beating me, but I was knackered and couldn't stay with him — pushed and pushed — then up the final straight got out-sprinted by a specky Liverpool bloke (Roger Harrison) — what a bloody blow to my ego — out-sprinted! — God, I was knackered — I know no reason why."

The next Saturday I got 4th in the Parbold Hill race, ran a week of 91 miles, raced the M.A.C. relay at Heaton Park on the Saturday

". . . I had an awful day in the Northern . . ." Here leading Andy Etchells.

and a 6th place, 3,000 metres track race, in about 8 mins. 30 secs. on the Sunday, then took a low mileage week, 69, leading up to the National.

For the first time I was doing "the diet" for a short distance race. Monday and Tuesday, both of which were hard training days and Wednesday I ate little carbohydrate, Thursday, Friday and race day, high carbohydrate. Friday night I drove to Luton to stay with a local athlete Dave Collier. I was determined to do well. I didn't, and wrote in my training log:

Sat. March 1st 1975 E.C.C.U. Champs — Stopsley — Luton. *Lovely course, good going, one hill, my sort of course. Feared the start and couldn't look forward to pushing myself — we had a good pen (20) on the right hand side, with the first bend a right hander — it was a bit chaotic at the start — Bang! the maroon went up, charge! — the announcer saying, "A sight to be seen . . ." — worked my way over to the right, out of trouble — at the bend I had Gerry North near me — was about in the early 100's — round then down the hill on dry plough, then along the track — got through to the 80's but lost an awful lot up the hill — had been struggling up till then, but really died up the hill — at the top got going again and passed a few runners — Bill Robinson, someone called Clive, Rick, a Shaftesbury Harrier (wearing Nike) — down the hill again, and got through to 60's and then about 55th — then died again on the hill — people just sweeping past and away — out of sight — Bill Robinson, Altmann, Jeff Norman — was almost resigned to dropping back to the 100's — had passed Steve Kenyon, but he ran away up the hill — got going again on the flat — down the hill I passed Tony Byrne — got behind Tony Birks — followed them against the wind — passed Alan Spence and then **at last** Roger Harrison (Liverpool) — pushed up the hill — got Rushmer — a Stoke lad — followed "Clive" — just behind Mike Tagg — speeded up and up — but what was the point of a sprint — let Tagg and Clive go — got 43rd — well, a sad day for* *me — I'll never make the England team again — my sort of course, diet, preparation and they all ran away! Kirkham went to 14th after passing me at 4½ miles! Felt sad — and sorry — I've lost it — God, it had to come, but I don't like it.*

43rd in the National.

The Friday after that I left Courtaulds. I didn't see the manager, but the lads and lasses gave me a great send-off and wonderful gifts — I'm still using the electric shaver. A huge card had been signed by all the lab and works staff and was inscribed on the back: "Presented by Ken Meldrum in the King's Head, Friday March 7th 1975". There followed a list of gifts, including "and several pints of ale"!

I was free. It would be a good while before I could pay myself a wage from Ron Hill Sports Limited, the business would have to be built and all funds ploughed back before that happened. And until then I had my returned superannuation contributions to live off. We would manage, we never went out; I brewed my own wine and beer and May had always looked after our clothes, so they would last as long as we needed.

But now I could plan ahead to next year's Olympics in Montreal and would use the rest of 1975 to enjoy my freedom to travel and to experiment with the marathon. I had my weekly schedule sheet for 1975 in my training log and was able to pencil in the races for the whole of the year and plan accordingly. With the private invitations I had had already, the season began to take shape with far more marathons than I had undertaken in one season before: April 21st, Boston; May 19th, Ankara, Turkey; June 15th, Debno, Poland; August 3rd, Montreal (pre-Olympic marathon); August 30th, Enschede, Holland. Five marathons in four months. But I wouldn't run them all hard; I would alternate one serious race, with "the diet" and a hard effort, with an easy, fun-type race. The fun-type races would be Ankara and Montreal, I didn't want to win the pre-Olympic race anyway. And I would round the year off with a return to Maryland early in December.

In the seven weeks between my disastrous National run, and Boston, I did only two very long runs, 21 milers, and only twice exceeded 80 miles a week. The weekly miles ran, 37, 56, 72½, 80½, 74, 84, 79½. This reduction in mileage came naturally as I no longer had to run to work and back, where the shortest possible run was 6½ miles. Now I was happy with just a three mile morning spin with a second session of 6 to 9 miles at lunchtime or in the afternoon or evening. I had to find new training routes and tended to head down to the valley containing the River Tame and the Peak Forest canal as I didn't particularly like training on the hills in the other direction from our home, and I ended up with some good summer courses, mixtures of road and paths. At least twice a week I put in hard sessions of fartlek or timed efforts on my wristwatch, and every weekend I raced more or less locally at distances usually up to 10 miles. Almost automatically I sought weekly competition to test myself, after all I'd always been a runner, but I also looked on these short races as really good speed training as without the stimulus of competition I could never push myself that hard.

Very rarely did I miss a weekend race even if I was "resting" and I was still up there in the results. After the "National" I raced the Manchester University Cross-Country Club Championships (3rd),

Manchester University Cross-Country Club. Golden Jubilee Year.

the Sutton '7' (2nd), the Newcastle '7' (4th), Easter weekend the Salford '7' (6th, Friday), the Rivington Pike Fell Race (4th, Saturday), and the "Chas Kendall" 15 Km at Barrow (a rather knackered 15th, Monday), the next weekend a 6¼ mile leg of the Northern Road Relay, and finally, the weekend before Boston, the Chris Vose '10' at Warrington (4th, in 49:18).

Another factor which ensured I got to races regularly was business. Whenever I raced I took gear, running shorts, running shoes etc., in the back of my car to sell afterwards. This always helped to bolster our mail order sales.

CHAPTER SEVENTEEN

My second trip to Boston was jointly sponsored by Colgate-Palmolive of the U.S.A., which Kathy Switzer, the women's winner of Maryland, had fixed for me, and Tom Ashton, a Bolton garage proprietor, who was assisting a team of Bolton Harriers marathon runners to go there. After my 2:10:30 record in 1970 I had said I would not return except possibly for the 100th anniversary of the race in 1997, but the temptation to travel to this famous race was too great, and who knew, maybe I could win it again? Also Ron Hill Sports Limited were the importers of Nike shoes from the U.S.A. and Nike had a factory in Exeter, New Hampshire, about an hour away from Boston. Nike's development manager, Jeff Johnson, himself a runner and an excellent photographer whose pictures of the Boston marathon appeared each year in 'Runners' World' magazine, had offered to put me up at his home, so this could be a business trip too.

May looked after the business whilst I was away, opening the mail, getting out the shoes, and other items, parcelling them up, addressing and stamping them, and finally carting them down, by hand, in big bags to the local post office in Gee Cross. I did the banking when I got back as the size of the takings only merited doing this once a week. Nevertheless, we had moved the business out of the loft into the spare bedroom and the garage was rapidly filling with stock, the fruits of reinvesting all of the profits.

The 1975 Boston Marathon was on Monday, April 21st, Patriots' Day, and the T.W.A. 707 carrying the Bolton team of myself, Tommy Parr, Kenny Mayer, Vince Regan and Graham Bennison touched down at Boston's Logan Airport at 1.15

Boston.

295

p.m. local time on Tuesday 15th. To greet us there was my old friend, Jock Semple, a couple of reporters and Jeff Johnson. After photographs and interviews the lads were taken to their Copley Square Hotel and Jeff drove me through the New Hampshire country-side to his home. Jock had told me Drayton was running again, but he wasn't getting any younger. Neither was I!

Jeff Johnson lived by himself in a peaceful single storey wooden house, amongst pine trees by a small lake. The wood smelled lovely inside, he had lots of books and I didn't mind at all when he had to go to work and I was left alone. I was able to work myself, planning advertising and orders for when I got back to England. But I got to see the Nike set-up there, visiting the warehouse and the factory in Exeter where they made me a special pair of green lightweight pigskin shoes for the marathon. Training was pleasurable on those country roads lined with trees, and the low carbohydrate part of the diet passed fairly easily on Wednesday, Thursday and Friday before the race.

Saturday night Jeff had some friends over including Rick Bayko, editor of a magazine with a circulation of 250 called "Two" (later to become "Yankee Runner"), for what was becoming a tradition amongst American marathon runners, a spaghetti dinner — bags of carbohydrate. I made the sauce with minced beef, onions, bay leaves and the Baykos' home-grown frozen tomatoes. It wasn't bad.

Sunday night, the night before the race, we spent quietly. Jeff took me in his car to a derelict farm shack in the woods off the road. We poked around but it was getting too dark to look properly for anything old; just 1947 newspapers blowing about. I dug up a couple of small conifers, which I brought back to England, probably illegally, and planted them in my garden. They came to an untimely end when on a visit from my brother Norman, his youngest son Darrell came running down from the garden to the house shouting, "Look what I've got dad, a tree!" We returned to Jeff's house and I slept well that night.

Race day was cold. And there would be a following wind. Shortly after 7.00 a.m. I was out for a 1½ mile jog and stretch, followed by coffee, two jam butties and vitamin pills. Jeff's co-coach with a local girls' team, Cynthia, drove us to Hopkinton and the gym. It was very, very crowded as we forced our way to the V.I.P. changing rooms, "GIRLS LOCKER ROOMS". There I met a lot of old friends as I spun out the hour and twenty minutes before the start; Clive Longe, the G.B. decathlete, there as the Bermuda team manager for Raymond Swan; Dave Hemery, Pat McMahon, Jock Semple and Jerry Nason, reporter with the Boston Globe in 1970, now retired. At 11.30 a.m. they kicked us out of the gym. I jogged a little, felt good and headed for the start. The crowd of runners was incredible; there were over 2,000 starters. I had to push my way across gardens and through hedges to get up to the start line. It was still cold; people were wearing gloves, tights, even polythene bags over their bodies. I had a chance to win. Drayton, I thought, would be my main opposition. I signed a few autographs; had a couple of pictures taken. I felt nervous behind the rope at the start, on the extreme left so I could stay out of trouble; my face was screwed up. I felt somehow vulnerable, all those people staring, pointing, shouting. For God's sake, let's get on with it. I gave my track suit to Jock Semple. The starter was up a ladder. He wouldn't give a count down. The rope was dropped, then "Bang", we were away.

The start. Boston. 1975.

The start was a good one for me; pretty fast and out of danger from the pursuing masses, but after the first half-mile I knew there would be problems for me. We came to a hill and I was having to work like hell to get up. There seemed to be nothing in my legs. It was the same at every small hill. I was having a bad day.

I managed to stay with the leading bunch for about 6 miles, the bunch that mattered. Some idiot had blasted off and had stayed ahead for about five miles only to die a death. Someone called "24 minutes" at 5 miles with Steve Hoag, whom I'd met at Kosice, Drayton, a swarthy Puerto Rican, De Jesus in a dark green vest and red shorts, Tom Fleming, Richard Mabuza from Swaziland, a guy in a white T-shirt wearing a headband and white gloves, and another guy with a white vest and red shorts.

At 6 miles the bunch split and I couldn't go with them. Drayton

JEFF JOHNSON

Framingham — 6 miles.

JEFF JOHNSON

With Tom Fleming and Richard Mabuza.

was away. The white T-shirt and gloves following him. Then De Jesus and the red shorts in tandem, then Mabuza and me 6th. The next 6 miles I ran alone, hoping I would begin to run better, but I was just forcing it, pushing, pushing all the way. Just before half-way, Tom Fleming came up to me and led me for a while: "How're you feeling Ronnie boy?" he said. "Knackered and I'm hanging on to you," I gasped. Shortly after he left me.

Again I was alone, now in 7th position, trying to stride and cursing my bad run. The energy just wasn't flowing to my legs. The crowds were giving me tremendous support, but it did no good. Added to this, my new shoes, which I hadn't broken in properly, were giving me blisters under the ball of my left foot and on the big and fourth toes. Shortly before the Newton Hills, Steve Hoag swept past and away out of sight. 8th. Christ, how many more were going to come past? Just after that I passed Mabuza. 7th.

I had really suffered on all the hills up to 17 miles. The Newton Hills were murder! I just had nothing left in my legs to force me up them. On the last steep climb I felt as though I was tip-toeing, barely moving at all, and I was surprised and relieved that hordes of runners had not gone past. Over the crest and I let gravity take me down the steepish hills until the long flat run into the finish. The sun was shining strongly now, everyone finished with sunburn on their backs. I relaxed and strode out, there was De Jesus coming back fast. At 22 miles I passed him, "Vamos," I said, then tried to push on as strongly as I could. I just wanted to get to the end. There was a hell of a following wind blowing, bits of paper and plastic cups were overtaking me, tumbling along the wide empty crowd-lined streets. At 23 miles I spotted Jerome Drayton, wearing one of my mesh vests standing at the side of the road.

"Come on, Jerome," I shouted. "Bloody finish it, if you have to walk!" "Good luck," he replied quietly. He didn't make it. That put me 5th. I ran on, seemingly moving quite fast with that tail wind, I was catching the guy with the red shorts; it was something to aim for, keep my interest alive, even though I couldn't increase my efforts. As we turned right before the final left hand turn into the finishing straight, I got in right behind him. People were shouting his name. Tom. He heard me there. I thought I could take him, but no, he speeded up, I tried to respond, but there was nothing in my legs, I was shot at. Up the last road to the finish I was weaving a little from side to side and gladly crossed the line to slow to a walk, refuse a yellow blanket, and march quickly, annoyed, into the Prudential Building. The result:

JEFF JOHNSON

". . . gladly crossed the line . . ."

1975

1.   William H. Rodgers (Great Boston Track Club) 2:09:55
2.   Steve Hoag (Twin Cities Track Club) 2:11:54
3.   Tom Fleming (New York A.C.) 2:12:05
4.   Tom Howard (Richmond Kajaks) 2:13:23
5.   Ron Hill (Bolton Harriers) England, 2:13:28

The white T-shirt and gloves had won it and my record had been broken by someone I'd never heard of: Will (Bill) Rodgers. He was quoted: "I don't put myself in the same class with a runner like Ron Hill — a world class man, but I definitely would like to get on the Olympic Team."

The Boston Herald American said, "The man whose record was wiped out on the chill, wind aided course, England's Ron Hill, finished 5th yesterday in a highly respectable 2:13:28 when you consider his advancing years (36)"!

In my training log I wrote, ". . . *very disappointed as it was a 2:08 day if ever there were one"*.

Model of the Montreal Olympic complex shown at the Boston Marathon.

The Ankara marathon was exactly a month later, Monday May 19th. My training after Boston went 61 miles, no race; 70 miles, 7th in the Wigan '6'; 86 miles, 1st in a track 3,000 metres at Eccles beating Jeff Norman in a sprint in 8:37.5; and finally 75½ miles, the week before the race. My friend Ismail Akcay, the Turkish marathon runner, had been trying to get me to run in Ankara for years and now it was happening.

The trip was going to be a little bit of a holiday, departing on Friday, racing on Monday, returning on Wednesday. I was hoping to get some sun on my back; a lot of the time it rained! I was up at 5.45 a.m. to train and to put in a few hours' work on the business, before journeying to Turkey. A lift in a car from a caller/customer to Stockport railway station, train to London, tube to West London Air Terminal, bus to Heathrow, plane to Istanbul with team mate Max Coleby and a team manager, change planes on the tarmac, plane to Ankara airport and finally car ride to the Otel Ersan. The team manager's bags had been lost! Just before midnight Max and I stumbled out for a three mile run on rough roads with a taxi behind us giving light. I almost broke my left ankle on a big rock in the gloom and was limping for ages afterwards.

Ismail showed us round Ankara and took us to his home. Another old friend popped up too, Yoshi Honda, the happy interpreter from the Fukuoka Marathon, Japan, now working in Ankara. It's a small world!

May 19th, a national holiday in Turkey, was a day for a youth

Ankara.

festival including parades and games in the big stadium with the marathon as a centre-piece, starting and finishing there. This year the rain caused so much flooding that everything but the race was cancelled. So it was to an almost empty stadium that we were conducted by taxi arriving at 8.45 a.m. We expected a 9.20 a.m. start. The sun came out which made it warm and humid; that didn't worry me too much, it wasn't a serious race; also a sore throat and bad chest which had come on in Turkey didn't seem important. 9.20 a.m. came and went and only when we began to ask questions did someone tell us that the start had been changed to 9.55 a.m. There didn't seem much opposition, a couple of Polish runners, a Rumanian, Huseyin Aktas and a few of his fellow Turkish runners. Not many more than a dozen starters. I told Max that I wouldn't be doing any leading.

With the cinder track flooded, we did a lap of the grass, whilst what crowd there was threw paper darts on to the track. I went straight to the back and was joined there by Aktas. Three Turks, hares, bombed off, but the wise men ignored them and we jogged along nicely through 5 Km in 16:59, with only a crew-cut shepherd boy, Ahmet Unal, wearing a yellow vest and blue cut-away shorts, and bearing a distinct resemblance to Ian Stewart, some 50 or 60 metres ahead. We ran up and around the Ataturk mausoleum, then down into Ankara centre. On this downhill stretch Max and I opened our legs and forced the field to stay with us before dropping back to let the others lead uphill out of the city. The sun had gone, but it was overcast, close, and sweaty on the hills. I was glad of my halter neck mesh vest.

Orzel, Unal, Coleby, Aktas, Hill

The city streets were crowded with spectators and they were calling the name "Aktas" and even "Akcay", though he wasn't running. As we left the city the shepherd boy was reeled in just before 10 Km, and a group of five of us, the white capped Pole, Orzel, bringing up the rear, headed out on to the straight undulating road to the turn. It felt really easy, jogging along, so easy that after taking a sponge I was able to lob it into the air and jump to head it to the side of the road.

The shepherd boy moved off once; I said to Max, "Let's cover that break," and we easily accelerated, pulling Aktas and Orzel with us, until we were together again. A huge white spherical radar dome looked over the turn, which was just before 25 Km, at the bottom of a hill. Max and I turned together; I was going to force the pace back up the hill, but it suddenly felt hard so I dropped back, waited until the top, then I began to wind it up into the slight headwind. We lost the shepherd boy. The course was deceptive and there seemed to be a lot more uphill on the way back. I was surprised as I expected a flat course from Derek Clayton's record, in 1969, of 2 hrs. 17 mins.

Leading now I looked down the road and could see huge black clouds approaching. As we passed 25 Km it began to rain, and I began to feel sick; a nauseous feeling just lurking in my stomach. I just kept pushing on, hoping it would pass. Aktas put in a burst on the opposite side of the road, which we more or less ignored, after which he dropped back and we never saw him again.

The nausea didn't go away; it got worse, though I tried to maintain my pace. "I'm feeling bloody sick, Max," I said; and he replied, "Aye, I'm going through a bad patch too at the moment." A steep hill approached and I was off the back. Orzel seized his opportunity and was away, opening a gap on Max too. At the top I strode out after him, dragged Max through with me and got behind him, sitting right on his tail. By now it was thundering and pouring down with rain. On we went until approaching 35 Km the sickness got the better of me. I half stopped, ran on again, then stopped to vomit on the grass of the central reservation, bringing up vile tasting bright greeny yellow bile. Starting to jog again, I looked up to see Orzel was now 70 yards ahead with Max 20 yards behind him. "That's it," I thought, "but I'd better get moving or Aktas will catch me."

At first I ran to hold my position; looking ahead, they weren't gaining ground; then I began to feel strong and with that lot off my stomach I began to chase, powerfully striding through the puddles, to give all I could, whatever it might bring.

I went past Max, fast, without a word, and was now at a roundabout at the top of the main road near our hotel. The water was flowing down the street at a terrific rate and was at least three inches deep. Left, down the road now, splash, splash through the brown water, until half way down I caught the Pole. I checked him out; he seemed to be making an effort. I wasn't waiting for him; I went. For 100 yards he seemed to stay right behind me; at the bottom of the road a bloke leaned out of his car and said, "You have 10 metre lead." That spurred me on, I pushed like hell. I heard someone from a car say, "Classic race"; I groaned to myself, "It's not over yet." Even the Pole's coach, riding in a car near me, was leaning out shouting, "Bravo, Hill." Bombing on through the rain, I took a left turn, under a railway bridge, and started the climb to the stadium. The nausea was returning; the sickness welling up more and more. Could I hold on, could I make it?

Into the stadium. Half a lap to go. Swallowing, swallowing, trying to control my rising stomach, I just managed to cross the line; dashed to the left, and was sick again. What a lucky win! Result:

1975

1. Ron Hill (Ingiliz) 2:21:25
2. Max Coleby (Ingiliz) 2:22:02
3. Kazimierz Orzel (Polonyah) 2:22:07
4. Huseyin Aktas (Turk) 2:22:40

In 9th position with 2:29:44 was Veli Balli, later to become a Boston Marathon winner!

Max was sick all night and the next day, Tuesday; not through too many beers either. There must have been a bug about, as on the journey from Euston station on Wednesday, I too began to feel ill. At first I thought it was the travel and the marathon and nearly revised my schedule for the rest of the year. It could only have been a bug but it scared me and I thought for a few minutes I was going to die sitting in my seat on the train, as my heart started to feel tight and was missing beats. On the 2½ mile run I did when I got home I "felt really tired and rough". There was one month to go before the Debno marathon in Poland, a serious one this time.

I was over the illness within a week and after an easy 60½ miles finished 3rd in the Otley '8' to Steve Kenyon and Martin Dell of Leeds. The next week of 75 miles contained a little fartlek and I didn't race the weekend, preferring to sell gear at the A.A.A. marathon and watch the race in Stoke-on-Trent. Tony Simmons was stopped by cramp at 22 miles and Jeff Norman won the race in 2:15:50 with Keith Angus (2:16:14) 2nd, and Colin Kirkham (2:16:22) 3rd. "No danger," I wrote in my diary, looking ahead to the 1976 championship, which would be the trial for the Montreal Olympics. Instead I raced on Wednesday evening, following my long run of 20 miles on Tuesday, and got 2nd place behind Frank Davies of Liverpool in the Birkenhead '5'. 81 miles in that week brought me to departure for Poland, and the Debno marathon.

We were all very excited as this was going to be a family trip and after sorting out tickets, East German transit visas and Polish visiting visas we were ready to go. The Debno organiser, Henrik Witkowski, had invited me to his race when I was in Kosice, Czechoslovakia, despite my disastrous run there. He had shown me a photograph of the first prize, a huge crystal vase, one metre high, which had been a perpetual trophy, presented each year to the winner then returned. If I won it this year, it was mine to keep! My travelling expenses would be given to me in Polish money and had been agreed at the cost of two return tickets, London to Warsaw. My permit from the B.A.A.B. I kept firmly in my passport as the last paragraph read: "It is understood that Dr. Hill is travelling at his own expense and the question of reimbursement of travel and/or accommodation costs does not arise." We were going on holiday.

Both May and I being away from our mail order business meant that there would be no service for two weeks. We were both always concerned over keeping people waiting, and on departure day I wanted everything up-to-date and was up at 5.15 a.m. and out for a 3 mile run after a cup of coffee. Until May made me ham and egg at 8.30 a.m., I was busy answering queries by letter, paying bills, and assessing sales so that I could place forward orders for Nike shoes. After breakfast I was flat out getting out pending orders for mesh vests, a consignment of which had arrived the day before, sending out foreign orders, and clearing out all that day's orders until 12.45 p.m., when I did a 7 mile run as fast as I could to save time. Immediately I drove down to Hyde Central Post Office with all the parcels and had to pay £4 to have all our mail held for two weeks.

It was 4.35 p.m. when after furiously packing the van all afternoon, we dropped two last parcels at Gee Cross Post Office and headed off for Harwich. I estimated the journey was about 150 miles, but was way out; it was more like 230 miles. After motoring gently down the A1, I realised we were going to be late and bombed it in the Transit van until I almost ran out of petrol, nursed the van for ages until I found a garage open, filled up and bombed it again, arriving in the dark, 9.30 p.m. at a deserted embarkation area to see the ship's lights far out to sea. We'd missed the boat!

We ate fish and chips out of the paper, put the van on a deserted car park outside the town centre and at 11.30 p.m. settled down to try to sleep, with me across the front seats. Around 2.30 a.m. I sensed a car circle us and go away. At 3.15 a.m. a police mini arrived. This time a copper got out, tapped on the window, took our names, address, occupation and he examined my tax disc. I explained our situation and he said he would try to let us know the time of the morning boat to Holland. I was just asleep when he came back at 4.00 a.m. and asked if he could have my autograph!

We easily got a boat the next morning for a good crossing with a group of about 25 race walkers including Colin Young and Bob Dobson. From the Hook of Holland we drove to s'Gravensande for a surprise visit to young Jacques Valentin. I wanted to find a road race for the next day, Sunday, but all we could discover was a 5,000 metre track race in Rotterdam. That would do. Jacques' parents fed us, his sister Ine gave up her room again for May and I, and Steven and Graham slept in the tent pitched in their back garden, with Jacques' little brother Eric for company.

In the 5,000 metres race, on a hot day, running in a borrowed pair of Jacques' spikes, I struggled a bit and all I could do was sit in on a young Dutch runner until the home straight when I outsprinted him for a 14:52.0 victory. I got no applause, even a few boos and hoots, and I myself felt bad about winning a race that way. By 3.00 p.m. we were off via Utrecht and Arnhem into Germany, stopping after 5½ hours' driving at a camp-site by a river and canoe centre near a town called Herford. We put the tent up and I went to sleep after a couple of Newcastle Browns.

Monday we drove on from 9.45 a.m. through West Germany, into East Germany, and on to the Polish border at Frankfurt-an-der-Oder, arriving almost dead on 5.00 p.m. as arranged, driving at the stipulated 20 k.p.h. over the river bridge. In Poland, three men looked on as grey uniformed customs women perfunctorily poked in the boxes of camping gear at the back of the van, then waved us through. The three men approached and gave me four red carnations. We had arrived.

One of the men, 18-year-old Arkadivsz Janowicz, "Eric" for short, was our interpreter, and he got into our vehicle and we followed a fawn coloured van about 40 minutes to Debno. It was like stepping back in time, lots of cobbled roads in the towns, in the country people working in the fields, and mainly horses and carts on the road. We were led to the "Pamerania" tourist hotel, category 3. It looked pretty run down; our room, 11, was on the first floor and contained four separate tubular army type beds with sagging three part straw mattresses. It was the best room in the hotel as we had a shaky looking balcony overlooking the courtyard at the back, where I parked the van. After one night we brought up our air beds to sleep on as the straw mattresses nearly broke my back, and not wishing to keep trailing out for breakfast we brought up the Gaz cooker and ended up virtually camping in the room. I'm not complaining; it was fun.

Our meals we took in a restaurant at the top end of town and these inevitably proved difficult as we couldn't understand the menu. If we ordered one thing, we seemed to get another. Salad was

"Pilca?" "Pilca?"

always just cucumber with sour cream. Of the list of half a dozen drinks there was usually only one "in stock". Beer or "orangeade", which in fact was cherryade, or "Cokta Pola", a kind of cola drink. The shops had no tomatoes, green salads or fruit at all.

Our lads with new friends at the lake.

We enjoyed ourselves during the five days before the race. I found a small lake in a forest on one of my training runs and we went there, sometimes twice a day, to lie in the sun and Steven and Graham immediately found friends in a group of kids from Debno who borrowed their football pointing, saying, "Pilca?" "Pilca?" and thanking us in English. One of them with a well shaven head we christened "Kojak", his pals called him "Gangster". Eventually we were ferrying about eight extra kids home at the end of the day.

I trained hard for the race and did the "diet"; low carbohydrate, Tuesday, Wednesday, Thursday, with hard sessions on the first two days, high carbohydrate Friday, Saturday and race day. I was going to give the organisers the best I could. After all they had paid me 19,000 zlotychs to cover my expenses. Unfortunately, Henryk Witkowski would not be there to see me run. He was in hospital following a bad car accident and Thursday we went to a hospital at Szeczin to visit him. His chest and head were in a huge plaster cast and at first he had been completely paralysed but now he could move his hands and feel sensations in his legs.

It seemed a long day, Sunday, as the race didn't start until 4.00 p.m. On my 2 mile run at 9.00 a.m. I felt "indifferent". There were runners from Greece, Denmark, Russia and several Eastern European countries. We paraded, marching to the square, Swiatowida Platz, me following the sign "ANGLIA"; there were speeches, and we lined up for the off. They are very proud of their marathon in

Will it rain?

Debno and everything is done to produce a fast time. The course consists of two laps of the square, 250 metres, plus five laps, almost straight out and back, exactly 8,389 metres to give 42,195 metres, the metric equivalent of 26 miles 385 yards. At the far end of the lap there is a specially built tarmacadam loop off the road to allow the runners to turn round without losing too much speed, and if the weather is hot they spray the whole course with water before the race to cool it down.

This wasn't necessary in 1975 as it rained before the start. A rocket exploded to start the race, and almost as we finished the two

The start— Debno.

laps of the square another exploded in the air about 5 metres away, almost bursting my eardrums. I felt the shock waves pass over my body! I was near the front as we headed up the main street of Debno and moved out to the left so that Steven could get a picture of me. I had been very nervous before the start, but now I felt better. After only 800 metres it looked like it would be a race between myself, two East Germans, and Jensen of Denmark. I ran as I felt and took the lead; it seemed a good pace and the footsteps behind began to fade. I heard them talking, and it looked as though they had decided

". . . headed up the main street . . ."

to let me go. Perhaps someone said that I had blasted off last year in Kosice and blown up, but I didn't feel that it was that fast.

I strode out well and at the first turn round I had almost the length of the turning loop, lead. I headed back past the oncoming runners, under the tall windless trees, and saw 15:00 at 5 Km. This was fast but I had no idea how accurate the splits were going to be. Into town again and there were lots of cheers. "Bravo!" "Bravo!" Around the square, "Dabei, Dr. Hill!" Out again and I had a good lead leaving

"Around the square . . ."

town reaching 10 Km in 30:24. On the second turnround I seemed to have increased the lead even more; I was still feeling good and went through 15 Km in 45:32, still well inside five minute miling. Into town for the second time and on the way out my lead was much

". . . and tried to relax."

bigger. There were three runners in the chasing pack, one in a navy blue string vest and two in white string vests. Just before the third turn was the half-way point; 1:04:25, not bad. I turned; the three following runners were still together.

I was beginning to feel tired and tried to relax, I was getting hot and took a couple of sponges, hoping they wouldn't make me feel sick, as I had been in Ankara. After the third trip into town, I appeared to have increased my lead still further, but heading out for the fourth turn I had a little bad patch and slowed slightly. After this turn I saw only one follower, he had broken away from the other two, or had I lapped him? I couldn't be sure, I was getting tired. At 30 Km I felt really tired.

Round the square for the last time and heading out, my lead had been really whittled. It was a Polish runner, Lengowski, chasing me; he obviously wasn't a lapped runner. I tried to remain calm on this last lap; it started to rain, which was a blessing, but I was feeling flat footed, my left arch was starting to hurt and I had one or two twinges of cramp. After the 5th and final turn, Lengowski was less than the loop behind me, and I had to concentrate all my efforts on pushing forward. I reached 40 Km and thought to myself, "1¼ miles to go." A race official leaned out of a car and said, "Victory, Hill." I wasn't so sure. The Russians' coach in a car, motioned me to keep going. Leaving the tree lined road for the last time and entering the streets of Debno, I knew I had got it. Fifty yards from the tape a girl gave me a bouquet of flowers and my legs almost gave way. I crossed the line. 2:12:34.2. I was really back! Roll on next year!

After two cups of tea, a pale blue sash was hung across my chest on the podium and we walked back to the hotel. The only bath was occupied by someone I assumed hadn't finished the race and I got into my sleeping bag. I didn't feel like moving for the rest of the night, but the presentation was at 9.00 p.m. It was pouring down outside and we had to get a lift in a police van to the local sports hall for the ceremonies. On arrival, a committee member took me on one side, to a small room. All the officials were there, and I thought, "Bloody hell, there's going to be some problem with the expenses."

"There has been a tragedy," one of them said.

"Christ," I thought, "I was right."

"The first prize has been broken," he continued.

On moving the metre high crystal vase from display in a shop window, to the hall, someone had dropped it. It was a pity, but that was that. They gave me two extra smaller crystals instead. I went back to May, had three bowls of beetroot soup, a lot of soft drinks to re-hydrate and then started on the vodka. I got a radio for another prize, which I swopped for a crystal bowl, and I bought another crystal, hoping to sell it and recoup some of my expenses.

We stayed until Thursday morning. After a post-race celebratory breakfast on Monday, at which we drank sweet Polish wine, and every country, including May and I, had to sing a song, a lot of our time was taken spending the zlotychs, mainly on things we might be able to sell back home. We bought training shoes and hooded tops, but it was like having hit the pools; we had to spend the money as we couldn't take it out of the country. Vodka, gherkins, tablecloths, dolls, rugs, stamp albums, soup dishes, clothes for the kids. We had boxes of stuff. We bought Eric a pair of jeans and a denim waistcoat as a present. The rest of the time we spent at the lake with our lads and their Polish friends. The last day we had lunch at the restaurant; as we came out each of the kids we had been bringing back from the forest gave May a flower.

Thursday we left early. On my run at 5.00 a.m. I flushed a hare and two grouse. We gave three pips on the horn as we passed Eric's house, then drove to the border with the Polish customs lady tut-tutting at all the boxes in the back of the van. We crossed into East Germany and on into West Germany after an inspection by East German border guards, including under the engine with a mirror mounted on wheels. Across to Willich, near Krefeld, where we visited and had a beer with my brother Jeff, now based in the Army there, and finally into Holland, Venlo, where we camped a couple of days. We stayed one night at the Hook of Holland and sailed Saturday for Harwich, finally getting to bed in Hyde at 1.45 a.m.

CHAPTER EIGHTEEN

The next day I won the tough Rossendale half-marathon in 77°F heat from Alan Spence and Jim Alder with 69:15.

There were six weeks to go until my next marathon, a "fun" one this time, the Pre-Olympic marathon in Montreal. It was a family trip, arranged by myself. I wanted to see the Olympic course first hand, and the B.A.A.B. had no plans to send a marathon runner there, although they did cough up £250 towards my expenses in January 1976! Most of my training up to that race was easy running, but lots of races.

I ran 59½ miles to the Y.M.C.A. 20 Km race, where I finished 2nd to Ricky Wilde in 61:01. I sat on Steve Kenyon for the last half of the race and as we reached the final field he said, "Just what I don't want, this," so I promptly outsprinted him. 69 miles to the Hyde '8', 2nd again to Ricky Wilde. 82½ miles, including a Thursday night 5,000 metres, 14:36.0, victory at Leverhulme Park in a Bolton Track League race, to the Salford '5' where I had a bit of a stinker, feeling sick for some reason or other and finishing 7th in 24:09. 81 miles to the Rivington Cup 5,000 metres at Bolton, 5th in 14:26.6. 84 miles, including a win in the Rochdale 10,000 metres road race, Tuesday night, and 3rd in another Bolton Track League 5,000 metres, Thursday night, to the Harwood '8', near Bolton, on Sunday July 27th where I got 2nd to Steve Kenyon, with Mike Freary 3rd.

Monday night's training session was a three miler in Mount Forest, north of Toronto, in Canada, from the house of Peter Lever, ex-Bolton Harrier who with his wife, Kim, was visiting England! We really enjoyed the relaxation there. The house was out in the country and had a stream in the huge garden. We sunbathed, cut the grass, ate well, and drank a little beer. With the temperature in the 90's, and the clear sun on my shoulders, training in just a pair of shorts on deserted dirt roads, spotting beautiful coloured butterflies, was pure pleasure.

Peter and Kim arrived Thursday night, and Friday, Peter drove us to Toronto for us to catch the 11.40 a.m. "Rapido" for the 5 hour 20 minute train ride to Montreal. We got a taxi to the University of Montreal and everyone there was so helpful. We had two lovely rooms, all of us were "accredited", with special passes containing our photographs. The weather in Montreal was hotter than Ontario, probably just touching the 100 deg. F mark as I jogged out for a two mile run, meeting Hugh Sweeney III, from New York, one of our mail order customers.

Race day, Saturday August 2nd, was no cooler. I drank plenty of fluids during the day and hoped that five days would have been enough to acclimatise to the heat a little. I learned that the seven Japanese runners had been there for three weeks! The start was at 4.30 p.m., and at 3.00 p.m. we joined the other marathon runners on a big blue and white, air conditioned bus with tinted glass windows. When I stepped off at Parc Etienne Desmarteau, it was like walking into a furnace. It was still 100 deg. F at 16 Km in the race. The humidity was high, 88%, and the temperature remained in the 90's well after the race had finished around 7.00 p.m.

I had been writing to a runner, Mike Sudlow, an ex-Sale Harrier who had been at Sheffield University around the time I was at Manchester. They were putting us up for a few days after the race. I had a mental picture of him and recognised him immediately as he came over with his wife, Jenny, to introduce himself. He had a new pair of Nike lightweight road-race shoes, specially made for me and delivered from the U.S.A. to Mike for speed.

Only 18 runners faced the starter's pistol. Seven were Japanese, of whom I knew only one, Akio Usami; there was Lesse from East Germany who I thought would go well in the heat, Cindolo of Italy, two Finns, an unknown Kenyan, Sirma, Reveyn of Belgium, three Americans, individual entrants, and surprisingly only one Canadian, Schamburger who dropped out after 25 Km. Mercifully the pace was slow and I stayed near the front; I had no intention of racing this one; I wanted to survive.

I'd done no warm up but started to sweat as soon as we began to move. I was on the tail end of 10 runners through 5 Km in 16:50, and

"I was on the tail end . . ."

"I stayed with the group . . ."

it seemed reasonably easy. Trotting along to 10 Km I moved out from behind the bunch to allow the breeze to blow over my skin, and through the holes of my blue and white mesh vest to cool me. My second 5 Km took me 16:57, and at the refreshment station I grabbed a wet sponge and my drink. The drinks were in special bottles and had been taken refrigerated to the various feed stations. I needed to drink and lost some ground trying to get the liquid down, but quickly made it up.

I stayed with the group, happy to be still there, and noticed Lesse dropping at 14 Km even though the pace was slowing, 17:16 for my 5 Km split to 15 Km. We never saw him again; he retired at 20 Km and was taken to hospital suffering from complete dehydration. At 15 Km I missed my feed bottle, groaning, but luckily a man dashed after me and thrust it into my hand. I had difficulty drinking again, but I made sure I swallowed as much as possible then accelerated slightly to make up for lost ground. I was expecting someone to break any minute and I knew I would go off the back if that happened. I survived the next 5 Km in 17:27, grabbed my drink, gulped what I could and handed the bottle to Reveyn. My worst fears came true and I started to slip behind the leaders until I was 50 or 60 yards down. I was really struggling, I was running on a road called L'Acadie, a long uphill drag away from the river, there was no shade, the sun was shining on my neck and back and there was a slight following wind which meant I was running in dead still stifling air. I put my head down. I had to finish. Suddenly from the side of the road appeared Toivola, one of the Finns. He had had to make a dive for the bushes, and quickly he left me and caught the leaders. But perhaps they had been over-ambitious up the hill and by 25 Km, with a 17:22 split, I was back on again. Here there was a sharp right then left turn, and a period of light relief as one of the traffic cops, noisily, and too closely protecting the runners at intersections, rode up L'Acadie on his huge machine with lights and aerials all over the place, missed the turn and fell off his bike trying to reverse direction. I got my drink again, and a sponge squeezed all over my head and neck so that the water cascaded down on my vest, Union Jack shorts and racing shoes giving temporary refreshment. There was a slight rise here and, freshly sponged, I took the lead. This broke up the bunch, but as we approached a bigger hill, an over-pass, one of the Japanese went away. I wasn't chasing; I had my pace and a trio of myself, Toivola and Usami detached ourselves in his wake. The uphills slowed my 5 Km split up to 30 Km, to 17:59, but at this stage I took a lot to drink, waiting for the downhill sections where I wasn't having to breathe so hard, and squirting the liquid into the side and bottom of my mouth before swallowing.

Stretching our long legs downhill, with Parc Mont Royal on our right, Toivola and I slowly drew away from Usami who pattered along wearing a back-to-front white cap. As we swept down steeply to the centre of Montreal I held back for the company of the Finn over the last four or five miles. At 35 Km, with the latest 5 Km having taken 17:05, I felt I was the stronger of the two of us and even offered him a sponge when he missed one. I could see the leading Japanese was coming back. At 37 Km I suddenly became tired and had to switch roles, tucking in behind the Finn, thankful for the shade of the buildings along Sherbrooke Street. Together we caught

The finish — 2:26:01.

315

the Japanese runner dead on 40 Km, 17:10 for that section. I hoped we would go past him as we turned on to Pie IX Road, but he latched on. I didn't want a fight.

Near the finish there was a rise up to the track. I'd had it. I didn't want to win anyway and be labelled a possible favourite for the Olympics next year, so I backed off the pace and let the other two race away. On the track I watched the Japanese run away from Toivola over the last 200 metres. The results:

Toivola, Mizukami, Hill.

1.	N. Mizukami	2:25:45.9
2.	J. Toivola	2:25:50.5
3.	R. Hill	2:26:01.4
4.	A. Usami	2:27:04.8
5.	J. Reveyn	2:31:20.3
6.	T. So	2:32:38.7

Only 12 runners finished out of eighteen, seven of them Japanese. I was well pleased. If I could run like that after my busy summer schedule and without the "diet", if the conditions were like this next year and I was perfectly prepared, who knows.

Mike gave me a cold beer, my rectal temperature was 103.6°F, but I recovered quickly and felt fine. After a press conference, packing, and chatting, we all left for Lennoxville, near Sherbrooke, in Mike's BMW Bavaria. A flashing sign read: "10.40 p.m. — 86°F".

August looked like being a tough month, culminating in the Enschede Marathon, August 30th, exactly four weeks after Montreal. I was defending my title in this bi-annual marathon classic in Holland. This would be my last serious marathon of the summer campaign, and would be preceded by the Geraardsbergen half-marathon, August 23rd, and the Locomotion '20' in Darlington, August 16th. Meanwhile we rested in Quebec, or I tried to. Mike was a fast trainer and although we ran only four miles, after a couple of days he had me gasping and I had to let him go on whilst I jogged 2½ miles. Mike was on holiday from teaching at college and we went sightseeing, one day barbecuing in Mt. Orford Park with a friend, Gaetan Breton and his wife Nicole. We borrowed their canoe and Graham and I had a long paddle across the placid lake, before we all walked to the top of the mountain for some magnificent

Mike and Jenny Sudlow with their family and mine.

views. Friday we returned to Montreal, taking a train from there to Toronto where we stayed a couple of days with ex-Yorkshireman Bob Moore, now married. His wife Jane had just had a daughter. Saturday I finished last and rather ashamed, in a 3,000 metres at Oshawa, in bare feet on an asphalt track in 8:49.0. I had forgotten my flat shoes!

After sightseeing in Toronto we flew back to England through Sunday night and eased back into work Monday. We were in bed at 8.45 p.m. when a knock came on the door; a guy wanted to buy a pair of training shoes. After he had gone, the phone rang twice, but I refused to answer. Having the business at home was getting a bit much.

The week following Montreal I ran 68½ miles including the 26 miles of the race. The week after, back in England I logged 58½ miles and followed up the Oshawa embarrassment with a Wednesday '6', in Bolton Harriers "Around-the-Town" race. I got 3rd to club-mate Steve Kenyon and Frank Davies of Liverpool. I felt tired most of the time in training and was nowhere near fully prepared to take on Ian Thompson in the Locomotion '20' at Darlington on August 16th. The organisers, including Max Coleby, had gone to a lot of trouble to get me there, and on a tough hilly course I spotted immediately that Thompson was in a serious mood as he belted it from the start. I was soon with him, followed by Alan Domleo, but could only hang on until 7 miles, when on an extra steep hill, the pair ran away. I tried and tried on the out and back course but at 13 miles realised that the chase was useless, stopped for a drink, and cruised home nursing my left leg where I was getting groin pains. Alan gave Ian a real scare, losing out only on the sprint with 1:42:28 to 1:42:25. That long race at the start of the week boosted my total to 71½ miles, and I set sail from Hull to Zeebrugge, for me to challenge the half-marathon in Geraardsbergen once more. This week Steven and Graham stayed with my parents in Blackpool; May and I were free as birds driving towards Enschede in the big Ford Transit van and camping during a beautiful, hot, sunny week. But first the Belgian half-marathon. The only runner I knew in the field as we massed in the railway square, the loud-music-playing-fairground at our backs, was Jose Reveyn, 5th in Montreal. For once the start felt reasonable, but soon a runner called Schoofs started putting in bursts and eventually took Reveyn with him. At the end of the first of three laps this pair had 30 yards lead and I had someone called De Maesschalk trailing me. Towards the end of the second lap we caught and left Reveyn. However, a runner in red came past so quickly I couldn't believe he was in the race. I thought he was training. I was amazed when I learned he had gone through to win the race with 1:00:52, 18 seconds in front of Rik Schoofs. His name was Leon Schots. My partner, De Maesschalk, actually shunted me into the lead for the last lap, but from the traffic lights at the top of the hill in the main street, about 400 metres from the finish, I dropped him by 4 seconds to record 1:02:36.

We had long celebrations on Saturday night, both in town and back with our hosts, Alphonse and Alphonsine at the Oudenberg-hof. Later on the whole committee came up, and we talked, drank pils and trappist beers, and danced until 4.00 a.m. Sunday morning we went down to the town to join the local athletic club in a parade round the streets, but it rained and after a couple of glasses of pils it turned into a bar crawl following Augustine and Walter and the rest of the committee. We were impolitely one hour late for Alphonse's rabbit lunch, I was unfit to drive, and we stayed an extra night in Belgium.

A thunderstorm deafeningly rattling the roof of the van heralded our departure for Holland and the roads were winter white with hail, but later in the day we reached perfect summer weather. We camped in Otterlo and then Diepenheim. The sun, training on sandy forest trails and canal banks, the early to bed, at sunset, and the fresh outdoor food made the low carbohydrate stage of "the diet", Monday, Tuesday and Wednesday bearable. I remained a little stiff and weary, with pains in my left hamstring, even off "the diet". Friday we drove to Enschede, found Mr Wolsink at race headquarters and followed our hosts, Henk and Beryl Van Gelderen, to their beautiful home, off Vlierstraat, right on the marathon course, on the outskirts of town. At night we attended the formal reception of the runners at the Town Hall. It looked like being a tough race with Will Rodgers, who had won Boston this year in

Camping at Diepenheim.

2:09:55, wearing a crumpled T-shirt, taking the mantle of favourite, followed by Neil Cusack of Ireland. In all, twenty-two countries were represented.

Saturday morning I did a one mile run, to stretch, mentally rehearse, and look at the weather. After my comparative success in Montreal, I was looking for a hot day. It looked like I might get it. At 9.30 a.m. I had bread and marmalade and coffee, then went for a medical. I met two Bolton team-mates, Tommy Parr and Kenny Mayer, in town as we bought stamps, postcards, sweets for our kids and six litres of red wine to take home. It was getting hot. Back at Henk's house I had a drink of lemon squash at 11.50 a.m. followed by tea and two slices of bread with jam. In the bedroom I wrote my postcards, training log and travelling diary. From the garden I watched the parachutists landing in the Diekman Stadium, had a shave, put on my gear and left at 2.05 p.m. for the start. This was at 3.00 p.m. I missed the parade of athletes, and after wetting my hair and arms from a tap, I sat on a bench at the track-side waiting, my mind elsewhere, until the gun went.

The temperature was 79 deg. F. It was sunny and stayed that way for the whole of the race. I forced my way to the front of the pack and stood on the line to the extreme right.

Bang! We were off! A cloud of black dust was raised as the big field of almost 300 runners circled the track a lap and a half then funnelled through the tunnel and out on to the roads. I stayed on the outside, out of trouble, and gradually worked through to the big group of leaders over about 1½ miles, carefully cutting the corners and minimising distance. There was a slight headwind on the way out. Just before 5 Km on a loop through the high-rise apartment buildings I had to jump over a bucket someone had placed in the side of the road. Morales of Honduras, just behind, hit it.

The pace seemed easy enough and I moved towards the front of the group, led by Fredriksson, a Swede, wearing a small cap and orange vest and shorts. I looked around the rest of the runners, then glanced at my arms and shoulders. I didn't seem to be sweating a lot. Will Rodger, sporting No. 1, was wearing a pair of maroon shorts and a lilac T-shirt with "BOS-TON GBTC", hand written on the front. He looked reasonable, but No. 25, Neil Cusack, with beard and a shock of thick black hair, wearing a green mesh vest, with the shamrock shield badge of Ireland on the front and, I was happy to note, a pair of my freedom shorts, looked terrible; sweat was pouring off all his body. It was amusing to see him dashing, almost obsessionally to get sponges, whichever side of the road they were on, darting this way and that. I too, took the sponges, whenever they were convenient, squeezing them over my head. My hair was not shorn as in other years but long and thin and carrying and holding the water over the back of my head. The tail end of the group was Max Coleby, Bob Lunnon, Sandy Keith, Brenton Norman (Australia) and Ferenc Szekeres (Hungary).

Rodgers went up and did some leading, and it was puzzling to see him running wide round all the bends instead of cutting the corners. At 15 Km he actually stopped for a drink, but he didn't do it again. This wasn't Boston where he had time to stop, drink, tie his shoe-lace and still run 2:09:55! I didn't take a drink at 15 Km but strode on comfortably encouraged by the shouts of knots of spectators along the road. "We want Hill," "Elef" — Eleven, my number.

I took my first drink at 20 Km picking out my specially marked ex-Montreal bottle and didn't lose any ground as I downed the dilute electrolyte drink. In the confusion, grabbing for drinks, the field split up and Sandy Keith in white vest and green shorts took the lead. It was easy for me to stay with him on the underpass and through the crowded, noisy, twisting, cobbled streets of Haaks-bergen. It was easier still as following, I cut the corners, and he went the long way round. By this tactic I got the lead, but put him back up there to take the turn ahead of me. The clock said 1:08. After turning, I glanced up. The field had split up completely. They were

Drinks at 15 Km.

well strung out, and surprise! Rodgers was off the back!

Keith seemed to push it harder, along the cobbles, the crowds cheering, avoiding the oncoming runners, past the funfair and the church, and out of town again. Now there were big gaps in the runners coming towards us, and in the comparative quiet Keith seemed to slow as I hit a rhythm and started to drop him. Somehow, at 25 Km I missed my drink and had to dash back a few metres to retrieve it. He overtook me again, so I settled in behind him until I'd

321

1st. 2:15:59.2.

taken enough liquid, cast the bottle into the edge of the road at my right and settled down to a rhythm again. About 1 Km later I moved out and began to move away. I hit a great pace and was running well and easily, looking for whatever sparse shade there was from the roadside trees.

At 30 Km I took my last drink; 35 Km seemed to take a long time coming, but I knew I was well ahead then, and I was fully aware, striding well, concentrating and using the course, taking sponges wherever possible. I knew I had it in the bag. The Van Gelderens' house was just before 40 Km. I saw the family there, raised one finger and smiled, then put my head down for the finish. At 40 Km I saw "2:08", and thought that the record was out of the question. But the win would be nice. Along the dual carriageway, I could see the stadium to my right, up the cobbled road with huge crowds, right along the dirt back road, and right into the tunnel and stadium. I saw 2:15 on the illuminated clocks and knew I could get the record. I finished off with a sprint that was no trouble at all, right fist held high and smiling. 2:15:59.2, and on a hot day, well inside the course record of 2:16:54.2, set on a rainy day. Roll on 1976! The result:

1. R. Hill (England)   2:15:59.2
2. S. Keith (Scotland)   2:18:43.0
3. B. Norman (Australia)   2:20:27.0
4. B. Watson (England)   2:20:54.4

Relaxing with the Van Gelderens.

Clapping the tail-enders in.

Henk took us back to Vlierstraat and gave May and I a couple of beers. In the lowering golden sun, we sat tanned from the year's travelling on two camp chairs at the road side and clapped the tail-enders in.

Enschede was the end of my summer campaign. The end of a successful season experimenting. I'd had some good wins and a 2:12 marathon on 65, 70 and 80 miles a week, rather than the 100 plus I had previously thought necessary. I was confident again of my capabilities and now it was time to plan ahead to next year's Montreal Olympics.

I needed a couple of weeks' rest, then I would train for a 10 mile road race in Amsterdam on October 18th. After another easy week I would train for six weeks to bring me to a peak for the defence of my Maryland Marathon title on December 7th. That would round off 1975. The next serious objective was the Olympic Marathon Trial at Rotherham on May 8th. After Maryland, four weeks' rest, six weeks' training, four weeks' rest, then an eight week build-up should see me fit for that. Afterwards, four weeks' recovery and a final build-up would see me at my best for the Olympics.

Featuring in these plans were trips to sunnier climates in the winter, to give me a break and provide hot weather training as race conditioning. I needed to have May with me on some of these trips for harmony and the so necessary peace of mind, and of course I wanted to have my family with me in Montreal. All of this would take money, which unfortunately I did not have. The meagre profits from the business were going into buying stock so that we could give the best possible service and boxes of running shoes and shorts occupied first the loft then the garage, all of it, next the spare bedroom and finally the entrance to our house. Apart from the clutter, May was worried because the stock wasn't insured, and after looking for some time I found an almost derelict double shop in Market Street, Hyde, which I thought we could work from. I took out a bank loan to purchase it. The repayments made it even less possible to draw on the company's finances and also I was about to take on Andy Etchell's dad, Jeff, as our first employee, albeit on a small salary. There was a little money left in the Mayor of Bolton's 1972 Olympic Preparation Fund, but that would not go far. I needed a sponsor. Meanwhile the plan went forward.

The Scotch Produce Centre, a local firm, sponsored me with meat through 1975.
But first — catch your cow!

My left hamstring was sore through September weeks of 54½, 53, 62½ and 67 miles, and I finished usually in the first five or six in weekend minor road races.

At the end of September, I met my sponsor. Barry Williams, a hammer thrower, had appealed on T.V. for a sponsor, and on enquiry Joe Lancaster, the journalist, discovered that the B.B.C. had had three responses to the plea, but had done nothing constructive with them. Joe knew of my predicament and contacted one of the interested parties, David Green of Radlett in Hertfordshire.

On September 28th, after presenting my report of the Pre-Olympic Marathon in Montreal to a conference of National Coaches in Hendon, London, it was with a great deal of nervousness that I parked my old Transit in the drive and knocked on the door of David Green's house. I need not have worried; he and his wife, Ruth, made me feel at home. David was the boss of a company called Chilton Machinery and after talking for a while he said he was willing to sponsor me up to Montreal to the tune of £2,000. There were no strings attached; he wanted nothing more than to help a British athlete. It put my mind at rest.

Another three weeks, 86, 71 and 59½ miles, and all I could finish in Amsterdam was 15th, but I had run 48:32 for the 10 miles and easily beaten Commonwealth Marathon Champion, Ian Thompson. A week of rest later, on October 26th, I ran a personal best, 24:28, finishing 2nd to Pete Griffiths, in the Gale Fell Race at Littleborough near Rochdale, and through November built up for the Maryland Marathon with weeks of 68, 77½, 86, 82 and 84 miles, with a taper down week of 65½ miles including "the diet", before the race on December 7th. Two weeks before this race I had lost my title, and my record, in the Brampton to Carlisle '10' where Nick Sloane of Blackpool and Fylde A.C. ran 45:50. However, despite having to stop and tie my shoelace, I got 2nd with a respectable 47:02.

Travelling to Baltimore was a full day affair, arising at 5.45 a.m. for a 3 mile run, flying British Airways to London, TWA to New York and Allegheny to Baltimore to take my second run of the day from the beautiful Cross Keys Hotel at midnight. I could easily have called it 7.00 p.m., local time, and gone later but I wanted to stay on English time so as not to upset my system. I had with me a small vacuum flask I had bought in Poland and each morning after my 9.00 a.m. (4.00 a.m. local time) run I collected it from the hotel desk full of hot coffee plus milk, sugar and a bowl of cereal. I put all the lights on in my room, imagined it was daytime and after breakfast did some work. Naturally I tried to get to bed before midnight — 7.00 p.m. local time.

This year the organisers had brought in some opposition in the shape of two bearded Irishmen, Neil Cusack, whom I knew well, and little Mike Keogh, a six-mile specialist runner. They both lived in the U.S.A. and were both members of the Florida Track Club. More highly rated by the Americans was John Vitale, who had recently hammered Frank Shorter in a tough 15 mile road race. I had been hoping for an easy, ego boosting win, but was happy to take what would come.

After warming up in the corridor of the Eastern High School, I put Vaseline on my legs and arms for warmth and at 10.30 a.m. local time faced the initial hill on 33rd Street for the off. I was wearing No. 1 on a singletized yellow Maryland Marathon T-shirt, Union Jack shorts and green gloves. Both Cusack, No. 7, and Keogh, No.

8, wore socks on their hands to hold off the worst chill of the dry freezing day.

In the first mile up, then down, 33rd Street, the record field of 734 starters stretched to leave Ron Kurrle, 2nd last year, leading Keogh, Cusack, Vitale, a local runner and myself in the vanguard as we turned left into Hillen Road and a slight headwind all the way to the turn. Immediately the two Irishmen went to the front and after 3 miles Cusack started putting in bursts up the long climb to Perring Parkway. We covered these increases in pace easily and at 4 miles he dropped back leaving a local boy heading us until the course levelled at Putty Hill Road and somehow I was shunted into the lead. I didn't mind; I was feeling reasonable and just relaxed as I had no desire to dominate the race yet. The local runner came up again and I sat on him until the top of Satyr Hill. Here I relaxed and let gravity carry me speedily down the steep, twisting road ahead of the others, wanting to worry them.

Mike Keogh leads.

At the bottom I looked round. The field was split wide open. Cusack was about 30 yards down, and I let him catch me. He didn't go ahead and made me lead until Keogh and Vitale, in all white, including gloves and wearing No. 6 caught us. They overtook and pushed ahead on Loch Raven Drive until at 9 miles Cusack really started pushing the pace. For 2 miles he was almost sprinting up the hills, with me right behind him and Vitale coming with us, then I forged ahead and kept up a good relaxed pace in an attempt to

". . . I forged ahead . . ."

control the race. We hit the turn in 1:08. Keogh had been dropped.

On the comparative flat alongside Loch Raven Reservoir I stretched the other two, taking a five yard lead at times, but up the first long hill at 15 miles I could feel my calves tightening, and by the top Vitale was 15 yards ahead. Over the crest, I caught him easily as I strode out downhill, and Cusack caught the pair of us. His heavy breathing was punctuated by a peculiar sniffing noise.

As we raced on towards the bottom of Satyr Hill I took the lead again and heard the sniffing getting fainter and fainter. Up Satyr Hill I knew I was going to suffer; my calves were completely tight, I had to run on my heels and Vitale moved easily away until at the top

". . . Vitale moved easily away . . ."

327

". . . I was up to Vitale."

he was 75 yards ahead. Cusack almost caught me and as the hill levelled out I thought I might have to stop as cramp was grabbing the backs of my thighs. On the flat and downhill my muscles relaxed and amazingly within a mile I was up to Vitale. I thought he had been too ambitious up Satyr and had blown it, and I tried to go past at 20 miles. No chance; he locked on to me and together we started the long gentle descent towards the finish. My legs were threatening to cramp again; I was running carefully; I decided that the only way

". . . watched him fly down to finish . . ."

I could win was to out-kick him. I just hung on to him, trying to relax and keep the pace as gentle as possible. My breathing and upper body were great, but my legs were hurting so much. Up and down the switch-backs of Hillen Road we ran stride for stride, turn right into 33rd Street and up the long climb, with less than three-quarters of a mile to go, I thought I could feel him tiring. Suddenly he spoke, "Are we going to finish this thing together?"

"No, we'd better make a fight out of it," I replied.

The pace increased slightly to the crest of the hill and a sight of the finish. I kicked and jumped him. Immediately I discovered that my legs were dead and crampy. I led for 30 or 40 yards, hoping, then felt him brush me and go past. I lost co-ordination and helplessly watched him fly down to finish in 2:17:02, 4 seconds ahead of me.

Well it had been a long year. I hadn't really rested since En-schede. My time was better than last year. I was on course. Now I could rest.

2nd. 2:17:06.

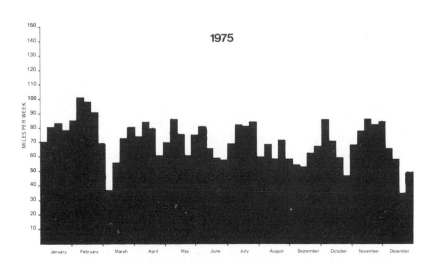

1975

CHAPTER NINETEEN

A celebratory, boozy, 58, 34½, 49 and 54½ miles finished off 1975 and 1976 was ushered in with a resolve of virtually no drinking until the Olympics were over. I got 13th in the Lancashire Cross-Country Championships at Witton Park, Blackburn, which wasn't bad and the day after May and I flew out to the Canary Isles, the Park Hotel Las Margaritas at Playa del Ingles on Gran Canaria for 8 days. A Northern Holiday Tour Company said they would give me a one-third reduction on the price, to help me in my Olympic preparation. It was to be in the form of a refund. I'm still waiting.

Gran Canaria was a beautiful place, but I rather over-reached myself there, running 6 miles every morning, much of it over soft sand and initially being surprised by the nude sunbathers! I enjoyed my longer runs, inland, mainly following a road up into volcanic hills where goats fed and miniature trees grew, each square yard of the ground looking like a Japanese Bonsai garden. During morning runs I saw a group of young German runners on several occasions. God, we were way behind in Britain!

The sun was good, I had some 11 hour sleeps, and I didn't touch a drop of alcohol, even when there was free wine at the meals. The day we were leaving I set out for a long run. The map I had bought misread the land and I ended up running for 3¼ hours, about 28 miles and that whole week gave me 101 miles, and sore hamstrings.

When we got back, the leaky roof of the shop had been sealed, and I was able to start doing some runs from there. Another 90 miles and I was 7th in the East Lancs. Cross-Country Championships. Sunday I ran 20 miles. The weather was cold and miserable in the next week, as I tried to train hard, 83 miles. This weekend I raced in Mezidon with a Bolton team of Mike Freary and Keith Darlow. I was shattered and trailed in 11th. My legs were O.K. but my heart felt tired. After the race I broke my alcohol fast at the "Vin d'Honneur" and dinner. Tuesday I ran 21 miles and felt shattered all week for 81 miles to the end of January.

In England we were going through a freezing spell, and I was glad to get away for the sunny weather of Coamo, Puerto Rico and the Half-Marathon of San Blas, with Keith Angus as team mate. Keith did everything I did: training, exercises; except he talked more. But not quite as much as John Chaplin, a Washington State University coach, managing some Kenyan runners. Keith beat me in the race, 24th, 25 seconds ahead of my 27th. Amazingly, Jack Foster at 42, finished 3rd, behind two South Americans Perez and Mora and over

5 minutes ahead of us two Englishmen! I had run 67 miles in the week to the race, during which my hamstrings had been troubling me, especially the right one. I felt peculiarly flushed for a long time after the hot race. Things were not going right and I decided to bring my rest period forward a week.

On my return I was not too happy. My back was sore and I felt depressed. I lost my resolve and Thursday night drank a fair bit of home-brewed beer followed by whiskies. Saturday, after a 51 mile week, I got 5th in the Parbold Hill race. 4th was Jeff Norman, last year's winner of the A.A.A. marathon. I didn't have a good race at all. My training log records: *"on the big road hill Cooper passed me — Curran — Leigh — I felt absolutely dead — ill — whole body shattered — heart too."*

The next week I ran 44½ miles. I was working night and day. During the day on orders, at night with Jeff Etchells renovating ceilings and floors at the shop, a dusty blackening job; I needed the home-brew after. Two further weeks of easy running 54½ and 63 miles took me into March and to the start of my build-up without any serious races.

On the last weekend of that rest period I gave a slide show in Bolton, organised by my own club to try to raise a little more finance for my "Olympic Preparation Fund". Three hundred people were expected. Thirty turned up, and they raised £13.65. Thank you!

After my first week's build up of 69 miles I ran the National Cross-Country Championships at Western Park, Leicester. That day I sent off my resignation to Bolton United Harriers and an application form to rejoin my first club, Clayton-le-Moors Harriers. On the three lap course at Leicester I started absolutely dead last, standing behind all the 1,300 runners. I was 200th after one lap, 140th after two laps and finished 107th. The second week of my build up was an easy 65 miles. I was working very, very hard on the business and renovations. The third week of 75½ miles I introduced some speed work on two days, but my hamstrings still felt sore, and the work load at my job increased considerably as Jeff Etchells had to go into hospital for an operation on his ear. I was really flogging it, May and I doing every aspect of the job, including me having to transport the workmen to finish the refurbishing jobs.

Still we weren't yet a shop, and I was able to just lock up for May and I to fly to The Hague and the "City-Pier-City" Half-Marathon at the weekend. I didn't fare brilliantly and was 9th in 1:04:10, less than a minute behind Revejn's winning 1:03:24. Chris Stewart was 2nd (1:03:25) and Jeff Norman 3rd (1:03:29). I had put in a good hanging-on effort. Six weeks to go for the trial. Things were coming on.

Family portrait. March.

Unfortunately my employee Jeff Etchell's week in hospital turned out to be two, an extra week for convalescence, and I had to cancel a racing trip to Israel at the eleventh hour, something I'd never done before. I had an easy run with Andy Etchells on Monday afternoon following the half-marathon in Holland. My training log records: *"heart felt extemely tired all the way — pressure of work or Saturday's race."* On Wednesday: *"4— mile course — easy running — again heart was tired through pressure of work and problems — should have done an 8."* After a week of 76½ miles I finished way down in the Pendle Fell Race.

The work was getting to me as I was having to do almost everything, working Saturdays and Sundays, day and night. May helped as much as she could, but when orders received were entered, assembled, packed, stamped and taken to the post office, I still had to write purchase orders, answer queries, give quotes, cash-up, write adverts, and collect a lot of goods, driving round all over the place.

When I got to bed, often I couldn't get to sleep, eventually having to get up for a couple of whiskies and lemonade, before falling asleep at 1.30 a.m.

On Tuesday, April 6th, in the middle of an 80 mile week, things began to pick up: *"8 mile course — number stride fartlek up to 50 and down x 2 — heart still feeling pressed but running a bit better than usual."* That week I got a sore throat and a bad chest. One of the reasons for the frenzied activity, even though Jeff was now back at work, was that we were driving to the South of France for a fortnight of hot weather training starting at the weekend, and I wanted everything in the business straight. On Saturday I finished 7th in the Chris Vose '10' with 49:33. Fairly reasonable. We were leaving Sunday.

I had so much to do that day that I was up at 4.00 a.m., felt too knackered to do anything, and had to go back to bed until 7.45 a.m., when I had two shredded wheats then ran 20 miles. We packed the Transit in a hurry, dropped all last minute messages at Jeff's at 2.00 p.m. and drove to Southampton for the overnight ferry to Le Havre. At 6.20 a.m. the next day we were driving through the early morning mist towards Pont Tanquarville.

Things didn't go as planned. I thought we would take a scenic route down to the Mediterranean but it turned out very, very slow. We spent two nights in small hotels before we saw the Mediterranean near Narbonne, and then it was windy and raining. Also we had forgotten to pack our big tent. I could have cried. We stuck it out there, alone and shivering on a camp-site before Friday, we drove up to Lyons for a half-marathon. Even with travelling I managed 89 miles that week.

Naturally, with our luck, the weather in Lyon turned out scorching and I slumped to 3rd in around 1:10, behind Fernand Kolbeck and an unknown to me, Margeritas. I was all in. Sunday we bombed down to Cavaliere on the Cote d'Azur, leaving the sun behind and meeting swampy, puddly ground and grey waves on the Med. This was turning into a nightmare and next day we travelled north to Orange, where at last we had three days of sun and I was able to bang in three good 12 miles runs before journeying on again north, to La Ferté Bernard, and more freezing weather.

It was another half-marathon, Bonnetable to La Ferté Bernard. I had a better run than Lyons. Barry Watson was there with three Southern runners I hadn't met before, Steve McHale, Roger Brown, and Pat Gallagher. I didn't think there was much opposition and started far too casually allowing Watson and McHale to get away. My 5 Km splits read: 15:40, 15:20, 14:46 but I could only manage 3rd with 1:06:19 to Watson's 1:05:24 and McHale's 1:05:54. After the race I thought to mself, "Enjoy it, Barry. In two weeks' time I'll hammer you in the marathon trial." I'd clocked 89½ miles my second week in France. We were home by Monday lunchtime, to more freezing cold weather.

I was determined nothing would go wrong and for two weeks deliberately only worked mornings. May got a sore throat, so for two nights I went in the single bed in the spare room to avoid catching it. Wednesday I drove to Rotherham and met Mick Hague, one of the organisers, who showed me round the marathon course. It was my last big week, 92 miles.

There was one sharpening race left, the "International Zucker-lauf" 10 Km in Ameln, Germany. On May 1st I flew out to Dussel-dorf, coincidentally on the same flight as Klaus Gerlach, who had been a good friend of mine as head of the Dyestuffs Division of Bayer U.K., and was now returning to Germany permanently. I stayed in the beautiful house, in a forest, of Herr Werner von Langen and his wife, and in the race on Sunday ran 5th, with 29:59.8, and was knackered at the end. My brother Jeff who was stationed not far away watched the race. The von Langens gave me lovely white wine with the dinner of roast pheasant and salad, and afterwards we put in an appearance at the official reception where I chatted to Neil Cusack and Danny McDaid from Ireland, Brenton Norman from Australia and Jukka Toivola of Finland, all of whom had raced the 25 Km competition the same afternoon. I had a few beers and foolishly smoked three cigarettes. Neil raised his eyebrows, but I said, "Don't worry. You'll see. I'll make the Olympic team next Saturday." Christ, what a time for bravado! And the fags made me feel bad the next day, Monday, the first day of "the diet". I didn't touch another drink until after the trial.

That day I ran 6 miles in the morning, getting lost in the forest, and a hard fartlek session at lunchtime before flying home. Tuesday I ran 3 miles in the morning then 8 miles at night at Stockport Harriers' track in Woodbank Park, running sets of 2, 4, and 6 x 400's with 400 interval. I was really tired on the last three; "the diet" was working. Wednesday I ran three and a six and felt quite good, even though it was the third day of "the diet".

On Thursday morning's 3 miles my legs felt very tired, but I was a lot better on my lunchtime 3½ miles from the shop. Friday morning I felt very tired when I woke up and stayed in bed until 7.50 a.m., then ran 3 miles in full track suit. After all the bloody cold weather we'd had, it was now warm. And beautifully sunny too, for training, as I trotted 2 miles at lunchtime in vest and shorts. In the afternoon I loaded the van with stock for selling after the race on Saturday and went home at 5.00 p.m. I went to bed at 10.30 p.m. and slept very well.

Staying in bed until 9.00 a.m. on race day made me feel well rested and after a 2 mile run I had one shredded wheat, two jam butties and a cup of tea. It was a warm morning. I had a shave, a bath, and cut my hair on the forehead. Later I sat in the sun and shaved my legs, but noticing the time, I hurriedly packed my bag, had another jam butty and cup of tea at 11.30 a.m. and all the family of us left in the van at 11.50 a.m. Just before Penistone, I felt some wheel knock, stopped the van and examined the tyres. I was dreading problems at this hour, but could see nothing and drove carefully the rest of the way. It was disturbing and worrying me, but we reached the Sports Centre safely at 12.50 p.m., 40 minutes before the start.

After parking, I pushed through the crowds to the reporting desk. All the feed bottles had been taken away. Sportingly, Dave Allen, of Manchester Athletic Club gave me five of his and I filled them with dilute "Accolade", rushed out to the distribution car to find it had gone. Another official said he would get them to the feed points for me and I stuck clear identification labels on them. I would need them as the weather had turned out very hot. Hundreds of people were wishing me luck and my dad came to wish me all the best.

I pinned a silver St. Christopher medal my mother had given me to my number. I had on a new white mesh vest and Union Jack shorts, I wet my hair under a tap and went out to find a bus to the start, not bothering with a track suit in the heat. I was one of the few on the last dark green, double decker, corporation bus up to the start, and once there I just had time for a quick pee and jogged to the starting area with Jim Alder, who I noticed was going grey. We merged into the crowd of runners and Jim said, "Are you going to the front then?"

"I don't know what you mean," I replied.

"Are you going to the front?" he repeated.

It dawned on me. I was facing the wrong way in the narrow street. The start was in the other direction and we were at the back! We forced our way to near the front and stood as officials tried unsuccessfully to get the anxious runners back over the genuine start line. Suddenly we were off.

From behind the front line I found myself in around 40th position at an uncomfortable pace on a hot sunny day with little wind. I didn't feel loose, even running downhill. The sizeable crowds were shouting, "C'mon, Ian," and I could hear youngsters' voices calling "C'mon Wrighty"; Trevor was almost a local boy anyway. For over 2 miles I was 30 yards adrift of the leaders, and Jim Alder warned, "This is 2:10 pace!" Gradually I moved up until at 5 miles I was in a group of about ten athletes, and the time was sub-25 minutes. But I was hanging on; the running wasn't coming easily.

5 miles.

". . . I couldn't respond . . ."

At 7 miles Ian Thompson took off and Barry Watson went with him. There was nothing I could do but hang on to the second group. Encouragement was coming all around the course, "C'mon Colin," "C'mon Norman Deakin," and "C'mon Ron and Jeff" from the Manchester area supporters.

At 9 miles Jeff Norman stirred things up, I couldn't respond, and Trevor Wright, Chris Stewart, Bernie Plain, Keith Angus and Tim Johnston went with him. A thought flashed into my mind, "What

". . . grabbed my first drink at 10 miles." From my dad.

am I going to do with all my spare time now?" but within a mile I was on them again and grabbed my first drink at 10 miles. A shade over 50 minutes. Turning right, a camera car obstructed me, and furious, I hurled my half full feed bottle scoring a direct hit through the driver's open window.

I kept going with this group for some distance, hoping, and even led a little at 13 miles where there was another feed station. But warily I dropped back to follow, having just got over a bad patch. Trevor Wright and Chris Stewart were off the back, and our group was 40 seconds down on Thompson and Watson. I felt relaxed and felt I might just do it, as I knew the first three must certainly go to Montreal. I took another drink at 16 miles.

At 17 miles Jeff Norman came from the back of the bunch and set off down the road after the two leaders taking Plain and Angus with him. I had only one pace and watched helplessly as Angus, wearing No. 3 on his red Ron Hill vest, disappeared up the road, along with my chances of Montreal.

One of the Keily family came alongside in a van. "Go on, Ron, you can do it." I just shook my head. I was feeling desperately tired, and my left thigh was painful and stiffening. I was alone, in limbo, knowing that I would have to suffer all the way home with no reward. I grabbed my next drink at 19 miles and gulped it down to minimise the suffering and attack on my body. A mile later I glanced up and saw that Plain was coming back; he'd blown it. Slowly, slowly, I caught him and passed him at 21½ miles. Encouraged and with only 4½ miles to go I began pushing on. I could now see Thompson up ahead, and coming back. Head down, pattering along in the gutter, I overtook him just after 23 miles. "Keep it going, Ian." "Go on, Ron."

Three miles to go and I was fourth. In a queue of slow moving cars to my right I heard shouts of encouragement from Trevor Wright, Don Faircloth and Arthur Walsham. "You can do it." "Remember Athens." I was flying now.

337

On the pavement to my left a yellow pullovered Hammy Taylor. He was keeping with me, downhill, urging me on, "Lean into it." "Go." "This is the big one." A camera car was shadowing me on the right. I stretched my legs.

Then I saw the Leisure Centre, the finish, and not another runner in sight. I knew that was it. Keith Angus was coming up the home straight as I swept down on to the track for the last lap. I heard the loudspeaker, ". . . one of Britain's greatest marathon runners . . . most popular . . ."

The banner says "FINISH". It really was the finish for me.

A brave face?
With mother, Steven and May.

Result:

1.	B. Watson	2:15:08
2.	J. Norman	2:15:17
3.	K. Angus	2:15:55
4.	R. Hill	2:16:59
5.	B. Plain	2:18:52
6.	A. Keith	2:19:02
7.	I. Thompson	2:19:07

CHAPTER TWENTY

Ironically, fourth prize for the race was six silver plated goblets on a silver plated tray. So that I could celebrate? I smiled ruefully.

We set off back, May and the boys, my mother and dad in our van, and just over the M1 motorway we stopped for a drink at a pub called The Travellers, with Harry and Sylvia Smith. I sank two pints of Stones Bitter. It would have been much more but I was driving.

I was acting as if it were just another defeat, but in my heart I was massively disappointed at having missed my fourth Olympics. May was right, though I would not admit it, when she said that the tremendous pressure of work had affected my running. I would

May in the kitchen of our Highcroft, Gee Cross, house.

probably now never win an Olympic medal of any colour let alone the gold medal. The gold medal which would have brought me the ultimate triumph of my career, personal glory, and surely financial rewards from which my family would benefit. The Commonwealth Games of 1978 and the 1980 Moscow Olympics were a long way off, but I would certainly be giving them a try. After all Jack Foster of New Zealand would be 43 in Montreal — I would be 42 in Moscow — and perhaps if I could only reduce my work-load in the business I might be able to do it. There was an off-chance that I would still go to Montreal as Arthur Gold, expressing his sorrow at my disappointment, had said I was first reserve, but that was a forlorn hope.

Meanwhile, I would have to adjust my life and look for new goals. I asked David Green to pass on my sponsorship to Barry Watson, the new champion.

The Olympics were at the end of August, so I would stay fit until nearly then in case by some miracle I was called upon to compete. There had been a furore in the press at Thompson's non-selection, but four days after the trial I heard it confirmed on the radio that I was first reserve if anything went wrong with the selected three.

To stay fit, and because I yet knew no other way of life, I raced practically every weekend, and the highlights of my year were in races abroad, taking May along wherever possible.

Travelling put pressure on our running gear business as turnover was growing and the premises were slowly becoming as much a retail shop as a base for a mail-order business. We had a new shop front fitted, a damp course installed and the walls plastered. Jeff Etchells pulled down sagging ceilings and replaced them, along with floorboards which had rotted under the leaking roof. My dad spent most of his holidays painting the storerooms above the shop for us.

". . . a new shop front . . ."

Jeff collected empty wooden Chinese pig bristle boxes, which smelled of mothballs, from a paintbrush factory and we stacked them and used them as storage shelves. This space was supplemented by shelving prised from an empty shop on a demolition site. Everything had to be done on a shoe-string.

My office inside the shop.

Dave Ellison, a runner from Keswick, came down with his family later in the year to join the company on the retail side, but despite May's help too, the manpower never seemed to keep pace with the increasing work, and by the end of the year I was going back to the shop at nights to try to keep up with jobs. Before that, much of my evenings had been spent working on our garden, putting up fences and concreting, etc.

With the subconscious disappointment of failing in the trial, which must have affected May too, and the pressure of work, right through until the end of the year stomach pains plagued me, often in races, the symptoms almost certainly of an ulcer. The disappointment and pressures precipitated continual rows between me and May.

But life went on. Graham, now 11 years old, started his secondary education at Greenfield School, Hyde, and Steven, 13, was progressing well at Hyde Grammar School. As winter approached they both helped me gather a quick harvest of elderberries and hawthornberries to make home-made wine.

My racing results for 1976, after the Marathon Trial on May 8th, .are listed below:

May   23 "Ernest Harper" '10'. Stannington, Yorks. 7th. 53:05. (1st. R. Bailey 51:14).

It was a well known fact that certain runners around the world were being paid a lot of money to race. When I arrived at this '10', not exactly an unknown, I was informed that I had sent 5p short on my entry fee, my name was at the top of a list. I would not get my number until the 5p was paid!

May 29 Congleton '4', Staffs. 12th. 20:34. (1st. Alan Blinston 20:02).
　　30 Rossendale Half Marathon, Lancs. 2nd. 67:20. (1st Roger Harrison 67:16).

Rossendale Half Marathon.
Hill, Harrison, Byrne.

St. Maurice Half Marathon.

June 4 Burnley '4', Lancs. 13th. 19:58. (1st. Mike Freary 18:34).
　　13 St. Maurice Half Marathon, Switzerland. 2nd. (1st. Albrecht Moser).

The invitation for this race came from an acquaintance, Bernard Voeffray, I had met in the cross-country race at Mezidon, France, and whilst there I met for the first time Noel Tamini, founder of the Spiridon Clubs, and publisher and editor of Spiridon Magazine.

June 16 Swinton '6', Manchester. 2nd. 29:41. (1st. Frank McGuire 29:26).
　　19 Freckleton Half Marathon, Lancs. 4th. 65:52. (1st. Roger Harrison 65:31).
　　25 St. Gallen, Switzerland, Relay Race. Four Man International Team v. 125 Townspeople. 1st.

Last minute advice for Chris Stewart
(rt.) and myself at St. Gallen.

This race was great fun. I was teamed up with Chris Stewart (G.B.), George Kaiser (Switzerland) and Victor Mora (Colombia) — on his way home after training in Italy. The lap, through streets, was more than 800 m. Commencing at 3.30, Victor ran 10 laps then cleared off back to Bogota, while the three of us left ran first 15 laps each, then four sets of five laps, ending with two laps apiece. I had the fastest individual lap time of 2:29 and our team won by five laps, the race finishing in the dark at about 9.30 p.m.

June 27 Y.M.C.A. 20 Km, Manchester. 8th. 65:01. (1st. John Calvert 63:15).
July 4 Hyde '8', Cheshire. 2nd. 40:29. (1st. Graham Ellis 40:24).

Hyde '8'. 1st. Graham Ellis 40:24, me 2nd. 40:29.

July 10 Eccles '10', Manchester. 2nd. 51:47. (1st. Derek Blakeley 51:45).
11 "Mather and Platt" '6', Manchester. 1st. 28:14.

This double proved I was in good form and after winning the second race someone told me that the day before, Keith Angus, one of our Montreal Marathon trio, had twisted his ankle so badly, whilst warming up for a race, that he had had to drop out. I waited anxiously for news that I was called up as a reserve, but none came.

1976

The story goes that Keith had to go to London to be examined by a specialist who told him that he HAD NOT TO RUN AT ALL until he got to Montreal, then he could train for the marathon which was on July 1st. So much for the reserve! I helped with the commentary on the marathon from the BBC studio in London, noting in my diary "our boys absolutely nowhere in sight — pathetic performances".

The Olympic Marathon results were:

1. Waldemar Cierpinski (G.D.R.)   2:09:55.0
2. Frank Shorter (U.S.A.)   2:10:45.8
3. Karel Lismont (Belgium)   2:11:12.6
4. Don Kardong (U.S.A.)   2:11:15.8
5. Lasse Viren (Finland)   2:13:10.8
26. Jeff Norman (G.B.)   2:20:04.8
31. Keith Angus (G.B.)   2:22:18.6
45. Barry Watson (G.B.)   2:28:32.2

All the British boys had gone down with colds.

July 21 Heywood '5', Lancs. 5th. 27:20. (1st. John Calvert 26:58).
Aug. 8 Sierre-Zinal, Mountain Race, Switzerland. 6th. 2:53:00. (1st. Aldo Allegranza (Italy) 2:46:33).

I drove to this classic race with May in our Ford Transit van, arriving in Zinal on Tuesday before the Sunday race. We had a scare on the motorway near Lausanne when, driving through a tunnel, sprays of hot rusty water suddenly spumed into the front seat. I had already seized up one engine this year through putting no oil in, and anxiously cruised in neutral down to a lake-side garage where happily a mechanic reconnected a loose hose and charged me less than £1.

"Raclette" at Zinal.

344

The drive up to Zinal on narrow twisting roads, precipitous drops at the side, was hair-raising and ensured that we stayed at the camp-site up there until time for returning. The weather was marvellous. Sun during the day, clear freezing at night. And we had good company — specialist fell runners (the men that is) from near home — Harry and Sheila Walker, Pete Walkington and Carol, Mike Short and Ann, John North and Alan Heaton of Clayton-le-Moors Harriers.

Friday we laughed our way, on white wine, through a "raclette" at the home of Jean-Pierre, the local bus-driver, and his wife, joined later by the mayor and Jean-Claude Pont, the race organiser. On Sunday, I was pleased with my performance as the race involves a total climb of around 7,000 ft., 4,000 ft. of this coming in the first three miles, and only Harry Walker of the Britons beat me. Poor Ian Thompson, on a real downer, finished over an hour behind me.

Aug.	15	Stockport "2-4-6", Cheshire. 3rd. 30:22. (1st. Keith Darlow 29:45).
	19	Clayton-le-Moors A.G.M. 5,000 m. Track. 1st. 14:58.0.
	28	Cheshire 10,000 m. Track. Stockport. Guest. 1st. 30:40.4.
	30	Rotherham 3 miles. Track. 4th. 14:27.9.
Sep.	1	Linotype '5', Altrincham, Cheshire. 11th. 24:05. (1st. Frank Davies 23:24).
	4	E. Cheshire '7', Ashton-under-Lyne, Lancs. 2nd. 34:55. (1st. Steve Kenyon 34:14).
	11	POLYTECHNIC MARATHON, Windsor. 3rd. 2:18:14. (1st. Bernie Plain 2:15:43).
	17	BERCHEM MARATHON BELGIUM. 4th. 2:23:38. (1st. W. Van Renterghem (Belgium) 2:19:01).

This was the closest I had ever run two marathons — six days apart — and at half-way in the second race I thought I was going to win. Over the last 15 kms stiffness, then tiredness set in and I suffered very much at the end.

Sep.	22	Saddleworth '6', Lancs. 2nd. 29:57. (1st. Tony Byrne 29:48).
	25	Eccles Pike Fell Race, Derbyshire. 1st. 18:44. ON MY 38th BIRTHDAY.

Stockport "2-4-6", 3rd.

"Poly" Marathon. Me 3rd. 2:18:44, Plain 1st. 2:15:43, Joslyn 2nd. 2:16:56.

Oct.   16 Manchester University Cross-Country Relay, Wythenshaw Park.

I ran the first leg for Manchester University Vice-Presidents' team, then continued for the other five laps recording 10.04, 10.42, 10.44, 10.53, 10.47 and 10.26, with only four of the teams of six runners in front of me at the end!

24 NEW YORK MARATHON. 10th. 2:19:43 (1st. Bill Rodgers 2:10:10).

New York City Marathon.

The first of the New York City spectaculars, starting on the Verrazano Bridge and taking in the five boroughs of New York. On a freezing day I worked through steadily after 5 minute miling it to 8 miles until I was 13th. After 18 miles, where I passed Ian Thompson, I got very tired and managed to pass only a Puerto Rican and Richard Mabuza (Swaziland) to finish 10th. The field of 2,000 runners had only been equalled by the famous Boston Marathon.

New York, 10th. 2:19:43.

Oct. 31   Gale Fell Race, Littleborough, Lancs. 6th. 24:55 (1st. Colin Robinson 24:11).

Nov. 6   Manchester League Cross-Country, Boggart Hole Clough. Guest. 1st. 34:04.
     7   Black Lane Ends Fell Race, Lancs. 4th. 30:39. (1st. Harry Walker 29:45).
  20   Harold Doggett Handicap Cross-Country, Boggart Hole Clough. 3rd. fastest 24:56. (1st. J. Calvert 23:56).
  28   Geraardsbergen Cross-Country, Belgium. 7th.

Dec.   5   MARYLAND MARATHON, USA. 3rd. 2:20:23 (1st. Bill Rodgers (USA) 2:14:22).

Bill Rodgers ran a great time on this course with Tom Fleming 2nd and me just breaking away from Barry Brown over the last mile to get 3rd of the 1,200 competitors. After a tasty cocktail reception at the penthouse apartment of race patron Victor Frenkil, and a few beers with Les Kinion and his team at their local fire station, I decided to travel back to New York that night with Fred Lebow and Paul Fetscher in Paul's prized Mercedes. Half-way, they switched drivers and Paul fell asleep on the back seat until about 15 miles out

347

of New York, when the engine started to boil up. Paul was none too happy with Fred as the vehicle limped into the city with frequent stops to top up with water. The next day Fred asked me if I would help him next year in signing up European runners for his marathon.

Dec.   12 Stoodley Pike Fell Race, Todmorden, Lancs. 3rd. 18:38 (1st. M. Weeks 18:00).

          26 Brinscall Road Relay, Blackburn, Lancs. 3rd leg. Lost one place.

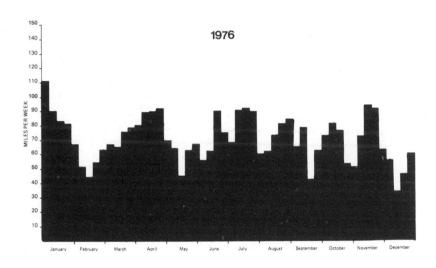

CHAPTER TWENTY-ONE

Through 1977 our running gear business continued to grow. I moved out of the shop floor to use an upstairs store room as an office and we moved the mail-order business to an upstairs room too, with Jeff Etchells doing the day-to-day work in that department. My dad spent more of his holidays painting the six rooms above the shop floor.

The shop itself was improved with a proper sign above the windows and new shop fittings, and on the 14th May we had an official shop opening with my old friend Dave Bedford cutting the tape. Dave Ellison continued working in the shop and we had to take on a Saturday lady, a family friend from our Romiley days, Elsie Conway, to cope with the extra work on that day. May too helped a lot with serving and cleaning which was not easy with two growing boys to look after. I was little help in the home as the brunt of the increasing business work fell upon my shoulders.

By July I was working seven days a week and going back every night to keep up with all the administration and paper work.

The official opening of our shop. Dave Bedford with young admirers.

Jeff came back occasionally to clear backlogs but I took that upon myself too if he got behind. On Dave's day off, Tuesday, I had to serve in the shop all day.

In addition to domestic business we were beginning to export, and also branch out from retailing into wholesaling, initially mesh vests and Nike shoes which we imported from the USA. This looked like growing quickly. One customer in Holland, Michel Lukkien, was already taking a lot of Nike shoes from us, and I was actively looking to rent another building to use for warehousing. Bill Rodgers, who had opened a shop in Boston, ordered some clothing from us and the future looked promising for increasing our turnover.

349

1977

It was in November that I had visits from my Mexico Olympics team-mate, Mike Tagg, now working for a large textile company, and phone calls from someone in Nike, which were obviously leading to an attempted takeover of our U.K. distributorship of Nike shoes. This alarmed and worried me after all the spade-work we had done introducing this line to the British market, but I pressed on regardless.

I was on a treadmill. Having the responsibility did not bother me too much, it was having to spend all those hours keeping up with the jobs that was unenjoyable. I was even knocked up by the police at 5.00 a.m. on Christmas morning to go and see to the alarm at the shop which had been set off. A false alarm, thankfully. It was definitely no good for our family life and led to many rows between May and myself. The only time I could spend in the garden or on the house was an odd hour between getting back from the shop at night and having my daily two or three drinks of shandy made from home-brewed beer or something stronger.

My aim was one day to have staff who could virtually run the business for us, leaving us the freedom to direct. It was obvious I could not do everything myself and the company was growing. Without deliberately setting out to increase in size, it was happening. Towards the end of the year I advertised for a personal assistant.

Despite this frenzied activity at work there was no let-up in my running programme and I trained twice every day and raced practically every weekend.

British Marathon Squad patron, David Green, with his family — and mine.

When I had failed to make the 1976 Olympic Team, the sponsorship I had been receiving from David Green, a Herefordshire businessman, was passed on to Barry Watson. Out of David's generosity the idea of a British Marathon Squad was born, to provide cash for food, equipment and travelling to British marathon runners, and David became the patron.

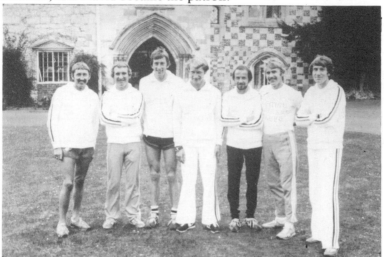

Bisham Abbey. l. to r. Ron Hill, Keith Angus, Dave Cannon, Bernie Plain, Barry Watson, Ian Thompson, Chris Stewart. (Missing is Jeff Norman.)

The venture started off well and the first training/discussion meeting was held at Bisham Abbey in September. Unfortunately, with the appointment of a National Marathon coach, the impetus to raise money to support a squad appeared to die away, and within a couple of years our dream had vanished.

Many of the trips were abroad and the change of routine accompanying these visits to foreign countries sweetened life a little. Whenever practical I took May with me and, just once in this year, Steven and Graham. The race was Marvejols-Mende in France, in July, and although they enjoyed most of it, I'm sure sometimes they were bored. They were approaching an age when they did not wish to be tied to the things that we did.

One of Graham's few races.

351

1977

May too began a little training which was almost regular, setting out with me in the mornings and returning after one mile. Graham showed a slight interest and during the summer came with May and myself on Tuesday nights to the track at Woodbank Park to run with the big, friendly crowd of Stockport Harriers. We often took Graham's mate, Stuart, and two of our friend Elsie Conway's daughters with us in the van.

One of our excursions abroad, to Rhodesia for the Rhodes Marathon, turned out to be the trip of a lifetime, but I will describe that within the list of my races for 1977:

Jan. 8   Lancashire Cross-Country Champs., St. Helens. 13th. 37:29. (1st. Geoff. Smith 36:11).
    15   Mid-Lancs. Cross-Country League, Blackburn. 6th. (1st. John Calvert).
    22   Inter-Club Cross-Country, Warrington. 1st. 26:42.
    29   E. Lancs. Cross-Country Champs., Stockport. 7th. 38:38. (1st. Alan Blinston 37:48).
Feb. 6   San Blas ½ Marathon, Coamo, Puerto Rico. 30th. 69:34. (1st. M. Yifter 62:56).

San Blas ½ Marathon. l. to r. Watson, Heatley (manager), Hill, Angus, Norman.

    12   Northern Cross-Country Champs., Leeds. 23rd. 37:35. (1st. Alwyn Dewhurst 36:27).
    20   Cambourne ½ Marathon, Cornwall. 3rd. 68:50. (1st. Dave Collins 66:37).
    26   Manchester University Cross-Country Champs. 2nd. 30:57. (1st. Laurie Reilly 30:08).
Mar. 5   National Cross-Country Champs., London. 71st. (1st. Brendan Foster 43:49).
    12   Clayton-le-Moors Cross-Country Champs. 2nd. (1st. Paul Livesey).
    20   RHODES MARATHON, SALISBURY, RHODESIA. 1st. 2:24:07; 2nd. Gordon Shaw 2:31:33; 3rd. Zonga Tapfumenayi 2:33:31.

Happily, May went with me for this race, which was sponsored by OK Bazaars, and no expense was spared to make this a dream visit for us. Everyone made us welcome: Joe Davies, managing director of OK Bazaars, the road running fraternity and especially our hosts Len and Joyce Keating who accepted us into their home like family.

With Len and Joyce Keating and family.

We arrived there on Tuesday for the race on Sunday, giving little time to acclimatise to the time change, the 5,000 ft. altitude and the heat. To minimise the effects of the latter, the race started at 6.30 a.m. This was 4.30 a.m. UK time and meant getting out of bed at 2.30 UK time the morning of the race; not an easy thing to do! The course was quite tough with a few hills and much of the route was on 9 feet wide dirt roads.

6.30 a.m. start.

At start time the weather was fairly cool with light cloud, but that early in the morning I felt knackered and my stomach was hurting a bit. I got off quickly on the slightly uphill road and for half-a-mile had two Africans with me — one of them talking a bit — but then I took off, striding and breathing well, and quickly built up a lead. At 5 miles I clocked 26:30 and by 7 miles (36:58), managing the hills well, had a lead of about 2 minutes. Ten miles went by relatively easily in 51:30.

". . . and quickly built up a lead."

A novelty of this marathon was that I had a "second" and Bert Barrett did a great job supplying me with drinks or sponges whenever requested. I took a light sponge just before the 500 foot climb between 11 and 13 miles and ascended well, breathing fast. After a swift run down the other side I began to worry somewhat about

". . . took my first liquid at 15 miles."

"... sponging ... regularly."

drinking and took my first liquid at 15 miles. Little was swallowed. At 16 miles the day began to heat up and the terrain got hard, with a long gradual climb into the sun, necessitating sponging and drinking regularly. The road levelled out a bit at 18 miles. At 19½ miles I began to drink Coke plus salt. The road seemed to be slightly uphill all the way home and I felt my pace was dropping drastically, but I pressed on taking drinks and sponges every 1½ miles. Despite slowing, in fact I was pulling away and won by 7 minutes and 26 seconds, my biggest winning margin, the previous having been Maryland, 1974, when I won by exactly 7 minutes.

OK Rhodes Marathon, Rhodesia. 1st. 2:24:07.

Relaxing after the OK Rhodes Marathon.

Tuesday we were sent off on a four day tour by air to Lake Kariba and the Kariba Dam, the Wankie Game Reserve, including two animal spotting safaris, and finally Victoria Falls. The sights and hospitality we encountered were unforgettable.

Carribea Bay Hotel, Lake Kariba.

Kariba crocodile farm.

Above: Wankie Game Reserve.

Right: Victoria Falls.

After two days back with Len and Joyce and a 10 mile road named in my honour, we spent a couple of days with Harry Schubert, a runner, and his wife Rita, in Gatooma where I lectured to, and we trained with a group of African runners employed by the Rio Tinto Mine.

Start of the Ron Hill '10'.

3rd. in the Ron Hill '10'.

Early morning run with Rio Tinto Mine workers — Gatooma.

Track session at Gatooma.

May running with Joyce Keating — Salisbury.

1977

Our final six days in Salisbury included a trip by air to Fort Victoria, where Len was doing his stint in the army, and the mysterious Zimbabwe ruins. Every night in Salisbury we visited someone's house for drinks and a meal, completing our stay with a marvellous farewell party at the Monomatapa Hotel. What a wealth of happy memories we brought back with us.

Right and below:
The ruins of Zimbabwe.

Mar. 27	Ron Hill '10', Salisbury. 3rd. 52:01. (1st. Kenyus Tembo 50:37).
Apr. 3	Mashonaland 5000 m Track, Salisbury. 6th. 15:40.0 (unofficial).
9	Rivington Pike Fell Race. 10th. 17:26. (1st Alan Blinston 16:31).
16	Chris Vose '10', Warrington. 14th. 50:37. (1st. Dave Brennan 48:38).
28	Cretes-de-Spa, Belgium. 2nd. 70:40. (1st. Alan Blinston 70:08).
May 1	Wigan '6'. 26th. 31:34. (1st. Geoff Smith 30:10).
7	Sam Crossland '10', Oldham. 1st. 51:49.
15	Rochdale 10 km. 4th. (1st. Steve Kenyon 31:07).
21	AMSTERDAM MARATHON. 14th. 2:26:07. (1st. Bill Rodgers 2:12:46).

360

Mashonaland 5,000m. 5th.

Amsterdam Marathon, 14th. 2:26:07.

I don't know what went wrong here. I tried to go with the leaders and lasted only 2 miles. Feeling weak all over my pace got slower and slower and the 10 km between 30 and 40 km took 39 minutes. My log records: *"felt dreadful when I finished — just had to lie down"*.

361

Jun. 11   POLYTECHNIC MARATHON. 2nd. 2:16:37. (1st. Ian Thompson 2:14:32).
    26   YMCA 20 K., Manchester. 9th. 62:56. (1st. Steve Kenyon 60:38).
July 2   Annan '12'. 4th. 62:40. (1st. Ian Thompson 57:55).
     3   Skiddaw Fell Race, Keswick. 12th. 69:32. (1st. Alan McGee 64:44).

The night before the Skiddaw we were up until 2.00 a.m. drinking with our friends Harry and Sylvia Smith and Jim Alder and his mates, in Annan. At the start of the race I wanted to be last out of the field but at a bottleneck gate climbed a fence and leapt off to land in a hidden hole, badly spraining an ankle and cutting my knee. It was very pleasing to get through to 12th without walking any of the way. The ankle gave me a few weeks' pain.

July 17   Bagnols-les Bains 6½ K., France. 2nd. 19:42. (1st. Moisoniet).
    24   Marvejols-Mende, France. 8th. 1:27:33. (1st. P. Liardet 1:22:11).

Ready to go — to Mende.

Rob Towler (extreme left) with us and his friends — Mende.

Chateau near Mende.

This was the last time the family of four of us had a holiday together, driving in the Ford Transit van all the way from Le Havre to Mende in one go, almost 500 miles. This was 10 days before the main race and we camped and toured around this beautiful area, sometimes in the company of Rob Towler, a customer of ours who lived in Strasbourg. We visited the Gorges du Tarn, Mont-Lozere and the wonderful caves of Aven Armand.

Unfortunately I had a disastrous race in the heat, dying on the hills, despite the encouragement of Jean-Claude Moulin the race director and seeing my name painted on the road, "Allez Ron Hill". On the downhill I started to pick up a few people and eventually got through to 8th. Rob Towler collapsed about 300 m from the finish and had to spend the night in hospital, thus missing the rather wild celebration dinner with rough red wine that was only just drinkable!

Marvejols—Mende, 8th.

363

1977

Aug. 7   Barnsley '6'. 20th. 33:09. (1st. Steve Kenyon 30:53).
    14   "Weets" Fell Race, Barnoldswick. 8th. 31:42. (1st. D. Slater 30:34).

A comment on how I felt in most races, then, from my training log:

"Why am I so knackered at the start? Just can't go any faster and all sorts of blokes are in front of me. Breathing feels bad, legs ache, stomach aches, head feels pressure. Breathing flat out."

Aug. 20   Zottegem 23 K., Belgium. 5th.
    27   ENSCHEDE MARATHON, Holland. 9th. 2:21:21. (1st. Brian Maxwell 2:15:14).

On this occasion we toured in the Ford Transit van with Harry and Sylvia Smith. For the Zottegem race we stayed with our old friends Alfonse and Alfonsine at the Oudenberghof, Geraardsbergen. After the race, where I had never seen such corner-cutting in all my life, Harry passed out at the presentation. I was worried as he fell back into my arms but luckily he had only fainted from the heat and soon revived enough to drink his share of "Oud Zottegem" beer at a reception in the town hall afterwards.

Camping with Harry and Sylvia Smith — Enschede

From Belgium we went to Germany to visit my brother Jeff and his wife Isabel in Willich, where he was still stationed with the army. From there we went to Enschede and camped until just before the marathon when May and I moved to lodge with our friends the Van Gelderens.

However, this time they did not have the winner staying with them. On a hot day, 24 deg. C, I was able to keep with the leaders for 10 km then had to let go, slipping further and further behind until at about 25 km I was 21st. After 30 km runners began to come back to me and I got through to 9th but with a poor time of 2:21:21.

Enschede Marathon — with Harry Smith at the start.

Sep. 4 Frodsham Hill Race. 15th. 26:10. (1st. Ricky Wilde 24:07).
      7 Linotype '5', Altrincham. 18th. 24:01. (1st. Ken Newton 23:09).
     17 Lantern Pike Fell Race. 7th. 31:43. (1st. Ricky Wilde 29:12).
     18 Manchester and District Road Relay. 4th fastest. 9:40. (Fastest Ricky Wilde 9:16).
     23 Stockport Harriers Club Champs. 1,500 m Track. 3rd. 4:15:0.
     24 Burtonwood Road Relay. 18:47. (Fastest Steve Kenyon 17:32).
     25 Stockport Harriers Club Champs. 800 m Track. 2:18.2.

Stockport Harriers Championships (I ran for them on the track only). 800m. 2:18.2.

Oct. 1 Northern Road Relay, Wakefield. 56th fastest. 19:49. (Fastest Steve Kenyon 18:45).

Oct.   2   Stoodley Pike Fell Race. 16th. 18:30. (1st. Ricky Wilde 16:54).

The start of John McDonagh's Stoodley Pike Fell Race from the Top Brink Inn, Lumbutts, near Todmorden.

Stoodley Pike, 16th.

Oct. 9   Sedan-Charleville, France. 8th. 77:17. (1st. Rik Schoofs 73:47).
      15   Manchester University Cross-Country Relay. 9:58. (Fastest Ricky Wilde 9:25).
      23   NEW YORK CITY MARATIION. 18th. 2:20:00.9. (1st. Bill Rodgers 2:11:28).

For my second visit to the New York City Marathon I stayed at the Mayflower Hotel, opposite Central Park, and shared a room with that master of travel and the telephone, Chris Stewart. This time there were 4,823 starters, and almost a million spectators. My training log: *"did some stretching and a little jogging warm up — orderly start and a pretty fast one — Chris Stewart off like a scalded cat — I went with the leaders fairly hard up the Verrazano Bridge then got my breath back down the other side — took the lead off the bridge — 2 miles at 9:45 — lead changed a good few times — Orzell (Poland), Mora (Colombia), Kolbeck (France) — but stayed up there with the group — Rodgers (USA), Viren (Finland), Kardong (USA), Drayton (Canada), Cusack (Ireland), Plain (Wales), and a few others — up the hill at 9 mls. I dropped off — Ryffel (Switzerland) went with them — Fleming (USA) and Ken Moore (USA) went back — struggled on and sat with Moore and Kardong for a couple of miles — Plain went back — then Thompson (England) went through with Fleming — couldn't stay with them — began to lose ground badly — up the bridge with the carpet (Queensboro) a couple passed and went away — up 1st Avenue a corridor of spectators only 2 yards wide along the blue line — hardly room to spit — caught a Finn, Spik, at 20 miles, and we stayed together for about 3 miles, then Ron Wayne (USA) shot past going very well — just keep on plodding into Central Park — caught one bloke here as we left the park — then caught Victor Mora with 400 m to go — could see Viren ahead but got 2:20:00.9 very disappointed — fair bit of headwind on the course — and it was warm later on — had to take water on my head — even had to stop once for a drink of Body Punch — disappointing"*.

My expectations seemed to be far higher than my capabilities at the time.

Oct. 30   Gale Fell Race. 4th. 24:43. (1st. Jeff Norman 24:06).
Nov. 6   Black Lane Ends Fell Race. 5th. 30:29. (1st. Harry Walker 28:52).
      12   Mid-Lancs. Cross-Country League, Burnley. 8th. (1st. John Calvert).
      19   Inter-League Cross-Country Race, Rochdale. 10th. (1st Dave Brennan 24:09).
Dec. 4   MARYLAND MARATHON. 4th. 2:24:50. (1st. Gary Bjorklund 2:13:46.4).

The organisers made me a special number for my 4th appearance in this race — 1234. Having finished 1st, 2nd and 3rd in my previous races I was fated to finish 4th. I had an awful run for some reason — perhaps I was short on mileage. My log sums it up: *". . . relaxed up Satyr Hill and managed it well! but at 20-21 mls. my legs really tired*

1977

*— dreaded the last 5 mls. — at 22
mls. Kardong was being sick —
that put me 3rd — tried to hang
on — dying for a feed station —
got one at 23 mls. — stopped and
walked and drank a full cup of
ERG — Bruce Robinson went
past — kept going — just — with
1 mile to go I was asking how far
the man behind me was — 200
yds. — 150 yds. — 100 yds. —
"on your tail" — made it to the
top of the hill and had to sprint
like hell to hold 4th — was very
tired at the end — almost in a
state of collapse".*

Maryland Marathon, 4th.

Dec. 17   JOE STEELE ROCKET CITY MARATHON, HUNTSVILLE, ALABAMA. 2nd. 2:17:40. (1st. Steve Bolt 2:17:35).

I travelled to this marathon, on Wednesday before the Saturday race, Manchester to New York, via Prestwick, J.F.K. airport to La Guardia, then New York to Huntsville via Knoxville. To keep up the sequence of running twice a day (once on Sundays) since 1964 has been logistically difficult at times. On this journey I had to run from J. F. Kennedy airport, changing in a toilet, leaving my bag at a British Airways' desk, in pitch darkness and pouring rain, on muddy grass verges with huge cars spraying up waves of unrefreshing puddle water. It was "cold and depressing — very miserable". Arriving at Huntsville at 3.00 a.m. (9.00 p.m. local time), there was no-one there to meet me and red eyed and exhausted, I curled up on a luggage bench in the airport terminal. An hour later, following 5 minutes of glancing at me out of the corners of their eyes and whispered discussion, Ray Roberts and Harold Tinsley concluded that it was not a tramp lying there, but the marathon runner they had come to collect.

Harold put together the most detailed race booklet (80 pages) I have ever seen, and Ray along with his fine family — Pat his wife, and Sandy, Ray Junior and Greg — were my hosts. The whole event was really friendly. Russ Boon, partner of Joe Steele, a realtor (estate agent) and major financial sponsor of the race, painted "humorous" signs and placed them round the course. At the bottom of the only major uphill on the course was a sign "RON'S HILL" and at the top "YOU MADE IT".

368

The race started in rain and low cloud and my final time was certainly aided by the 1,000 ft. downhill run between 4½ and 10 miles. Around 12 miles the rain had stopped and I pulled away from

Leading Steve Bolt and Ed Leddy.

Ed Leddy and Steve Bolt. Just after 22 miles Bolt caught me again, gained about 100 yards, but by 24 miles had lost his advantage. I felt really comfortable and sat on him. At 25½ miles he started to kick and I could have gone with him but the back of my right leg locked in cramp and it took a few seconds before I was running freely. But too late. I lost by 5 seconds.

From that incident I have scar tissue in that muscle which starts to be painful towards the end of long races.

Despite the downhill, the 2:17 was a nice way to end the year.

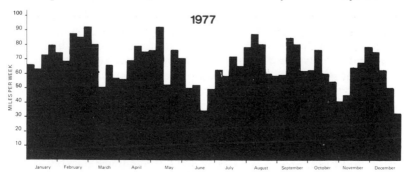

CHAPTER TWENTY-TWO

At the very beginning of 1978 I took on a runner from Oldham and Royton Harrier, Julian Leah, as an assistant on the mail order side of the business. Growth was continuing and our accountant, Danny Herman, informed me that using a "Simplex" VAT book was no longer sufficient to keep proper accounts and that we would have to move over to some kind of double entry bookkeeping system. This would have been impossible for me to handle from a time point of view and early in February I took on another Oldham Harrier, Mike Deegan, to keep the books.

This extra help was doubly necessary as I was at last making serious preparations for writing my autobiography!

On the retail side of the company, although takings at the shop continued to go up, by the end of the year we were on our third manager. It was proving difficult to find someone who lived up to the exacting standards of May and myself with regard to service, tidiness, cleanliness, enthusiasm, loyalty and imagination. Nevertheless by November we had looked at Manchester city centre as a place for retail expansion. However we found that the overheads would be too expensive, and decided that the satellite towns would probably be more realistic.

On the wholesale side, having just rented a large building for warehousing shoes, it became obvious that the transfer of the Nike distributorship to the company Mike Tagg worked for would be "Hobson's choice" and the compensating contract I was offered was non-negotiable. We decided to use the building anyway for overflow stock from the shop and in fact I prepared a little room in there to get away to write my book in peace. About May I moved in and started researching — training logs, diaries, press cuttings — then writing. I found it an exhausting occupation and many times emerged for a run with my head spinning and floating.

In June we took delivery of the first new car we had ever "owned"; in fact the company was leasing the vehicle. It was a silver Rover 2,600 and it was to serve us for exactly four years.

But it was impossible to entirely divorce myself from work. I often went back to the shop at night with May, cleaning and tidying, and was constantly loading, unloading and arranging stock at the warehouse, which as winter hardened grew extremely cold.

My most important race in 1978 was the trial for both the European and Commonwealth Games, held at Sandbach on May 7th. I

Loading stock into our new Rover.

built up my mileage to around 90 miles per week but just over two weeks before the race caught a chest infection and had to go on anti-biotics. The "diet" didn't appear to help me in the race where I ran 2:20:02 for 24th place. That was it — for the rest of the year I rarely went above 70 miles per week. On September 28th I became a veteran, officially, but vowed that it would be a long time before I ran in "vets" only competitions. I was still interested in "open" competition.

My total races for 1978 were:

Jan.   7   Lancashire Cross-Country Champs., Liverpool. 22nd. 40:31. (1st. Steve Kenyon 38:05).

      14   Mid-Lancs. Cross-Country League, Blackburn. 6th. (1st. John Calvert).

      29   BERMUDA MARATHON 1st. 2:26:13. (2nd. Kerk Lazarides 2:26:37).

Feb.   5   San Blas ½ Marathon, Coamo, Puerto Rico. 27th. 70:24. (1st. Henry Rono 64:46).

These last two races were on the same trip with May. The Bermuda Marathon had been arranged by my old friend Peter

Bermuda Marathon — start.

371

Lever, now teaching on the island. We were treated royally, staying at the beautiful Southampton Princess Hotel and touring the island on a "moped". The day of the race was very windy all the way back from halfway and I sat on Kerk until he got cramp at 24 miles, watched him for another ½ mile, then dashed away.

Bermuda Marathon . . .

. . . following Kerk Lazarides.

Bermuda Marathon, 1st. 2:26:13.

We flew on to Puerto Rico and stayed with a family in Coamo. I have never run well in the San Blas race and ran my worst ever this time. Whilst there I met Dr. Norb Sanders, a U.S. marathon runner and friend, Noel Tamini of Spiridon and Norb's friend Matteo, who lived in Haiti. After the half marathon we flew to Haiti and stayed a few days in Matteo's house, high above Port au Prince. In fact there was only one way from Port au Prince, that was up! We enjoyed one long run together from there — further up from Matteo's house, and the scenery was almost like Switzerland.

Long run, Haiti, Matteo, Norb Sanders and me.

Preparing for . . .

. . . Carnival in Port au Prince, Haiti.

Trails End Marathon — start.

Trails End Marathon — leading, but eventually 3rd. 2:22:44.

Feb. 25 TRAILS END MARATHON, Oregon. 3rd. 2:22:44. (1st. Sam Williams
2:21:44).
Mar. 4 National Cross-Country Champs., Leeds. 221st. (1st. Bernie Ford 41:34).
18 Clayton-le-Moors Cross-Country Champs., 4th. (1st. Paul Livesey).
25 Rivington Pike Fell Race, 13th. 18:15. (1st. John Calvert 16:55).
May 7 SANDBACH MARATHON, 24th. 2:20:02. (1st. Tony Simmons
2:12:33).

Sandbach Marathon, 24th. 2:20:02. Don MacGregor (208), Andy Holden (164).

Bolton 10,000m, June 10th.   *Stretford Track League, 3,000m.*

May 28   Burnley '3½', 8th. (1st. John Calvert 17:53).
June 4   Clitheroe Fell Race, 13th. 54:25. (1st. Ricky Wilde 48:58).
     10   Bolton, 10,000m. track, 7th. 32:52. (1st. Gerry Helme 30:23).
     11   Bolton '6', 33rd. 33:09. (1st. Steve Kenyon 30:12).
     18   Northern Track League, Bolton, 5,000m. track, 3rd. 15:32:0.
     20   Stretford Track League (B) 3,000 m., 4th. 8:44:0.
     21   Swinton '6', 4th. 30:43. (1st. Frank McGuire 30:17).
     25   Y.M.C.A. 20 K., 23rd. 64:41. (1st. Graham Ellis 61:23).
July 2   Hyde '7', 10th. 35:33. (1st. Graham Ellis 33:36).
     5   Sale '6¾', 7th. (1st. Mike Deegan).
     9   Altrincham '10', 13th. 52:18. (1st. Graham Ellis 49:27).

Altrincham '10', 13th. 52:18.

July 11 Stretford Track League (A)
3,000 m. 8:39:7.
30 Northern Track League,
Stretford, 5,000 m. 1st.
15:07:2.
Aug. 1 Stretford Track League, (A)
3,000 m. 8:44:0, (B) 3,000 m.
8:58:4.
20 Stockport "2-4-6", 13th.
30:00. (1st. Steve Kenyon
28:08).
22 Stretford Track League, (A)
3,000 m. 8:46:3.
23 Saddleworth '6', 9th. 29:50.
(1st. Gerry Helme 28:04).
24 Clayton-le-Moors A.G.M.
5,000 m. 1st. 15:20:0.
26 Harold Wood '8', Wigan.
10th. 39:34. (1st. Dave Brennan 37:40).

*Selling gear from the back of the van.
Stockport "2-4-6".*

Harold Wood '8' — start.

Harold Wood '8' — 10th. 39:34.

377

1978

Aug. 30   Rochdale 10 K. 8th. 32:25. (1st. John Calvert 31:06).
Sept. 2   Hollingworth Lake Road Relay. 7th. fastest. 21:49. (Fastest Gerry Helme 20:50).
      3   Frodsham Hill Races, 8th. 26:29. (1st. Graham Ellis 24:55).
      6   Linotype '5' Altrincham, 8th. 24:12. (1st. Mike Tagg 23:27).
      9   East Cheshire '7', Stalybridge, 9th. 36:02. (1st. Ricky Wilde 35:14).
    10   Cheshire League, Gatley, 3,000 m. track. 3rd. 8:58:8.
    17   Eastham Burco '7', Fleetwood, 7th. 34:46. (1st. Mike Freary 33:38).
    23   Stoodley Pike Fell Race, 9th. 18:24. (1st. Jeff Norman 17:22).
    30   Seedhill, Burnley, 3,000 m. 1st. 9:05.8.
Oct. 7   Lancs. Road Relay, 15:21. (Fastest Steve Kenyon 13:59).
    14   Manchester University Cross-Country Relay, 10:08. (Fastest Hugh Jones 9:30).
    22   NEW YORK CITY MARATHON. 19th. 2:20:24.3. (1st. Bill Rodgers 2:12:11.6).

This time marathon running had really arrived with around 11,400 starters having to use both sides of the Verrazano Bridge. I was 2nd veteran to the great Jack Foster who got 6th in 2:17:28.9.

Oct. 29   Gale Fell Race, 4th. 24:45. (1st. Colin Robinson 24:11).
Nov. 5   Black Lane Ends Fell Race, 6th. 30:33. (1st. Mike Short 29:30).
Dec. 2   MARYLAND MARATHON, 2nd. 2:22:38. (1st. Jeff Bradley 2:19:36.2).
    10   Todmorden Harriers Christmas Handicap, 4th. (1st. Colin Robinson).
    16   JOE STEELE ROCKET CITY MARATHON, 4th. 2:19:36. (1st. Steve Bolt 2:17:03).

Joe Steele Rocket City Marathon. With my hosts' family, l. to r. Greg, Sandy, me, Ray jnr.

Joe Steele Rocket City Marathon, 4th. 2:19:36.

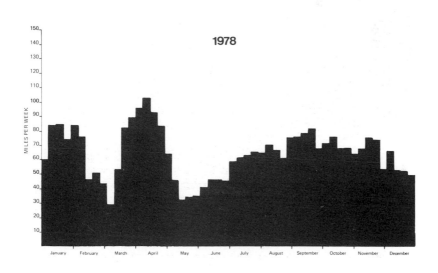

CHAPTER TWENTY-THREE

At the end of 1978, it got so cold in my little room at the warehouse we were renting, that I could no longer write there and had to abandon it in favour of the spare bedroom at home. The first draft of my book was complete by the middle of February, but there progress stopped, due mainly to pressure of business work. A little polishing of the manuscript ready for dictation was attempted in July but again work took priority for the rest of the year.

Things began to move fast and by the middle of the year we had taken out bank loans to purchase the lease on a shop in the precinct at Droylsden, and to buy both a shop in Stalybridge and an old plumber's workshop on Tower Street, Hyde. This last building was

Tower Street, Hyde.

renovated, converted to offices, warehousing and a base for the mail-order business, which we transferred from our Market Street shop. As the wholesale side of our company was expanding rapidly with the Ron Hill designed running gear, we changed the name of our retail mail-order and specialist running shop to "RUNNING WILD". It would have been stupid to blatantly compete against our wholesale customers. The general sports shops at Droylsden and Stalybridge we named "SPORTCARE & FITNESS". I did not want them to trade in my name; their success would have to come through the service offered.

Not unnaturally these developments did not come cheaply and although everyone, the staff, our kids and my dad put time in on painting and cleaning, the brunt of the work fell on May and myself. It meant we were going back working every night and most weekends too, which up to July led to continual stormy rows. My escape? — booze, home-brewed beer and my stock of duty-free — but only at nights. Towards the end of the year, with a couple of breaks for travelling together to races abroad, things settled down. We started to look for a bigger house and in August I set my heart on an old property — very run down — in Joel Lane, only about 600 yards away from where we lived. We had often admired the balcony outside one of the bedrooms as we walked past and, it may have been fate, the house had a carved stone on it which read "Arnold Hill — 1822", Arnold being an anagram of Ronald.

The lads were growing. Graham came occasionally to the track at Stockport on Tuesday nights but his interest was waning. We did not want to push him. He ran for the school team, but somewhat unfairly was continually pointed out as "Ron Hill's son". Steven, to our disappointment, was building up an interest in punk rock, an unhealthy interest in our eyes, with dyed hair and weird clothes. He possessed physical talent and had won his grammar school cross-

country championships by a large margin, off no training, "just to show the ones that trained how it was done". He didn't run again after that. At the end of the summer term he passed eight 'O-levels', but shortly after his return to school he was sent home for inappropriate dress. Not surprisingly really — narrow canvas black pants, boots, no tie and dyed black hair thick with Vaseline. To May's grief and my fury, he would not compromise, nor return, and he was lucky, later, to get a job in a laboratory.

Our company still had problems finding good retail staff, that is conscientious people with common sense. At 3.10 a.m. Boxing Day, there was a rata-

Jogging through injury (knee) at the World Veterans Championship, Bolton, with a boyhood friend (minus some weight) George Bell, now a Clayton-le-Moors Harrier.

tat-tat on our front door. The police. Someone had driven a van through the shop window at Droylsden and the manager, the key holder, could not be raised! I had to go.

However much toil there was I managed to run twice a day. About the middle of March my right knee started to give a lot of pain, below the knee-cap, the patella tendon, I believe, and this "injury" was not clear by the end of the year. However, I managed to race well on the roads. I tried a little track racing during May and June, but without specific training the results were disappointing. After September, the three marathons I attempted were all very difficult to handle and produced slow times for me. My performances were diminishing at an unhappy rate.

The story for 1979 was:

Jan.   6   Lancashire Cross-Country Champs., Manchester. 26th. 38:53. (1st. Andy Holden 36:23).

      13   Mid-Lancs. Cross-Country League, Blackburn. 3rd. 33:46. (1st. John Calvert 33:32).

Feb.   4   National Business Houses Cross-Country Champs, Horwich. 12th. 33.27. (1st. Steve Kenyon 31:42).

National Business Houses, Horwich. Chasing Mike Short.

      10   Northern Cross-Country Champs., Blackburn. 93rd. (1st. Steve Kenyon 39:28).

      18   MARDI-GRAS MARATHON, New Orleans. 3rd. 2:15:46. (1st. John Dimick 2:11:54).

      25   3rd OLYMPIAD MARATHON, St. Louis. 4th. 2:29:45. (1st. Tim Rollings 2:26:02).

A long and varied trip, this one, with May. In New Orleans we stayed with a family, Diane and Bill Reddock. Because of a police strike, the city-centre course could not be used and the race took place over the Lake Pontchartrain Causeway, the longest bridge in the world, 24.2 miles, dead straight and with just four or five humps in the middle. I never realised that concrete was harder than asphalt

National Business Houses. 1st Team "Under 500 Employees"
l. to. r. Mike Deegan, Ron Hill, Des Austin, Julian Leah.

Mardi-Gras Marathon — start.

for running, but know now after those 24.2 miles. There was a following wind and I might have run faster than 2:15 if the race mile markers had been accurately placed. Towards the end they were nearly a mile out and I was despondent thinking another 2:20 plus performance on the cards. Plodding, after losing second place to John Gregorio, I turned a corner, thinking I had over a mile still to go, and there was the finish.

A running store owner, Jerry Kokesh, had invited me to St. Louis and we stayed with another family, Jerry and Peggy Adams, before my second marathon in seven days. The day was literally freezing,

with a gale force wind blowing. Towards the end I nearly lost fourth place to a runner in full jog-suit, and had to whip myself to get under 2:30. After, I couldn't unbend my arms, and May had to put me in a hot bath to thaw me out.

After St. Louis we flew to Reading, Pennsylvania to stay with Tom Fry, the president of Dolphin, an athletic clothing manufacturing company. I was seeking a licensing agreement for manufacturing the Ron Hill line in the U.S.A., but as it turned out Dolphin's capacity was fully committed. A pleasant diversion, though, and we were entertained well.

3rd. Olympiad Marathon, St. Louis. Nearing the finish.

Mar. 3 National Cross-Country Champs., Luton. 399th. (1st. Mike McLeod 47:10).
 10 Manchester University Cross-Country Champs. 1st. 32:32.
 18 East Lancs. Cross-Country Champs., Ashton-under-Lyne. 7th. 45:10. (1st. Alan Sladen 43:11).
 24 Clayton-le-Moors Cross-Country Champs. 1st. 35:15. (2nd. Dave Wilson 35:40).
 25 Chris Vose '10', Warrington. 20th. 52:54. (1st. Adrian Royle 49:24).
Apr. 7 Pendle Fell Race. 22nd. (1st. Harry Walker 30:49).

After this race we called at my brother Jeff's and picked up a black and white kitten, christening it "Penny", after the race.

Apr. 14 Rivington Pike Fell Race. 9th. 17:44. (1st. P. Ravald 17:03).
 22 Great Hameldon Hill Race. 8th. 28:39. (1st. Ricky Wilde 27:36).
May 7 Northern Track Champs., Stretford. 10,000m. 13th. 30:37. (1st. Geoff Smith 28:03.6).
 8 Stretford Track League. 1,500m 4:14.1, (B) 3,000m 9:01.9.
 27 Northern Track League, Stretford 5,000m 3rd.
 29 Stretford Track League. 800m 2:05.3, (B) 3,000m 8:58.0.
June 10 Northern Track League, Bebington. 5,000m 1st. 15:08.8.
 16 Northern Champs. Stretford. 5,000m track 15:25 (unofficial). (1st. Nick Lees 13:35.2).
 17 Cheshire Track League, Stockport. 3,000m 3rd. 8:53.0.
 19 Stretford Track League. 1,500m 2nd. 4:10.3, (B) 3,000m 8:58.7.
 20 Swinton '6' 8th. 31:04. (1st. Pete Ravald 29:46).
 24 Y.M.C.A. 20K, Manchester. 11th. 62:29. (1st. Bill Domoney 61:17).

March 3rd. The National, Luton. 399th.

July   1   International Vets. 25K, Brugges, Belgium. 2nd. 80:32. (1st. John Robinson 80:31).

This was my first all-vet race and I must say I felt really out of place at the start. Because of several plane delays it was almost midnight when I got to Brussels and I had to find a hotel, then get the first train in the morning to Brugges, arriving about an hour before the start. After two miles some guy took off, we all let him go — I thought it was a tourist, and by the end of the first lap (of three) he was out of sight. After 10 kms. I took off and slowly pulled the tourist back until he was only 40m ahead entering the football stadium for the finish. For show and not really kicking, I put on a sprint and got within 4m of him at the end. When he turned round I realised that it was an old rival, John Robinson from New Zealand, whom I had last raced in Christchurch, in 1974.

This race is a "classic" event, over a beautiful course, organised by Jacques Serruys, a runner and editor and publisher of "Fit Veteran".

July   8   Danis Berglauf, Switzerland. 20th.

I drove with May to Heathrow to fly to Switzerland and as I got out of the car my right knee gave way. I could hardly walk, never mind run, and downhill was agony, but I struggled as best I could to 20th place.

July   10   Stretford Track League. 800m 2:05.9.
        28   Northern Track League, Bolton. 5,000m. 2nd. 15:13.4. (1st. Eric Rannicar 15:09.2).

With the Montreal Marathon coming up a month later I had expensive microwave and ultrasonic treatment on my knee in Manchester. To no avail. The pain stayed.

1979

Aug. 11   Harold Wood '8'. 13th. 40:08. (1st. Steve Kenyon 37:06).
    19   "Weets" Fell Race, Barnoldswick. 27th. 34:17. (1st. Dave Slater 31:24).
    26   MONTREAL MARATHON. 19th. 2:25:50. (1st. Balcha 2:11:35).

I was almost in tears from the pain in my knee whilst training
there and was not too disappointed with my run in extreme heat, as
Bill Rodgers and Tom Fleming were not far in front, and I passed
Tony Simmons near the end.

Montreal Marathon. 19th. 2:25:50.

May and Graham went with me on this trip, Graham mainly
because at the time he was a fanatic plane spotter. After the race we
spent a relaxing sunny week at the cottage of our friends Mike and
Jenny Sudlow, in Ayer's Cliff.

Sep. 9   East Cheshire '7', Ashton-under-Lyne. 8th. 36:31. (1st. Steve Kenyon
       34:02).
    16   Eastham Burco '7', Fleetwood. 20th. 35:30. (1st. Dave Black 32:41).

Eastham Burco '7'. After Bernard Lloyd (Wigan A.C.).

386

Sep. 22   Hollingworth Lake Road Relay. 22:03. (Fastest Colin Robinson 21:30).

25-30   THE TOUR OF UMBRIA.

May came as my manager to this "Settimana Verde" (Green Week) or Giro Dell' Umbria, Umbria being a picturesque, hilly department in the middle of Italy, to the north of Rome.

Sep. 25   Ponte S. Giovanni — Ponte Patolli, 15K. 4th. 44:33.8. (1st. Silvano Penzo 43:33.6).

My 41st Birthday. This was not the original course. Earthquake damage in the town where we should have finished had caused its cancellation. I thought it might be a tactical race, but it was "eyeballs out" all the way. The runners after 22nd. position got stopped for over a minute when railway level-crossing barriers came down!

1st Stage, chasing Penso.

Sep. 26   Cascata delle Marmore — Sangemini, 20K. 10th. 66:56.5. (1st. Alessandro Cervigni 63:40.7).
After two stages: 6th. 1:51:30.3. (1st. Cervigni 1:47:54.5).

The start at Cascata delle Marmore.

387

2nd Stage. The chasing group.

As the day before, the runners charged off before the gun. It was hot and I quickly tired. I thought I would get a rest when our group encountered the white poles of another level crossing — this time catching us, but they were under, over, scrambling across the railway lines and I was dropped. The final 5 km of climb was murder. I had been off alcohol up until this, but it was not doing me any good, so I went out and bought three large bottles of beer after the race.

5 km. climb to Sangemini.

Sep. 27   Acquasparta — Todi, 22 K. 4th. 73:35.6. (1st. Penzo 72:28.5). After three stages: 4th. 3:05:05.9. (1st. Cervigni 3:00:47.3).

The start was delayed 20 minutes because of a funeral in Todi. A much better run for me, this, but the last 2 km got steeper and steeper until I thought I could see steps ahead!

Sep. 29   Gualdo Tadino — Gubbio, 24.5 K. 1st. 82:08.5. (2nd. Franchi 82:21.1). After four stages: 2nd. 4:27:14.4. (1st. Penzo 4:24:14.2).

The day of rest had been welcome. Everyone was saying I would win this one as it was the longest stage of the tour. There was a 40 minute delay before the field started itself. I battled it out with Cervigni, Penzo and Massimo Franchi under the sweltering sun. Just after half-way Cervigni, the race leader, dropped out with a blister! Penzo fell back with 5 km to go, and up the last steep hill to Gubbio (God, those hills!) the shadow of Franchi disappeared behind me. It was sweet victory.

Sep. 30 Torgiano — Perugia, 19.5 K. 4th. 61:05.3. (1st. Mario Rossi 59:44.7).

I was so stiff and tired before this final stage, that I could hardly warm up. About half the race was flat, then there was a 10km climb into Perugia. A huge group left me at the start, but my position gradually improved, despite jumping a level crossing with officials furiously waving their arms, and I held on to second place overall.

Final positions were:
1. Penzo, 5:25:13.0
2. Hill, 5:28:19.7
3. Rossi, 5:29:03.9
4. Franchi, 5:29:07.1
5. Tomaszewicz, 5:34:07.8

The tour was a marvellous idea and event and some lively, if short-lived friendships were struck up with two Poles, Tomaszewicz and Glinieki, and a Portuguese, Antonio Moreira.

Finish of the 3rd. Stage at Todi.

Oct. 6 Northern Road Relay, Liverpool. Passed 4.
7 Cutlers Cross-Country Relay, Sheffield. Passed 12.
21 NEW YORK CITY MARATHON. 45th. 2:23:20. (1st. Bill Rodgers 2:11:42).

This time, around 14,000 competitors and a false start. I stood at the line, as did Bill Rodgers and Ken Moore until the cannon fired, and had to force my way through the crowds who had gone before time. It was a poor race for me, even though I had been on "the diet" and I was happy to see the finish. My body ached all over.

Central Park — N.Y.C. Marathon.

New York City Marathon, 45th. 2:23:20. Thankfully over!

Oct. 28   Gale Fell Race. 9th. 25:30. (1st. Jeff Norman 23:59).
Nov. 4   Black Lane Ends Fell Race. 9th. 33:22. (1st. Harry Walker 31:50).

SHAUN LIVESEY

Black Lane Ends Fell Race, 9th.

Nov. 25   Rombalds Moor Fell Race, Skipton. 22nd. ca. 37 mins. (most of the field got lost).
Dec. 2   MARYLAND MARATHON. 5th. 2:23:37. (1st. Jeff Foster 2:19:26).

Maryland Marathon, 5th. 2:23:37. Toivola (No. 2), Vainio (No. 3).

Fate was bringing my sequence up-to-date — 1st, 2nd, 3rd, 4th, 2nd (in 1978 as an anomaly), now 5th. Two Finns, on their way to New Zealand for winter training ran. Toivola was 4th and Vainio, 1978 European 10,000m Champion, was 7th.

    9   Todmorden Harriers Christmas Handicap '6'. 4th. 31:32. (1st. Colin Robinson 31:13).

   15   JOE STEELE ROCKET CITY MARATHON. 17th. 2:24:14. (1st. Kevin Brower 2:17:32).

"Another awful run . . ."

Another awful run with weary, weary legs. All I could think of was whether I would beat the time I had done in my first ever marathon, 1961, which was 2:24:22.

1979

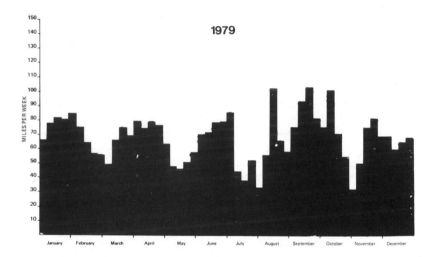

CHAPTER TWENTY-FOUR

1980 proved to be something of a hectic year for us. Throughout the twelve months I put a lot of solid work into dictating what I had written of my autobiography on to tape so that this could be typed up, correcting the typed manuscript, and completing the researching and actual writing. This part was done by mid-July. The original version of the book was to have ended at 1976, when I failed to get into the Olympic team for Montreal.

This continuous project was fitted in around arranging the purchase of a "new" house in Joel Lane. To say it was run-down is an understatement, and we tried to do a lot of work before we moved in, but major jobs like fitting new windows and double glazing, completely replacing the central heating system, and knocking out the old kitchen units and having them completely refitted had to be done once we were in. It almost drove May mad, as most of the workmen involved appeared to have no respect for property whatsoever. Ron McAndrew, a fellow runner, helped us with the design and purchase of a new kitchen.

We moved in on August 11th and with the property came a cat. We had seen this scruffy "tortoise" coloured animal on our pre-purchase visits to the property, as it would come mewing out of the bushes. Once we were in, it became obvious that this was *her* home, and we took her in, christened her "Sammy", by accident, and she

Son Steven with May.

has become a lovely talkative cat. Our other "mog", Penny, wasn't too happy about the new addition to the family, and it has taken them ages to adjust to each other.

Steven got made redundant from his job, worked in our Hyde shop for a while, then found other employment in a laboratory. Graham continued his secondary education at Greenfield Street, Hyde.

September 17th was our 20th Wedding Anniversary. I bought May some flowers; we never ate out, but we couldn't even enjoy the bottle of Pomagne I had bought to drink with our tea, as the kitchen fitters were working overtime to finish patch plastering. May was still doing a little, fairly regular running, early in the mornings.

The company on both the retail and wholesale side continued to expand. We bought the business and lease on a sports shop in Denton, and began to take on agents to sell our gear to other shops countrywide. We exhibited at major sports goods exhibitions in both Birmingham and London, and continued to make a little headway into exporting, even sending goods to Hong Kong! Across the business we tended to employ runners, some coming, a few going — Stan Curran, Gerry Helme, Steve Kenyon, Graham Richards, Malcolm McBride, Steve Pegler — we even converted people to running, for example shop manager Duncan Martin.

Mike Deegan became far more than the book-keeper I took him on as, and was able to accept a lot of responsibility for the day to day running of the company. This was absolutely essential to me because of my preoccupation with the mammoth autobiography. In October we made him a Director of the company.

Perhaps because of all this activity and pressure, my running hit rock bottom. I ran only two marathons, one in January and one in December, both in the U.S.A. and both in just under 2hrs. 28mins.

During 1979 and early 80 I had been saying that I would run the British Marathon trial for the Moscow Olympics on the basis of: "If you don't try, you don't find out." During the first months of the year it became obviously plain that I would have no chance, and I merely watched the race at Milton Keynes, which was won by Ian Thompson with Dave Black second. These two were picked for Moscow along with Bernie Ford who had been pre-selected as a result of a previous fast race.

I remember sitting in front of my television on August 1st, watching the Olympic Marathon, won for a second time by Waldemar Cierpinski of East Germany, waiting for a British runner to finish. None did. I wrote in my diary: *"all three of our marathon runners dropped out!!! — disgusting."*

As usual I raced a lot, but was finding myself so tired that at the end of June I decided I needed a long term "rest" and elected to run just 60 miles a week for the next year. I was convinced that all the years of training I had done, combined with 60 hard, hard marathons, had worn me out. I didn't know if this "rest" would bring it back, but I couldn't think of anything else. In November, Dr. Ian Adams and Dr. John Humphries in Leeds, gave me a thorough check-up and testing. My hope was that they would find something amiss that they could easily rectify. Their report disappointed me. Nothing was radically wrong and I was quite deflated when John Humphries added that my results for "power", tested on a "force plate", were the lowest they had ever recorded!

1980's race results were:

Jan. 5 Lancashire Cross-Country Champs., Blackburn. 30th. (1st. Dave Lewis, 42.43).
      12 ORANGE BOWL MARATHON, Miami. 12th. 2:27:28. (1st. Ken Misner 2:18:31).

This was a wonderful sunny trip in the middle of winter for May and I. We stayed with race director, Basil Honikman, and his wife Linda in beautiful Coral Gables. The race itself proved to be very difficult. It was a scorching day and I got so bad near the end that I seriously considered walking! Joyce Smith collapsed just before the finish and had to be helped over the line. Her condition afterwards had everyone worried, but happily she recovered.

We hired a car and drove across the Everglades to the Gulf Coast then headed north, finally to Bradenton Beach where we sunbathed and collec-

O.B. Marathon, 12th. 2:27:28.

lected beautiful sea shells. I had rather a scare that night. The two of us had a jog and purchased some chilled wine and beer, which we drank before going out to dinner at "Harbour House", where you could have all you could eat for $5.95. After the meal and another three or four beers we went to bed. I don't know whether it was the combination of seafood and alcohol, but in my diary I wrote: *"woke up in the early hours with a frightening headache — got up to go to the toilet and thought I was having a heart attack — pains*

1980

across the chest in a spasm and a blinding white headache — thought I was going to collapse".

I'd had similar pains a couple of years previously. Hopefully it hasn't done any permanent damage, but it makes me wonder.

Jan. 26 East Lancs. Cross-Country Champs., Atherton. 33rd. 37:00. (1st. Steve Kenyon 34:11).

Feb. 3 National Business Houses Cross-Country Champs., Horwich. 16th. 32:57. (1st. Steve Kenyon 29:53). Ron Hill Sports Race Team 1st. (2nd. I.C.I.).

9 Northern Cross-Country Champs., Durham. 49th. 54:13. (1st. Nick Lees 49:30).

16 Parbold Hill Race. 15th. 36:45. (1st. Dave Brennan 35:03).

Mar. 8 Manchester University Cross-Country Champs. 1st. 32.08.

12 Lincs. Services League, R.A.F. Cranwell. Guest. 3rd.

15 Leeds University Past v Present. Guest. 5th.

29 Afcent — Brunssum Cross-Country, Holland. 36th. (1st. Steve Jones 31:23).

30 Stiphout 20 K, Holland. 6th. 67:22. (1st. Tom Larmit 65:15).

*Ron Hill Sports Race Team at the Stiphout 20 K.
l. to r. Stan Curran, Mike Deegan, Gerry Helme, Ron Hill.*

Apr. 1 Stretford Track League. 800m. 2:16.7, (B) 3,000m. 9 mins +.

5 Rivington Pike Fell Race. 9th. 17:45. (1st. Andy Taylor 16:35).

7 ASVAC Centenary Road Race. 20th. 23:32. (1st. Andy Armitage 22:00).

13 Chris Vose '10', Warrington. 18th. 51:22. (1st. Hugh Jones 48:22).

17 Altrincham Track Races. 10,000m. 1st. 31:22. (2nd. Jeff Norman).

20 Great Hameldon Hill Race. 10th. 28:36. (1st. Dave Lewis 27:04).

23 Blackburn Track Races. 1,500m 4:18.7, 3,000m 9:07.9.

26 Manchester University Track relays. 1,500 m 2nd. 4:16.3, 3,000m 1st. 8:54.8.

May 4 Silverstone Relays. Two legs. 14:27 and 14:43. (Fastest Andy Caton 13:42).

6 Stretford Track League. 1,500m 4:12.0, 3,000m 9:02.4.

7 Blackburn Track Races. 1,500m 4:22.6, 3,000m 9:10.5.

11 Darwen Moors Fell Race. 7th. 78:43. (1st. Ricky Wilde 75:52).

14 Fallowfield Track Meet. 3,000m 2nd. 8:57.5.

18 Earby Fell Race. 3rd. 34:01. (1st. Harry Walker 32:32).

May 21 Manchester University Sports. 5,000m. Guest. 1st. 15:15.0.

24 Julien Saelens Meet, Brugges. Vet. 5,000m. 1st. 15:26.4. (2nd. E. Van Ranst 15:32.7).

June 1 Saddleworth Fell Race. 25th. 22:06. (1st. Andy Darby, 19:17).

3 Stretford Track League. 800m. 2:10.5, (C) 3,000m. 3rd. 8:49.6.

4 Blackburn Track Races. 1,500m. 3rd. 4:16.4, 3,000m. 5th. 9:04.2.

7 Tockholes Fell Race. 8th. 33:00. (1st. Pete Ravald 31:19).

11 Murphy 10K, Bingley. 15th. 31:09. (1st. Graham Ellis 29:33).

15 Lyme Fell Race. 10th. 38:50. (1st. Ricky Wilde 34:32).

29 International Vets. 25 K, Brugges. 6th. 83:33. (1st. John Robinson 81:38).

April 5th. Rivington Pike, 9th.

Int. Vets. 25 K, Brugges. Me, May and the winner, John Robinson.

This year I took May to Belgium with me and got there two days ahead of the event, as opposed to last year when I arrived about one hour before the start. My race was far worse. It may have been the ultra-strong coffee at breakfast which made me feel sick, but I had a disastrous run, three minutes slower than the previous year.

July 6 Hyde '7'. 17th. 36.02. (1st. Ricky Wilde 33:20).

July 23 Rochdale 10K. 6th. 32:40. (1st. Pete Ravald 31:28).
26 Northern Track League, Warrington. 3rd. 15:26.4. (1st Graham Richards 14:57.1).
Aug. 9 Harold Wood '8'. 20th. 40:32. (1st. Dave Cannon 37:06).
12 Stoodley Pike Fell Race. 21st. (1st. Alan Sladen 16:49).

Aug. 17 "Weets" Fell Race, Barn-oldswick. 13th. 34:06. (1st. Roy Bailey 31:42).

Stoodley Pike Fell Race, 21st.

23 World Vets. Champs., Glasgow. 10K 9th. 32:49. (1st. Roger Robinson 31:09).
27 Saddleworth '6'. 6th. 29:57. (1st. Pete Ravald 28:49).
28 Clayton-le-Moors Harriers A.G.M. 5,000m 1st. 15:28.0.
31 Frodsham Hill Races. 26th. 27:10. (1st. Ricky Wilde 24:25).
Sep. 2 Sun Life Assurance '5', Bristol. 9th. 26:37. (1st. R. Partridge 25:21).
6 Foulridge Fell Race. 7th. 29:17. (1st. Jeff Norman 28:22).
14 Eastham Burco '7', Fleetwood. 30th. 34:40. (1st. Barry Smith 32:44).
28 Hollingworth Lake Road Relay. 22:24. (Fastest, Dave Singleton 21:18).
Oct. 4 Northern Road Relay, Liverpool. 22:05. (Fastest, Richard May 20:18).
5 Cutlers Relay, Sheffield. Lost one place.
11 Lancashire Road Relay. 15:20, 52nd fastest. (Fastest, John Woods 14:18).
19 20K of Paris. 27th. (1st. Mike McLeod 62:53).

SHAUN LIVESEY

'Weets' Fell Race, 13th.

Paris, l. to r. Mike Deegan, me and May, Stan Curran, Graham Richards, Paul Cornou.

Here we had a Ron Hill Race Team entered: myself, Mike Deegan, Stan Curran and Graham Richards with May as team manager. There were 17,000 runners in the race, starting at the Eiffel Tower at 3.00 p.m. At 2.30 the runners were there straining at a rope and I said to Michel Jazy, one of the race directors, "Are you sure the start is at 3.00." "Definitely," he replied.

We went away to warm up. At 2.49 we were taking off our jog suits when we noticed a silent solid mass of heads bobbing off down a narrow path. Someone said, "I don't remember there being a jogging event on as well." Then it dawned on us; they'd gone off early! We joined in — could hardly move, but, incredibly, moved right through. Mike was 20th, Stan 21st, and Graham about 40th. My 27th was pleasing as for three miles I was passing people in tracksuits and women, and I didn't pass 60-year-old Alain Mimoun (Olympic Marathon Champion of 1956) until four miles.

After this race I started to grow a beard. Just for a change.

Oct. 26 Gale Fell Race. 15th. 26:23. (1st. Jeff Norman 24:25).
Nov. 1 Kiwi '15', Holmfirth. 8th. 78:30. (1st. Graham Ellis 74:22).
       2 Black Lane Ends Fell Race. 46th. 36:10. (1st. Andy Taylor 31:04).
       9 Harwood '8'. 15th. 38:11. (1st. Kevin Forster 35:54).
      15 Mid-Lancs. Cross-Country League. Burnley. 12th. 36:30. (1st. Andy Taylor 34:38).
      22 Brampton — Carlisle '10'. 8th. 51:08. (1st. Kevin Forster 49:04).
Dec. 7 MARYLAND MARATHON. 7th. 2:27:56. (1st. Jerome Drayton 2:19:45).

I wanted to do well in this race as I had always been well received in Baltimore. It was my 7th consecutive appearance which meant that well over 10% of my marathons had been here in Maryland. I did the "diet", but to no avail. The course had been changed to give a downtown, indoor finish, which meant that the notorious Satyr Hill, the up part, anyway, came a lot earlier in the race which should have been easier. I died over the last 10 miles, even though it was mainly downhill. My training log describes the performance and me: *"bloody disgusting and hurting all over"*.

What had gone wrong with me, I don't know, but that was the end of my affair with the Maryland Marathon.

The beginning of the end of my affair with the Maryland Marathon.

Maryland Marathon, 7th. 2:27:56.

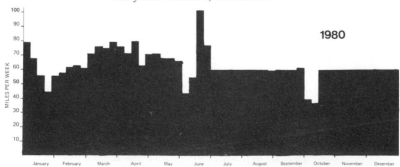

CHAPTER TWENTY-FIVE

It was perhaps fortunate that I was in the middle of a long term "rest" of 60 miles per week as 1981 seemed to produce an increase in pressures rather than an easing. On the personal side, the house we had bought was providing a tremendous amount of work right through from January to December. We had to fell a huge willow, transplant shrubs and move stones and soil to make room for a double garage at the side of the house. I put up a false ceiling in pinewood in our big kitchen and a similar one on the upstairs corridor. I tiled the shower-room, bathroom and kitchen, knocked out an old fireplace in the lounge and built a new one from old bricks salvaged from demolition sites.

My dad working on the outside of our house.

May, in addition to keeping the house clean, clearing up after my work and looking after the two boys was bagging and labelling running shorts, which saved our firm a lot of money, until well into the next year when the quantities became far too big for her to handle. Graham followed Steven into outlandish modes of dress and appearance, his "punk" look only being accepted as he was now at the more liberal "college". Having finished his normal secondary education, he was studying an extra year to get 'O' levels.

We opened our fifth shop, "SPORTS FEET" in Manchester city centre, and built an extension to the Hyde shop which almost doubled its size. On the wholesale side the Ron Hill Sports line developed further in the U.K. and we also took on a distributor in Norway, Nils Jebsen, who May and I met when I was there for a race, one in Ireland, Mel Buckley, and one in Greece, our friend the marathon runner Kerk Lazarides. We exhibited at the famous Munich ISPO Exhibition in September, doing it "the hard way", or rather the least expensive way, driving there by car and camping! It was a success. We also started a magazine: "The Running Wild Newsletter" which was later to become "Running Review".

Driving to ISPO, Munich.

After a run, May and I with Lasse Viren at ISPO.

My autobiography began to come to fruition this year. Having left complete manuscripts with several people, the consensus of opinion was that the book would be far too long to be commercially viable. I wanted it to a be a commercial success if possible, but reading it through, with a view to condensing it, I could see nowhere to start cutting. My decision was to leave it as it was, but to publish the work in two parts. A slick "commercial" piece was not what I had been creating. I wanted to leave behind a small piece of history, a detailed account of a running career, an account it is unlikely any other runner could emulate. This decision to have two books also gave me the opportunity to include many, many photographs which hopefully would add to the historical value and interest of the work.

The time spent on the book, which we were to fund and publish ourselves, involved correcting manuscripts, going through the photographs of newspaper files, friends, family, own collection and sports photographers, having the book printed on to galley sheets, correcting these, cutting these up into pages and fitting in the photographs with captions and credits and finally correcting the page proofs. Unfortunately we ran out of time and the finished books arrived far too late to take real advantage of the Christmas market.

All this various work was fitted around several trips abroad and led to the following quote in my diary for December 17th, after having returned home in the evening from our weekly shopping: *"— didn't feel like doing any work when we got back — similar lethargic, depressed state of mind — cold (illness), cold (weather), unfitness, all the work on the house? — getting me down"*.

On the running side, the trips abroad were interesting and produced some reasonable performances, but the 12 months of 60 miles per week was not bringing me the expected freshness I believed it would. In July our company organised the "Chesters Tour of Tameside", a six day series of races in which I personally finished 7th overall, but which did not produce one self-satisfactory performance in the whole week. Sixty miles per week were not regenerating me, and after the Tour I decided to reduce my mileage still further to 35 miles per week for six months. A spin-off from this was that I was able to run with May every morning. Four months of this much reduced training prompted this statement in my diary: *"Not training is frustrating. Easy to slip into a soft way of life. Easy to avoid competition when results are poor due to unfitness. Progressive loss of desire to compete with detraining."* It was the biggest "rest" I'd had since injury in 1974, and before that probably 1958.

My racing results for 1981 were:

Jan 10 Savannah ½ Marathon, USA. 4th. 68:30.6. (1st. Benji Durden 65:31.2).
17 ORANGE BOWL MARATHON, Miami. 15th. 2:22:55. (1st. Benji Durden 2:12:33).

May and I enjoyed a 13 day tour to these two races, which included a lot of variety. Savannah, Georgia, was icy cold and I didn't envy those runners who were entered for the full marathon and had to continue for another lap after our race was over. We stayed in the luxury of the magnificent De Soto Hilton Hotel. I had intended to hire a car in Savannah and drive to Miami, but before we left I couldn't for the life of me find my driving licence and without that a hire-car was impossible.

We decided to go by train and stop off in the middle of the

journey at a town called Sebring. We left behind the hard frozen weather but it was still cold when we reached the huge Kenilworth Village Lodge and Motor Inn. We were practically the only ones staying there and were invited to help ourselves to chille con carne from a cast-iron cauldron heated by an open wood fire. We stayed just one night before boarding the slow, slow monster silver train for Miami.

Our lodging was again in the home of race director Basil Honikman and his wife Linda, enabling us to enjoy the company of the runners from all over the world — Japan, Denmark, Sweden — as well as some of the best U.S. runners which this race attracts. The start and finish this year had been moved to the famous Orange Bowl Stadium, and the gun fired at 7.00 a.m. We were blessed with cool weather and I had one of my better marathons for some time, winning the Masters (Veterans) division of the race.

Orange Bowl Marathon, 15th. 2:22:55.

Feb. 1 National Business Houses Cross-Country Championships, Horwich. 16th. 32:08. (1st. Laurie Spence 30:04).

For the second year Ron Hill Sports Race Team took the team prize, and again with the same number of points as I.C.I., but having a superior last counter!

Feb. 22 International Cross de Longwy, France. Veterans Race 1st. Senior Race 8th.

Mar. 15 National Veterans Cross-Country Champs., Birkenhead. 13th. 34:15. (1st. Tecwyn Davies 32:47).

I think "veterans" running is a great movement and it has obviously been a real driving force in keeping people in, and bringing

National Vets. Cross-Country, 13th.

people back to the sport. At 42 I was not prepared to go chasing vet.'s prizes and championships as an end. The state of my fitness (and maybe ability) as shown by the above result, would have made it futile anyway. At present the races I would like to challenge as a veteran are those in faraway places, championship races at events which I have long since discarded in open competition, for example 1,500m, 5,000m and 10,000m track, and maybe team races. However, I have to admit that in many open races the challenge of being the first veteran, within the general competition, has been a definite motivation,

Mar. 22   Taipei 15K. 4th. 46 mins.+. (1st. So twins, 43 mins.+).
     29   COAST OF CHINA MARATHON, HONG KONG. 1st. 2:34:35. (2nd. Bill Pegler 2:46:33).

Another exciting tour for me and May even if the most time we got for sightseeing was half a day on a double decker bus in Hong Kong. We were invited there by Andy Blunier who imported our clothing into his shop and was editor and publisher of "Asian Runner" magazine.

We extended our journey to Taiwan and were looked after there by Bob Morgan, an American runner who had an export business in Taipei. We were looking for possible manufacturing sources there. Bob introduced me to the Taipei "Hash" which got us off the beaten track in our running! The night of the run I had to leave the Hash House booze-up and dinner at the "Waltzing Matilda" at 9.30 for an emergency visit to a Chinese dentist. I had an agonizing toothache which could only temporarily be assuaged by swilling it with ice-cold Taiwan beer. What he thought seeing me enter his surgery with a tall bottle of beer in my hand was likely equalled by

405

what I thought when I saw his antiquated equipment. At first he wanted to drill without anaesthetic, but I insisted that he give me an injection, presenting me with a fright as he bent the hyperdermic needle trying to fill the syringe. He drilled my tooth to release the pressure, relieved my pain, and he had my heartfelt thanks. Imagine trying to get dental treatment in Britain at 9.30 on a Saturday night. He charged me about £5!

The Taipei Hash.

"Down — down" time!

The marathon in Hong Kong started very early and was pretty hilly. I thought I was flying but my splits told me differently.

Coast of China Marathon — start.

Coast of China Marathon, 1st. 2:34:35.

Suffering terribly with sore legs over the last 7 miles I thought I must surely be caught. However, I doubled my lead over the final stretch. The 2:34:35 was my slowest-ever time, but the victory represented my largest ever winning margin, 11 mins. and 58 secs. In my other 64 finishes, only once had I recorded outside 2 hours 30 minutes and that by 24.2 seconds in the Christchurch Commonwealth Games in 1974, when I was injured. Another barrier had fallen. From now on I would not worry so much about finishing outside 2:30. It broadened my scope for future marathons.

Apr. 18 Rivington Pike Fell Race. 32nd. 18:12. (1st. John Wild 15:35).

Something was sadly wrong with my running. I wrote in my log: *"Even walked; for the first time in 20 years."*

1981

Apr. 20   Great Hameldon Hill Race. 28th. 29:28. (1st. Andy Taylor 26:19).

May 3   Northern Vets. Track Champs., Nelson. 1,500m 1st. 4:30.3, 5,000m 2nd. 16:20.9. (1st. Colin Robinson 15:51.6).

     9   GRE Gold Cup, Stockport. 10,000m 2nd. 31:49.8. (1st. D. Singleton 30:44.8).

   23   Elby's Distance Classic, 20K, Wheeling, West Virginia, U.S.A. 38th. 66:45. (1st. Bill Rodgers 60:09).

   25   Cotton Row Run, 10K, Huntsville, Alabama. 20th. 32:38. (1st. Kent McDonald 29:43).

   30   Norwegian Mountain ½ Marathon, Beitostolen. 1st. 65:51. (2nd. Tormod Saetre 67:03).

These last three races were part of one hectic trip. The 20K is sponsored by the Boury brothers, who own the Elby's chain of restaurants. Wheeling, West Virginia is a quiet little town on the Ohio River, but what a field Hugh Stobbs the race director had assembled — Bill Rodgers, Rod Dixon, Tom Fleming, Kevin Ryan, Benji Durden, Louis Kenny, Ed Mendoza, Gary Fanelli, Robin Holland and Britain's Malcolm East, together with a host of other top Americans.

It was hot and hilly and I was blown away after the first mile. On the mile and a half "29th Street" Hill I seemed to go backwards and almost panicked near the top when I thought I heard "first woman" somewhere behind me. "God," I thought, "don't let Patty Catalano beat me." It was a false alarm. I recovered a bit downhill and more or less held my own on "Chicken Neck" Hill and finally "Wheeling" Hill. Incredibly, there were 37 people in front of me.

Early next morning saw me on the way to Huntsville, Alabama for the Cotton Row Run 10K. Huntsville/Decatur Airport serves two cities. The airline hostess announced "Decatur" and I stayed on the plane. Immediately we took off I became an "override". It took me 5 hours, via Birmingham and Atlanta, to get back to Huntsville at 5.30 p.m., having left the hotel at 6.30 a.m. I jogged 3 miles and felt knackered. I felt no better the next morning for an 8 o'clock start. The temperature was already in the 70's and I felt completely legless in the race. My heart and limbs were tired and it was a strain all the way. I finished 20th overall, 4th veteran.

Less than 24 hours after arriving back from the U.S.A., I was driving to Heathrow, with May, to catch a plane for Oslo for a further 3½ hours' journey to Beitostolen. The start of this race was on a road between 2 metre snow banks, and ice covered the puddles in the ditches. Surprisingly I ran away from 3 challengers, of the 900 starters, on the only uphill section of the course and set a new race record by nearly 3 minutes.

June 20   Borgholzlausen, 10 miles, Germany. 34th. 51:11. (1st. Steve Kenyon 46:11).

   28   International Veterans 25K, Brugges. 4th. 81:34. (1st. Antonio Villa-neuva 78:33).

CHESTERS TOUR OF TAMESIDE

July	5	Nike '7'. 9th. 38:51. (1st. Stan Curran 34:19).

July 5 Nike '7'. 9th. 38:51. (1st. Stan Curran 34:19).

6 Mountain Equipment Hill Race, '5½'. 12th. 29:41. (1st. Alan Sladen 27:34). Overall 7th. 65:32. (1st. Alan Sladen 62:08).

7 Adidas, Run Across Tameside, '11'. 12th. 59:45. (1st. Andy Darby 56:50). Overall 10th. 2:05.17. (1st. Alan Sladen 1:59:14).

9 New Balance, ½ Marathon. 6th. 67:18. (1st. Alan Sladen 64:37). Overall 8th. 3:12:35. (1st. Alan Sladen 3:03:51).

10 Running Magazine Cross-Country, '6'. 7th. 33:15. (1st. Alan Sladen 32:05). Overall 7th. 3:45:50. (1st. Alan Sladen 3:35:56).

11 Brooks Canal Race, '9'. 6th. 46:45. (1st. Colin Kirkham 45:12). Overall 7th. 4:32:35. (1st. Alan Sladen 4:21:52).

1st. Stage, in conjunction with Dave O'Leary's Hyde '7'.

Organised in a rush under the sponsorship of Chesters Brewery the race was a tremendous success, especially amongst the competitiors. Being greatly involved with the organisation, down to helping set the courses on the day of some of the races, my own performances were less than satisfactory to me. I had to push to be second veteran, with Pete Lomas and Dave Attwell pushing me. Colin Robinson was way ahead in this category, finishing 4th. overall in 4:29:39.

It was after these events that I decided to have 6 months at around 35 miles a week, to try further to regain freshness.

Stage 3, 12th.

Final Stage, Tour of Tameside, Canal Race.

July 26 Northern Track League, Stretford. 5,000. 4th. 15:21.1. (1st. C. Moore 14:27.5).
Aug. 16 Weets Fell Race, Barnoldswick. 25th. 33:44. (1st. John Wild 30:44).
     22 Northern Track League, Stockport. 4th. 16:01.1.
     27 Clayton-le-Moors Harriers, AGM 5,000m. 5th. 16:10.0. (1st. Brian McKenna 15.44).
Sept. 5 Springbank Road Races, London, Ontario, Canada. Masters '6'. 5th. 30:38.3. (1st. Terry Manners 28:39.5).

Oct. 4 Hollingworth Lake Road Relay. 23:10. 32nd. fastest. (Fastest Paul Campbell 21:31).
 10 Lancashire Road Relay. 16:05. 71st fastest. (Fastest Dave Singleton 14:47).
 11 Cutlers Relay, Sheffield. 10.08. (Fastest Mike Deegan 9.09).
 18 20K of Paris. 46th. 64:25. (1st. Radhouane Bouster 57:35).

Despite getting off with the "star" runners at the front, I finished 19 positions worse than the year before. A result of detraining. May ran her furthest ever and finished happy and undistressed in just over 1hr. 50m.

20K of Paris, 46th.

May's 20K of Paris.

Oct. 25 Gale Fell Race. 15th. 26.43. (1st. John Reade 24:35).
Dec. 6 Todmorden Harriers Christmas Handicap '6'. 5th. 32:40. (1st. Ian Clarkson 30:57).

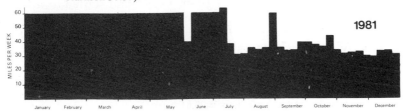

CHAPTER TWENTY-SIX

Things did not slow down in 1982. Having got Part One of my autobiography out of the way, I had to catch up with the paperwork piled on my desk and also stand in firstly, as advertising manager and then as magazine editor due to people leaving. New people joined, runners again, Keith Rothwell for advertising and Simon Smith as editor of "Running Review".

The "running boom" had arrived in the U.K., with the size of marathon fields and the number of actual marathon races mushrooming. We opened a new "Running Wild" shop in Farnworth, and decided to consolidate our retailing position at that. Runners, Jack Haslam and Ron Filer, joined us to manage

May in training — early 1982.

shops. Our biggest growth, and growth potential, is on the wholesale side with expansion of the Ron Hill Sports Line to incorporate new designs of clothing and now, running footwear. Business has been coming to us, without us actively searching for it, and excitingly this is happening in the export field as well as at home.

The "boom" has presented many other opportunities, all of them requiring time. I am at present a consultant to Adidas on the footwear and running side, and our own company has become involved in race organisation and running tours.

As with any occupation there are boring tasks to be carried out, but I am fortunate in being able to combine my career and my running. In January I completed my 1½ years' "rest" and started to train again, building up the mileage. I even purchased a set of weights and a special exercise bench; however, although I am sure that this type of training will be useful to me, it is one thing that will have to wait a little longer. I simply have not had the time to use them! The biggest motivating factor for getting fit after my "rest" was to compete well once more, hopefully being able to duck under 2 hrs. 20 mins. for the marathon. But in addition I am fully aware of the necessity of keeping my name in the public eye as a means of promoting our company. My trips abroad, which provide some highlights to the year, especially when May comes with me, are all "business" trips in some way or another.

Before the London Marathon in May, my mileage topped 100 per week on four occasions and I was rewarded with a 2:20:57. I thought I might get better later in the year but the opportunity never arose. The second Tour of Tameside, in July, proved I was going well, with 4th place overall, and I was hoping to carry this fitness forward to the Rio de Janeiro Marathon in August. However, the organisers failed to make firm bookings for our flight and we stayed two nights at Paris Orly airport unsuccessfully trying to get on a plane to Brazil. Some friends and customers of ours, Paul Cornou and his wife Raymond, invited us to stay with them at their country cottrage, but the weather was cold and even the excellent white wine did not compensate us for missing Copacabana Beach.

My season deteriorated after that. I became ill with *another* sore throat and chest infection and I have just ticked over till now, October, when I begin 8 weeks' "rest". I am convinced that these recuperation periods are absolutely vital to me.

Every morning I run with May. She is up to 4 miles now, and in July completed her longest ever run, at Brugges, 25K, that is about 15½ miles. Graham our youngest son has just started work for our company.

In August a full-time start was made to complete "The Long Hard Road", bringing it, as advised, right up-to-date.

May, Graham and
"Sammy" the cat.

413

Race results, 1982:

Jan.   9   Race of the Americas, 10K, Miami. 42nd. 33:22.1. (1st. Alberto Salazar 28:03.5).

Sonesta Beach, Key Biscayne.

May and I were on our third trip to Miami which had now become a "festival of road running" and included a 10K race, one week before the Orange Bowl Marathon. We stayed on Key Biscayne at a beautiful hotel, the Sonesta Beach. It was the nearest we had come

Training 26 miles in 2:40.

May's 10K.

to a holiday for years. In the 10K I was at my utmost for many a year but was not prepared for the shock of 2 women beating me. It had never happened before and I was helpless as Charlotte Teske (32:49.7) and Wendy Smith (33:02.3) ran away from me. May ran 54:10. A week later I was quite pleased to "train" through 26 miles of the marathon in 2 hrs. 40 mins.

Jan. 23 Mid-Lancs. Cross-Country League, Upholland. 62nd. (1st. N. Miller 33:10).
     30 East Lancs. Cross-Country Champs., Horwich. 30th. (1st. Bob Shorrock 33:18).

Mid-Lancs. C.C. League, 62nd.   *E. Lancs. C.C. Champs. 30th.*

Feb. 7 National Business Houses Cross-Country Champs., Horwich. 30th. 33:07. (1st. Steve Kenyon 30:09).

'B' Race Team: Me, Tom McNally, Malcolm McBride, Duncan Martin.

Ron Hill Sports 'A' Race Team were 1st. overall, and Ron Hill Sports 'B' Race Team (including me) were 1st. in the under 500 employees division.

Feb. 13 Northern Cross-Country Champs., Birkenhead. 292nd. (1st. John Woods 38:51).

19 BAHRAIN MARATHON. 2nd. 2:35:30. (1st. Saad Mubarak 2:34:37).

The invitation for this race, sponsored by Cathay Pacific Airways came via Jeremy Bell, a runner with the British Embassy. A dreaded sore throat and chest infection had hit me just before the Northern and I was coughing badly right up to the marathon. I thought I could win it in 2:35 and in fact ran this time but didn't bargain for a young Arab runner, Saad Mubarak, who was only going to do 15 miles for training, then decided he could win it, blasting away from

Training in Bahrain.

Bahrain Marathon — start.

Mubarak takes off.

me with about 3 miles to go. Third in the race was Gordon Shaw, whom I had last competed against 5 years previously in Rhodesia. My time was some kind of record — my slowest marathon ever!

I enjoyed the visit immensely — it was the 32nd. foreign country I competed in — the Bahrain Hash members looking after me well.

Mar. 6   National Cross-Country Championships, Leeds. 580th. (1st. Dave Clarke 42:09).

I couldn't believe this bad a run here. Illness — post Bahrain marathon?

Mar. 13   Manchester University Cross-country Champs. 2nd. 32:45. (1st. Hamish McInnes 32:35).

"EASTERRRUNS", GUERNSEY. April 9-12.

Apr. 3   Cross-Country '5', L'Ancresse Common. 9th. 25:07. (1st. Steve Kenyon 23:22).
      10   Milestones '6'. 10th. 32:04. (1st. J. Asse 29:12).
      11   Midland Bank ½ Marathon. 6th. 68:20. (1st. Steve Kenyon 61:52).
      12   Commodore '3'. 12th. 15:12. (1st. J. Asse 13:59).

Guernsey — start of the Milestones '6'.

Apr. 18   Great Hameldon Hill Race. 12th. 29:48. (1st. Dave Lewis 27:36).
      27   Haigh Hall '5', Wigan. 11th. 25:22. (1st. Gerry Helme 23:30).
May   2   Knowsley ½ Marathon. 19th. 72:59. (1st. Steve Kenyon 62:18).

1982

May 9 LONDON MARATHON.
39th. 2:20:57. (1st. Hugh
Jones 2:09:24).

Maybe an indicator of what I
might be capable of if only I had
the time to seriously consider
my training again; the time, and
possibly self-motivation.

May 16 Wigan '6½'. 19th. 31:36. (1st.
Gerry Helme 29:36).

23 Saab 10K, Manchester. 28th.
31:16. (1st. Steve Anders
28:34).

29 Elby's Distance Classic 20K,
Wheeling, West Virginia.
20th. 67:45. (1st. Jon Sinclair
61:37.1).

Eighteen positions higher
than last year but 1 minute slower
on a roasting morning!

KEITH IRVINE

London, 39th. 2:20:57.

3 Boston Marathon Winners in Wheeling: Bill Rodgers, Amby Burfoot, me.

Jun. 5 Norwegian Mountain ½ Marathon, Beitostolen. 3rd. 65:33. (1st. Aland
Per Knut 65:02.2).

Eighteen seconds faster than last year, but 2 positions down. I
just let them go at the start and never pulled them back.

June 19 Christie Univs. v. Cornell and Penn. 5,000m. 5th. 15:49.9.

20 Reebok 10K, Bolton. 19th. 31:47. (1st. Ian Gilmour 29:21).

27 International Vets. 25K., Brugges. 11th. 84:26. (1st. Tim Johnston 80:05).

May ran 2:33:56 in this race, Mysteriously my own performance
was a disaster.

July 3 National Vets. Track Champs., Cudworth. 5,000m. 2nd. 15:35.1. (1st.
John Etchells 15:20.2).

4 Hyde '7'. 16th. 36:01. (1st. Mike Deegan and Keith Irvine 33:47).

7 Golden Hind '6', Stockport. 7th. 26:57. (1st. John Davies 25:10).

Right: Norwegian Mountain Half-Marathon.

Below: National Vets. 5,000m. l. to r. Hill, Carroll, Grubb, Etchells, Wainwright.

CHESTERS TOUR OF TAMESIDE
July 18 Nike '7'. 10th. 36:23. (1st. Paul Campbell 34:43).
    19 Mizuno Hill Race, '5½'. 6th. 29:24. (1st. Paul Campbell 28:07). Overall 7th. 1:05.47. (1st Paul Campbell 1:02:50).
    20 Adidas Run Across Tameside, '11'. 6th. 58:50. (1st. Eric Williams 56:30). Overall 5th. 2:04:07. (1st. Paul Campbell 1:59:55).
    22 New Balance ½ Marathon. 4th. 66:36. (1st. Eric Williams 65:00). Overall 4th. 3:11:13. (1st. Paul Campbell 3:05:15).
    23 Surf City Cross-Country, '6'. 7th. 32:03. (1st. Paul Campbell 30:48). Overall 4th. 3:43:16. (1st. Paul Campbell 3:36:03).
    24 Athletics Weekly Canal '9'. 6th. 46:27. (1st. Stan Curran 45:17). Overall 4th. 4:29:43. (1st. Paul Campbell 4:21:56).

I wrested the veteran's yellow vest from Colin Robinson on the 4th stage. Colin was running worse than last year and me, far better. I relaxed on stages 1, 3 and 5 but ran almost as well as when I was really trying! A slightly bigger Tour this year and again much enjoyed by the competitors.

LEN SYKES

3rd Stage, Tour of Tameside, leading John Turner (Holmfirth).

RON GOODYEAR

Final Stage, Tour of Tameside, leading Mike Dooling (Liverpool).

July 27 Stoodley Pike Fell Race. 28th. 18:06. (1st. Alan Adams 16:42).
Aug. 18 Trawden Hill Race. 2nd. 38:36. (1st. Roger Brewster 38:35).
   25 Saddleworth '6'. 27th. 30:25. (1st. Dave Topham 28:04).
   26 Clayton-le-Moors AGM 5,000m. 4th. 15:52.0. (1st. Roger Brewster 15:27.0).
Sept. 12 Olympialauf 25K, Munich. 6th. 86:26.

Ten years after my Olympic Marathon I once again finished 6th. on the roads around the Olympic Stadium. This time I wasn't serious, taking time out from the ISPO Exhibition, and wearing training shoes rather than racers.

   25 Burtonwood Road Relay. 19:18. 53rd. fastest. (Fastest Karl Harrison 17:43).
   26 Todmorden '6'. 6th. 32:51. (1st. Denis Quinlan 31:37).
Oct. 3 Hollingworth Lake Road Relay. 22:13, 16th. fastest. (Fastest Pete Eaves 21:18).
   17 20K of Paris. 42nd. 63:48. (1st. Jacky Boxberger 57:47).

1982

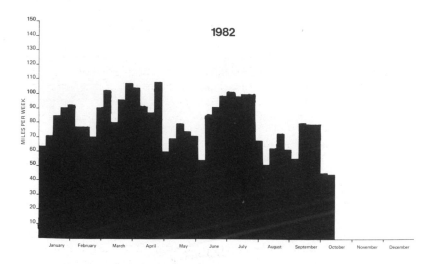

NOT REALLY THE CONCLUSION

At last "The Long Hard Road" is finished. I never realised the amount of work that would be necessary to complete a project like this, or how mentally draining it would be to relive and write the experiences of my career. Now it is over. I'm relieved and happy to get it out of the way. That period of my life is wrapped up; and I can look forward to the future with optimism.

In producing this autobiography my intention was to teach as well as entertain. The mistakes *I* made are there for runners to learn from and hopefully not repeat. I too can begin to use the condensed information to improve my own performances, because although I am fully aware that advancing years inevitably produce a slowing of times, my own demise has been too rapid and the purpose of my further training will be to decrease the downward slope of my performances, perhaps even reverse the slope in the next few years.

My consecutive "streak" of runs: twice a day (once only on Sundays), since December 1964, is still intact and will remain intact, barring accident for many years to come. I enjoy running. It maintains the health of my body and mind and is a barometer of my physical condition. At the time of writing I am approaching 100,000 miles of recorded training and racing. I hope to go on for a second 100,000.

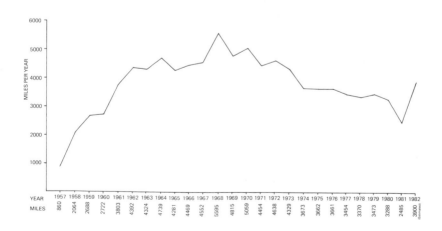

YEAR	1957	1958	1959	1960	1961	1962	1963	1964	1965	1966	1967	1968	1969	1970	1971	1972	1973	1974	1975	1976	1977	1978	1979	1980	1981	1982
MILES	860	2064	2688	2722	3803	4392	4324	4739	4281	4469	4552	5595	4815	5059	4454	4638	4329	3673	3662	3661	3454	3370	3473	3288	2485	3900